Peak States
of
Consciousness
Volume I

Institute
for the Study
of Peak States

"Methods for Fundamental Change in the Human Psyche"

Peak States of Consciousness
Theory and Applications

Volume I

Breakthrough Techniques
for
Exceptional Quality of Life

First Edition

Grant McFetridge
with
Jacquelyn Aldana,
Dr. James Hardt
and Zivorad Slavinski

First Edition
First printing, 2004

National Library of Canada Cataloguing in Publication
    Peak states of consciousness : theory and applications / Grant McFetridge ... [et al.].
    Includes index.
    Contents: v. 1. Breakthrough techniques for exceptional quality of life
    ISBN 0-9734680-0-9
    1.Consciousness.   2.Peak experiences.   3.Mental health.   I. McFetridge, Grant, 1955-
BF311.P3175 2004   153   C2004-900146-9

Institute for the Study of Peak States Press
3310 Cowie Road
Hornby Island, British Columbia
Canada
V0R 1Z0
http://www.peakstates.com

Contents

Books from the Institute for the Study of Peak States Press

The Basic Whole-Hearted Healing Manual (Third Edition) by Grant McFetridge and Mary Pellicer MD.

The Inner Peace Process, 2002. (A training video, 2 hours, VHS).

Peak States of Consciousness: Theory and Applications, Volume 1: Breakthrough Techniques for Exceptional Quality of Life by Grant McFetridge with Jacquelyn Aldana, Dr. James Hardt, and Zivorad Slavinski.

Peak States of Consciousness: Theory and Applications, Volume 2: Extraordinary Spiritual and Shamanic States by Grant McFetridge with Mary Pellicer MD and Adam Waisel MD.

Peak States of Consciousness: Theory and Applications, Volume 3: Applying Peak States to Research and Healing by Grant McFetridge. (forthcoming).

Silencing the Voices: From Mind-Chatter to Schizophrenia by Grant McFetridge (forthcoming).

To order, go to: www.peakstates.com

Introduction to Volume 1, First Edition

Welcome to the exciting new field of peak states of consciousness.

As you read these words, new breakthroughs and discoveries are being made worldwide in this new and rapidly growing field. My name is Grant McFetridge, and I'm the research director and co-founder of the Institute for the Study of Peak States. Like many in this field, we've been working for nearly two decades, making progress that in the last few years has crystallized into new approaches and a new paradigm. I hope this book gives you a taste of the wonder of this time in history, with its camaraderie and excitement. More and more technique developers are making breakthroughs and sharing their results in a selfless effort to improve the field for everyone.

This book is a survey of the field for the interested lay person, a more in-depth look at the some of the most significant approaches now available, and a training manual for our own Institute projects. This text was originally written as a collection of lessons for students. We've rewritten it for publication in order to make it available for anyone who is interested in exploring this topic. In particular, we hope that others will use this material to improve on our results, incorporate our findings into other processes, and significantly improve their own and their clients' lives.

This text is both theoretical and experiential. We include our current processes and short examples from real people's experiences. Rather than making this just a dry list of facts and processes, we've also included our own personal experiences as we slowly worked out how our experiments and discoveries fit together in a coherent whole.

This volume explains the underlying mechanism for many peak states of consciousness.

One of the most important contributions of this book is a simple model of how peak states, peak experiences, altered states, biology, religion, spirituality, shamanism, and psychology fit together into one simple underlying framework. Up to now, the various types of data and realms of human experience have been treated as separate subjects, with information from other fields generally ignored as irrelevant by investigators. Our model has numerous times allowed us to predict processes and phenomena that at the time we had not heard of or uncovered. We call our framework the 'developmental events model for peak states, experiences, and abilities', or the 'developmental events model' for brevity. In this volume, we focus specifically on the developmental events for triune brain peak states of consciousness.

This volume gives all the current approaches for acquiring peak states that we know of.

The other key contribution of this book is a world-wide survey of the new generation of techniques that have recently become available. We're very blessed to have chapters written by breakthrough process developers in this new field, describing their own work and the approach they used. As of this writing, we know of no other processes than the ones listed in this book, although doubtless we have missed some of them in a field that is so rapidly growing and changing.

As this field is so new, our contributors focus on their own processes and models without any integration with each other. This will change with time, as we're all tremendously excited to share our work with each other to develop new and better processes.

You do not need to know any particular therapy to understand this book.

Although much of the material in this book comes out of break-throughs using the new power therapies, we have deliberately chosen to keep this a book about peak states and not about therapy or therapeutic techniques.

However, you might find it helpful to know something about the effective yet simple meridian power therapy EFT (Emotional Freedom Technique). Two of the approaches for acquiring a peak state in this volume, PEAT and IPP (Inner Peace Process) use it in unique ways to get their results. The EFT manual can be downloaded from www.emofree.com.

Many of the processes given here are experimental and some may be potentially dangerous.

This book is about the state-of-the-art in inducing and investigating peak states of consciousness. Thus, we've covered finished and tested approaches such as the 15-Minute Miracle, PEAT, IPP, and so on that are safe and effective. However, we've also included Institute processes that are still very experimental. As we are doing original research and these are our first generation tools, many are not yet tested or optimized for the general public. We've chosen to include them for the benefit of other investigators in this field of study in the hope that they will build and improve on our work.

Thus, the experimental processes haven't been tested on large numbers of people and so they should be considered potentially dangerous. We've included them for educational purposes only. They should only be attempted under trained supervision, with the understanding that any-thing that happens is at your own risk and responsibility.

There are currently three volumes in this series.

Volume 2 covers extraordinary spiritual and shamanic states of con-sciousness. Among other phenomena, we examine fundamental ques-tions about God and the planetary consciousness we call Gaia. This book covers many states that rarely occur in the general population. We show how to use them to generate simple processes for healing and peak states that can be used by people in average consciousness.

Volume 3 on advanced healing techniques covers relevant peak states of consciousness and how to use them effectively. This volume in this se-ries is designed specifically for people who are using our discoveries to heal emotional and physical issues or discover the cause of several severe dis-ease processes. It is intended to follow on to our book *The Basic Whole-Hearted Healing Manual* by Grant McFetridge and Mary Pellicer MD which can be downloaded from our site at www.PeakStates.com.

Expect revisions in the future.

This is a work in progress, and should be considered as such. These books describe cutting-edge research work that is still happening as you read this. We feel we've moved into an incredibly important area of re-search that has never been seen before, so it will be in its teething stages for years to come. With this in mind, in the text we've tried to indicate when we are not sure about the meaning of some result, or give alternative hypotheses. However, we do expect that as time goes on we will find that we've made errors or find that what we thought was happening was actu-ally something else. Occasionally we're in the position of the storied blind men touching the elephant in different places and trying to come up with an accurate description of the animal. So, in the future expect to see new editions that update our findings, correct our errors, fill in unintentional omissions, and revise our nomenclature.

Grant McFetridge
Hornby Island, BC, Canada

The Institute for the Study of Peak States
5808A Summitview Ave #120
Yakima, WA 98908 USA
250-413-3211

This book is dedicated to my father, John McFetridge MD,
whose loving encouragement and financial support
during the early stages of this work
made it all possible.

Acknowledgements

This work has come out of the enthusiasm, pain, struggle, and suffering of literally thousands of people—friends, associates, and clients. I'd like to specifically acknowledge the contributions of some of these individuals here:

All the present and past volunteer staff of the Institute—Frank Downey, who believed in me, spent time to support me, and kept me encouraged even when we made no progress for long periods of time; Kate Sorensen of Trauma Relief Services, who worked with me on the beginnings of this work, and shared my excitement around the initial discoveries; Wes Gietz, whose pioneering work verified the hypothesis of key developmental events for peak states; Deola Perry PhD, who tested much of this work on herself and came up with the Perry diagram to communicate triune brain fusion states; Marie Green PhD, whose financial and personal support and enthusiasm made this work possible and who made challenging the current paradigm much more fun; Dr. Mary Pellicer, my workshop co-instructor and general sounding board; Dr. Adam Waisel, who has applied this work on himself while working in virtual isolation from the rest of us over the past few years; Scott McGee, who expanded the image descriptions in Chapter 8 and the chakra ball material; Preston Howard, who found the key to the Wholeness state; Matt Fox, who has followed through in applying our work; and Joel Sanders, who volunteered his time to make the first ISPS website, through which many new friends and colleagues found us.

All the members of the first Radical Physical Healing class who persevered via email and phone to test the lessons that were the core to this book, and whose financial contributions made it possible to write—especially Adam Waisel, Eddie Kendrick, Jorge Aldana, Maarten Willemsen, and Richard Hunt.

All our Whole-Hearted Healing workshop participants, who allowed us to test our developing processes on them—especially Jerry Pegden, who tested our work, made significant financial donations, and continues to encourage us all; and Colleen Engel, who also tested my work and donated financially.

My co-authors in this volume—Jacquelyn Aldana whose enthusiasm is an inspiration, and who kindly contributed a chapter on her methods for this book; Zivorad Slavinski, who has independently made major discoveries that have relevance to our work, and was willing to share his results with us in a chapter for this book; and Jim Hardt, who gave me hope those many years ago that what I was exploring could be understood from a rational, scientific perspective.

To those professionals I've had such a delight sharing ideas with as we created new methods, and who are pioneering such a huge changes in the field of psychology—Gary Craig, whose development and sharing of the Emotional Freedom Technique has single-handedly changed the way people view healing; Larry Nims, the inventor of BSFF whose friendship I've greatly enjoyed and who showed me the value of listening; Gerald French of the TIR Institute who showed me the parallels between TIR and WHH, and whose humor still delights me; Terry Larimore, for her friendship and the sharing of her work on prenatal stages and trauma; David MacQuarrie MD, from 'A Place Two Be' day retreat center who independently tested the Inner Peace process; Harold McCoy of the Ozark Research Institute for his kindness and the opportunity to teach at his facility; and Melvin Suhd, whose Association for the Whole Person has given us a legal vehicle under which to continue this work.

The volunteers, contributors and editors who made this book possible —Paula Courteau for testing the procedures in this volume, making new discoveries, and helping me write an understandable text; Dhyani Jo Sinclair, who edited the text for me without charge. (Any mistakes are due to my own last minute changes and not her work!); Sudha Putnam, a dear friend who also helped edit the book without charge; Star Love who did the cover graphics; and Tantra Bensko who did the cover photo; Maura Hoffman, Janet Taylor, and David Burnet who shared their knowledge of other peak state processes; Jim Bisakowski who helped with the final text layout and all the other arcane aspects of publishing; Bruce Rawles, who has supported this work in many ways, from encouragement to website and software assistance; and Fred and Lorraine Lepper, and Dan Bruiger, in whose beautiful island homes most of this was written; and finally, the many people who willingly contributed their own personal experiences to this volume.

Naming conventions

In a number of cases we've had to choose names for various peak states. In general, we've tried to pick names that reflect the most obvious or dominant characteristic of the state. We could have named the states based on what caused them, in cases where we knew, or we could have named them for the main ability that the state conferred. We decided that it was more important to make the nomenclature accessible to the general public and recognizable from personal experience, rather than create a jargon based on more abstract criteria.

In cases where there was a difference in the characteristics between men and women for the same state, we arbitrarily chose the dominant characteristic that was found in men even if it wasn't as dominant in women. An example of this is the 'Underlying Happiness' state, where both sexes have underlying happiness with a loving feeling, but in men the happiness dominates, while in women the loving feeling dominates.

In cases where there are different characteristics for the same state when combined with other states, we chose the characteristic that appeared the most often in the general population. An example of this is the 'Brain Light' state which is perceived as if gentle sunlight were inside one's body for most people, but when combined with the 'Sacred' state, creates a bright fluorescent black internal light.

Occasionally, the state already had an existing name that is generally recognized, for example the 'Beauty Way' state from Native American tradition. Although it was tempting to use our own choice for the state name, we generally went with the older, more common name if it was well enough known.

Legal Liability Agreement

IMPORTANT!
READ THE FOLLOWING BEFORE CONTINUING THE TEXT!

The material in this book is experimental and in many cases has not been tested on large groups of people. It is provided for educational purposes only, and is **not** intended to be used by the general public as a self-help aid. The processes in this book are included for the benefit of other professionals in the field investigating these phenomena, and are not meant to be used by lay people without **competent and qualified supervision**. As this is a relatively new and specialized field of study, even most licensed professionals do not have adequate background and training in both prenatal and perinatal psychology and power therapies.

It is possible, and in some cases probable that you will feel extreme distress, both short and long term, if you use the processes in this book. As with any intense psychological process life-threatening problems might occur due to the possibility of stressing a weak heart, from activating suicidal feelings, and other causes. Although we've tried to indicate the more hazardous processes, and the ones that we consider relatively safe, this does not mean that you won't experience serious or life-threatening problems with any of the processes in this book. The possibility that you may die from using these processes **does** exist.

Given what we've just said, the following common sense statements constitute a legal agreement between us. This applies to everyone, including licensed professionals and lay people. Please read the following statements carefully:

- I, any people associated with the Institute for the Study of Peak States, and the other authors in this text cannot and will not take responsibility for what you do with these techniques.
- You are required to take complete responsibility for your own emotional and physical well-being if you use these processes or any variations.
- You are required to instruct others whom you use these processes on, or use variations of these processes on, that they are completely responsible for their own emotional and physical well-being.
- Use these techniques under the supervision of a qualified therapist or physician as appropriate.
- You must agree to hold harmless myself and anyone associated with this text or with the Institute for the Study of Peak States from any claims made by anyone who you use these or variations of these processes on, yourself included.

Continuing on in this text constitutes a legal agreement to these conditions. Thanks for your understanding.

Chapter 1

Current Paradigms in the Study of Exceptional Quality of Life and Mental Health

Introduction

The Institute for the Study of Peak States (ISPS) has accomplished a breakthrough into an entirely new field of knowledge. This field is the study of peak states of consciousness, a field that is virtually unknown and unsuspected in the dominant paradigm of our culture. As odd as it may seem to some of you, none of the current social and academic models of human psychology and behavior recognize that many people live their daily lives in quite different kinds of consciousness, far superior to those most of us live in. Our Institute calls these kinds of consciousness 'peak states', and there are a number of different ones. This is one of the key conceptual breakthroughs we've made that allows many apparently unrelated phenomena in psychology, spirituality, healing, and shamanism to be understood in a new way.

We will be covering background material in this chapter. After years of working with laymen and healers, I've found that it is absolutely necessary to do this. People have an amazing number of different and often conflicting beliefs about what we'll be describing in this book. These beliefs, if not addressed, cause people to ignore, distort, or deny data and experiences that relate to this topic. If these paradigm conflicts are not brought to awareness, the material that we teach is partially or completely blocked. You might enjoy looking to see if your beliefs are listed. As the chapter progresses, I'll try to address these often unconscious belief conflicts. Some of these beliefs are self-evidently incorrect, but others are not so obvious and will require you to read the following chapters in order to understand the flaws.

For example, a number of people walk out of my lectures because our material is in conflict with their religious training. Some are Christian, some are following gurus, but the reaction is the same. Others leave because these concepts make them feel very deeply afraid for reasons that they can't even describe. Others are psychologists, who after years in the field had decided that this couldn't be true, apparently because it would have invalidated years of effort. Whatever the particular reason, this problem occurs in the majority of our students. Very few people are able to absorb this information immediately.

In this chapter, I'll briefly describe a variety of topics from very different traditions that relates to the existence of peak states. Note, perhaps from your own experience, that each of these groups ignores conflicting data from the other groups, and no one is trying to put this material in a comprehensive whole.

Example:
> There are well over 30 distinct and often contradictory psychological models taught in my graduate psychology school. None of them can be used to successfully heal mental illness or explain the whole gamut of psychology. And none of them attempts to include data from shamanic or spiritual traditions. At this time, there is no unified theory in psychology. Stanislav Grof's model is probably the closest to a unifying model, but because it contains shamanic and spiritual experiences, it is generally not included in the university curricula.

Definition - Paradigm

The axioms, assumptions and preconceptions at the core of a given theory or world-view. A paradigm is a pattern or an example of something. The word also connotes the ideas of a mental picture and pattern of thought. Thomas Kuhn uses the word to mean the model that scientists hold about a particular area of knowledge. Kuhn's famous book *The Structure of Scientific Revolutions* describes his view of the stages through which a science goes in getting from one paradigm to the next. The process of seeing things within a paradigm is "built into the nature of the perceptual process itself," Kuhn says, referring to the anomalous playing card experiment. In this experiment, he swapped the colors of the playing card suites and people couldn't see it. Kuhn says that "once it has achieved the status of paradigm, a scientific theory is declared invalid only if an alternate candidate is available to take its place." Internal psychological forces cause a person to reject or ignore data that doesn't fit their unconscious paradigm, and also establishes the way that a person tries to solve problems.

The Events That Shaped
the Way Psychology Looks at
Exceptional Quality of Life

In this section, we briefly describe the events that have shaped the changing paradigms about exceptional quality of life and exceptionally mentally healthy people. Rather than a story of a smooth evolution from the dominant paradigm of the '50s, we see a series of new paradigms appearing as revolutionary new techniques and data become available.

Before we go any further, it is important to understand the distinction between exceptional 'quality of life' and exceptional 'mental health'. In years past the academic psychological community tended to view people's inner experience from the single perspective of poor, normal, or exceptional 'mental health'. The idea was that a person with exceptional mental health basically had everything going for them, and no other distinctions were emphasized. However, in the last few years this idea has been supplemented by the concept of an internal 'quality of life' that is independent of outside circumstances (for example, having continuous feelings of joy, happiness, peace, optimism, and so on). In essence, internal quality of life refers to how good people feel inside of themselves. This concept of life quality is something that people find much more meaningful and desirable for their own lives over abstract ideas about exceptional mental health.

In the chapters that follow, we will often use the historical convention of referring to exceptional mental health as synonymous with, or the cause of, exceptional internal quality of life. However, in my opinion the two concepts as currently defined in the field of psychology are not necessarily the same, although they can be in some circumstances. A person can experience themselves as having an exceptional quality of life, yet still have emotional, relationship or job related problems that need healing. Obviously, an exceptional internal quality of life makes these sorts of issues much easier to deal with. Contrast this with a person who has exceptional mental health characterized by a lack of emotional, relationship, or job issues, yet lacks these previously mentioned inner feelings. They would still be subtly dissatisfied with their lives, as it's not the absence of pain that makes life worth living but rather the presence of these wonderful internal feelings.

> ## Definition - Internal quality of life
>
> Refers to a person who has one of a variety of inner feelings that are experienced as pleasurable and make living feel worthwhile. Happiness, peace, joy, and so on are examples of these types of feelings. Almost any of the peak states of consciousness (see Appendix A) make a person feel they have an exceptional quality of life.

The Origins of Humanistic Psychology

Historically, psychology, like medicine, has held the underlying assumption that health is the absence of disease. This model is still dominant to this day, but during the 1960s another model started to come into existence—that mental health should be understood by looking at exceptionally healthy individuals. There were many contributors to this change, but for our purposes the best known was Dr. Abraham Maslow, one of the founders of Humanistic Psychology. He popularized a phenomenon he'd noticed and called 'peak experiences'.

Have you ever had a moment in your life where you felt very, very different and wonderful? Everything seemed to be exceptionally perfect, time slowed down as if you were a child again, or some other aspect of what was going on was so remarkable and unique you've never forgotten it? Maslow defined these peak experiences as having some but not necessarily all of the following characteristics:

- very strong or deep positive emotions akin to ecstasy,
- a deep sense of peacefulness or tranquility,
- feeling in tune, in harmony, or at one with the universe,
- a feeling of deeper knowing or profound understanding,
- ineffability, a sense that it is a very special experience that would be difficult or impossible to describe adequately in words.

The experiences might spontaneously occur while being surrounded by exceptional beauty, or during a physical event like running a race, or for a variety of reasons or no particular reason at all. Dr. Maslow found that there were quite a large variety of different peak experiences, although all made the person involved feel better than normal, and usually much, much better. Generalizing broadly, Humanistic Psychology was formed to look at both this phenomenon and that of exceptional mental health, in order to try and help people improve their lives. This was the start of the 'human potential movement', where the assumption was that people had incredible potential that could be either developed, or unblocked.

Although an immense number of techniques, methods, practices, and therapies came out of this movement, the bottom line was that researchers still did not understand what caused peak experiences, why some people experienced them and others not, or any way to rapidly and permanently have them for oneself. In fact, the idea that these experiences could be lived permanently as a state of being was doubted—and many felt that living in a permanent 'peak experience' would actually be a debilitating problem in day-to-day life. In essence, the humanistic psychology approach to peak experiences was a failure, and did not result in the hoped-for breakthroughs.

Cultural Changes and Transpersonal Psychology

The confusion about the experiences and states a healthy person should expect grew worse as the years went on, as more data from various spiritual, religious, psychological, and shamanic groups accumulated. The concept of 'altered states' from isolation tanks and drug experimentation also came into our culture during this period, along with the implication that states outside that of average, waking consciousness were dysfunctional in daily life. In our work, we find that people still often confuse 'peak states' with their ideas about 'altered states'.

Outside of psychology, writers like Carlos Castenada and Michael Harner popularized shamanic traditions involving those types of unusual experiences. This was just one of the many other approaches to unusual states of consciousness that became available during this period.

Example:
> Dr. Michael Harner uses drumming to put students into a trance, which he calls a 'shamanic state of consciousness'. From there, they can move their consciousness into other 'shamanic' worlds, or around this one.

Example:
> Robert Monroe was a pioneer in the study of the out-of-body experience. He used sound at slightly different frequencies in each ear in order to put people into a state of consciousness where they could go out-of-body. These experiences allowed travel in this world and into other 'realms' of existence.

Example:
> D. E. Harding, while hiking in the Himalaya mountains, had the experience of losing the sensation that he had a flesh-and-blood head. He lectured about it and described it in his book, On Having No Head.

A huge variety of ancient and modern spiritual traditions became accessible. New spiritual groups talked about spiritual experiences and states, but they often disagreed about what they were, if there was more than one, or even whose were the best. The idea that everyone who followed different spiritual practices would all come to the same state became a 'new age' belief, although this is easily shown to be false when different spiritual practices are actually followed to their conclusion. This conflict between traditions is hard to spot, as it's not common that spiritual seekers go far enough in several traditions to encounter this problem. And in most if not all of these traditions, the student is expected to take what is told to them without question or analysis.

The problem of spiritual teachers abusing their students also became very common, which was hard to understand or accept. Rationalizations for this phenomenon abounded, especially since many people had the idea that spiritual growth involved a smooth progression from 'average' to 'enlightened'.

Example:
> Samadhi is a 'higher' state in some yogic Indian traditions. Although there is a perennial problem of isolating a description of what this or any 'spiritual' word means, in this case there is general agreement that samadhi is a state of exceptional peace, timelessness, and a radical decrease in the need to breathe. Yet, in the Zen tradition this state is considered a problem, and students are directed to avoid it. See Chapter 5 for a description of what causes this state.

Example:
> Kundalini yoga espouses the virtues of raising the kundalini energy in the base of the spine for spiritual growth. Other traditions have no knowledge of this experience, and so ignore it if it occurs in their students.

As techniques such as meditation for stress relief and personal growth came into the popular culture, a number of people using them encountered a whole variety of unusual spiritual and other strange experiences that didn't fit *any* of the models that people had, either in psychology or in traditional spiritual lineages. Because of all this, another branch of psychology called Transpersonal Psychology was formed to study these even more unbelievable experiences and states. Dr. Stanislav Grof, using results from his LSD and breathwork experiments, was one of the driving forces behind this movement.

The '70s and early '80s saw a huge burst of enthusiasm for this work in exceptional experiences, but by the '90s a change occurred. The initial enthusiasm for understanding and having peak experiences was waning, with the pioneers feeling they'd gone as far as was possible. The hoped-for results had not materialized. From our Institute's perspective, this was because the early models that were developed or borrowed from various religious traditions were fundamentally flawed and could not be used to solve the basic problems.

Conflicting beliefs:

- A permanent 'peak experience' would be dysfunctional in one's life if acquired.
- Humanistic and transpersonal techniques can induce peak experiences, but only temporarily. This is the best that can be expected.
- The only alternatives to average consciousness are achieved with shamanic or chemical techniques, called 'altered states' of consciousness. These states are not compatible with everyday life.
- A healthy person is in average consciousness, but with the ability to temporarily experience other kinds of consciousness.
- People are basically all the same, except for the mentally ill.
- Spiritual states are reserved for enlightened beings. When they occur, the average person would 'ascend', or simply vanish from the earth.
- Real spiritual teachers would never harm their students—or if they did, it would be to help the student evolve.

The Development of 'Power Therapies'

By the '90s a change outside of the areas of humanistic and transpersonal psychology was taking place, involving radically effective emotional and physical healing. A group of therapies, all invented independently, was starting to become available. Dr. Charles Figley of Florida State University (the originator of the term Post Traumatic Stress Disorder) forced the acceptance of some of these therapies into mainstream psychology in 1995 and named them 'power therapies'. These originally included EMDR (Eye Movement Desensitization and Reprocessing), TIR (Traumatic Incident Reduction), VKD (Visual Kinesthetic Disassociation), and TFT (Thought Field Therapy). Since then a host of derivative techniques has become available, EFT (Emotional Freedom Technique) being the best known. The field is still in turmoil around this topic, as conventionally trained therapists and academic psychologists resist these new processes—for the simple reason that they're too good to be true from a conventional perspective.

These therapies also introduced a key change in the current paradigm of psychology. These therapies not only heal a tremendous number of conditions that had never been successfully treated before, but usually do it in time spans that can be measured in minutes to hours. The methods focus on healing traumas, which have been found empirically to be the cause for most of the mental and many physical problems that people suffer from. The importance of trauma is something that the dominant model almost completely ignores. In fact, in three years of graduate and doctoral school psychology, I can recall the existence of trauma mentioned only once or twice, and only in the limited context of post traumatic stress disorder.

Thus, these power therapies have created a change in what therapists believe is possible in the professional field of physical and emotional healing that humanistic and transpersonal psychology never did. These tools are unbelievably fast, simple, and effective, and people are starting to question their cultural assumptions because of stunning personal experience. This change in expectations has also affected our Institute, as it has created a new climate with therapists and other healers who are willing to look at what our Institute's Whole-Hearted Healing technique can do—and who then feel comfortable using it when it lives up to its claims.

Most healers using power therapies are not searching for a peak state—in fact, most probably don't believe it's possible. The dominant model in the profession at the present time is that people will feel better as more and more traumatic material is healed, and usually there is truth to this. Yet, these techniques often cause people to feel dramatically better for various lengths of time, more so than can be accounted for by removing their current pain. During or right after finishing the healing session, a significant percentage of clients also report having all sorts of spiritual and shamanic experiences that they had never heard of before or didn't believe in. Still these wonderful moments almost always soon pass.

Conflicting beliefs:
- Therapists work to bring people back to average consciousness, which occurs when trauma is minimal or well suppressed.
- Average consciousness is the best that can be expected.
- There is no way to help people feel better other than eliminating traumas one at a time.
- Trauma is irrelevant to most of people's problems.
- Psychological healing is a slow and difficult process that usually is not successful.

Data Relevant to Exceptional Quality of Life

The assumptions that psychology makes towards mental health as described in the previous section have shaped the kind of questions that people ask about the phenomena that they see, the data that they're willing to look at, and the models that they propose. In this section, I'm going to examine the relevant phenomena that are often ignored even in psychology, because they don't fit the patterns of belief that people have.

Spontaneous Peak Experiences

Let's look more closely at Dr. Maslow's 'peak experiences'. We'll focus on those that occur spontaneously, rather than those induced by the variety of techniques popular in humanistic and transpersonal psychology. Generally, these spontaneous experiences are brought on in moments of pleasure, visual beauty in nature or the world, intense crisis, or occasionally for reasons that aren't immediately obvious. The fact that they apparently happen spontaneously turns out to be both a clue to their cause, and also a block to understanding. Why is it a block? Since many people have had these unasked-for moments, they tend to assume that they are either given to them by 'grace', or that some things in the universe are just not meant to be understood. Plus, it's easy to make the assumption that since they had a peak experience without doing anything in particular, this is how it's done and 'working' to get it back is the wrong approach. These people generally feel that effort and pain are incompatible with peak experiences.

A lot of research went into trying to categorize these states, partly to try to get enough data to look for patterns and reason out the causes of them. This approach was unsuccessful.

Although a huge variety of peak experience exists, there is one similarity common to all these moments—they are characterized by *less* tension than the person normally experiences. This turns out to be a major clue to understanding what causes them.

Example:
> A woman in one of my workshops who had never had a peak experience had absolutely no idea what I was talking about. I ran her through the Inner Peace Process induction (a technique to put people into a particular permanent 'peak experience'), and she had a hard time putting the drastic difference in how she felt into words. Note that she immediately slept deeply for the first time in years over the next few nights, as the tension in her body had vanished.

Conflicting beliefs:
- Peak experiences are not meant to be understood, and simply exist for some fortunate people.
- Anything involving pain, discomfort, or effort is incompatible with peak experiences.

Peak Experiences as a Byproduct of Psychological Healing

As I've mentioned, some therapists occasionally see people move into temporary peak experiences at the end of their work with the client. This occurs at times with some of the older intense experiential therapies, such as breathwork, deep bodywork, or regression therapies. However, it happens much more frequently when using the new power therapies. For example, I regularly saw my clients have peak experiences, sometimes very dramatic ones, that lasted from minutes to days after sessions of Whole-Hearted Healing (WHH) therapy. Yet, almost without exception, the peak experiences do not last. This gave me a very strange data point when I was trying to understand what was going on. Clearly, healing trauma can *sometimes* put people into peak experiences, but not predictably or for a long duration. For the moment let's just hold this observation in mind as raw data. I tried to take careful notes of what they'd healed that did the trick, but I didn't find any obvious patterns at the time.

As an aside to therapists, I would like to note that when using a power therapy to completion, the client *should* go into a peak experience that we call Inner Peace at the end of the trauma sequence if you did your work correctly. Getting this experience is a way to verify that you've successfully come to completion on a trauma. This experience is characterized by feelings of calm, peace, and lightness (CPL), the lightness being the feeling you get when you take off a heavy backpack. This is actually how the present really feels emotionally if you are in it.

Oddly, researchers in the psychology field do not recognize or discuss the existence of peak experiences in clients even when these occur in front of their eyes! As I've mentioned, power therapists see them all the time, yet ignore them as either incomprehensible or not meaningful. They consider them just part of the normal variability of the human condition, rather than seeing them as a distinct step into another state.

Originally, I developed the Whole-Hearted Healing power therapy to investigate the mystery of peak states of consciousness. If you're interested, you can download the manuals from our website at www.PeakStates.com. Using WHH led to the initial breakthroughs, and now that we understand what we're trying to do, we use a variety of the power therapies for the work. These power therapies have allowed the breakthrough in solving the mystery of peak states of consciousness.

From our Institute's perspective, healing trauma is a lot like pulling pitchforks out of people who are in hell—when you're done, they're still in hell, they're just more comfortable there. Don't misunderstand—the work these paradigm pioneer therapists and healers are doing is vital and necessary to millions of people. But what we'd really like is a way to change people so that they're in a continuous peak experience, a state of higher functioning than normal. We'd like to put people up in a condo in heaven first, then deal with whatever is left over...

Conflicting beliefs:
- Healers using power therapies try to bring people to health, defined as 'average' consciousness. Experiences outside of 'average' are ignored as temporary aberrations.

Religious Experiences and States

In the West, our thinking about peak states is dominated by our history with Christian religious beliefs mixed with a few of the other dominant world religions. Our upbringing tells us that people who live in peak states of consciousness are few and apparently quite unusual. Thus, we are taught about saints and other exceptional people whom God has apparently specifically chosen, who after years of struggle, apparently sent by God as a test to see if they're really worthy after all, essentially win the 'spiritual state' prize. Jesus spending forty days in the desert or Buddha sitting seven days under the Bodhi tree come to mind. Our personal experience and observation of other people generally supports the view that a 'spiritual' state is difficult to achieve—in spite of our best efforts, sometimes even heroic efforts, we don't normally get there ourselves, and in fact often fall short of our ideals of virtuous behavior. Often, we see that as people get older, they generally get more and more restricted internally and further and further away from exemplifying the religious virtues, so we tend to believe that's just the way life is, a curse of aging.

Thus, from this bias in our religious and social conditioning, we unconsciously assume that these states are given to those who are intrinsically exceptionally worthy or sometimes make themselves worthy, or both. Thus, if we work hard, are nice to people, pray a lot, get a dash of grace, and so on, we become happy, good and blessed people also. This unconscious bias makes seeing the truth of what causes peak states much, much harder.

Our Western cultural background complicates matters. Mixing our religious cultural background with a strong work ethic, we tend to believe that unusually positive states of consciousness, especially ones with a 'spiritual' aspect to them, can only be achieved by hard work. Or perhaps by direct intervention, 'grace', from some higher source, usually because we've been really good. Or, because we assume that we're intrinsically 'bad', we don't believe we can have or even deserve to have any better states. These beliefs, although often contradictory, can often be found in the same person.

Example:
> One of my clients, a Mormon, when she developed unusual spiritual states under my training, wanted to block them because in her tradition women couldn't have this sort of thing and she feared she would be excommunicated if she was found out to be possessing them.

Example:
> A friend of mine, a woman who had been sexually abused as a
> child, followed Yogananda's teachings. She refused to do anything
> to heal her traumatic issue that involved pain or discomfort, be-
> cause of her religious belief that it would go away if she believed,
> prayed, chanted, and was devoted enough. The problems related
> to this early trauma did not leave her in the fifteen years I knew
> her.

Conflicting beliefs:
- Higher states result from grace, and nothing a person can do can induce them—except, perhaps, by leading a virtuous life.
- Most people, such as ourselves, should not hope to be touched by
  grace. In fact, it would be presumptuous towards the Deity.

Spiritual Experiences and States

One category of peak experiences that is often ignored by people in the
psychological healing field can be classified as 'spiritual' experiences (and
states). Spiritual experiences are ignored or rejected by the vast majority
of psychologists because most of this data is outside of the dominant paradigm, and because there is no adequate model for understanding the phenomenon. Although the field of transpersonal psychology was founded to
explore this area, its descriptions and classification schemes are difficult to
understand, and no comprehensive model arose. Dr. Stanislav Grof's
work attempted to be a comprehensive model of psychology and spirituality, but, although a huge step forward, missed part of the solution. For example, it can't be used to deal with the dominant problems of mental
illness. The biggest omission was in failing to recognize the importance of
the triune brain, without which many underlying mechanisms cannot be
understood. Classification schemes, such as that of Ken Wilber, have not
proved useful in understanding underlying causes or assisted in developing ways to acquire the states.

Like many of you, when I was trying to understand the phenomena of
peak states and exceptional mental and physical health, I did a lot of experiential work in a variety of classical and modern spiritual paths, such as
Zen, yoga, Almaas's work, etc. Repeatedly, I encountered blank looks
from the teachers when I described experiences and states of consciousness that I'd had. Worse, all of my teachers rejected the importance of any
experience they didn't recognize. Additionally, the states that each
teacher from different traditions considered important were *not* the same.
Finally, just finding out the characteristics of the states they desired was
difficult. I could never tell if this was to increase the mystique of their
teaching, or if they hadn't experienced them themselves, or what was going on—and I still can't. However, from my personal experience in a huge
variety of spiritual states, they all can be described to some degree or

other, if by no other means than by their effects on a person's actions. Some bring drastic physiological changes, others have drastic psychological effects, and so on. For example, the word 'enlightenment', although used in our culture quite often, has no identifying descriptors tied to it, and hence has no real meaning. Our culture assigns it a meaning based on our preconceptions about spirituality.

Example:
> I can still recall my surprise when I went into samadhi for four straight days, while still teaching electrical engineering classes—and found I would only take a slight breath of air every 10 to 15 minutes when I wasn't needing air to talk! The state was stable, but eventually I figured out a way to return to average consciousness.

Example:
> For the first 30 years of my life, when I would close my eyes at night, the inside of my head was completely filled with bright white/golden light. It had the intensity of Hawaiian sunshine. In fact, the light radiated from my body a few inches also. I assumed this was normal, and in fact didn't even notice it was there until it faded over a period of a few months during my thirties. The contrast of change allowed me to recognize its existence.

Conflicting beliefs:
- Spiritual experiences are delusional.
- Spiritual states cannot coexist with mental illness.
- Spiritual teachers know all about the meaningful spiritual states and experiences.
- All spiritual practices are designed to bring us into a state of enlightenment.

Spiritual Emergencies

However, we can look at an area of study that has direct bearing on our work, and unlike spiritual states in general, is very well documented from a descriptive and experiential viewpoint. This is the area of spiritual emergency that Grof pioneered in the early 1980s. In general, these experiences are outside the norms of our culture, and are either intrinsically a crisis (e.g. demonic possession), or create such a big change in the person that they can become a crisis, hence the name 'spiritual emergency'. The internal distress can be as simple as a conflict with deeply held religious beliefs, to problems that are outside the dominant culture's belief system. Another reason spiritual experiences can become a crisis is when one leaves one of these spiritual 'peak' states and feels overwhelming loss and grief, feeling that average consciousness is like going to hell, and despair that the state might not return. More gradual versions of many of these experiences also occur, but are often not distressing to the individual because they have time to adjust. We recommend reading the books on spiritual emergency listed at the end of the chapter for more information on this topic. Our work in this area, which sometimes disagrees with others in the field can be found in our book *The Basic Whole-Hearted Healing Manual*, or on our website at www.PeakStates.com.

Example:
> The 'Spiritual Emergence Network' started by the Grofs is a free phone referral service run by volunteers for people in these types of crisis. A huge variety of calls came. For example, one person called because she was hearing what people were thinking without being able to shut it out. Several classmates in my psychology program were spontaneous 'channels' but couldn't control or stop it.

Example:
> The rate at which a positive spiritual experience occurs can be a problem. A man suddenly realized that we are all one. He then threw off his clothes and ran down the main street proclaiming it, and was picked up by the police and delivered to a hospital. This awareness came too suddenly and overwhelmingly for him to handle it properly. Fortunately, the psychiatrist involved recognized the state, did not drug him, and three days later he was fine, his experience balanced against day-to-day life.

Example:
> Kundalini awakening experiences are often very disruptive to the people involved. My own girlfriend developed it, and the symptoms were so strange she feared that she had a major medical problem. She also found it nearly impossible to sleep for almost six months. The experience was hellish for both her and myself, partly because we had no idea what was going on.

For example, so many people were experiencing kundalini awakening that excellent diagnostic criteria were developed in the '80s. One caution on this particular experience, however—many of the writers on the topic tend to ignore the diagnostic criteria and throw virtually every state into the 'kundalini' pile. This tendency seems to be particularly a problem with writers that had experienced kundalini themselves, oddly enough. Kundalini, although unusual, in my experience shouldn't be considered a peak state as it is invoked unconsciously by people in an attempt to heal themselves. However, kundalini often evokes unusual temporary peak experiences.

To review, Grof's classification structure of spiritual emergency includes many categories which we wouldn't remotely consider to be peak states, such as demonic possession, channeling, alien abduction, past lives, near death experiences, etc. One category called Psychic Opening covers psychic abilities which are probably a byproduct of peak states. They become a crisis if these abilities become uncontrollable. Other categories are crises that directly involve peak states, such as shamanic crisis, psychological renewal through activation of the central archetype, and unitive consciousness.

These 'spiritual emergency' states are generally the result of meditation, although there are other triggers such as life-threatening events, extreme physical exertion, sleep deprivation, childbirth, sex, loss, and life failure, to list the major causes. Rarely is one of these spiritual emergencies 'spontaneous'.

Conflicting beliefs:
- Spiritual states are only for special people, not ourselves.
- Spiritual states can only be received from God, at 'his' whim. Nothing we do matters.
- Spiritual states are only given to us if we work hard at being virtuous.
- We develop from average consciousness towards spiritual states and perfection.
- People are not born into spiritual states.

Definition - Spiritual emergency

Spiritual emergencies are not crises of faith. Instead, they involve very disruptive and disturbing episodes of experiences that are outside of our cultural belief systems. Often, people have these sorts of spiritual experiences without major upsets in their lives, but for some people the experience is too abrupt and extreme, particularly when it is completely unknown and frightening. When these spiritual experiences become a crisis, they're called a spiritual emergency.

In the early 1980s, Dr. Stanislav Grof wrote the primary book on spiritual emergencies, and gave a 12-part categorization that became standard to the field. A number of experiences are not covered in his categories, but it's still a very adequate map of the field. He and his wife Christina also started a free phone referral service in the US to put people who were experiencing one of these spiritual emergencies in touch with therapists who knew about them.

In the late 1990s, this phone service was picked up by Dr. Brant Cortright at the California Institute for Integral Studies. Another organization for Canadians was also started in the late 1990s.

Invulnerable Children

Have you ever noticed that some people just seem to be happier, healthier, more successful, able to weather life's ups and downs more easily than you do? I think we all have, and of course there are a variety of reasons. In the current psychological paradigm, it's believed that these people had better childhoods, had fewer traumas, better genetic backgrounds, better friends, and so on. In this model, it boils down to two factors—better genes or a better environment. And recently a third element has been added: better prenatal care.

However, our cultural idea that nurture is the dominant influence on one's degree of mental health was discovered to be wrong when longitudinal studies of children 'at risk' because of traumatic early environments (poverty, neglect, abuse) were made. These studies in the '60s, '70s and '80s, quite against expectations, found that a small group of 'at risk' children lived through their terrible childhood experiences and yet flourished anyway. Although the statistics are hard to determine from the studies, the group of flourishing children is somewhere between 1/10 to 1/3 of the studied 'at risk' population. They became known as "invulnerable children" (later termed "stress resistant" or "resilient" children). The existence of these children caused a tremendous furor, because some people interpreted the data as saying that trying to help 'at risk' children was pointless, since apparently the environment didn't make any difference. Of course, that argument was ridiculous since only a minority of children could be put in that category.

One might suppose that these invulnerable children were just fortunate in life's genetic lottery, but even more puzzling was that occasionally some of these children as adults would suddenly stop being invulnerable, and have the same difficulties that the others who were not invulnerable were having. This invalidated the genetic explanation, since their genes hadn't changed. No explanation was discovered, although conventional theory guessed that there might be a threshold of accumulating trauma, different for different people—the straw that broke the camel's back idea. Yet, a number of these adults were living in pretty good situations by that time and no longer exposed to significant trauma, which invalidated that hypothesis. In the years since the initial discovery of the invulnerable children, a tremendous number of papers have been written trying to fit these children into the dominant model, but a close look at the criteria they use and the results they get quickly shows that this just doesn't work.

Oddly, this phenomenon of invulnerable children gets virtually no teaching time in psychology school, probably because it is completely outside of the current paradigm. In that, it's a lot like the placebo effect, which is also ignored in medical schools because it too is outside of the dominant paradigm.

Experiments on 'learned helplessness' with animals bear a striking resemblance to this phenomenon of invulnerable children. In the original experiments by Steve Maier, Bruce Overmier and Martin Seligman, dogs were given inescapable electric shocks. After they learned that nothing they did mattered, they no longer tried to escape the shocks even when it became possible to do so. However, about a third of the rats and dogs tested did not become helpless but instead never gave up, no matter what was done to them. Are these simple shock tests on dogs and rats comparable to complex human 'at risk' situations? Perhaps, and in both cases the percentage of invulnerable children and optimistic animals is remarkably similar.

Conflicting beliefs:
- Bad childhood environments will always create behavior or personality problems later in life.
- The degree children are nurtured, have good genes, and have good prenatal care predetermines their degree of mental health and stability.

Key Points

- People live their lives with a group of beliefs that filter what they are willing to look at and define acceptable activities. Even obvious contradictions are ignored. Each of these groups of beliefs is called a paradigm.
- Several paradigms about mental health have appeared over the last five decades due to the development of new techniques and the acceptance of previously ignored data.
- In the last twenty years, data on spiritual emergencies, resilient children, peak experiences, and spiritual states has accumulated that cannot be explained by the current paradigms.

Suggested Reading and Websites

On invulnerable children
- E. J. Anthony and B.J. Cohler (Eds.), *The Invulnerable Child*, Guilford, 1987.
- E.E. Werner and R.S. Smith, *Vulnerable but Invincible: A longitudinal study of resilient children and youth*, McGraw-Hill, 1982.

On peak experiences, peak abilities, and unusual states
- The Exceptional Human Experience Network at www.ehe.org. They study out-of-the-ordinary experiences with reviews of relevant books.
- Stanislav Grof MD, *The Adventure of Self-Discovery*, State University of New York Press, 1988. Dimensions of consciousness and new

perspectives in psychotherapy and inner exploration. A good coverage of his work on birth trauma and transpersonal experiences, for lay people and professionals.

- Stanislav Grof MD, *The Cosmic Game: Explorations of the frontiers of human consciousness*, State University of New York Press, 1998. An excellent look at fundamental issues from his years of work.
- Stanislav Grof MD, *LSD Psychotherapy*, Hunter House, 1980. For professionals, it covers in great depth unusual experiences that can be encountered in psychedelic therapy.
- D. E. Harding, *On Having No Head: Zen and the rediscovery of the obvious, revised edition*, Inner Directions Foundation, 2002. Describes what it feels like when the sensation of the skin boundary vanishes.
- Abraham Maslow, *Religions, Values, and Peak Experiences*, 1976. A classic in the field, one of the books that started the Humanistic Psychology movement.
- Dr. Raymond Moody Jr., *The Light Beyond*, Bantam, 1988. A sequel to *Life after Life*. Both are on the Near Death Experience by the man who first described the phenomenon. Written for a general audience.
- Dr. Raymond Moody, Jr., *Reunions: Visionary Encounters with departed loved ones*, Ivy Books, 1994. A very fascinating account of his discovery and adaption to the present of the Greek process for communicating with the dead.
- Michael Murphy, *The Future of the Body: Explorations Into the Further Evolution of Human Nature*, Jeremy P. Tarcher, 1992. A survey collection of material from a variety of sources on unusual abilities and experiences circa the 1980's.

On power therapies
- Power and energy therapies articles at www.psychinnovations.com.
- Leslie Bandler, *Solutions: Practical and effective antidotes for sexual and relationship problems*, Real People Press, 1985. It covers the power therapy VKD from the Neuro-Linguistic Programming approach.
- Gerald French and Chrys Harris, *Traumatic Incident Reduction (TIR)*, CRC Press, 1999. A well written manual for the TIR power therapy.
- Fred Gallo, *Energy Psychology: Explorations at the Interface of Energy, Cognition, Behavior, and Health*, CRC Press, 1998. One of the first survey books in this field.
- Grant McFetridge and Mary Pellicer MD, *The Basic Whole-Hearted Healing Manual*, The Institute for the Study of Peak States Press, 2000. Covers the WHH regression therapy.
- Francis Shapiro and Margot Forrest, *EMDR: The Breakthrough Therapy for overcoming anxiety, stress, and trauma*, Basic Books, 1998. Covers the EMDR power therapy.

On shamanic states
- Foundation for Shamanic Studies, the organization that Michael Harner founded at www.shamanism.org.
- Tom Brown, Jr., *Awakening Spirits*, Berkley, 1994. His only book so far on his shamanic techniques, based on his first level of training. Recommended.
- Michael Harner, *Way of the Shaman: Tenth anniversary edition*, Harper, 1990. A classic in the field, describes the shamanic journey approach to shamanism.
- Sandra Ingerman, *Soul Retrieval: Mending the fragmented self through shamanic practice*, Harper, 1991. Written by Harner's colleague, an excellent coverage of the soul stealing and loss phenomenon.
- Hank Wesselman, *Spiritwalker: Messages from the future*, Bantam, 1995. An very well written account of an anthropologist and modern shaman communicating with a future life time.

On spiritual emergencies
- Spiritual Emergence Network at www.ciis.edu/comserv/sen.html. Treatment, referrals, and descriptions of spiritual emergencies.
- Treatment, referrals, and references for Canadians in spiritual emergencies can be found online at the Canadian Spiritual Emergence Service at www.spiritualemergence.net/pages/home.html.
- Emma Bragdon, *A Sourcebook for Helping People in Spiritual Emergency*, Lightening Up Press, 1988. Focused on procedures for helping people in these crises.
- Stanislav Grof MD, *Spiritual Emergency: When personal transformation becomes a crisis*, Jeremy P. Tarcher, 1989. The formative book in the field, with articles by a variety of key authors.
- Yvonne Kason MD, *A Farther Shore: How new-death and other extraordinary experiences can change ordinary lives*, HarperCollins, 1994. Well written book on spiritual emergency.

Chapter 2

Peak States of Consciousness as the Cause of Exceptional Quality of Life and Mental Health

"You never change things by fighting the existing reality. To change something, build a new model that makes the existing model obsolete."
— *R. Buckminster Fuller*

Introduction

In the last chapter, we looked at key data that is anomalous or contradicts current beliefs. In this chapter, we'll describe a simple conceptual breakthrough that explains that data in an elegantly simple and useful way—the idea of peak states of consciousness.

With this understanding, exceptional quality of life and mental health occurs because the person is in one or more peak states of consciousness. These states have identical characteristics for everyone who has them, and people can be in them most or all of the time, even from birth. This concept may sound trivial, but its lack is a huge stumbling block to the field of psychology which has almost completely stifled progress in the core objective of improving people's lives.

Grant's story
Why I Investigated Peak States

Why did I look in this direction of peak states of consciousness? Because until I was 29 I lived in one, a radically different kind of state from that of average people. Since I had always been in it, I just considered it normal, and didn't think that I was much different from anyone else—rather, I was just as painfully aware of my own failings as most of us are. The ways I was different didn't really stand out in childhood, but became more and more pronounced the older I got. For example, as the years went on, I became extremely frustrated because I could not understand or predict how people were going to react to things—what people did just didn't make any sense to me. I tried to understand, and in a breakthrough moment at age 24, I suddenly realized people must be afraid, and that this generalized fear was projected on whatever was going on in their lives, causing them to act in the ways that they did. It was difficult for me to understand, as it was so outside of my own experience.

As I got older, I tried to share the way I was, especially with my wife, but with no success. Not being able to help others live in the way I was living caused me great distress. Lacking any other model, I assumed the differences must be cultural, as I was a Canadian living in the US with an American wife, and on top of that I was part of the alternative lifestyle movement.

All this changed when I was 29. During a divorce, I suddenly lost my state. The difference was dramatic, so much so that it felt like I'd been kicked out of heaven and sent to hell. I now realized exactly how tormenting and painful average consciousness was. I'd always assumed that a person could just 'let go' of their issues if they really wanted to. I had no idea that this just wasn't an option for most people. Now I was like everyone else, and I couldn't get back to what I'd had no matter what I did.

The changes were obvious and dramatic. My past suddenly had a lot of emotionally painful memories. I started to dream most every night, something that I had almost never done. The sense of being alive and feeling the aliveness in things around me vanished. Spiritual truths, which had been so obvious I could never tell why people bothered to talk about them, suddenly became something I had to be told about and memorize. I could feel anxiety and a lack of safety in myself at all times. I started to judge people, rather than just be curious as to what they were about. From my perspective now, I had lost the state we call 'Walking in Beauty' or 'The Beauty Way' (the name is from the Native American culture).

Over the next ten years, I tried to get back what I'd lost. This was no minor loss, as I considered suicide a number of times—I felt life was not worth living in average consciousness. As part of my state had involved intuitively knowing spiritual truths, I assumed various spiritual traditions must know about what I had lost and how to get it back. This turned out to be false, as none of the teachers I worked with recognized what I was talking about. In fact, they tried to get me to say that what I was searching for was worthless and a distraction, that if it had had any value, it had been just a stage and should be left behind. Eventually, I found out that shamans recognized the state, but that they didn't have any good ways of inducing or recovering it.

I searched for years. Finally, I realized if I was going to understand what I'd lost, and get it back, I was going to have to do it myself. There was no one out there that I could buy it from. This was the genesis of the Institute for the Study of Peak States.

My own experience of living in a very radical peak state most of my life taught me several key things about them. This gave me a tremendous advantage in trying to understand them, and the ability to ignore the dominant paradigm, since I knew it was false from hard personal experience. First, I knew that there were stable states of consciousness far outside the norm. Secondly, I knew you don't have to 'practice' or 'be nice' or 'pray' or 'be good' or do anything in particular to get or stay in peak states of consciousness. In fact, as a child I fought with my brother and sister, wasn't nice to my parents, didn't go to church or believe in God, or anything else that could be considered as making me worthy of a peak state (especially one which had considerable spiritual overtones, where I effortlessly knew spiritual truths that others spend their lifetimes studying!) Years later, during my experimental phase, I entered more and more different states of consciousness. To my surprise, I discovered that there were quite a number of them, all radically different from each other.

My intuition said that trauma was the key to understanding why people didn't have peak states. To better study this, I developed the Whole-Hearted Healing therapy. I used it both to understand and to eliminate trauma from my life. I figured that since I wasn't able to solve the problem with a flash of genius, I'd just have to eliminate all traumatic material out of my consciousness and hopefully the answer would eventually become obvious. This eventually worked and led to the material in Chapter 4.

Natural Peak States

Let's turn our attention to something in our own lives that might give us the answer to the question, "Why do some people have exceptional mental health?" Try to recall one of your peak experiences. Wouldn't it be amazing to be able to live your life like that every day, not just for the short time you had it? What if many of those amazing adults you know or invulnerable children you've read about were in just such a type of nearly continuous peak experience? That would surely cause them to seem more resilient and happier than the rest of us, although unless you had some sort of test for it this explanation might be easy to overlook. Rather than explaining away the data as some sort of dissociative disorder in these invulnerable children, we propose that these kids are actually mentally healthier than the average person. And sure enough, it turns out that a small percentage of the general population, not just those put under extreme stress as children, do live in a nearly continuous peak experience, something we call a 'peak state'. The existence of these peak states is one of the key discoveries we've made. The second part of this discovery is that there is a large number of distinctly different states, and each kind of state has characteristics that are the *same for everyone*. Those invulnerable kids were almost certainly in a long-lasting (although maybe not 100% of the time) peak state of consciousness, one in which trauma didn't affect them as it does 'average' people.

Our culture predisposes us to assume there is a developmental sequence of peak states that one can go through to reach the goal of exceptional mental health. Thus, one would give up previous states, or build on previous states like mastering advanced mathematics. However, this hierarchal idea about peak states is in general incorrect, with the exception of triune brain states as described in Chapter 5. In fact, there are a number of unrelated states of exceptional mental health that can be reached. This is because there are a variety of unrelated peak states of consciousness, and they are all quite different from each other. These states can also be acquired in combination. It's as if the possible states are like marbles, and although one can pick up a single marble, one can also collect an assortment of different ones.

The existence of natural peak states often escapes our notice. A small percentage of the population is gifted with various peak states without having done anything in particular, generally from the cradle! These are the people who just seem to be happier, healthier, more functional; their life is simply better, they're nicer than average... I'm sure you can think of several examples from your life. Since they had these states from early childhood, clearly all the models and beliefs involving 'inner growth' do not apply—they had them from before the time they could talk, after all! And it can't be genetic; this as shown by the loss of 'invulnerability' in some adults. What causes peak states will be covered in Chapter 4.

Interestingly, we don't generally recognize that these people are in a peak state, and often neither do the people in it. Since our culture doesn't recognize this phenomenon, we just chalk it up to a good early environment, good genetics, few life traumas, a good personality, and so on—essentially, the 'good nurturing' environment model. Or we might call it denial of real life.

Example:
> A woman in her fifties lived in a household with her husband and sister. The husband was happy all the time, the sister was very accepting and easygoing. The woman, who was plagued by painful feelings and memories, believed that the other two were in denial about their lives, based on her own experience. In fact, she tried to help them 'get in touch with their feelings', so that they would be more like her. We put her into the Inner Peace state, and she realized from her own experience that they were not in denial, but in fact were living life in a much more wonderful way than she had ever had. She spontaneously apologized to the others for her behavior and attitude within hours of achieving her own peak state.

Thus, one of the Institute paradigm's conflicts with our dominant cultural assumptions is due to our recognition that some people have peak experiences that range from part to nearly all of their daily experience. Oddly, both Humanistic Psychology and Transpersonal Psychology completely overlook this phenomenon! (Conventional psychology denies the existence or possibility of peak experiences at all, of course.) I have absolutely no idea why, but the current paradigm says that only peak 'experiences' exist, and no work is done *at all* to identify those people who live in continuous peak states.

Of course, a number of people have been described in the psychological literature who can do unusual, non-ordinary things—Jack Schwarz who can run a knitting needle through his arm without any injury jumps to mind—but aside from doing brain wave tests, investigators have held the unspoken underlying assumption that either these people are completely unique, or they are just like anyone else but have some sort of unusual ability, perhaps like perfect pitch, and they only have this occasionally. That these people might be in a continuous type of peak state is not even considered.

Once you realize that peak states exist, and that people sometimes move in and out of them, you can usually easily identify individuals who have them most or all of the time. These people are usually unaware that they have a peak state, it's just how their life is, although they are aware that other people seem to be a lot more messed up than they are.

Chapter 13 gives a number of personal accounts involving peak states of consciousness. Appendix A contains a list of peak states we've identified so far and our estimates of their occurrence. The two most obvious and significant of the naturally appearing peak states are called the 'Inner Peace' state and the 'Underlying Happiness' state. The Inner Peace state has several characteristics, but one of the most important for this discussion is that people who have it experience their past without any emotional content. They experience the present with an underlying sense of calm, peace, and lightness that exists even when they feel their feelings. Such a state does tend to make one's life drastically better, no matter the past or present circumstances. The other state, 'Underlying Happiness' is just that, as the person in it feels a sense of happiness continuously in the background. In women, this state expresses itself with happiness combined with a strong loving feeling.

Conflicting beliefs:
- People who are usually happy or exceptional are actually in denial about the problems in their lives. In psychological terms, they have dissociated from real life.

An Example of a Lifelong Beauty Way State

Bruce has had the Beauty Way state (a composite state that includes Inner Peace) as long as he can remember. It gives a sense of peacefulness without any feeling to past trauma, and a sensation of aliveness in oneself and in the world. He also has some of the Underlying Happiness state although he feels the Beauty Way part is stronger. We had the opportunity to work together for a number of years, and from my perspective it was not only a pleasure but a relief—he was calm and cheerful no matter what was happening around him, unlike so many of our other colleagues in our high stress job situation. We used a question and answer format for his contribution:

"What is the state like?

Hard to describe, but it is an unshakeable serenity that does not depend on anything external, or internal, for that matter.

Why would people want your state?

It enables one to feel compassion for real human challenges, yet not be stymied by them. Most of the time I'm able to feel a concern, do what I can to remedy as appropriate (respond wholeheartedly), and then move on to the current situation.

How did you get it, or did you always have it?

I feel this state has evolved over this lifetime and still "in process" but getting deeper all the time, generally.

What is the difference between yourself and someone else without the state?

Nothing really; I just choose to feel a peacefulness more and more in spite of circumstances.

What problems are caused by having the state?

Sometimes I can be perceived by others as being unfeeling, yet in fact, I actually am free to feel more deeply. I just have been learning not to become attached to the feelings and let them flow through me somewhat spontaneously, while the "background serenity" remains.

Would you recommend the state to others, and how much?

Definitely, and 100%.

Does the state make you feel special, unique, isolated?

Not really, although sometimes when I see folks get emotionally manipulated by events (without really feeling them) I can feel a bit isolated, but not in any real sense, because I feel compassion, including for myself.

Has your state had any effect on your health, i.e. still get sick a lot, rarely sick, aging, etc.?

I'm rarely sick, and see discomfort as a feedback mechanism from the creator as a divine blessing to be heeded immediately. I used to procrastinate responding, and now when I get a momentary "twinge" I pay attention and change course appropriately."

The Differences Between Peak Experiences, Peak States, and Peak Abilities

Before we go any further, I would like to clear up a potential area of confusion in our use of vocabulary. In this text, we differentiate between peak experiences, peak states, and peak abilities.

- A peak experience is a brief experience that is extremely positive or uplifting, outside of the range of average experience, as detailed in the previous chapter.
- A peak ability is an ability, either physical or 'spiritual', that is also outside the range of average experience.
- A peak state is a *long lasting* peak experience in everyday life, hence the use of the word 'state', implying something that is stable and continuous.

When we speak about peak states, we sometimes use the modifiers 'stable' or 'unstable'.

- A stable peak state is one that the person keeps without any effort or technique. If he loses it, usually due to some outside stress, the loss is only temporary and the state returns automatically, usually when the stressor is removed, without any effort on his part.
- An unstable peak state is one that requires technique or outside circumstance to maintain. If the state is lost, some sort of intervention is required to recover it. For example, an intervention might be a time in nature, a focus on love or the divine, and so on. The phrase also applies to a peak state that was lost and not recovered, the implication being that the required intervention was not known by the person who lost the state.

Although all peak states can be considered peak experiences if they don't last very long, not all peak experiences can be peak states. By this I mean there are a large number of peak experiences we can have that are not changes in our inner being, rather they are actions or experiences of our inner being. For example, you might have had an out-of-body experience that takes you to a non-physical 'place' that was simply overwhelmingly beautiful. Afterwards, when you spoke about it you would most likely say that you had an amazing peak experience. But it wouldn't be a peak state as it didn't involve a long lasting change in your consciousness here in the real world. Your experience was about going somewhere temporarily, not something that was now a continuous part of your life. Even if it were possible to make the experience permanent, you and your family would call it a disaster, not a peak state!

How do peak abilities fit into this? Notice that in the previous example, you probably needed to have a peak state (even if only temporarily) to be able to have that specific peak ability of consciously getting out of body. Particular peak abilities come with certain peak states. However, we suspect it's possible in some limited cases to have a peak ability without an accompanying peak state.

It turns out there is a beautifully simple explanation for how all the transpersonal and spiritual experiences, states, and abilities fit together, which we'll explore in detail in Chapter 4.

Mental Health and Peak States

A key misunderstanding often comes up about mental health with people who are curious about our work with peak states of consciousness. It has to do with our culture's assumptions about what mental health is. Most people assume mental health is the absence of overt mental illness, and that 'ordinary' or 'average' people are mentally healthy. Actually, from our model ordinary or average consciousness is also one of mental ill-health. We will be going into great detail about this in Chapters 4 and 5, but for now we'll just say that peak states are not extra qualities added onto ordinary consciousness. Instead, peak states are our birthright. We as a species are designed to have these states as our normal way of being. Unfortunately, since people with peak states are in the minority, our society's beliefs about mental health have been formed by looking at a distorted picture. To exaggerate for clarity, the situation is a bit similar to inmates of an asylum looking at each other to decide what mental health is. They then assign the label of exceptional mental health to the few staff members.

In this text, we use the word 'average' or 'ordinary' to describe people without any peak states. We use the word 'normal' to describe someone with some or all possible peak states, as this is a state of health. We use these terms in the same way that your eye doctor does—20/20 eyesight is considered to be 'normal' (i.e., your eyes are working properly), yet the average person needs corrective lenses.

Example:
> A woman had been spending years working on her healing. When I offered her the option of going into a peak state where her painful emotional past would just vanish, she refused. She felt that this was somehow cheating her inner work, and that a healthy person didn't need those states.

Example:
> During a conference, a deeply religious woman had this reaction to the peak states paradigm: "People have come to earth to suffer to learn a lesson. Even if you could put them in a painless, effort-

less and peaceful state, it would be wrong." I told her that although I shared this concern myself in the beginning of this work, I've never found any evidence to support this idea. However, to my great surprise, instead of learning a lesson, I found we are here to accomplish a purpose. In several cases that I've seen, a peak state was necessary to even have a hope of fulfilling the purpose. Although I don't know the outcome of our conversation, I'd like to think I gave her hope for a better life.

Conflicting beliefs:
- Average consciousness is a state of mental health.
- A peak state is an avoidance of spiritual growth.

Existing Applications of Peak State Theory

Rather than trying to achieve peak experiences and states directly, several innovators have observed people in these states and tried to codify how they act in order to improve the lives of average people by teaching them these behaviors. The clearest example of this that I know of is Marshall Rosenberg's process for successful interpersonal conflict resolution, described in the book *Nonviolent Communication: A Language of Compassion*. He found people in these unusual states, watched how they naturally interacted, and derived rules that guided their state's normal behavior.

Another application involves using states of consciousness without realizing that they exist. Gay and Kathlyn Hendricks have developed a body-centered therapy that uses the 'Underlying Happiness' state to facilitate change in their clients. They use a variety of techniques in their therapy, which can be found in the book *At the Speed of Life*. They get their clients into the correct state by teaching them how to love themselves. They do an exceptional job of explaining how to do this (and consequently putting their clients into the state they want) in the book *Learning to Love Yourself* and its companion volume *The Learning to Love Yourself Workbook*.

Another application of peak states is in the Whole-Hearted Healing therapy for healing trauma. The therapy works by using steps that can be done by people in average consciousness. These steps simulate a much faster and easier healing process that uses a peak state called the Hollow state. The therapy is described in *The Basic Whole-Hearted Healing Manual* by Grant McFetridge and Mary Pellicer, or on the website www. PeakStates.com.

Encountering Conflicts With a New Paradigm

I recommend approaching our work like we at the Institute for the Study of Peak States did. We're a bunch of hard-core skeptics, but we were willing to look at anything if it moved in the direction of solving the problem of understanding and acquiring peak states. The bottom line is, does it work? Anything else is just refinement. That is the only criterion we use. None of us are comfortable with some of the results we're getting—after all, we share the Western paradigm too—but they come up in our work whether we want them to or not. Thus, be skeptical. But suspend your preconceptions and try it out. If it works, there must be something there.

This is the heart of a paradigm shift. A paradigm tells you how to live life and solve problems, and it also tells you what to ignore as being irrelevant or false. This works fine as long as it solves the problems adequately. A new paradigm comes into being when the old one fails to solve a significant problem, or fails to allow you to respond successfully to changing external conditions. Thus, we get examples like the Swiss watch makers who actually invented the battery-operated watch, but it didn't fit their paradigm of a watch being a mechanical device. Only ten years later the whole Swiss watch industry was virtually eliminated by the Japanese and US semiconductor firms who didn't share their paradigm.

However, when you're in a paradigm it's almost impossible to tell, as it feels true. To give this idea visual impact, let me paint a word picture. Imagine that you've gone to the South American jungle because there are reports of cures of an incurable disease by a native shaman. You go there and sure enough, people are getting cured, something you really were convinced was impossible. This is the first paradigm conflict. After you recover from that, you watch what he does. You pick out the parts, like the awful-smelling concoction, and since your paradigm says drugs cure things, you find out how it's made and try it out. If it works, fine, it matched your paradigm and you continue on your way. If it doesn't, then you're in another paradigm conflict. You look at what else he's doing, and you notice that he chants a lot. So in desperation, you try that violation of your paradigm, and amazingly it works. After you get over that, you eventually discover a totally unknown phenomenon that you label 'hypnosis', and find that the concoction only relaxed the patient. I'm obviously making up this example, but in the 1800s hypnosis was outside of the current paradigm, and I'm sure it bothered people then just as much as paradigm violations bother people now. Notice too that the explorer didn't have to give up his whole paradigm, just the parts that were blocking his ability to see what was really going on. The Swiss who lost their jobs didn't have to give up the parts of their paradigm that told them how to eat, go to work, pay their bills—just the part that said that the best way to make watches was with machinery.

The Institute for the Study of Peak States (ISPS) Paradigm

So far, we've identified many conflicted beliefs about peak experiences and states of consciousness. But what is *our* paradigm? Briefly, it is:
- Peak experiences can be had continuously.
- Some people can have a peak state without having healed anything.
- Peak states are not something you have to work toward achieving, like getting an advanced degree or some sort of prize for leading a virtuous life. Instead, they're your natural state.
- Even though you may be in a peak state, you need to learn how to use all its qualities effectively.
- Any given peak state doesn't make you perfect. Other people don't necessarily notice that you are in a peak state. You still have areas of dysfunction, until a state is achieved with no more trauma of any type.
- All the data in biology, psychology, and spiritual/shamanic experience has to tie together perfectly. Everything must be explainable from one underlying model.
- The scientific method applies perfectly to this problem. Hypothesis, experimentation, models, verification, prediction, and a LOT of reality checking are required.
- Virtually everything people say about the problem is wrong.

In Chapter 4 we'll explain what causes peak states in great detail. But for completeness, I'll list the rest of our paradigm now:
- The reason most people don't have peak states is due to specific kinds of trauma.
- Anyone can have peak states permanently, it's just a matter of eliminating the correct type of trauma.
- Even correctly healing the underlying problems does not keep you continuously in peak states. Your remaining problems kick you out of them temporarily while they're being stimulated by the internal or external environment.
- You have already had most and probably all peak states *in utero*—you've just forgotten.

Conflicts With the New Peak State Paradigm

In the section, I'd like to specifically address some of the concerns that people have raised with our peak states paradigm when we describe our work in workshops and conferences. Many of these concerns are ones that we ourselves once shared, and only over time did we come to have a different viewpoint. I hope you find it useful to see these issues addressed all in one place when thinking about this new paradigm.

Conflicts With General Western Cultural Assumptions

Because of the subject and content of our work at the Institute, people sometimes assume that we don't share everyday cultural beliefs. Nothing could be further from the truth! I did my graduate work at Stanford University in electrical engineering before moving to psychology, and several of my associates are MDs. We only came to the paradigm in this book slowly and I might add with great resistance. Yet we had to look at all of the data, not just what felt comfortable to us in order to create practical, real-world models with practical solutions. On a personal note, it's now hard for me to relate to mainstream assumptions about mental health anymore. They've been slowly eroded away by 15 years of work in this area of peak states and healing. I am still impressed that people who approach our work for the first time are able to suspend disbelief long enough to listen to us.

What are some of the issues people encounter? One of the first is the very concept of peak experiences—some people have never felt one, and have no idea what we're talking about. Unless they have one themselves, they can find the whole concept difficult to accept—after all, our culture doesn't do so.

Another issue is around the specifics of our work. Fortunately, the developmental events model for triune brain peak states is compatible with mainstream Western cultural beliefs. However, the details can be a problem for some people. Cutting-edge work being done with techniques involving *in utero*, sperm or egg trauma is unknown to most people. The fact that the fetus, sperm and egg are self-aware and can suffer is beyond what most people have been taught to believe. Interestingly, many people, especially ones who work outside of medicine and psychiatry don't have as much difficulty accepting this as I would have expected. Apparently they assume we're experts and leave it at that.

Probably the biggest credibility hurdle we face is when we move to material that is generally only discussed in traditional spiritual or 'new-age' contexts. I'm referring to experiences of past lives, chakras, meridians, the Creator as seen during a near death experience, and Gaia, just to name a few. The only way I know to overcome this hurdle is to give people personal experiences, which is why we include techniques to do so in these books. It was tempting to delete these concepts when we wrote for the general public. However, the simple elegance of our model and how it encompasses all of the unusual phenomena we know about in one simple framework is extremely important for people who are working in this field. Thus, I chose to include it all and accept that some people will decide not to explore this work because of this choice.

Evaluating the Credibility of the New Paradigm

How might a person judge our credibility? Personally, if I've already heard about something from a lot of people I already know and who can vouch for it, I'm much more inclined to actually pay attention. Unfortunately, this option isn't available to us as our work is too new and too ground-breaking—only a relatively few specialists in this field know about it.

Another way to gain credibility is by charging high prices. However, we've chosen to make our work either available for free via the website or inexpensively in book or workshop form. Unfortunately, our culture has a conviction that cost and value are tied together, even though intellectually we know this isn't true. The unconscious assumption is "It costs a lot, it must be valuable" along with its opposite, "It's free, it must be worthless."

An interesting variation of this cultural assumption about money occurs when it's mixed with ideas about spirituality. A woman at a conference felt that our ideas about peak states must be wrong for what to her felt like an obvious reason—as we were not making large sums of money, our work was invalid. She felt that if we were really able to bestow 'instant spiritual states', as she interpreted our work, Deepak Chopra's 'seven laws of spiritual success' would immediately apply and we would all be wealthy. We have not found that people in peak states are typically affluent, although they tend to be successful in life in whatever way is important to them. Some states do appear to help people manifest what they want in life, whether it's money or something else. (See Chapter 10 for a technique that often has an impact in this area.)

I hold the hope that giving away fast, simple processes that actually work to put people into peak states with the reliability we've measured might make cause people to rethink the whole issue. A number of such processes are covered in this book.

Conflicts With Specific Spiritual Paths

At conferences, we often meet people who have already left the mainstream cultural assumptions behind and have chosen to follow one or more spiritual, religious, or shamanic traditions. Although I expected that our work would appeal to these people, this isn't always the case.

A close friend of mine wasn't interested in hearing details of my work—as he said, from his perspective, our approach didn't have heart, and so he'd stick with his Bhakti meditations. We do take a Western scientific approach to our work, involving as it does statistics, measurement tools, and testable processes. Since we're basically doing research and development, very few people have the temperament or background to work with us. However, we're also working out simple ways to get the same results without having to learn the details of our work, as the process in Chapter 9 illustrates. Our work is about love and compassion, but more than love is required. Mother Teresa loved the people she helped, but she also used practical skills to actually, physically help them.

Another man I deeply respect for his contributions to the field of healing felt our work couldn't be true, because the idea of peak states was in conflict with his understanding of the Course in Miracles. He felt, from

our casual conversation on the topic, that if what we said was true a person in such peak states would simply vanish from the earth. Although he
had no way to know this, most of the peak states that people can have are
ones that they've already had *in utero*. This is fortunate, for if we had to
study for peak states like learning calculus, how many people would be
willing or able to do so? Instead, we just have to recover what we've lost,
which is an entirely different kind of process.

Conflicts With the Concepts of Enlightenment and Self-Actualization
Another more general objection to our model of peak states has to do
with the concepts of enlightenment and self-actualization. A number of
people have said to me that they had no interest in our work because those
other goals were all they were interested in. Our work feels irrelevant to
them. However, what are their goals? Let's look at the word 'enlightenment' first. Our culture has a vague idea that there is an extremely valuable goal represented by this word, but unfortunately no one I know has a
clear, verifiable definition. As it's used today, it's a word without real
meaning.

The situation gets even more confusing when several spiritual practices are followed. Various groups that teach spirituality disagree on what
one should be working towards, and fail to acknowledge the validity of
other traditional spiritual paths. From our perspective, we see a number of
totally different and important states that different spiritual traditions focus on to the exclusion of others. For example, Gurdjieff's goal is different
from that of a Native shaman which is different from that of a Zen monk
which is different from that of a Taoist healer. Thus, we get yogis focusing
on the their spiritual states, but dying of terrible diseases. We get shamans
healing diseases and connected to the planetary consciousness, but ignorant of the states the yogis work towards. We have Buddhists focusing on
the Buddha mind, but ignoring Taoist longevity and healing practices.
And so on.

However, reflect a moment on the amazing, unique times we live in.
The twentieth century has brought great changes to the world's spiritual
paths by making their differences available for scrutiny. We're no longer
limited to one acceptable religion in a small geographical area.

Our work shows that people who are on a path of spiritual growth go
through many peak states of consciousness. In fact, from our viewpoint
these states should accumulate in a person. As of this writing, our idea of
an ultimate state is not a state at all, but rather a simultaneous combination of 'ultimate' states from many traditions. As far as we know, our view
that the goal of spiritual practice is to acquire a composite of many states is
unique.

The idea of enlightenment can cause another kind of confusion when
we discuss the peak states paradigm. Many people continue to unconsciously assume that there is really only one peak state, even though we
emphasize that there are a variety of very different ones. They assume that

we're talking about various degrees of inner serenity, a serenity that is independent of the events in one's life. Although there are states like this, there are also a huge variety of other peak states that don't give a feeling of serenity. I can point to people who are in a peak states where they feel happy all the time, yet can still be angry, sad, or whatever simultaneously. Making this distinction conscious can really help when presenting this material.

As far as self-actualization is concerned, this word has a little more of an objective definition. People in a variety of peak states exhibit the characteristics found in the literature on this concept. Apparently, our approach of achieving it, sort of by the back door as it were, is difficult for people to grasp at first. The states exhibit these qualities—one doesn't have to work to acquire the qualities of self-actualization directly if one moves into certain peak states.

Conflicts With the Paradigm of Spiritual Teachers

Another group of people who have strong reactions to our work are those who follow teachers or gurus, be they alive or deceased, and are actively doing spiritual practices or other self-improvement processes.

Many people have spent years learning a process or spiritual path and making a personal relationship with a teacher. Others have never had a personal relationship but rely on the writings of the teacher. These people can sometimes feel that if what we say is valid, then their teacher would have spoken about it to them already. For some, to even listen to our paradigm can feel like a betrayal of their teacher. And if they start to consider that we might be correct, it can feel as if they've wasted years of hard work for nothing. After one has given trust to a teacher, one expects him or her to keep one's best interests at heart and be totally knowledgeable and competent. Particularly with traditional spiritual practices, to consider the idea that generations of teachers might not have known everything relevant can seem sacrilegious.

Even the best spiritual teachers are like any specialists, and often can't keep up with material outside of their area of expertise or lineage. It's similar to seeing a medical specialist we like—if he can't help us, we go to others who may know more or who have different training. For example, twenty years ago Stanislav and Christina Grof brought to the world's attention the problem of 'spiritual emergencies'. Yet, even now, many meditation teachers are still unaware that meditation can trigger these events in some people. New ways of solving problems and healing people are being invented on a regular basis, ways that have never been seen before. A synthesis is happening on a world-wide basis that simply was never possible before and, as in the field of medicine, information overload has become a major problem.

Many people have encountered this conflict between teachers and their own experience. When we're looking for the truth, or the way, or whatever label we put on it, we generally start with the traditional forms that are offered. I had a similar conflict between what I was discovering and what my teachers were saying. If you've found yourself in this dilemma, I can only suggest doing what worked for me, a sort of common-sense approach to these issues. When I look at a teacher or a spiritual path, I look for inconsistencies with what I've learned elsewhere. I also look at the larger picture. Have the teachers really got their act together spiritually, emotionally, and physically? Do they have amazing personal relationships and marriages? Do they contribute, work, play, have fun? Do they get sick? Can they heal themselves and others? And so on.

A Loss of Hope for Deep Inner Change

Over the years, I've met a number of motivated, dedicated people who have done workshops, learned techniques, practiced a variety of spiritual paths, and yet continued to feel that nothing had worked for them. By the time they encounter our work, they may feel rather hopeless and, reasonably enough, this time they want to know how our work is any different. First of all, it's not just about 'our' techniques—rather, it's about a new way of looking at what people are really searching for. This book covers a number of techniques, developed by different people following different approaches to accomplish a similar goal—living in peak states. As I've said before, the new techniques have a much better track record for giving peak states in comparison to the previous generation of techniques. However, even these amazing new processes are not going to work for everyone. This field is still in its infancy, and success is not assured. Perhaps the best way to go is to try a variety of peak states techniques and so increase your odds of success. Organizations are starting to appear that plan on testing these and other processes for effectiveness so you can pick the processes that give you the best chances, but this movement is still in its infancy. We hope that in a few years you will be able to look up any given process in a 'consumer report' for psychological processes, but for now you don't have that option.

Let me address this issue in a different way, from just our perspective at the ISPS. What is totally different about our approach, the developmental events model, is that we are deriving the underlying theory of peak states—how we lose them and how to reclaim them. You can read about this, learn it by yourself, and even invent entirely new techniques on your own to solve the underlying problems we've discovered. We didn't start with a technique that worked, we started by exploring the problems that people have, derived underlying mechanisms, and then invented techniques to fix the problems we discovered. As time goes on we expect that we and other motivated people will devise faster and simpler techniques. However, our work is rather analytical, and still in the research and development stage. People can be put off by this, as it's a bit like learning electrical engineering rather than just using what engineers have done to throw the light switch on. Fortunately, just like those engineers have made light switches that don't require knowing calculus, we and other developers are making simple processes that can be used by the general public.

Our focus on underlying mechanisms has another benefit. People are complex, with a whole variety of reasons that might cause them difficulties in having peak states. Since we know what we are trying to accomplish and we understand many of the underlying mechanisms, we can sit down and usually figure out a way around a person's unique problem. Or people can do it for themselves, which I feel is very empowering.

Key Points

- One of the most important points in this book is that there are peak 'states' of consciousness. The dominant paradigm in both our Western culture and in psychology causes people to not think of the idea of peak states of consciousness as the explanation for a variety of personal and professional experiences. Generally, people's beliefs, regardless of data, would contradict this explanation if it were presented to them.
- Psychological, spiritual, and religious traditions focus on different aspects of enhanced mental health and ignore or reject conflicting data from each other. Most people come to accept this state of affairs as normal. No unifying theoretical explanation is publicly available that encompasses all known phenomena.
- A peak state is a peak experience of long duration, although not necessarily continuous.
- People can be in relatively permanent peak states of consciousness from birth.
- There are quite a large number of possible peak states with different characteristics.
- Any given peak state has identical characteristics for everyone.
- Peak states are states of increased mental health.

Suggested Reading and Websites

On current applications of peak states of consciousness
- Gay and Kathlyn Hendricks, *At the Speed of Life: A New Approach to Personal Change Through Body-centered Therapy*, Bantam, 1993. An excellent coverage of their body centered therapy techniques. Recommended.

- Grant McFetridge and Mary Pellicer,   M.D., *The Basic Whole-Hearted Healing Manual*, third edition, Institute for the Study of Peak States Press, 2003. A training manual for professionals and laymen in the Institute for the Study of Peak States regression process for healing trauma.
- Marshall Rosenberg, *Nonviolent Communication: A Language of Compassion*, Puddledancer Press, 1999. The best conflict resolution process that we know of. Their website for training and more information is at www.cnvc.org.

Chapter 3

Current Techniques for Acquiring Peak States of Consciousness

Introduction

A quiet revolution is occurring as new approaches and techniques for giving people peak states of consciousness are appearing from every part of the world. Many of these process developers already incorporate the concept of peak states in their personal paradigms. They build on traditional approaches and the previous generation of breakthroughs, older techniques that are in general unknown to most professionals and lay people. The techniques in this new generation are faster, more effective, more stable, and work for a much higher percentage of the general population. Unlike older techniques, many of the current generation of procedures can be finished in hours to days; others require only occasional brief maintenance sessions. Some of the best in the current generation of processes are described by their creators in Chapters 8 through 12.

This chapter will briefly cover both the older and the newer techniques that we know about. This material is particularly important to professionals, as it gives a feeling for the current state of the art in this field. It also allows technique developers to look at other approaches and the different phenomena they exploit so as to incorporate them into their work. We also expect interested readers to follow up on any technique that they find that looks intriguing. However, this field is in rapid change with new methods being created and old ones being improved, so be sure to check with the process developer for any changes before relying on the information in this chapter.

In years to come, we can imagine providing the name of the process, the contact information, the peak states that the technique confers, the percentage of the general population that it works on, and its degree of permanence. However, at this time the field is too new and changing too rapidly. Even basic issues like state names and their characteristics are still in flux. Methods for verifying what states a technique confers and how to measure technique effectiveness are still being derived. Even an understanding of the underlying mechanisms is generally absent from these techniques.

In this chapter we are grouping the techniques by the underlying approach they use for their effect. This gives a historical perspective to the lay person, but our primary reason for doing this is to give technique developers an awareness of alternative approaches. Interestingly, although in many cases the approaches can be combined together to make them faster and more effective, this is generally not yet done. We can roughly categorize the approaches used as: 1) the conscious choice (psychological) approach; 2) meditative (religious) practices; 3) induction (shamanic) techniques; 4) the mind/body approach; 5) the trauma-healing approach; and 6) the resolving dualism approach. Other categories could be formulated, but as of this writing we find these the most useful.

Technique Selection Criteria

I chose to include peak state techniques for this chapter based on the experiences of our colleagues and students, and discussions with people from organizations doing consciousness work. Since this field is so new, this is about the only way to even find out what techniques are available! Where possible, I tried to find out if the technique worked for many of the participants, even if it didn't work for the person involved. I rather arbitrarily excluded techniques that didn't appear to work for at least an observable number of participants, unless the technique was designed for a rare state difficult to acquire. Clearly, this biased the list towards the newer generation of processes, although I included older, less effective ones if I felt they were historically important or contained a valuable approach. If your favorite approach was omitted or identified as less effective, or a technique you detest was identified as very effective, please recognize the necessarily limited nature of this data. As time passes, we expect this situation to improve.

Techniques that are specifically designed to give peak states are very rare and generally easy to spot. However, a huge number of healing techniques exist and some of these can sometimes give peak states as a byproduct of their process. Because of the current dominant paradigm, most healing therapy inventors don't recognize the existence of peak states or the desirability of having them, and their techniques reflect this bias. Because of this, I had to omit almost all healing therapy processes as irrelevant to this book. As this field matures, I expect that some of these developers will shift their orientation to include peak states.

I excluded lists of gurus or teachers with whom a peak state can sometimes be acquired simply by being in their presence, perhaps while doing a spiritual practice. Except in rare cases the effect is temporary and leads to the problem of people needing to follow the guru around to maintain the state.

Classifying States as Either 'Spiritual' or 'Shamanic'

In general, the states that the methods try to achieve fall into two broad groups, which we might call for simplicity 'spiritual' (or religious) states and 'shamanic' states. We can generalize the two orientations by saying the states involved either focus outward to God (the spiritual states) or inward to the body (the shamanic states). The spiritual states have to do with our undying 'spiritual' self and the realm that it is from. For example, Yogic, Buddhist, Sufi, and Christian practices all tend to focus on this type of state. In contrast, shamanic states are involved with the body and the real living physical world. Examples of these states would be from Taoism, Native American traditions, practices focusing on being aware of the earth as a living being, and physical healing methods like Chilel Qigong. Of course, any given practitioner may encounter the whole range of states, but the traditions tend to identify one group over the other as meaningful or significant. Also, any given tradition will usually specialize on a subset of the total number of states available in their orientation.

It should be clear that historical need drove the choice of states. At the risk of oversimplifying, shamans were more focused on the health and survival needs of their tribe. Spiritual practices focused more on issues that were not directly tied to survival, coming as they were from societies where hunting and gathering had been replaced by agriculture and settled communities. The states in each group reflect these needs.

Which group of states is more important? From our perspective at the ISPS, they are all important to one degree or another. Different states allow us to feel differently, to have different kinds of perceptions, or to do different things. Fortunately, states can be accumulated and so we don't have to choose one at the expense of losing another. However, I recommend that both the general public and professionals first acquire the triune brain fusion states which are found in shamanic traditions. These states are described in Chapter 5. In my opinion, even partial versions of these states have the biggest impact on day to day quality of life, especially for client populations that psychologists and psychiatrists see. Triune brain fusion states are also the foundation for many advanced healing techniques as described in Volume 3. I also recommend adding limited versions of the advanced spiritual and shamanic states described in Volume 2 to greatly enhance the triune brain states. For example, Jacquelyn Aldana's 15 Minute Miracle technique in Chapter 10 gives a well balanced combination of states that are particularly useful for manifesting in the world. Full versions of the states in Volume 2 can have such a major impact on a person's experience of self that we generally don't recommend people start with them. Even triune brain states can be a huge step for many people and can take a considerable amount of time to get used to.

The techniques in this chapter, although they tend to be specialized for either shamanic or spiritual states due to their historical roots, can often be adapted to both orientations. Because of this, in this chapter I chose to categorize techniques by the phenomena they exploit to give peak states rather than to categorize by the type of states they were originally intended to give. And realistically, determining the specific states the techniques can give is beyond our limited resources. I hope the classification scheme below will help technique developers and consumers combine different approaches together to increase effectiveness, efficiency, and scope.

Classifying Peak State Techniques by Approach

The following six categories cover the approaches that most peak state techniques use. As of this writing, we don't know of any technique that incorporates two or more of the approaches, although we anticipate this happening in the future.

The Conscious Choice (Psychological) Practices

The conscious choice approach, sometimes called the psychological approach, has several variations and a number of techniques. In its simplest form are techniques from individuals who have identified some characteristic, quality or attribute of the peak state they want, either from reading, observation of someone else, or from a momentary peak experience of their own. Then they simply decide to make an effort to experience the characteristic. In this approach, the characteristic is usually a feeling. Rather than getting a state and then experiencing its characteristics, they do the opposite. They deliberately choose and emphasize a characteristic from the state which in turn moves them further into the complete state. This approach can be very simple and useful for many people.

From our perspective, the drawback to this type of technique is that it only works for people who are already close to having the particular target state and can recognize the characteristic from their own experience in the past. As the ability to feel the characteristic depends on having had it enough to evoke it, for most people the more unusual states are not available using this approach. Even with relatively minor states it may be difficult to recall the sensation or feeling from it. The other drawback is that for many people in general the state is not permanent, but needs to be maintained by practice. In essence, you're fighting your tendency to return to average consciousness. Additionally, we sometimes see this approach backfire in people who are 'far' from the target state. They may instead try to repress contrary feeings, which can occassionally explosively erupt.

Example:
> One man I knew decided that he would just choose happiness (which is the peak state caused by body-heart fusion). Another man, after returning to the US after surviving Vietnam was so glad

to be alive he went into an almost continuous Beauty Way state (head-heart fusion) afterwards.

Example:
    In a more conventional 'psychological' approach, Mary Pellicer of our Institute decided to quit judging people, and after a number of months of practice went into the Inner Peace state.

Example:
    Another woman, with help, decided to look at all the reasons why she wasn't in the present, and this also brought her to the Beauty Way. Just bringing the reasons into consciousness did the trick for her, at least for a number of months.

There are a variety of techniques in this category. We've listed the ones we know about here, but there are probably a number of others.

From a classical religious orientation come techniques where the monk or lay person will get instructions to embody the quality of the peak state desired. Examples include Tibetan Buddhism and their meditations on the qualities of specific deities, and Christianity with its instruction to pray, meditate, and feel God's love. The problems of this approach are the same as described below in the section on meditative practices.

The shaman Tom Brown Jr. uses an interesting variation on this. He teaches a technique he calls "breath to heart". In this technique, the shaman deliberately moves his center of awareness (see Volume 2 for more on the center of awareness) into the solar plexus, which we believe forces a triune brain peak state. This technique uses a unique characteristic of the state, the location of the shaman's center of awareness, rather than a more typical emotional characteristic.

Gay and Kathlyn Hendricks teach a method that use the sensation of self-love to put their clients into the state we call 'Underlying Happiness'. Gay does an excellent job of describing the technique in the books *Learning to Love Yourself*, and *The Learning to Love Yourself Workbook*. As we've mentioned in the previous chapter, they use it primarily to facilitate their body-centered therapy healing techniques, and not as an end in itself. As far as I know they don't realize happiness is a distinct state of consciousness. Although the effect is temporary, their approach is fairly effective, and they give good alternative techniques for people who can't use their basic process.

Martin Seligman, an inspiring process creator from an academic setting is the author of *Learned Optimism* and *Authentic Happiness*. He gives methods for getting these qualities of optimism and happiness, although at this writing I don't know how effective they are. His work is also valuable from our Institute perspective because it contains questionnaires to evaluate one's level of optimism and happiness. However, as far as I know he is unaware that these qualities are the results of certain peak states, and sees them through the current psychological lens of the normal variation in human emotions. His work has started an entire approach in academic circles called 'positive psychology'.

In the last few years, Eckhart Tolle has created quite a stir with his book *The Power of Now*. His work has introduced the idea of an accessible and exceptional state of consciousness to the general public, and is doing a wonderful service in that regard. However, according to the minimal feedback I've gotten, his techniques for acquiring the state don't appear to be very effective.

The Avatar course by Harry Palmer is possibly the most well known of the processes in this category. His introductory book is *Living Deliberately: The Discovery and Development of Avatar*. The courses are fairly expensive, about $2500US for three levels of workshops, and their contents are kept confidential. We don't have estimates on his method's degree of effectiveness. From people who have taken the course, its primary focus is around the idea that you create your experience by your beliefs. The processes you are taught can give peak states as a byproduct. According to our sources the states are not permanent, and the processes need to be used and practiced on a regular basis. (Zivorad Slavinski has an equivalent process which he feels is more efficient and effective. The inexpensive manual can be purchased at www.spiritual-technology.com)

The best of this approach that I know of is by Jacquelyn Aldana, in her book *The 15 Minute Miracle*. It's fast, easy, and pleasant to do. Her approach is particularly good for manifesting positive experiences in your life, and I highly recommend what she teaches. Chapter 10 is written by her and goes into depth on her process. Lynn Grabhorn's *Excuse Me, Your Life is Waiting* has very similar material with enough of a different slant that some find it suits them better.

Meditative (Religious) Practices

The category that we call meditative practices overlaps with the other categories, but in general I am referring to meditation, prayer, good works, blessings of a guru, and so on. These techniques are generally used by religious or spiritual groups. One of the major drawbacks is that relatively few people are able to successfully use this approach. Even for people who can use them successfully, the techniques generally take a tremendous amount of time and energy over long periods of time. Another drawback is the need to continue to 'practice' the techniques to keep oneself in whatever state one has achieved.

As most of these approaches come from religious traditions, another major problem exists. Although this is not often recognized, different groups focus on different types of states as being important and tend to ignore or denigrate other states as distractions. This is a problem as the processes tend to invoke a variety of states, causing conflict between the practitioner and his organization. Worse, the criteria for the desired state are often not explicitly established or identified. Finally, these groups tend to promote the idea that only the hard working or select few can have the states in question, and create a conflict inside the average person about acquiring the state. For example, most people would feel it very egotistical or presumptuous to think about having exactly the state that Jesus or Buddha did.

The typical process for this approach tends to be a mixture of instructions to meditate and pray. Essentially, this approach requires one to feel relaxed and peaceful enough to get the state, which can be a problem for most people. The spiritual teachers teach based on their experience and the experience of their teachers, in general—it wasn't hard for them to do, so why would it be hard for you to do? As we're well aware, this approach isn't very useful for most people.

The shaman typically does a meditative process to maintain his ability to use inductive processes successfully when he needs to. (See the next section.) This usually involves staying in one of the triune brain fusion states described later in this book. These meditations in my experience involve activities in nature, which makes sense given the origins of the techniques. For example, Tom Brown's core meditation is 'wide-angle vision', a practice of using peripheral vision, combined with 'fox walking', a way of walking that keeps the body from being harmed when moving through the forest (see his book *Awakening Spirits* for details). Interestingly, Zen Buddhism also emphasizes non-directed seeing during walking meditations.

Example:
> Wes Gietz, a West Coast shaman comments on this: "Although it is much easier to maintain these shamanic abilities by staying in a natural environment, they are not necessarily lost if one returns to the city. What seems to be more important is continuous practice; in this respect the techniques resemble others that achieve or maintain spiritual consciousness through practice. In my personal experience, however, an hour and a half of solitude in the woods without a destination puts me into a peak state."

Another variation of this approach is to use the influence of the teacher to get the peak state. Again, it's pretty hit or miss, and once one is away from the teacher for any length of time, in almost all cases in my experience the state fades away. Interestingly enough, we believe that there is a way to put people into these states permanently, but I suspect this option isn't available to spiritual teachers because they don't understand what they need to do to make it happen.

A modern adaptation of meditation is the use of brain biofeedback to put oneself into peak states. After the training, this can be done at will. In our opinion, the leader of this field in the area of peak states and experiences is Dr. James Hardt. He does trainings through his company Biocybernaut, Inc. This approach overcomes most of the objections to this type of approach—it's fast, easily accessible, and doesn't have any preconceptions or stigmas attached to it. Dr. Hardt has written Chapter 12 which describes his work.

Induction (Shamanic) Techniques

This category of techniques uses processes to push the practitioner into a state of consciousness, generally temporarily. This category of processes not only induces peak states, but often other experiences that in the literature and in common usage are called 'altered' states. These techniques are generally not useful for the general public, but are very useful for healers and researchers. Although examples exist of people who used this type of technique and acquired states permanently, this is uncommon and usually occurs only after a long and difficult apprenticeship.

Shamanism in particular contains the most well-known historical example of this class of techniques. The methods include drumming, drugs, vision quests, and other body-centered techniques. Breathwork can be considered to be in this camp, although it overlaps as a mind/body healing technique. Using a variety of practices, shamans move into a variety of different states of consciousness. The shaman and anthropologist Michael Harner identifies these states by the single label of a 'shamanic state of consciousness'. After training, the states can be used for whatever purpose was intended. Shamanism in general is a very practical approach, and its techniques were developed to solve practical, real-world problems—finding hunting game or lost items, learning survival information, healing people's bodies and psyches.

Shamanic practices also tend to be divided into two types, based on what they're intended to accomplish. The target states are quite different. The Michael Harner approach uses techniques to get peak states which can be used to get 'power animals' or 'spirits' to assist. Tom Brown Jr., an Apache-trained Caucasian shaman, is a good example of the other approach. He teaches methods to move into states where one can do the work directly, from a recognition of one's own essential self. The techniques of these two approaches overlap, but not as much as might be supposed.

Several problems exist with the shamanic approach. First, these techniques tend to only work for a small group of people. People who are exceptional shamans are relatively rare. Generally, the best of the shamans already had the state they needed, or one close to it, and only required training in how to use it. Actually living in one of the more advanced peak states where you can do shamanic sorts of things at will is quite unusual. Secondly, these techniques have the same drawback that the conscious choice and meditative approaches do—for most people, continuous practice is almost always required. For example, as we mentioned above it's typical among Tom Brown Jr.'s students that when they leave the woods for any significant period of time, they find the induction techniques become less effective, and they lose their shamanic abilities or have them decrease greatly.

Shamanic drumming has been used for thousands of years to induce peak abilities, experiences, and short-term states. Michael Harner puts out an excellent collection of shamanic drumming tapes to induce his 'shamanic state of consciousness'. However, in our times of advanced technology, we find an approach called the binaural beat technique that gets similar results but works faster and on a larger percentage of the general population. In this process, they use audio tones on headphones that have a slight mismatch in frequency to create a 'beat tone' that induces brainwave frequencies in the sub-audible range. The best known example of this technique is the Monroe Institute Hemisynch process.

The Mind/body Approach

This category of techniques involves an insight into how the physical body and the peak states are related.

One mind/body approach is taken by a particular Sufi sect that uses body positions and motions to get very rapid 'spiritual' development (i.e., peak states). It's taught by Adnan Sarhan of the Sufi Foundation of America. I know that it is successful for a lot of people, but I can't tell you if it needs to be practiced to keep the state, or what percentage of the general population is successful with it. However, it does work for the people that I checked.

Doing mind/body practices as a lifestyle is a staple of several traditions. Dan Millman who wrote *Way of the Peaceful Warrior* could be used as an example of this type of thinking. Athletes who go 'into the zone' while doing intense physical competition would be another.

Tantric and Taoist practices with their emphasis on the body would also fit in this category.

The Trauma-Healing Approach

This group of techniques assumes that traumas are blocking people's peak states. There are two major models in this trauma-healing approach. The older model assumes that the overall impact of all a person's traumas summed together is the main block to having peak states of consciousness. In other words, the idea is that the total trauma 'load' weighs down a person and keeps them in a blocked or sub-functional state. The newer model assumes that only specific kinds of trauma block people's peak states of consciousness. Several variations exist on this newer model, depending on what the creator of the technique considered was the key type of traumatic material to heal. Some of the techniques that use this newer model are getting dramatic and rapid results.

Most of these approaches used to get disappointing results because of slow and inadequate healing processes, but in the last decade the new generation of 'power therapies' has radically changed this situation. The newest generation of techniques takes advantage of this breakthrough in healing speed and effectiveness. Of course, not every technique has been updated to take advantage of these new breakthrough healing processes.

The older simple 'trauma load' model is severely flawed for several reasons. First, from a purely practical viewpoint the groups I know of that use this model still use healing techniques that are relatively time-consuming and usually only moderately effective. Secondly, the sheer volume of trauma that a typical person has is prohibitively time-consuming to heal—and some material is resistant to any method. Third, most of the important traumas are *in utero*, which most techniques don't successfully address. Having said all this, the simple model can work for some people if they get lucky and accidentally heal the key material that was blocking their peak state, especially if they use modern power therapies. And of course they can feel a lot better as the number of painful issues they have decreases. However, based on statistical probability alone only a pretty dedicated person with a lot of spare time would have any hope of success. Probably the best known example of a process that uses this simple model is the church of Scientology, which I don't recommend for the reasons given and because of their emphasis on secrecy and money.

Leaving the simple model, we encounter techniques that work with personal issues in a more focused way. An example of historical interest is from the followers of Gurdjieff. They mix facing one's issues with mind/body approaches reminiscent of Sarhan's technique. This approach is particularly interesting to me because they figured out the triune nature of the brain. If you're interested, there are several books by students of his, or you might enjoy the movie "Meetings with Remarkable Men" about Gurdjieff's life. I don't recommend this approach in its current form. It requires virtually a life commitment as the time required for a peak state is pretty indefinite. There is also a degree of secrecy that I feel is counterproductive. As far as I know they haven't updated their methods with the latest generation of healing techniques.

Another organization created by A. H. Almaas (a pen name for A. Hameed Ali) uses what he calls the Diamond Approach. It's a combination of Sufi, Gurdjieff and older psychological healing techniques designed to heal blocks to particular emotions and qualities of being. The key problem they focus on is the existence of experiential 'holes' in the body. Although this is a relatively unknown phenomenon, virtually all of the new effective healing techniques occasionally bring this problem to consciousness by accident. Their approach is rather slow and expensive, requiring trained facilitators over many months with no guarantee of success, and for this reason I don't recommend it. However, their material is freely available and we may see great improvement if they incorporate the new healing processes.

The approach taken by our Institute is included in this trauma-healing approach. We target specific *in utero* traumas as the main blocks to peak states, as described in this series of books. We call our model the 'developmental events model for peak states' or for simplicity the 'developmental events model'. See Chapters 4 through 9 for details. Although we started with regression healing techniques which are slow and not useful for the general public, we've developed much simpler techniques using meridian therapies that exploit key phrases to heal *in utero* developmental event trauma. The process for the general public in this volume is called the Inner Peace Process and is in Chapter 9. It is free, only takes a hour or so, and is permanent for about 40% of the general population. An expanded version of the process that gives more triune brain peak states is in Volume 2.

The Resolving Dualism Approach

This category of techniques heal the effects of contrast or polarity to achieve a state. This concept is used in Yoga and Vedanta practices. However, in recent years effective new techniques have appeared that use this concept in new ways. This approach is of great and unique significance, and we expect to see a lot more done in this area.

An interesting and simple technique is called the Ascension Process. It uses focus over a period of time on a series of words that contain great contrast, like the words 'big' and 'small' do, to change people's state of consciousness. We've had good reports on the first stage of their process, although less so at the next levels. Like Avatar, their technique is not disclosed to the public and has a fee. Although it could be considered a 'meditative' technique from the way it is implemented, its underlying approach uses the model of this category.

Zivorad Slavinski's PEAT and DP-3 processes are a new development in the field. They are derived from an understanding of the concept of dualism. These state-of-the-art processes use meridian therapies to heal the conflicts that are at the heart of the loss of certain kinds of peak states. Although Zivorad uses a 'trauma healing' technique for his method, in this case EFT, I don't classify it as a trauma healing approach because it is exploiting what at least for now looks like a different phenomenon, and is just using a meridian therapy to do so. I highly recommend these processes. They are very fast, effective, and look to be permanent. Chapter 11, written by Zivorad, is about these techniques.

Background Material and Other Miscellaneous Approaches

In this section I'll mention a few techniques that I don't know much about, or that don't specifically target peak states, or are of background interest.

The approach started by Lester Levenson, creator of the Sedona method, is relatively well known. Lester used a focus on using love to heal and change the past. It can be described as a mixture of a healing technique and a peak state technique, although to my limited knowledge their technique doesn't explicitly focus on the peak state application of their work. Interestingly, from what I gather the technique taught by Lester's followers does not duplicate what Lester himself went through to get his peak state. There are audio tapes, a book, and workshops which can be found at www.Sedona.com.

Byron Katie has a healing technique that tends to put people temporarily into a state of unconditional loving. It's based on methods that heal neurotic projections onto other people. Her book, *What Is* describes her method. However, the technique is not designed specifically to give peak states, although it appears to make use of one.

Neil Slade has written several books, *Frontal Love Supercharge* and *Cosmic Conversations*, and can be found at www.NeilSlade.com. I have no personal experience with his work, but was told that his notion is that when you experience pleasure, especially with music, the three brains merge. His work is based on the ideas of T.D. Lingo. I have no information on estimates of effectiveness.

Laurel Nellin in his book *The Pathway: Follow the Road to Health and Happiness* focuses on changing people who are in a depressed or difficult state, and his process tends to get peak states as a byproduct. There is a brief mention of the triune nature of the brain and the effects of merging them, which is why we mention it here. However, I have no data on its effectiveness.

The books listed below are involved in one way or another with what we call peak states of consciousness. Some of the authors teach workshops but I don't know anything about their techniques if any exist or their effectiveness. Some of the books give background to the evolution of peak state techniques. As of this writing, none of these authors have well-known techniques or approaches yet, although several appear very intriguing.

Background material:
- Thomas Cleary, *Zen and the Art of Enlightenment*.
- Flora Courtois, *An Experience of Enlightenment*.

Potential peak state processes:
- Andrew Cohen, *Embracing Heaven and Earth*.
- Lee Coit, *Being: How to Increase Your Awareness of Oneness*.
- Douglas Harding, *On Having No Head*.
- David Hawkins, *Power Versus Force*.
- Leonard Jackobson, *Words from Silence: An invitation to spiritual awakening*.
- Tony Parsons, *As It Is*.
- Tarthang Tulku, *Hidden Mind of Freedom*.

The Choice Between Psychological Healing and a Peak State Technique

When would you choose a healing technique over a peak state technique? Does one replace the other? The answer is a bit complex.

Obviously, if things are going well for you presently, choosing just a peak state process would make sense. It would be like moving from a shack to a better home. Once there, something either physical or emotional can still come up in your life that needs healing, and at that point using a healing therapy would make sense. This would be like calling a plumber for a stopped-up drain in your beautiful new home. And since this sort of issue might cause you to lose your state as well as being personally painful, healing is definitely a good idea. Continuing the analogy, it would be a bit like having to move out of your new home because a big chunk of the roof was leaking—get the repair man over right away!

From my perspective, it makes sense to be prepared to do healing on yourself regardless of the peak state you may or may not be in. But I *do* recommend using the latest generation of 'power therapies' covered in Chapter 1 *first* if you need healing—using other techniques is on average far less efficient or effective, although in any given case there are exceptions. Some of you may not be aware that many of the power therapies are also 'self-help'—you can do them on yourself at home, although for some resistant issues guidance is needed. I recommend EFT, BSFF, and TAT in particular, although new ones are appearing all the time. Returning to our previous analogy, it's wise for a home owner to at least know how to use a hammer, saw, and screwdriver for easy repairs even if you don't want to become a plumber or roofer.

But how about people who start with significant physical or psychological difficulties? By psychological difficulties I mean problems like phobias, abuse memories, relationship issues, or in fact anything that you don't feel a sense of calm, peace, and lightness about. The meaning of physical issues should be fairly clear. Note that in the last few years the new generation of power therapy techniques can eliminate many problems that used to be considered purely physical. I recommend doing one or more of the newest generation of peak state techniques at the same time you're getting healing work done, and not waiting until the problem is gone—who knows when that might be? There are two main reasons—in many cases a peak state makes the problem vanish without any other work, giving you the dual benefit of the state without the problem. However, it's just as common to have the problem remain after acquiring a peak state, but with your overall life experience so improved the problem doesn't have the same impact that it did (depending on the peak state acquired, of course).

Unfortunately, in some cases the problem that needs healing also blocks your ability to acquire a peak state. In this case there is no getting around it—you need to get competent help to heal the problem. Note that some peak state processes that appear to not have done anything will then automatically put the person in the peak state once their current issue is healed. This is certainly the case with our own Institute's Inner Peace Process, for example.

How about using the healing techniques that also give peak states as a byproduct? Wouldn't using them cover both bases? First, it would depend on which healing process you choose—some only give a temporary peak state at best. Secondly, as I've said, these healing/peak state techniques are in general not as effective as the power therapies for healing, so it still makes sense to learn a power therapy or have one accessible to yourself.

My Recommendations on Techniques for the General Public

I recommend you try the state-of-the-art current generation of techniques first, if possible. I characterize these techniques by their speed, effectiveness, and the relatively high percentage of people they work on. They appeal to folks who just want results in a minimum of time. Interestingly, the techniques all work on different principles, which means to me that we'll probably see combination techniques in the near future. Note that by the time this book is published there will probably be new or improved processes available that are not in this list.

As of 2003 I recommend you try a mixture of processes. As none of them work on everyone, doing more than one increases the likelihood that something will work for you. And since the techniques don't all give the same states, using more than one technique may give you a larger set of states. Although more peak states are in general a good thing, I don't recommend the general public jump into the major states described in Volume 2 until they're comfortable with the states in this volume. For example, I've worked with a few people from the general public who had no background in this work. They asked to stop the Hollow process in Volume 2 midway so they could get used to the changes in how they experience their emotions and the world around them. Similarly, several of my workshop participants have requested detailed descriptions of what to expect from the Hollow state so they don't get surprised when they accidentally discover new qualities. I suggest using some restraint—examples of this adjustment problem when major new states are acquired too quickly can be found in books on spiritual emergencies.

A little selectivity on which techniques to try may be required on your part. Some of the techniques in this chapter are designed to give specialized states that in our opinion are probably not optimum for the general public to start with. For example, Tom Brown Jr.'s work is specialized for shamanic or survival applications, but is no less valuable for this reason. Likewise, Harding's 'headlessness' (covered in depth in Volume 2) might be something that you might want to explore after you have adjusted to less radical peak states.

I recommend exploring the techniques in the list that follow in the order given. The list is biased towards inexpensive techniques that can be done easily and give useful states to the general public.

- The Inner Peace Process described in Chapter 9. This process gives a relatively minor state that leaves one with a feeling of inner peace and eliminates all emotional content from traumas in our past (which is the cause of much of our daily suffering and the tendency to get 'triggered' in interpersonal situations). It's fast, simple, does not need to be repeated, free and can be done by oneself at home. However, the current process only works completely on about 40% of the population.

- The 15 Minute Miracle by Jacquelyn Aldana or an equivalent process. Chapter 10 is written by Jacquelyn about her work. Her method has the advantage of helping clarify people's desires and ability to experience more positive experiences in the world. Its minor drawback is that it needs to be done every day for a brief time, hence the title. It's particularly designed for the general public. If its style doesn't 'speak' to you, there are other methods similar to this by other people that could be used instead, such as Lynn Grabhorn's.

- Any or all of the 'conscious choice' processes, such as: Gay Hendricks' self-love technique; Seligman's optimism and happiness techniques; etc. Start with the free self-help choices first—remember, cost and value don't always go together.

- PEAT and DP-3 by Zivorad Slavinski. Chapter 11 is written by Zivorad about his work. It's fast and looks to be permanent. However, the DP-3 states might be a little too major for the general public to start with—I'd recommend consultation with Zivorad or his instructors to make that determination for any particular person. At this time, you need a trained facilitator to run the process, which can take minutes to hours. It's especially interesting to professionals and consciousness researchers.

- Use the new power therapies to eliminate every issue in your life. I recommend therapies that can be done for free at home, such as the energy therapies EFT or BSFF. This will improve your life and can sometimes give the added bonus of one or more peak states. This is also a reasonable choice if other techniques are not working for you. In addition, I've seen people accidentally heal the issues that were blocking the success of peak state processes.

- The brainwave biofeedback training process with Dr. James Hardt at the Biocybernaut Institute. Chapter 12 is written by James on his work. Unlike the other techniques, this one is relatively slower (i.e., a week with the training equipment) and much more expensive due to the staff time and equipment costs. However, it has the potential to work for people who don't respond to other approaches. It's also particular useful for people doing consciousness research.

Many of the other techniques in this chapter, at least the ones developed in the last twenty or thirty years are usually reasonably fast and effective on a significant percentage of people when compared to well-known traditional processes. As the point of all this is to improve your life drastically by giving you one or more peak states, if the latest generation techniques do not work for you, or are not easy accessed, I recommend trying out the older alternatives. And as we've said, the field is in such flux that any given technique might be drastically improved by the time you try it.

Other Organizations Evaluating Peak State Techniques

I'm sorry to say that at least as of this writing I know of no book, magazine, website, or article that does a summary of peak state techniques or attempts to evaluate their effectiveness. A few books do popularize small pieces of this peak state field, like Michael Hutchison's *Megabrain Power* which focuses on binaural beat and brain biofeedback methods. Along these lines, the magazine *What is Enlightenment?* is an enjoyable quarterly publication which discusses a few of these approaches, especially the older traditional spiritual ones.

However, this situation may soon change. In the last few years, a number of academic organizations have appeared that are focusing on "quality of life." Much of their focus is not on peak states of consciousness, as many don't realize the possibility other than intuitively. One such organization is the International Society for Quality of Life Studies at the Virginia Polytechnic Institute and State University. Other groups with a similar agenda are also appearing worldwide, a development that we find very exciting. Terminologies and measurement tools are still being created and no particular set has yet emerged from this nearly simultaneous worldwide movement.

Another group that deserves significant notice is Martin Seligman's "Positive Psychology," which is also focused on peak states of consciousness, although to my limited knowledge they haven't formulated their work in the way we do in this book. Their website is www.positivepsychology.org. Several books have been published along the lines that he started. I recommend Seligman's books *Learned Optimism* and *Authentic Happiness* in particular. Mihaly Csikszentmihaly, the author of *Flow: The Psychology of Optimal Experience* does studies on positive psychology at The Quality of Research Center at the Claremont Graduate University.

Other organizations are still in the planning stages. For example, the "Life Quality Enhancement Organization" in Switzerland is in the process of forming. They plan to evaluate healing techniques and peak state processes, and hope to become a "Consumer Reports" for this field.

I wish them all great success!

Key Points

- Two types of peak states can be roughly identified: 'spiritual' states which spiritual or religious organizations focus on that have to do with fundamental existential phenomena like the Creator or the Void; and 'shamanic' states that have to do with physical body phenomena like the triune brain system and Gaia.
- Peak state techniques can often be used to acquire either type of peak states, although generally they are not used in this way.
- For this text, we've roughly classified peak state techniques into the following categories: conscious choice practices; meditative practices; induction techniques; the mind/body approach; the trauma healing approach; and the resolving dualism approach. There is considerable overlap between the different categories, as different processes may incorporate more than one category of approaches.
- Different approaches for acquiring peak states tend either to require continuous practice, as in meditation; or to be used only a few times to make the state fairly stable without regular maintenance, as with trauma-healing techniques.
- A variety of organizations have recently appeared in this field of peak states. Terminology and evaluation techniques are still in the early creation stages. In academic circles this work has a variety of names, such as "quality of life" and "positive psychology".

Suggested Reading and Websites

Peak state processes
- Jacquelyn Aldana, *The 15 minute Miracle Revealed*, Inner Wisdom Publications, 2003. See www.15minutemiracle.com. Uses manifesting and focus on purpose to move into peak states.
- A. H. Almaas, *The Diamond Heart Book 1: Elements of the Real in Man*, 1987. A numbLifeer of follow up books are available. Their school has a website at www.ridwan.org/almaas.html.
- The Ascension process at www.ishaya.com. It uses meditation on key words.
- Hale Dwoskin and Lester Levenson, *Happiness is Free: And It's Easier Than You Think!*, Sedona Press, 2002. Their website is www.sedona.com.
- Lynn Grabhorn, *Excuse Me, Your Life is Waiting*, Hampton Roads, 2000.
- Dr. James Hardt at www.biocybernaut.com. Uses brain biofeedback.

- Gay Hendricks, *Learning to Love Yourself: A Guide to Becoming Centered*, Simon & Schuster, 1982.
- Gay Hendricks, *The Learning to Love Yourself Workbook*, Simon & Schuster, 1990. Contains a simple method to temporarily experience a loving, happy state.
- Byron Katie and Stephen Mitchell, *Loving What Is: Four Questions that Can Change your Life*, Crown Publishing Group, 2002. Their website is at www.ByronKatie.org.
- David Lang, editor, *Face to No Face: Rediscovering our Original Nature*, Inner Directions Foundation, 2000. A collection of Douglas Harding's talks and method.
- Adnan Sarhan at www.sufifoundation.org. He uses music and body postures in a technique based on Sufi traditions.
- Martin Seligman, *Authentic Happiness: Using the New Positive Psychology to Realize Your Potential for Lasting Fulfillment*, Free Press, 2002. His websites at www.psych.upenn.edu/seligman and www.authenichappiness.org contain very good assessment tools for these peak states.
- Martin Seligman, *Learned Optimism*, Knopf, 1991.
- Zivorad Slavinski, *PEAT and Neutralization of Primordial Polarities—Theory and Practice*, 2002, available from www.spiritual-technology.com. His process is called PEAT and it uses energy therapies on select core issues.
- Eckhart Tolle, *The Power of Now: A Guide to Spiritual Enlightenment*, New World Library, 1999.
- Eckhart Tolle, *Practicing the Power of Now: Essential Teachings, Meditations, and Exercises for Living the Liberated Life*, New World Library, 2001.

Popularized books on brain induction technologies (such as binaural beat and brain biofeedback)
- Michael Hutchison, *Megabrain Power: Transform your Life with Mind Machines and Brain Nutrients*, New York: Hyperion, 1994.
- Robert Monroe, *Journeys Out of the Body*, Doubleday & Company, 1973.
- Robert Monroe, *Far Journeys*, Doubleday & Company, 1987.

Life quality enhancement investigation & testing organizations
- The International Society for Quality of Life Studies at http://marketing.cob.vt.edu/isqols/
- The Life Quality Enhancement Organization, at www.LQEO.org.
- The Quality of Life Research Center at the Claremont Graduate University, http://www.cgu.edu/qlrc/about.htm.

Positive Psychology

- Martin Seligman Research Alliance, www.positivepsychology.org
- Lisa G. Aspinwall and Ursula M. Staudinger, editors, *A Psychology of Human Strengths*, American Psychological Association, 2002.
- Mihaly Csikszentmihaly, *Flow: The Psychology of Optimal Experience*, Harper Collins, 1991.
- Corey L.M. Keyes and Jonathan Haidt, editors, *Flourishing: Positive Psychology and the Life Well-Lived*, American Psychological Association, 2003.
- Karen Reivich and Andrew Shatté, *The Resilience Factor: 7 Essential Skills for Overcoming Life's Inevitable Obstacles*, Broadway Books, 2002.
- C.R. Snyder and Shane J. Lopez, editors, *Handbook of Positive Psychology*, Oxford University Press, 2001.

Chapter 4

The Developmental Events Model for Peak Experiences, Abilities and States

"I believe that what we've worked on has never been done before, and it's both scary and exciting."

—*Wes Gietz about the Institute work*

Introduction

In this chapter, we describe the ISPS developmental events model for peak states, experiences, and abilities. The next few chapters will then expand on this simple, basic model.

In essence, people who have been investigating exceptional mental and physical health have been asking the question, "What causes exceptional health?" and the corollary, "What can I do to get it?" The answer hasn't been forthcoming partly because the question itself has the flawed assumption that exceptional health is something that we have to work to acquire—so the problem cannot be solved. The correct question is, "What *blocks* exceptional health?" with its assumption that exceptional mental and physical health are our birthright and natural state. This seemingly minor change in the question turns out to be critical to the solution of the problem.

The answer to the question involves trauma and normal developmental stages or events that occur before and during birth. *In utero*, we have most if not all of our peak states of consciousness. As we go through certain critical developmental events, if they occur with trauma the trauma response is retained, although not fully activated while we're still *in utero*. After birth, these traumas are 'turned on' or continuously stimulated, and we lose the states and abilities that are our birthright. The implication is that healing these core developmental events would result in peak states of consciousness, and for the majority of people this turns out to be true. This model also implies another way to acquire peak states that also works— weaken or eliminate the 'trauma stimulation' mechanisms that are acquired at birth. These mechanisms are covered in Volume 2.

Finally, there are other mechanisms that block peak states of consciousness in some people. This is the area of our current research, and is covered in Volume 3.

Our understanding of peak states has been derived and tested in the best possible way—by seeing if processes based on the theory worked. I want to emphasize this—we derived the theory, then came up with methods to apply it. I can't express my pleased surprise when they worked as predicted! To demonstrate the validity of the theory in this book, we have included our fast, simple and effective "Inner Peace Process" in Chapter 9. Other applications of our model for acquiring peak states, experiences and abilities are scattered throughout all the volumes.

Grant's Story
A New Approach to Understanding Peak States

As you read in Chapter 2, I lost my Beauty Way peak state when I was 29. As the years went by, I also started to get very sick, to the point where I almost died. I had already been learning various spiritual techniques to regain my peak state, and this illness pushed me into also learning physical and emotional healing techniques. I found that these spiritual practices had no effect on my illness, in spite of my teachers' beliefs to the contrary. I nearly died before a friend of mine healed me using a modified version of Holotropic Breathwork™. It turned out that the cause of my illness was the tremendous despair I'd experienced at age 29, along with an unconscious decision that I could never have what I wanted in life, and that there was no point in continuing to live. These feelings were completely outside of my conscious awareness, to my stunned surprise. Releasing them caused my illnesses to fall away in weeks.

This experience made me realize that emotional healing was important. Six months or so later, I started to lose my joy at being alive after nearly dying. I eventually realized I was unconsciously asking myself the question, "If I really loved myself, what would I be doing?". About a month later, I realized the answer was that I would heal everything, not just what had been killing me. But how to do this? I started working with the healer and friend who had saved my life, Sheelo Bohm, and with Ron Mied, a healer I'd met at a conference for shamans earlier that year. My intuition said that trauma was the key to healing, and both Ron and Sheelo had processes focused on trauma. I knew of no other techniques that were effective enough for what I wanted, so I used Ron's insight on the out-of-body trauma images and developed the Whole-Hearted Healing technique.

My intuition told me that trauma was the key to the peak state I was trying to regain. Oddly, virtually everyone I knew tried to convince me that I was wrong about this. Even the data accumulated by groups working with trauma, like the Primal Institute and Stanislav Grof's people, didn't seem to support the idea. It was too hard to resist my own doubts and the emphatic friends who tried to put me on the paths that they had unsuccessfully taken—in many cases I had to end these friendships to follow my own inner knowing. As I healed myself, it became easier and easier to continue. I started having more and more unusual spiritual experiences and states as I experimented. I moved into a state where I became bright inside myself, and found that I could now access pre-birth memories at will. I soon left all my teachers behind and entered new territory.

One day, during the traumatic ending of another relationship, I lost my internal brightness and could no longer continue the exploratory work. So I turned to others who had the ability I now lacked, and used them as experimental subjects to continue the investigations. The work couldn't have been done without the assistance of these very courageous volunteers, in particular Kate Sorensen, Wes Gietz, Dr. Deola Perry, and Dr. Marie Green. We finally cracked the core problem. This quickly led to realizing how everything I'd ever experienced or read about fit together. This was one of the peak periods in my life! I finally understood what caused all those other states and experiences.

When we read books like this one, we often don't get a feel for the pain and struggle that people went through to make their discoveries. Our work has had moments of triumph, and times of deep pain and suffering as we slowly worked our way into the unknown. Wes Gietz has offered an account of his experience below.

I first met Wes in Victoria, British Columbia in 1996. Because he had the Inner Brightness state, and a background in shamanism, I persuaded him to work with me exploring my ideas about peak states of consciousness and developmental events. He was the one who first discovered the significance of conception for the Beauty Way state, and we shared tremendous excitement as we made breakthrough after breakthrough. One of the highlights of our work together was when Kate Sorensen, Dr. Perry, Dr. Green and I taught a workshop outside Salt Lake City, Utah, on the advanced healing techniques we were developing at the time. Finally, however, Wes had had enough. Our friendship remains unchanged, but his time in doing exploratory work is over. This is his story:

Wes Gietz's Story
"Dying in the Monolith" or "Why I Can't Do This Anymore"

I was guinea pig number 2. We started at the earliest moments of the physical existence of a human being. There were two components to that exploration—the sperm and the egg. The life journey of a sperm is pretty short; it begins when a sperm comes into being in the father of the child, and ends with the death (that is the sperm's experience) of the sperm at conception. For the egg, existence begins in the womb of the grandmother, when the fetus that will become the mother starts to develop the egg that will become you.

I remember going back past the moment of physical formation of the egg, and finding myself in a place of luminous blackness, where there were long slow waves of something I couldn't identify. Now, as I write this, I realize that they were moving in the direction of physical manifestation. I rode one of those waves into physical reality, becoming the egg with the formation of the egg brains.

Next, we worked on the traumas that were experienced by the sperm and the egg (we worked on these things separately). As you might imagine, the egg experienced many more traumas than the sperm because its lifetime, up to conception, is hundreds of times as long at the lifetime of the sperm, and because the egg goes through the gestation and birth traumas of its mother.

We worked our way through a number of traumas associated with development, then up to the trauma of the death of the sperm. This event has an almost paradoxical power: for the sperm, that event is death, but for the egg, it is both completion and invasion. The trauma that is experienced by the sperm as death is transferred to the egg when the brains of the sperm merge with the brains of the egg. (If it were just the absorption of the sperm by the egg, like something ingesting food, you wouldn't expect the traumas to last in the developing organism.)

Conception was for me the biggest trauma to that point. It was also the first time I died in the monolith... About 25 years ago, I read a science fiction story whose theme was built around the discovery of a featureless monolith on the far side of the moon. The astronauts who discovered the thing eventually found that there was a way in, through a seemingly opaque wall. However, they also found that when they went inside, something killed them and returned them to a particular place on earth.

Fortunately, these people could be resuscitated.

Human nature being what it is, the explorers decided that they wanted to know what was inside the monolith; so they sent in volunteers to explore. The explorers discovered that certain moves inside the monolith would get them killed, whereas other moves would enable them to continue moving.

The purpose became to map the inside of the monolith. As each person died and was sent back to earth, he or she was revived and asked to contribute whatever they could to the map of the inside of the monolith.

I don't remember the outcome of the story, but I do recall clearly that no one could be persuaded to go into the monolith and be killed more than three or four times. The parallel between this story and my explorations of the developmental journey of a human being should be clear, except that instead of being literally killed by the traumas experienced by the sperm, egg, and fetus, it felt like I was being torn to pieces in some emotional or spiritual fashion. The other parallel that holds true is that I can no longer tolerate experiencing these traumas. However, like the volunteers who helped to map the monolith, I hope that the pain I experienced doesn't have to be repeated by everybody making these journeys.

There are several other traumatic experiences during the growth of the fertilized egg towards a viable infant. They include implantation, the first cell division, any insults to the fetus as a result of the mother's experiences, and the birth itself. The birth experience comprises probably the worst traumas most human beings will endure in their lives—the moment they receive the message "Separate from the mother"; the first contraction; the delivery journey itself; the death of the placenta; and the first shock of the external world, including the existence of other human beings and cold. Those first two steps of delivery were for me the second and third times I died in the monolith.

After those experiences, with the intense pain of some of them, I have found that I now know that I can survive any spiritual or traumatic event. At the same time, after getting killed so many times in the monolith, I find I can't continue this exploratory work. The value for me is now in what I can bring to other work. Currently this includes teaching and healing in the tradition of Tom Brown Jr, practicing and teaching EFT, and applying the concepts of mentoring as brought to our society by John Young and the Wilderness Awareness School.

Had I known what it was going to be like, I don't know if I would have continued. But in retrospect, I consider this experience to have been of immense value to me personally. It has tremendously deepened my understanding of life from a spiritual point of view, and has made me more powerful and compassionate for myself and all humans.

Understanding Theories and Models

When someone generates a model, they hope to put what previously looked like a huge amount of unconnected data into a simple underlying structure. A good example is that of the Copernican revolution. Up to that time people looked at the night sky and saw very complex motions of stars, planets, and the moon. Historical illustrations of theoretical machines that tried to model the motion of the heavens were ridiculously complex. The assumption (theory) was that the earth was at the center of the universe, and this resulted in the inability to see simplicity in the structure, or predict as yet unobserved phenomena. But once the correct theory was deduced, with the sun in the center, it became a trivial problem to predict stellar motion and understand the difference between the planetary motions and those of the stars. The key concepts here are 1) the correct model explains all the data, and 2) the correct model allows one to predict the existence of undiscovered phenomena.

Increasing the detail of the model allows one to incorporate more and more subtle phenomena. For approximate results, the simple model is employed—for more precise calculations, the subtle details are included. Choosing which level of the model to work with depends on how accurate you want to be. In our previous example, the motion of the planets at the simplest model level is represented by balls moving in circles around the sun. If more exact results are required, the slight elliptical orbital motions are included.

Another way to see this concept of modeling is by looking at arithmetic. We have a process model of how to add numbers—it would be much more difficult if we had to memorize every possible combination of sums (the raw data) that we were going to work with, wouldn't it? Instead, we have a simple model that allows us to do it in moments.

The key to what we're doing in this book is to assume that there *is* a relatively simple underlying model which explains *everything* that is going on: one that incorporates the physical data, the spiritual experiences, the shamanic results—everything. In fact, if there is some fact that can't be incorporated into the model, it forces us to re-examine the model for errors or incomplete areas. If you know psychology or spirituality, you will realize that this is not what is currently done in the field—each of the models stakes out a little bit of the problem, then ignores the rest of the field. It's just like the blind men we spoke about in the introduction feeling the elephant and telling the others what an elephant is like—like a snake if touching the trunk, or a post if touching the leg, and so on. Worse yet, the men get into an argument and then ignore each other! We don't want to be like others working in this field—so as you read this book, what are the areas of your experience that the peak states developmental events model doesn't seem to explain?

New models are often accepted when they actually allow one to predict phenomena that have not yet been discovered, or derive practical techniques that actually work. If a theory (model) allows one to explain all known data and additionally predicts something that hasn't yet been observed, and then it's found when people start looking for it, the theory is much more likely to be correct. For example, Einstein's theory of relativity was eventually accepted because it actually predicted a phenomenon never seen before, in this case the bending of light as it passed the sun. A few years after he made the prediction the proof was discovered. It had never occurred to anyone to look for such a phenomenon before then because none of the other models predicted such a thing could occur.

Thus, we also test the model by looking for evidence of strange, unexpected things that our model predicts and that have never been observed before (because no one suspects that the predicted phenomena exist). For example, the simple Whole-Hearted Healing model predicts that blind people have 'visual' images of trauma, and sure enough psychologist Kenneth Ring wrote about this a couple of years later. So, I encourage you to take the ISPS peak states model and think about the implications—what phenomena does this underlying model predict that have never been seen before because no one was looking?

Understanding the Concept of Trauma

From an experiential viewpoint, trauma is an event that isn't fully experienced by the organism. This event's response is then stored and replayed when sensations similar to the original trauma are evoked in the present. Although trauma usually feels painful, to many people's surprise some traumas can feel pleasurable. This latter case occurs when a pleasurable feeling is too overwhelming, or when a pleasant feeling is being experienced just as a painful trauma suddenly occurs and gets associated with it. Nevertheless, it's a trauma when the response to a situation becomes stuck and future events evoke that earlier response, irrespective of the situation in the current circumstances.

For example, when a mouse sees the shadow of a hawk and jumps to the right, saving its life, most likely it's been traumatized, in this case scared nearly to death. In the future, when a similar sensation occurs, perhaps the flicker of the shadow of a hawk, the mouse continues to jump to the right, regardless of whether it's a good idea or not—because the trauma response tells it that this is what to do. From a biological viewpoint, this may on average have been a good strategy for mice, ensuring the majority would survive. But for humans rote trauma response is a disaster in our much more complex lives.

Although as laymen we tend to think of trauma as extending over time, in reality trauma is composed of discrete moments of time. These moments often form a chain of traumatic moments linked by their similar sensation content. Several therapies take advantage of this fact in healing, such as Body-Centered Therapy by Gay Hendricks, Traumatic Incident Reduction by Frank Gerbode, and my own Whole-Hearted Healing. An alternative definition of trauma is any moment in time when an out-of-body image is stored by the organism. This definition is used in the Whole-Hearted Healing therapy as its key to the healing process.

This traumatic event can be due to injury or other kinds of influences that don't appear to be obviously traumatic. Generational trauma, the personality 'shell', misunderstood Gaia instructions, and conflicts with tri-une brain self identities are examples of more subtle causes of trauma and are described in Volumes 2 and 3. Trauma can also cause even more trauma when it drives a person to get into situations that in turn create trauma. Well-known examples of this are projection and repeating dysfunctional patterns.

Trauma can be defined in an even more fundamental way. In a state of consciousness we call 'Spaciousness', trauma can be seen as a fold or distortion in the medium that underlies physical existence. Volume 3 goes into details on how to use this for healing.

When healed, the trauma moment no longer has the power to affect the present, and in fact the trauma moment no longer has any negative or positive sensations left to it when recalled.

The Developmental Events Model for Peak States, Experiences, and Abilities

There actually is a very simple model that explains *all* the data about peak states, peak experiences, and unusual abilities. Three elements come into play: 1) the existence of trauma, 2) critical developmental events *in utero*, and 3) acquiring the 'false self' or 'shell' at birth, which gives people the sensation of having a skin boundary (described in Volume 2). For this analysis, we will ignore other factors which are not as dominant, which are covered in Volumes 2 and 3.

Simply put, at specific moments during every developmental event in our growth (primarily in the womb and parents' ovary and testes), a spiritual experience occurs and/or an ability and/or state manifests. To clarify, examples of such developmental events are conception and implantation. (Even though these events are often called "developmental stages" in the study of fetal growth, in this text we'll be calling them "developmental events" to emphasize that the key moments that initiate a new stage are very brief in duration.) If the developmental milestone is completed without a trauma response, that particular spiritual experience, state or ability is available to us after birth. Certain kinds of states and abilities require a number of developmental events to occur before they can manifest.

If trauma occurs during a critical *in utero* developmental event, the fetus will for the most part still get the state or ability that is the result of the increase in organism complexity. However, during birth, certain kinds of experiences occur that continuously activate the trauma responses of the fetus' history. In particular, trauma responses that occurred during the developmental events that were critical for the states/abilities we're interested in will now act to pull the baby from its natural function. Rather than the baby's organism acting the way it was designed, the trauma responses override the baby's natural actions and substitute the actions that occurred when the trauma happened. And the state/ability is lost. The reason for this is covered in Volumes 2 and 3.

This principle isn't readily apparent because until recently there were no methods that could easily access those *in utero* experiences. Also, since the impact of these *in utero* developmental events was not realized by researchers, only the biologists were looking at these events. The few therapies that can access *in utero* experiences don't generally look at the developmental events unless they come up for some other reason. For more on the developmental events, I recommend the work of the psychotherapist William Emerson, who as far as I know hasn't yet made the conceptual breakthrough with regards to peak states that we have, but he is very close to it.

The developmental events model explains why there are different peak states. Different developmental events confer different types of states because of the particular changes the organism made to itself. Secondly, some states are built on earlier states as the organism became more complex. Thus, certain states are commonly occurring or easily acquired because they only require one or two developmental events to be experienced with minimal trauma. Other states require a number of difficult developmental events to be experienced without trauma, and hence are much rarer in the general population. And third, this is why some people have only partial states, or move in and out of them—the relevant developmental events were not completely trauma free. Current circumstances may activate more or less trauma response, moving the individual away proportionally from the full state.

Implications of the Peak State Developmental Events Model: Acquiring Permanent States

What might be the natural implications of such a model? The first one that leaps to mind is that if we go back and heal these developmental events, we should get the state that the event would have given us. The second major implication of the model is that healing developmental events can give states or abilities that are permanent. And sure enough, for the majority of our clients this approach works! This is in contrast to other kinds of processes, which are mostly trying to relax the trauma responses, and so must be continually 'practiced'.

This is a stunning result, because it means that if you want a particular state, or ability, or spiritual experience, you can go to the relevant critical developmental moment and heal it—and these developmental moments *are the same for everybody*. Once you have a road map with all the relevant developmental events, and a way to get there, and a way to heal them, in the majority of cases the client moves immediately into the desired result. It's very, very simple. In the course of our work we've mapped a number of these milestones, but I fully expect you will also be exploring and finding new ones.

Traumas that do not involve those critical *in utero* developmental events do not, in general, affect a person's state. The only exception that we've seen is experiential—a minority of the people we put into peak states have something we call a 'dominant trauma'. This is an issue in their lives that has such a huge impact on them that when we put them through a process to induce peak states, nothing happens until the dominant trauma is healed. Then they pop right into the target state. I'd estimate that this dominant trauma problem occurs in less than 10% of the people we see.

An understanding of how traumas connect is important in making a technique that gives peak states. For those of you not used to using regression therapies like Traumatic Incident Reduction (TIR), or Whole-Hearted Healing (WHH), let me explain more fully. We know from using those techniques and others that traumas that have a theme involving certain similar sensations 'stack' together. These later traumas are generally only traumatic because the first trauma lends its 'punch' to the current trauma experience. Any specific traumatic material connected by a similarity of sensation theme is called a 'coex' by Dr. Stanislav Grof. Therapists use this principle in their practice to save time, since they've discovered that healing the earliest trauma makes the later ones dissolve without any time wasted on healing them separately. However, there is an exception to this rule. If the later trauma also involves physical injury, it generally needs to be healed as a separate trauma. Thus, for our method of inducing peak states, we would also have to be able to find and heal these later connected physical traumas. Fortunately, they are not too common—most post-birth traumas are emotional in nature, not physical.

Example:
> Many spiritual paths use a variety of techniques to access what could be called God or the Creator. It turns out that at certain developmental moments, like conception and implantation, some of this 'Creator' awareness is incorporated into the suddenly more complex organism. Thus, it turns out that you can go to the Creator anytime if you return to the developmental moments where more of the Creator 'stuff' is added to the being. Once there, if you've healed it fully, you can access that spiritual experience/ability. Once you've healed all the related material, you don't even need to go into the past to that developmental moment to access the ability, as it will now be permanently available to you in the present.

Example:
> One way to merge with and retain awareness of all your past (and future) lives is to return to the moment when the egg is being cov-

ered as it first leaves the ovary and heal the relevant trauma. This is covered in depth in Chapter 7.

Let me emphasize this again—we don't have to heal everything to get the desired ability/experience/state—we only have to heal a couple of the *right* traumas! And these traumas occur at particular developmental milestones that are the same for everybody. This is the basis for one of the Institute for the Study of Peak States' methodologies. Of course, some people have complicating traumas later in life, like at birth, that act as additional blocks. However, there are not nearly as many of these as might be expected because if you eliminate the core trauma, the subsequent traumas dissolve automatically except for related ones involving physical injury.

How the Developmental Events Model Explains the Observed Data

First of all, how does the model explain the number of people in natural peak states? Relatively simple states like the Beauty Way have only one or two developmental milestones, and so occur with some small frequency (about 8% we think) in the general population. However, more drastically improved states require the successful completion of a number of developmental milestones. On a statistical basis, it's unlikely that a person correctly goes through any one particular developmental milestone without trauma. You can assign a probability that each developmental event (for example, conception, implantation, etc.) occurs successfully in the average population. The 'higher' the state, the more of these events that have to be done successfully. When you multiply these probabilities together (to get the overall probability), the average occurrence of people with these states rapidly falls to nearly zero. (See Appendix A on the estimated occurrence of these states.)

This simplest model assumes any given developmental milestone occurs either with or without trauma. From this, you could compute what percentage of the population is in any given peak state. In other words, you can determine how many people don't have traumas blocking peak states. This explains the relative scarcity of people who live in natural peak states all the time. An analogy might make this clearer. It's a very rare pinball (you) which makes it all the way to the bottom without hitting one of the barriers (traumas at developmental milestones). The more gates you hit, the less abilities and states you have, although which particular gates you hit does matter—some of them give you a lot of penalty points and some much fewer....

Now, let's complicate the simple probability model to make it more accurate. The reality is that the person might have not fully succeeded, but not fully failed either to get through any given developmental event without trauma. Thus, you find some people who during the course of their week move in and out of any given peak state because the developmental trauma event(s) was relatively minor, and/or because outer circumstances don't trigger the trauma response that blocks the state. Thus, we can complicate our simple model to make it more accurate by including the probability that the trauma was minor and won't cause the person to lose the state much of the time. Probability estimates can also be made to include this, and they're included in Appendix A.

Example:
> In my own case, if I felt a woman's disapproval, I'd lose the Beauty Way until that stopped, because it would trigger an underlying trauma response.

Now let's examine how our model explains all those temporary methods for achieving shamanic or spiritual peak states or experiences I described in Chapter 3. How do those work? Recall that the block to these states or abilities is due to trauma. If you use a process that relaxes the organism so that trauma responses are not stimulated, the state automatically occurs—*because it is your natural state, your birthright!* You are designed to have access to those experiences, and to live in the highest possible state. Thus, techniques that relax the appropriate parts of the organism allow the person to have the state temporarily, until the relaxation ends and the stored trauma information (which tells the organism to not be in its natural tension-free state) is replayed back into the organism.

This model also explains why some people find that certain spiritual or shamanic practices work for them, and for the rest of us they're a pretty futile endeavor. These folks can either relax their trauma responses extremely well, or the relevant trauma responses are pretty minor and they are at the edge of having the state anyway. It's also why the vast majority of people aren't able to use those techniques successfully, as most people really mess up the developmental events. If that's your case, no amount of meditation or what have you will do a darn bit of good. You're either a natural shaman or spiritual teacher (i.e., little early trauma), or not—you're already in the right state and only need to be educated in how to use it, or you can successfully use these techniques to stay in the right state. Thus the number of people who have or can get more 'advanced' states and abilities (i.e., a number of critical developmental events done successfully) is rare.

And how about those 'spiritual emergencies' I mentioned in Chapter 1? From the perspective of the model, people can go through a hellish experience on their way to a peak state because usually severe developmental events are being triggered. As the general public doesn't have the experience to recognize *in utero* or earlier traumas, most never take advantage of the newer power therapies—they just try and endure, hoping it will go away. Another kind of spiritual emergency occurs when a person loses a peak state. As I've said, this can feel like the person has been 'kicked out of heaven', creating depression and suicidal feelings. This usually occurs when previously suppressed developmental event trauma is activated, blocking their peak state. Other causes for this problem are covered in Volume 3.

Using our model we can also explain how shamanic techniques like vision quests, drumming, or drugs work. They temporarily shut off some of the trauma response, and the organism settles into more of a peak state. The practitioner often isn't aware that he's done this, because he often has a number of types of experience going on simultaneously at various levels of his being. In everyday terms, "all hell can break loose," so the connection between less trauma and what he's experiencing is not obvious. Examples of different levels of consciousness from your own experience might be that of the Creator or Void, as well as a variety of others which we'll be covering in Volume 2 such as the Sacred or Gaia. In addition, it's common with these types of techniques to experience parts of the unhealed developmental traumas, with often difficult and painful results. They are often chronically re-experienced because they are not recognized as *in utero* trauma and healed.

Example:
> Hank Wesselman in his book *Spiritwalker* describes a sensation of pressure when his consciousness shifts forward in time. Although there are several possible explanations, the most likely is that an *in utero* trauma that is relevant to this ability is being re-experienced each time.

Other Generic Blocks to Peak States

If we again complicate our model to increase its accuracy even further, we can look at the *types* of trauma that occur at a developmental event. The trauma might have been a more serious type, such as if a particular organ didn't grow properly, or a 'hole' is created, or a Buddha brain structure interferes, etc. (For an explanation of these latter terms, please refer to *The Basic Whole-Hearted Healing Manual*.) For these individuals, a healing process like WHH, which is more directed to these types of problems than simple processes like EFT or TAT, would probably be required.

In addition, we know that trauma in very early key developmental events (described in Chapter 6) will predispose a person to fail in most of the subsequent developmental events. We discovered this with several of our volunteers, who failed to successfully do nearly all of their developmental events—it was a miracle they survived. We've identified several of these sorts of trauma events, and healing them first make our processes much more effective.

In Volume 3 we'll be describing how to heal another of the most important reasons why the egg, sperm, and fetus have trauma during developmental events—acquired generational traumas from the father and mother's lineage.

Occasionally the father or mother unconsciously interfere with the developmental stages of the sperm, egg, or fetus. This is in addition to gross mechanical damage like poisoning, attempted abortion, injury from sex during pregnancy, and so on. Our client base doesn't encounter this unconscious interference nearly as often as the previously mentioned problems. We go into depth on this in Volume 2 and 3. We have some evidence that the converse is also true—a mother and father in some peak states unconsciously assist the developing sperm, egg, and fetus to experience developmental events without trauma. Interestingly, it appears that peak states and abilities often run in families. This mechanism, or a lack of interfering generational traumas would explain this observation. Clearly, this implies that mothers can make pro-active changes by improving their own state to help their unborn children.

Finally, one might note that in your non-traumatic fetal, sperm, or egg memories, you find yourself in peak states even though the underlying developmental trauma moments were not healed. And then after birth you (like virtually every member of the mammalian group) lose your peak states. There are several reasons for this: First, *in utero* the fetus generally feels fairly safe, and generally relaxes its trauma response except for moments where it's traumatized again. Secondly, the 'shell' acquired at birth activates earlier trauma. However, there is another fundamental reason, and just as the model predicts, it has to do with a developmental event that most people don't pass through correctly. This occurs at the first moment the fetus/mother starts the birth process, even before the first contraction. In Volume 2 you'll learn much more about this, and why it's so traumatic, but for now you can just tuck it into the back of your awareness.

'Music' During the Developmental Events

Each developmental event is accompanied by a certain kind of 'music' that can be 'heard' when some people do regression to pre-birth events. Although this music is not physically present, and could be described as being at a 'spiritual' level, certain kinds of acoustic music mimic the spiritual music well. In fact, developmental event 'music' probably provides the inspiration for many musicians.

We have incorporated this observation into our processes. To help the client access the particular *in utero* developmental event we want them to access, we choose music that is similar to the particular 'spiritual' music that occurs at that event. Fortunately, for any given developmental event, the 'music' that occurs during it is the same for everyone.

Incidentally, there is something that can be perfectly described as 'music of the spheres' from the ancient Greek tradition, but it has to do with archetypes and isn't related to the 'spiritual' music I describe above. The

music of the spheres has no harmony, every tone being completely independent of all the others.

Example:
> This observation about the developmental event music may also
> contribute to why techniques like Holotropic Breathwork require
> certain types of music in order to be effective. It's either done as a
> preselected rote choice of music, or a skilled practitioner will
> choose by intuition, or sometimes the client will just know what
> music will be helpful.

Example:
> We have found in our practice therapy clients who suddenly find
> themselves attracted to a particular musical piece. This is often be-
> cause there is a developmental trauma that is trying to come into
> their consciousness—the music they are focused on is a close ana-
> log to the 'spiritual' music at that developmental moment.

Practical Difficulties in Finding Relevant Developmental Events

In our research work, we regress to *in utero* and earlier developmental
events to see what peak states or abilities or experiences they are involved
with. Or we start with a target peak state and try and find the relevant developmental moments. Obviously, the first major hurdle is to even find
the moments that are relevant to the state we want to acquire. However,
there other difficulties to identifying relevant developmental events that
are not obvious.

First, when you or your client regresses to a given event, you re-experience what actually happened. At this point, most therapists assume that
what happened to one's early self was what was supposed to happen, with
or without the trauma. However, in reality the full change at the developmental event is blocked with trauma. If you are using power therapies like
WHH, when you heal these traumatic moments you find that your experience of the past event actually changes. Often, the major changes during
the event only happen as the last of the trauma is dissolved. During our
experiments we would go over and over the time interval of the developmental event, healing it further each time. Each time more changes would
happen. In other words, each time we'd use a power therapy to heal the
same trauma, something new would happen. After a number of repeats,
occasionally it was hard to imagine it was the same developmental event!
This changing of the experience is something that other investigators
might not expect, and could mislead them away from looking closely at
given developmental events.

The second problem is even stranger, and applies to peak states that
build on a succession of developmental events. If earlier, critical develop-

mental events are not done correctly, the developmental event you're investigating will only change so far, then stop. The potential outcome of the stage will not be fully experienced. Instead, a partial experience will occur no matter how much healing you do on it. Thus, doing the earlier developmental event first (if you know where they are) can allow the later events to go to a different kind of resolution. This can be witnessed by first healing the later stage, then the earlier, then returning to the later stage, and having more or different changes happen without any further healing on the later event being done. Of course, some peak states/experiences/abilities are due to only one developmental ("stand-alone") event, and earlier developmental event trauma isn't relevant.

The bottom line is that it's tricky work finding the stages and realizing their full potential. Having a map of the stages and what should happen saves a tremendous amount of time, and we have often wished we could have purchased one from someone else!

Using Different Types of Trauma Healing Therapies

There are a number of 'power' and 'energy' therapies available now that can be used to heal these developmental moments. We refer you to the reading list at the end of this chapter for descriptions, or our own *Basic Whole-Hearted Healing Manual* which also covers them. In particular, the WHH manual emphasizes healing a variety of unusual experiences relevant to this work.

Probably the biggest stumbling block to their use in this application is regressing the client to the correct developmental event. In Chapter 9 we'll show a method that bypasses this problem. The next biggest stumbling block is that, unless you know what is supposed to happen at the given stage, the therapist often stops the healing process too soon, before the more radical changes take place.

Another problem with some therapies to eliminate trauma response is that they can be reversed. That is, you can eliminate the trauma at a particular moment, but later some circumstance in the person's life will bring it back. It's a bit like those therapies acted like whiteout on a library card, so that the person couldn't access the trauma anymore. However, the book was still in the stacks, and if the whiteout got scratched off, the trauma book would become available again. In general, energy therapies like Thought Field Therapy (TFT) or Emotional Freedom Technique (EFT) fall in this category. However, these therapies are very useful, fast and simple, and don't often get reversed, so we use them in many of our processes.

One of the reasons why some power therapies are not reversible is that they actually change the past as the trauma is being healed. TIR and WHH are examples of this past-changing type of therapy. Fortunately, any healing modality that eliminates the trauma response also gives the desired result, even if it doesn't also change the past. EFT is an example of the type of therapy that doesn't change the past, yet for our purposes works well in most situations. This concept of changing the past is outside the bounds of our culture's current paradigm, of course, but comes up when experiencing some of the advanced material described in later chapters. A fuller experiential understanding of this phenomenon of changing the past will have to wait till the chapter describing the Realm of the Shaman in Volume 2.

Example:
> When experiencing a past life, occasionally one finds that one can change the course of events, or communicate with the person involved to change the course of events. Although one might argue that there is no way to prove this is actually possible, the converse is also true and does have an impact in our own lives—our past lives can also communicate with us, and influence our choices. This latter event can be quite a surprise when it happens. Hank Wesselman describes just such a situation is his books, and we see this sort of thing in some of our own clients. (Chapter 7 goes into this in depth.)

As your state of consciousness improves, it becomes easier and easier to heal your traumas. Thus, in general, it's to your advantage to acquire peak states as fast as possible as you do your work, to make it easier to heal the harder traumas.

When working with clients, we've discovered that it's difficult for them to heal a developmental event if you have any trauma in it yourself. Essentially, clients unconsciously look to you for safety around facing the trauma. If your trauma response at the developmental event is triggered, even if it is suppressed out of your awareness, the client can sense this and will resist facing the trauma. Thus, doing this work on yourself *first* is generally required. If you have the peak ability or state you are trying to bring your client to, chances are good that you have little or no trauma at the relevant moment. Once you have these peak states, you can bring others to them relatively easily because you know what the right traumas are, and you are no longer 'unconsciously' telling your client to avoid the pain of the developmental event.

However, there can be other reasons why you 'unconsciously' block your clients from going into peak states, even when you have them yourself. Unfortunately, other traumas can make you want to block other people's progress into these peak states, as I've discovered with a number of my students.

It is possible to heal the relevant traumas in another person without their conscious participation, if you know what to heal and have the ability. This is the fastest and most efficient way for one-on-one sessions. However, this approach can't be used on groups of people, doesn't teach underlying principles to students, and does not provide methods that a person can use for self-help.

What We Haven't Covered Yet

All the basic elements of the model are not yet in place. If you want to think about these pieces that will be covered in Volume 2, I'll give you a couple of questions that point to these parts of the model: why do almost all mammals and humans lose their peak states during birth, what is the sacred, how does it differ from the 'holy', what triggers the start of birth, what gives the sensation of having a skin boundary, and what is the 'I' that experiences during a near-death?

Key Points

- The key point of this book is that the current paradigm causes us to approach the problem of peak states of consciousness with implicit assumptions that make the problem unsolvable. Rather than asking "How does one acquire or learn peak states of consciousness?", the correct question is "What causes one to lose the peak states that are one's birthright?" This paradigm question leads to a realization that individuals have all the peak states *in utero*, and generally lose them at birth. This in turn leads to solutions that have never been seen before.
- The *in utero* baby has most if not all of the possible peak states and abilities. Its consciousness is quite different from that of the baby after birth.
- The *in utero* baby loses the majority of its states and abilities at birth. From birth on, developmental traumas that block peak states and abilities are activated relatively continuously.
- Only *certain* kinds of traumatic events are the root cause that keep people out of peak states, experiences and abilities. These traumas occur at particular developmental events in the person's life, and although trauma after birth contributes to the problem, most of the essential blocks occur during or before birth. These moments are identical for everyone, although the content of the traumas we experience can vary drastically.
- Different kinds of peak states occur because different developmental events lead to them. In addition, more 'advanced' peak states require the person to successfully complete a number of the developmental events. An analogy might be a pinball table—it's a rare ball that misses all of the obstacles on its way to the bottom, just as it's a rare human who makes it through all the developmental events without damage.

- Peak abilities and 'spiritual' experiences can be recovered by regressing to the appropriate developmental events and healing the trauma that occurred then. You can then have the experience again by just regressing back to that moment, although as you develop further you can go to those experiences at will without the need to regress.
- Although we're not certain of this, we believe that if the parents, especially the mother, were in a high enough peak state, the fetus would be born in at least as good a state, as she would see that it made it through without trauma. We suspect that even if she can't directly help her eggs and fetus, if she made it through correctly (or healed herself there later), the fetus will most likely make it also. The converse is also true, and we see in some clients the mother's unconscious actions during the developmental events can inhibit correct resolution of the events and cause trauma.
- Even though you may be in a peak state, other traumas can block your ability or willingness to heal others in order to put them in peak states.
- There are many critical developmental moments in a person's prenatal experience, and *each one* is accompanied by a spiritual experience which includes the 'sound' of a kind of music at the spiritual levels. This music is identical for everyone.

Suggested Reading and Websites

On fetal, pre-, and perinatal events and trauma
- Association for Pre- and Perinatal Psychology and Health, www.birthpsychology.com. Excellent material on the topic of *in utero* regression.
- Early Trauma Treatment and Trainings by Terry Larimore, www.terrylarimore.com. Her website also contains excellent material.
- Emerson Training seminars, William Emerson, www.emersonbirthrx.com. He is one of the leaders in pre- and perinatal psychology in my opinion.
- William Emerson, "The Vulnerable Prenate", paper presented to the APPPAH Congress, San Francisco, 1995, published in *Pre- & Perinatal Psychology Journal*, Vol 10(3), Spring 1996, 125-142. An online copy is at www.birthpsychology.com/healing/point2.html
- Michael Gabriel and Marie Gabriel, *Voices from the Womb: Adults Relive their Pre-birth Experiences - a Hypnotherapist's Compelling Account*, Aslan Publishing, 1992.
- Stanislav Grof, *The Adventure of Self-Discovery*, State University of New York Press, 1988. Excellent coverage on the stages of birth and other spiritual and shamanic experiences.

- Terry Larimore and Graham Farrant, "Universal Body Movements in Cellular Consciousness and What They Mean," originally published in *Primal Renaissance*, Vol. 1, No. 1, 1995. An online copy is at www.terrylarimore.com/CellularPaper.html
- Sheila Linn, William Emerson, Dennis Linn, and Matthew Linn, *Remembering our Home: Healing Hurts and Receiving Gifts from Conception to Birth*, Paulist Press, 1999.
- Elizabeth Noble, *Primal Connections: How our Experiences from Conception to Birth Influence our Emotions, Behavior, and Health*, Simon and Schuster, 1993.
- Bill Swartley, "Major Categories of Early Psychosomatic Traumas: From Conception to the End of the First Hour" from *The Primal Psychotherapy Page*. An online copy is at www.primal-page.com/bills-1.htm. Excellent with great references.

Images of sperm, egg, and *in utero* developmental stages
- *Journey Into Life: The Triumph of Creation* (a 30 minute video),1990, by Derek Bromhall, distributed by Questar Video, Inc. This is an exceptional video on the journey of the sperm, egg, zygote, and fetus. The material is filmed with the same viewpoint and image size that people recalling trauma around these events see.
- Lennart Nilsson, *A Child is Born*, Delacorte Press, NY, 1990. Still photos of the journey of the sperm, egg, zygote, and fetus. The images are of scenes that people recalling trauma around these moments see. Recommended.

Regression techniques and therapies
- Leslie Bandler, *Solutions*, Real People, 1985. About the VKD (Visual Kinesthetic Dissociation) power therapy.
- Gerald French and Chrys Harris, *Traumatic Incident Reduction (TIR)*, CRC Press, 1999. See also the website www.tir.org.
- Winafred Blake Lucas, *Regression Therapy; A Handbook for Professionals*, Vol 1: Past-life Therapy, Deep Forest Press, 1993.
- Winafred Blake Lucas, *Regression Therapy; A Handbook for Professionals, Vol 2: Special Instances of Altered State Work*, Deep Forest Press, 1993.
- Grant McFetridge and Mary Pellicer, MD, *The Basic Whole-Hearted Healing Manual*, 3rd edition, The Institute for the Study of Peak States Press, 2003.
- Francis Shapiro and Margot Forrest, *EMDR: The Breakthrough Therapy*, HarperCollins, 1997. See also the website www.emdr.org.

Specific energy and meridian therapies
- BSFF (Be Set Free Fast) - A simple, effective, and even faster energy therapy than EFT at www.besetfreefast.com.

- EFT (Emotional Freedom Technique) - A simple and extremely effective energy therapy at www.emofree.com. Contains links to other meridian therapies.
- TAT (Tapas Acupressure Technique) power therapy: www.tat-intl.com. Specifically designed for allergies as well as trauma.
- TFT (Thought Field Therapy) power therapy at www.tftrx.com. The original energy/meridian therapy.

Other effective therapies
- Foundation for Human Enrichment, the Somatic Experiencing therapy, www.traumahealing.com.
- Eugene Gendlin, *Focusing (revised edition)*, Bantam, 1981. See also the Focusing Institute at www.focusing.org.
- Gay Hendricks, *Learning to Love Yourself: A Guide to Becoming Centered*, Simon & Schuster, 1982.
- Gay Hendricks, *The Learning to Love Yourself Workbook*, Simon & Schuster, 1990. Contains a simple method to temporarily experience a loving, happy state.
- Gay and Kathlyn Hendricks, *At The Speed of Life: A New Approach to Personal Change Through Body-Centered Therapy*, Bantam, 1993. See also the Hendricks Institute at www.hendricks.com.
- Holotropic Breathwork, developed by Stanislav Grof, MD at www.breathwork.com.
- Primal Psychology Page (the International Primal Association plus others) at www.primals.org. Contains a variety of links.

Perry Diagrams and Triune Brain States of Consciousness

Introduction

This chapter introduces the Papez-MacLean discovery of the triune structure of the brain and shows how it is the basis for a large number of peak
states of consciousness. We call them as a group 'brain fusion states'.
These states are of particular importance, because they have a tremendous impact on our quality of life and sense of health. Continuous feelings
of happiness, peace, aliveness, effortlessness and wholeness are *caused* by
these states.

In this chapter we limit the triune brain model to just its purely biological and psychological aspects. This is adequate for understanding these
brain fusion peak states as well as a number of types of spiritual emergencies. In later chapters, especially in Volume 2, we add transpersonal elements to the model to explain other types of triune brain related peak
states.

We also introduce Perry diagrams, which allows the depth of brain fusion states and their underlying structural causes to be shown pictorially.
They both illustrate the principles of this chapter and allow clinicians to
record their client's type and degree of triune brain state.

States in this chapter:
- Sub-average Consciousness
- Average Consciousness
- Mind Shutdown
- Mind-Heart Shutdown
- Samadhi
- Heart Shutdown
- Inner Peace
- Underlying Happiness
- Communicating Brains
- Big Sky
- Deep Peace
- Hollow

- Wholeness
- Beauty Way

Grant's Story
Discovering the Triune Structure of the Brain

As I continued to heal trauma, eventually I realized the importance of trauma in the womb and birth. Aided by an unusual state
of consciousness, one of the 'inner brightness' states which
experientially fills one's body with clear white light, I healed the
feeling that life in the womb had been wonderful, a sort of garden
of Eden experience. Then I was then able to recall my entire womb
experience with clarity and ease—and the high level of trauma in
utero became clear to me. As well, I realized my state of consciousness in the womb was very peculiar, but at the time I didn't understand why it was so different.

Day after day I continued to eliminate womb traumas. During a
session of Holotropic Breathwork with Sheelo, I encountered an
experience that was stunning as well as traumatic. While I was in
utero during the last trimester, my mother had eaten something
that was toxic to my fetal self. As the toxins poured into my belly
through the umbilical cord, I felt my mind breaking away from my
body and heart awareness. This was a stunning experience to me
in the present, because up to this point I'd never considered that
my mind and body were self-aware, or in fact any different than
'myself'.

My mind consciousness found this new experience of separation a
shock. The body consciousness, after dealing with the toxins, tried
to reconnect with the mind consciousness, and could not. The
body figured that it must have grown the mind brain incorrectly,
and so tried to destroy it by cutting off blood to that section of the
body. However, the pain that this caused in the entire organism
quickly forced it to stop, and the situation of separation remained
that way for quite a while. There were now two aware 'selves' in
one body, but it wasn't like two people in one box. Even though
much of the sensory and internal information is shared, the mind
functions differently than the body consciousness and was aware
of this. In fact, I recall the mind taking a sort of naive pride in being able to think much faster than the rest, and trying to do its best
to help, like a child might. For example, it stored sequences of
words that the fetal body heard in the womb in a sort of infinitely
repeating loop, with unintentional negative consequences to its
ability to think easily. One of the most emotionally painful traumas (outside of birth) that I can recall involved shame (in the
mind) and anger (in the body) because the splitting allowed the
mind to initiate defecation in the womb, contrary to what the body
wanted.

A new and even more serious problem developed shortly after the split. My fetal self found itself unable to be always completely in the present, as previous trauma would occasionally disrupt its awareness. The first time this happened, it felt like something was pushing into the mind from the side, making self-awareness vanish in that area—quite a terrifying experience, and one the mind tried desperately to resist.

The next major catastrophe occurred during the birth process. During my birth, the body consciousness broke apart again into two selves. This time the heart brain (also called the limbic brain or the emotional consciousness) split away from the body consciousness. I can recall the heart splitting and going out-of-body to escape what was happening to my body.

By the time I was taken to the crib in the hospital, my sense of self had changed to what I'm familiar with now as 'average' consciousness. It's as if some sort of amnesia took place when I lost the internal brightness I'd had in utero.

Once I knew what to look for, I was able to return to those experiences repeatedly to understand what had occurred. Eventually, I realized that inside myself were three self-aware consciousnesses: the mind, the heart, and the body. In my adult 'average' consciousness they were split apart and competing with each other for control, while in utero they had been fused into one organism. I found that much of my dysfunctional behavior was due to this inner struggle between the brains, and in fact much of my outer world was a projection of this inner conflict. Each of the brains held an unconscious self-identity, like a child pretending it was a cowboy, along with an inner image of the other brains. For example, my heart was unconsciously pretending that it was my mother, while feeling that the body brain was an archetypal monster in the basement. Dysfunctional family dynamics accurately describe this inner power struggle and craving for acceptance.

As the months went on, I came to realize that the peak state I had been trying to regain was due in a large part to the degree of union, or fusion, between these biological consciousnesses. I also found that my discovery about the multiple nature of the brain had already been made by biologist Dr. Paul MacLean in the 1960s, who called it the 'triune brain model'. This was a great relief, since as far as I knew up to that point no one was aware of this fundamental brain structure. This breakthrough in understanding the real underlying biological dynamics in the psyche has only now started to make its way into the psychological profession.

As an aside, it is possible to go into a peak state where the brains can communicate with each other. This state occurs when the brains are just peripherally merged together, but separate enough to still have a separate sense of self in each one. It's a bit hard to explain, but 'you' can ask a question about an issue and be aware of responses from the head, heart, and lower belly locations—and they don't always agree! For example, one time while in this state, I asked myself if I should work on healing my solar plexus next. My heart said yes, and my body and mind said no. The next day they'd each reversed their decisions.

I also found I had the ability to shut the different brains 'off'. This led to a number of states of consciousness that were actually sub-normal, although they felt quite wonderful. These states are de-scribed in literature on spiritual emergencies and on specific types of mental illness. However, they were enticing because, although I would lose the abilities of the brains that were shut off, the inter-nal state was much more harmonious, as the separated brains stopped being in conflict. By analogy, it was a lot quieter in my dysfunctional family after I'd shot the other family members.

Years later, we also discovered the existence of more brain sys-tems, ones which are not normally recognized but had been identi-fied in early stages of the developing fetus.

Dr. MacLean's Three-Part Model of the Human Brain

A very neglected breakthrough in understanding brain biology forms the basis of a three-part or 'triune' model of the brain. In the 1960s Dr. Paul MacLean at the National Institute for Mental Health, expanding on the work of James Papez, described a three-part concentric layering structure to the human brain. The outermost layer is the neomammalian brain, the neocortex which is the seat of thought and most voluntary movement. The next layer inward is the paleomammalian brain, composed of the limbic system, the seat of our emotions and autonomic nervous system. In the innermost portion is found the reptilian brain, composed of the brain stem, midbrain, basal ganglia and other structures. Each brain serves dif-ferent functions with some overlap, but what Dr. MacLean postulates is that the integration, or coordination between the brains is inadequate, a genetic problem in our species.

For a complete biological description see Dr. MacLean's *The Triune Brain in Evolution: Role in Paleocerebral Functions*. For more information, see *Evolution's End* by Joseph Pierce, *Three Faces of the Mind* by Elaine De Beauport, and for summary information see *Maps of the Mind* by Charles Hampden-Turner.

Triune Brain Structure and Inner Experience

How does the triune structure of the brain apply to our inner experience? In everyday terms, we know these brains as the 'mind', 'heart', and 'body'. Each brain has different biological functions and abilities. The 'mind', or neocortex, is the part of ourselves we most often think of as who we are. It perceives itself in the head, and it is the part of ourselves that forms judgments, handles short-term memory, and does abstractions like mathematics. One of its primary functions is handling and manipulating audible sounds and language. The 'heart' is the limbic system in the brain, yet perceives itself in the chest, probably because this is the area of its primary biological responsibility and sensory awareness. It allows us to feel emotions, and be either positively or negatively emotionally aware of the presence of others. One of its primary functions is handling visual imagery. Finally, the 'body' consciousness (or 'hara' in Japanese) is composed of the tissues at the base of our skull, and probably other distributed systems in our body. It experiences itself in the lower belly, its area of major biological function. This brain gives us a sense of time and our ability to feel sexuality. We communicate with this brain when we do dowsing or muscle testing. One of its primary functions is handling physical sensations, and probably scent as well.

Independent Self-Awareness in Each Brain

The most difficult conceptual jump in Dr. MacLean's work is to realize that each of the brains is intelligently, independently self-aware. Because we tend to assume thinking requires words, it's difficult for us to realize that each brain actually thinks. In fact, unlike the mind, the heart thinks in sequences of feelings, and the body thinks in gestalt sequences of body sensations (described as the 'felt sense' in Eugene Gendlin's *Focusing*). By this, I don't mean that it's as if there were three people inside of us. Instead, since each brain is so different, we might compare this situation to that of a living stereo system. Imagine if the speakers (mind), tape deck (heart), and receiver (body) were each self-aware, each trying to run the show and puzzled because the other parts won't do what it wants them to. It would be hard to imagine how a stereo like this would ever manage to play music! And unfortunately, this is fairly close to the mark. Even though sharing much sensory data and awareness of each other's actions, each brain tends to be in denial about the existence of the others. In fact, the brains often come into conflict, even to the point of overtly or unconsciously attempting to manipulate and control each other. A simple example to illustrate this occurs when you're sexually attracted (the body consciousness) to someone you don't even like (the emotional consciousness), and are confused about the situation (the mind consciousness).

In most people, the brains interact like members of a dysfunctional family. Generally, one of the brains ends up dominating the others. People tend to lead their lives and act in ways that reflect this dominance. We've all seen extreme examples of people who are driven by their feelings, or totally oriented towards satisfying body sensations, or completely analytical, although the pattern is present to some degree in most people. This brain dominance shows up in various branches of therapy and psychology, due to the unconscious orientation of the originator of the therapy. Thus, different kind of therapies will tend to pick out one of the brain types for their particular process, giving us cognitive, emotional, or body-centered therapies. Brain dominance also shows up in career choices and preferred activities. It's likely that a combination of brain dominance and trauma is the origin of preferred learning styles—auditory, visual, or kinesthetic.

Current Applications of the Triune Brain Model

The triune brain theory is put to practical use in two main fields: advertising, where they understand that clients buy more readily if the heart (emotions / socialization) and the body (survival issues) brains are addressed, rather than the mind; and educational programs, where people found that addressing these two brains gets more information and knowledge into the students. Oddly, the field of psychology is almost completely ignorant of this brain biology, and no current mainstream psychological theories that I know of incorporate it. The current interest in 'emotional intelligence' does bring awareness of at least part of Dr. MacLean's triune brain model to psychology.

Trauma and the Triune Brain Model

The final element of the basic model involves the phenomenon of trauma. For almost everyone, remembered or forgotten traumas drive most of our behavior and emotional life, completely outside of our conscious awareness. Traumatic experiences are stored, and later 'played back' as outer circumstances trigger us. This playback is an entire bodily experience, as if our younger traumatized self is partially taking over our body. Although we habitually resist this process, this playback mechanism combined with severe early trauma results in the psychological phenomenon of the 'inner child'. From a biological viewpoint storing and automatically using our responses to traumatic experiences makes sense, since we survived the experience by responding in those ways. Unfortunately, what may have been a good evolutionary strategy for our animal ancestors is a tragic problem in our complex sapient lives.

Further, although the body selects the category of traumas retrieved via body sensations, it is the heart that indexes these memories by the trauma's initially experienced emotion (with an accompanying visual image) and performs the playback and record function. To continue the stereo analogy, it's a bit like we carry around a library of trauma cassettes and our heart is the tape deck. A variety of healing techniques discussed at the end of Chapter 4 use this basic understanding. For a more complete discussion on indexing, triggering, and connections between traumas, see: our *Whole Hearted Healing Manual* on using connected traumas to regress earlier in time; *The Adventure of Self-Discovery* by Dr. Stanislav Grof on the 'coex' phenomenon in Holotropic Breathwork, where multiple experiences are triggered simultaneously; and *Beyond Psychology* by Dr. Frank Gerbode on how traumas 'stack' and connect through time. (Note that Grof and Gerbode do not include the triune brain model in their work.)

This simple model of the psyche is compatible with Western cultural biases and explains many psychological phenomena. For another viewpoint on trauma and the triune brain biological model, I refer you to Dr. Janov's *The Anatomy of Mental Illness* or *The New Primal Scream*.

Body Consciousness Associations and the Developmental Events Model

I want to emphasize here one of the most important points in this textbook, a point that can be easily overlooked or misunderstood. In the previous section, we briefly described how the body consciousness 'thinks' as a series of body sensations. In this section, we're going to explore this critical facet of its consciousness and how it causes the peak state developmental events phenomenon to occur.

As the body brain is often referred to as the reptilian brain, people often get the impression that it is slow and stupid. The truth is just the opposite—it's not only self-aware, it is probably the smartest of the brains. However, it is severely limited by its biologically dictated thinking processes, and it is this kind of thinking that causes all of humanity as well as other species severe and tragic problems. As we said, the body consciousness thinks in sequences of body sensations. Extending this concept, when the body learns, it does so by 'associating' two or more sensations together. It does NOT use judgment like our mind brain does. In evolutionary terms, the ability to form judgments came much later after the mind brain evolved. These body brain associations that have no element of judgment are the cause of most of the problems in our lives, particularly the severe or life-threatening problems. In an extreme example, early *in utero* associations can be so inflexible that if they involve survival issues the person will actually die trying to follow through with what his body feels he has to do to survive, even though it may be in reality killing him. Although there can be other causes, addictions are generally due to this type of problem—the body is convinced from early association that it needs the addicting substance to survive, no matter that in reality it is slowly killing him and ruining his life.

Example:

It was years before I realized I was sexually attracted to angry women. I had mistakenly thought I was attracted to them in spite of their anger. The reason turned out to be a series of in utero traumas. In them, I was being physically hurt and struggling to survive while my mom was feeling angry. My body consciousness had associated my survival with being surrounded by the emotion of anger. These women had exactly the same tone of anger as my mom had had. In fact, if they ever stopped being angry, I would unconsciously stimulate them again into anger, because to my body consciousness it felt like I might die if that emotion wasn't nearby. My body used the mechanism of sexual attraction to make me behave in ways it desired. In Volume 3 we go into this trauma type in much more depth.

These body consciousness associations are the basis for a whole range of issues, including the existence of 'psychological reversal' discovered in the use of energy and meridian therapies. Those therapies don't work if the body brain feels it needs the problem because of some non-logical association. One of the major contributions of Roger Callahan (the developer of Thought Field Therapy) was his discovery of a method to shut this mechanism off temporarily so that healing can occur.

How does this body consciousness learning mechanism of association apply to the developmental events model of peak states? First, you must realize that the body consciousness is the primary brain and it has a disproportionate influence on us. What it wants has much more impact on the organism than what any of the other brains do. To illustrate, thinking that we're not afraid of public speaking with the mind brain doesn't mean anything in comparison to the sweating, out-of-breath, gut-churning weakness the body brain induces when we get up in front of an audience. Secondly, because sensations are paired and learned in early developmental events, after birth anything that feels similar to the body triggers these early trauma associations—even when the current circumstances are completely unrelated from a rational perspective. Thus, events that were purely biological in nature during these early events cause our bodies to apply what it 'learned' in seemingly irrational ways in the post-birth period. Because the developmental events are generally related to various peak states, any sensations in the present that are similar to the states in question activate any event trauma associations in the body brain—and it responds by acting in ways that feel similar to how it did in those events, which generally means it blocks the state from occurring in the present.

Finding the developmental events relevant to peak states and peak experiences is tricky since the associations are generally not obvious from a rational perspective. We'll see in this and following chapters many examples of how a developmental event is reflected in the present's loss of peak states and experiences.

Additional Brain Structures

The triune brain model fits our personal experiences of the mind, heart and body quite well. It also is quite useful in explaining a lot of the different kinds of material that we as therapists and healers encounter in our work. However, as my colleagues and I became more experienced, we found there were some brain interactions that we didn't understand.

Eventually, we realized that although there were three primary brains, there existed two more 'sub-brains', for a total of five distinct brain structures in post-birth human beings. And our observations turned out to reflect underlying brain biology—Dr. MacLean, in his text on the triune brain, identifies five separate brain structures forming on the early zygote's spinal cord.

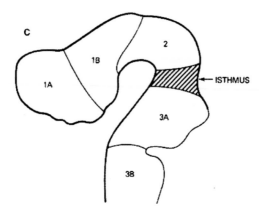

Figure 5.1: The fetal neural tube at 6 weeks with five main subdivisions. The forebrain is composed of the telencephalon (1A - "Buddha") and diencephalon (1B - "mind"), the midbrain (2 - mesencephalon, "heart"), and the hindbrain into the metencephalon (3A - pons and cerebellum, "solar plexus") and myelencephalon (3B - medulla, "body"). Drawing from *The Triune Brain in Evolution* by Dr. Paul MacLean, page 20, 1990.

The Solar Plexus Brain

The most important of these sub-brains experiences itself normally at the solar plexus, and so for simplicity we call it the 'solar plexus brain'. Like the other triune brains, it also has its own self-awareness. It appears to have a role in our connection to the physical universe and the nature of personal power.

Normally, this brain is merged and somewhat indistinguishable from the body consciousness.

The Buddha Brain

The other sub-brain is one we call the Buddha brain because of its experiential characteristics. Although it usually is merged with the mind brain, and hence indistinguishable, when it is split away it experiences itself centered above the physical head. When it is separate, it can feel like a massive Buddhist statue floating over one's head. One of the main functions of this brain is the creation of 'energetic' structures in the body. These structures, left over from trauma, often cause physical problems in the body. How to diagnose and heal this problem is covered in our *Basic Whole-Hearted Healing Manual.*

The Placental and Sperm Tail Brains

Another two brains exist but since they die off *in utero*, we don't normally refer to them in our normal post-birth description of the triune brain system. However, to our great surprise they are key to a very important triune brain state called Wholeness, and are also very important to *in utero* trauma. Chapter 6 and 8 cover these 'brains' in great detail.

The first of these is the organelle 'brain' that dies off during conception—it is in the tail portion of the sperm body. For simplicity, we call it the 'sperm tail brain'.

The second 'brain' is in an organelle structure in the egg which later develops into the placenta and dies during birth. Again for simplicity we call it the 'placental brain'. (Note that the placenta is part of the baby, not part of the mother.) The placental brain is intimately related to the solar plexus brain, but as of this writing we haven't yet defined the relationship.

Fusion of Brain Awarenesses Causes Triune Brain Peak States

Triune brain peak state characteristics and their strength are caused by the degree of connection that the different brain self-awarenesses have with each other. In other words, the states are caused by the different possible ways and amounts that the brains give up their separate self-identities to create new, composite identities. At one extreme are completely separate brain awarenesses, where the brains are unable to communicate directly with each other at all. People with triune brains separated like this are usually considered to have poor to sub-average mental health. At the other extreme, we have all the brain awarenesses completely fused together into a single awareness. This best possible triune brain peak state causes, among other things, an extreme feeling of effortlessness due to the lack of any delay or conflict between the brains.

Total fusion of the six brains (five in the body and the sixth in the placenta) into one awareness is our normal state as we develop in the womb. However, by birth the majority of the population has experienced disassociation of the brains, a state which we consider 'normal'. People spend the rest of their lives unconsciously searching for this internal fusion in their outer lives. They mistakenly search for this elusive 'something' in culturally-directed pursuits like jobs, relationships, or possessions.

A large number of other, quite different intermediate peak states occur from the possible combinations between the various brain awarenesses. We estimate about a third of the population has one or another of these intermediate triune brain peak states to some degree most of the time. Since they depend on how the multiple brain system is merged together, the states build up to the most inclusive one where all the brains are to-tally fused. However, some of the experiential characteristics change dras-tically when different brains fuse together. Intermediate states do not represent perfect health or balance—even though any one of them is far superior to 'average' consciousness. In other words, many of the states have unique characteristics that are not always incorporated into more complete states, but rather are superseded by new ways of being.

Many people have temporary or varying degrees of the state character-istics over time. This corresponds to the brain self-awarenesses changing their degree of communication or merging over time, due to outside trauma triggers or other factors. Of course, some people find that their state characteristics are unchanging, which means that the degree of un-derlying merging of brain self-awarenesses is fixed.

In the sections below are all of the significant triune brain fusion states that we know of. They represent groups of very different experiential state characteristics, which correspond exactly to different underlying brain connections. We've also given estimates of their occurrence in the gen-eral population, but the difficulties in testing, defining the degree of the state, and our small sample sizes could make these numbers quite a bit off. (Refer to Appendix A for a complete list of states and their estimated oc-currence in the general population.)

The Perry Diagram

As there are a number of brains, there are a huge number of possible ways and degrees that they can connect. Trying to analyze how the brain self-awareness interactions relates to experiential state characteristics at first seems like an impossible task, impossible to quantify. Fortunately, there is a very simple way to visually see the underlying dynamics that makes that task almost trivial. We call this visual technique the 'Perry dia-gram'.

This tool is derived from a perceptual ability that people have in the In-ner Brightness state of consciousness. In it, a person can actually 'see' his own (or others') brains self-awarenesses as glowing balls of light. The balls are brightest in the center and diffusely fade off at the periphery, without an abrupt edge. These balls are aligned along the vertical axis of the body. The body brain awareness in the lower belly, the heart brain awareness in the chest, and mind brain awareness in the head are typically the most vis-ible. Thus, for people in average consciousness there are three balls visi-ble, one at the lower belly, one at the heart, and one at the head. The balls that correspond to the solar plexus and Buddha brains are typically con-nected to or merged into the body and mind respectively, and so are not visible. Note that these balls of luminance are *not* Hindu chakras. Chakras 'look' quite a bit different, having rather geometrical shapes and definite structure.

One can explain the underlying dynamics of what causes a triune brain peak states by referring to how merged together these balls of light are. When we first tried to specify the states people undergoing our processes were in, and how much further the volunteers had to go, we were at a loss for something easily understood and reliable. Fortunately, Dr. Deola Perry soon came up with the graphical tool of using overlapping circles to represent the degree of fusion between the various brains' self-awarenesses, as one can approximate the edges reasonably well with an abrupt boundary. We've named this tool a Perry diagram to honor her contribution.

The Perry diagram uses the first letter of the common brain name next to the circle to indicate which it is. For the Buddha, we use Bu to avoid confusion with the body's B. For most cases, putting the labels on the diagram isn't really necessary—the body, heart and mind circles are obvious by inspection, with the Buddha and solar plexus assumed to be inside the mind and body respectively. A quick sketch just showing three circles in various degrees of overlap suffices in this case.

Figure 5.2 gives a 'visual' sketch of what can be seen in the Inner Brightness state, along with its equivalent Perry diagram. In this example, all of the brain awarenesses are completely disconnected from each other.

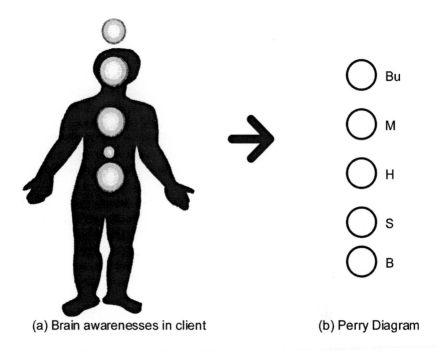

(a) Brain awarenesses in client   (b) Perry Diagram

Figure 5.2: Part (a) gives an idea of what totally separated brain consciousnesses look like in the Inner Brightness state. The Perry diagram equivalent is on the right (b). In this example none of the brain self-awarenesses are merged as shown by the spacing between the circles.

To my surprise, we found out quite early that people often only had partial peak state characteristics. Because in my own case I would go from average consciousness to a full state, I had incorrectly assumed it worked this way for everyone. Partial states can be understood by looking at the underlying brain awarenesses. How well the brains connect determines the degree of the state characteristics. One can 'see' this in the Inner Brightness state by noting how much the brain awareness spheres overlap and interpenetrate. When the spheres don't touch, a person has none of the peak state characteristics. The separation of the spheres gives a measure of how traumatized the brains are, but increasing or decreasing distance between spheres has no other experiential effect. It isn't until the spheres start to interpenetrate that peak state characteristics start to manifest. In terms of the Perry diagram, this is shown by partially overlapping the circles that represented the centers of self-awareness of the relevant brains. During our peak state induction processes, we would make these diagrams for our clients to show them how much progress they had made. The diagrams were also useful in keeping track of what additional degree and type of work our clients needed for full fusion of all their brains.

Once we saw how the proportion of interpenetration of the brain awarenesses determined the degree of the state characteristics, we thought we'd completely understood the relationship between state characteristics and brain dynamics. We now knew that we wanted, at this underlying level, to get the brain awarenesses to completely merge together. In terms of the Perry diagram, we wanted to get the circles to completely cover each other. However, in the course of inducing peak states, in some cases we could 'see' that the brain awarenesses were completely superimposed, yet people would not have the full characteristics of the state. This led to realizing that the brains could be in very intimate communion, but not quite to the point of releasing the last of their separate self-identities. Upon closer examination, we could see the resulting merged 'ball of light' of brain awarenesses was not really homogeneous but rather swirled like two flavors of ice cream mixed together. We call this intermediate step 'merging'. The degree of overlap of the circles in a Perry diagram indicates the degree of merging. When the circles completely merge, only a single circle now shows, so we put a comma between the brain labels to indicate which ones are there.

We call it 'fusion' when the brains fully release their self-identities, following Tom Brown Jr.'s nomenclature convention. In terms of our analogy, the flavors of the ice cream now mix to becomes a uniform color. To indicate fusion on the Perry diagram, we still completely overlap the circles, but now separate the first letters of the fused brains by a slash (/). The degree of fusion is indicated by putting a fraction or decimal beside the letters. In practical terms, the difference between merged and fused characteristics is minimal for most triune brain states. Thus, we rarely bother to include the percentage of fusion on the diagram. However, for some states fusion makes a big difference in the experienced characteristics. When working with a state where this degree of precision is relevant, the percentage is easiest to determine by estimating how much of a person's body has acquired the new characteristic that results from fusion.

Definition - Merged versus fused brain awarenesses

We use the term 'merge' to describe the action of interpenetration between the brain self-awarenesses, as shown by overlapping circles in a Perry diagram. We call the brains fully or totally merged when the brain awarenesses are completely occupying the same space, but still have some degree of individuality. This is shown on a Perry diagram with circles that cover each other.

Even though the self-awarenesses can be completely merged together, there is a further, subtle degree of surrender of separate selves that can occur among the brains. We call this complete union of awarenesses 'fusion', following the usage by Tom Brown, Jr. Although for most states there is little change in experiential characteristics due to fusion, in some states the change is quite dramatic.

For people who can 'see' the brain self-awarenesses, the two cases 'look' nearly identical.

Example:

> During one of our peak state processes, our volunteers can enter the Hollow triune brain peak state where all their brains fuse together into a ball located near the solar plexus. As the brains overlap and merge, the most obvious characteristic of the state, the feeling that one doesn't have any material body inside the skin starts to manifest. As fusion takes place, various parts of the body become 'hollow' first, i.e. the arms, chest, and so on. Finally, at total fusion, the body feels completely gone, as if there were only air, not flesh, inside the skin.

Another advantage of the Perry diagram is the ease with which one can see how the triune brain states, if present, are combined in a person. Since the states depend on which brains are combined, it becomes obvious at a glance what states a person has by the arrangement of the Perry diagram circles. It also becomes obvious what triune brain states are even possible! Instead of hunting for different groups of characteristics that identify potential new triune brain states, one can simply check off the list of different ways the brain awarenesses can be combined to be sure one has specified them all. This was quite an advantage for our work.

In the sections that follow, we'll be describing the various triune brain peak states with Perry diagram illustrations to show how the brain consciousnesses interact. The illustrations show the range of connection in the brain awarenesses that still give at least some degree of the particular state characteristics.

'Average' and 'Sub-Average' States of Consciousness

We start our explanation for the class of peak states that involve the triune brain structure with ones that are relatively familiar to us, so-called 'average' and 'sub-average 'consciousness. The key defining characteristic for these two states is the degree of connection between the solar plexus and body brain consciousnesses. In average consciousness, the two are at least communicating (the circles touch in a Perry Diagram) or fully fused (the circles are superimposed). In sub-average consciousness, the two are completely separated (the circles don't touch in the Perry diagram).

We also have some data that strongly suggests that having a solar plexus brain awareness separated from the body brain awareness actually inhibits other triune brain fusion states. Thus, people in a peak state whose solar plexus gets triggered into separation appear to lose their current peak state completely, even though the brains involved in the peak state have nothing to do with the solar plexus. We're still investigating this.

There is a degree to the characteristics of the states, shown in the Perry diagrams as depending on the degree of the underlying connection of the awarenesses. We've arbitrarily decided to separate the Average and Sub-average Consciousness states at the point where the underlying solar plexus and body self-awarenesses no longer communicate. In the future, with more clinical experience we may decide to shift the line between the two categories if it proves useful for clinical psychologists doing diagnosis.

'Average Consciousness' State

In average consciousness, the person does not have any peak states, triune or otherwise. Experientially, the heart, mind, and body brains interact like a dysfunctional family of three (or four if the Buddha is separated), with their own purposes and issues. At the underlying brain self-awareness level, the three main brains are disconnected from each other, indicated in the Perry diagram by the distance between the circles. However, the solar plexus brain awareness *is* either fused with the body brain awareness or at least still connected to it to some extent. We define the Average Consciousness state by this connection. In terms of the Perry diagram, the solar plexus and body circles range from just touching to being fully overlapped.

In this definition, we ignore any merging of the Buddha brain awareness with the mind brain. Perhaps in the future it would be useful to isolate it as a separate state, but at the moment we haven't done so.

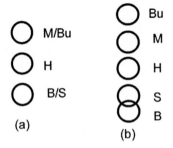

Figure 5.3: Average Consciousness state Perry diagrams. (a) represents the most common configuration, with the solar plexus awareness completely fused to the body. The state can range to (b), with the solar plexus barely connected to the body consciousness. Our current definition of Average Consciousness allows for the Buddha position to independently range from separate to fused.

'Sub-average Consciousness' State

Sub-average consciousness is characterized by the inability of the person involved to observe himself with any detachment. People in this state are often categorized as having some degree of mental illness. A person in this state believes and acts upon any trauma material that comes into consciousness without the awareness or ability to question it. This is an area that we intend to investigate further, but at least for now we believe it's caused by deep separation between the triune brains, especially the separation between the solar plexus and the body brain.

Let me emphasize the implications of this definition. If our limited observations in this area are correct, it implies that separation of the solar plexus and body brain awarenesses is the underlying *cause* of what we might call overall 'sub-average' mental health, albeit not the cause of an given specific mental illness. If so, and this looks to be very likely, it implies that techniques to heal this split might have tremendous, rapid impact on the mental health of large number of people who are suffering from moderate to severe mental illness.

The current definition allows the Buddha brain to be fused to the mind brain, separated, or in between these two extremes. Clearly, fusion of the Buddha is more desirable, but as of this writing we haven't determined what difference this makes. In the future we might want to separate this out into two states, but for now we lump them together.

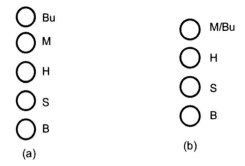

Figure 5.4: Sub-average state Perry diagrams. The body and solar plexus brain awarenesses don't touch. The degree of separation between awarenesses can vary. By our definition, part (a) and (b) give the range of the sub-average state, since the Buddha's degree of fusion isn't relevant to the definition.

Dysfunctional Triune Brain Shutoff States

We now turn our attention to a set of unusual states involving dysfunctional triune structures. This strange set of states can occur because the individual brains have the seldom-used ability to shut themselves off. During these states, the person loses the abilities that are primary to those brains. These states generally occur due to what that individual experiences as extreme trauma, or sometimes due to spiritual practices. Interestingly, we don't lose our ability to use language when these shutdown states occur.

The following three states generate calls to the spiritual emergence network as people wrestle with the conflict of losing key abilities that the brains have, weighed against the wonderful feelings of relief and 'spiritual' sensations the states give. These shutdown states feel good because they allow escape from the cacophony of three independent brains. As a healer, it is useful to point out that lobotomizing oneself to avoid pain is probably not in one's best interest. Explaining what causes the state, discussing the new techniques to heal trauma and how to live with more self-love as an alternative usually causes the people to decide to end the state. Simply desiring the aspects of oneself that have been turned off is usually sufficient to end these shutdown states.

We indicate this class of states on Perry diagrams by omitting the circle that represents the shutoff brain. We add the first letter of the name with a bar over it to indicate the brain consciousness is shut off or not present.

'Mind Shutdown' State

The state that occurs when the mind (cortex) shuts down has no particular name that I'm aware of, but it presents a very seductive yet problem-filled situation. The person experiences a sense of peace, calmness, feelings of simple joy in living and doing everyday tasks and connection to spiritual writings that is very profound. This occurs because internal conflicts the person experiences due to the independent actions of the mind cease. However, the abilities that the mind specializes in, short-term memory, mathematical ability, and the ability to form judgments (such as choosing between similar items in a store, or making a menu choice) are also suspended or greatly impaired. This internal lobotomy presents a real dilemma, as the individual wants the state to continue, but finds himself unable to work at most jobs. I've seen people stay this way for as long as a year.

Example:

> While experimenting with this state, I went to the local K-Mart to buy a cheap day pack. As there were about a dozen choices, I found myself unable to choose between them no matter how hard I tried. I stood there so long struggling to choose that the store detective came over to find out if I was some sort of criminal. I had the same trouble making choices at restaurants, so much so that I wouldn't go to one while still in the state. I came out of this state with the total appreciation of my ability to make judgments, in contrast to the new-age belief that judgments are a bad thing.

'Mind-Heart Shutdown' State

When we turn off both the mind and the heart, we are left with a state the Sufis call the 'Pearl Beyond Price'. This odd state is similar to the 'Hollow' state that results when the mind, heart and body are fused, in that we experience ourselves as if our flesh were made of air. In addition, we no longer feel like we have an edge or skin to our body—our awareness has no boundary at the skin. This lack of boundary is not due directly to the shutdown brains, but rather to another state that is triggered by the shutdown. It can also occur independently, as described in Volume 2.

However, unlike the 'Hollow', in this state our lower belly feels as if it were full, a bit like we'd eaten a large meal or were pregnant. We also lose the abilities of the heart and mind, such as being able to feel emotions, be emotionally aware of others, think analytically, and so on. Spiritual practice accompanied by feelings of dying and trying to escape our lives can trigger this state.

Example:

> While I was experimenting with this state, I found even the experience of washing dishes was extremely pleasurable. However, I wondered if I had entered some profound spiritual state, as my body had no boundaries at the skin. My entire body felt like it was made of air, not flesh. It wasn't till quite a while later I realized what I'd done, and that the boundaryless body state was a separate phenomenon. When I spoke to spiritual teachers about it, few rec-

ognized it and fewer knew enough about it to realize I was in a dys-functional state—instead, they assumed I had made a breakthrough into a 'higher' state.

'Samadhi' (Heart-Body Shutdown) State

When both the heart and the body consciousnesses turn themselves off, the state called Samadhi in the Zen Buddhist tradition occurs. One experiences a sense of peace and timelessness that is beyond anything possible to experience in normal consciousness. One finds oneself almost never breathing, probably because the need for oxygen metabolism to support the chemically-based thinking processes of the two shutdown brains is eliminated. Unlike the Mind Shutdown state, the individual can continue to work at most jobs, and in fact the memory and IQ are extremely enhanced. (One odd problem with this state is the ability to recall what we hear, such as music or conversation, so clearly it cannot be distinguished from the real thing. We can go into a state of continuous playback, but turning the playback off can be difficult.) Unfortunately, the ability to feel emotions, or connect with people other than intellectually is eliminated. Once in this state, the person can remain in it indefinitely. The desire to experience feelings again will turn the heart brain back on, and the body consciousness soon turns on spontaneously afterwards.

Example:

I went into this state playing an album by Sofia on my way to my teaching job at a university. There was a textbook in advanced engineering that I'd had great difficulty in understanding, and had quit at the fifth or sixth page. In the state, I found my IQ so greatly enhanced and my memory so nearly perfect that I could now read and understand the text at about the same speed as reading a novel. I also experienced that every moment in time was infinitely long, and that I had more than enough time to do everything that I wanted to do, including spend time at the local cafe. This latter effect was quite puzzling to me, as I'd always before been pushed to the limit to get my lessons ready and homework graded in time. I also had almost no need to breathe—at rest, ten or fifteen minutes between slight chest breaths was typical.

'Heart Shutdown' State

When just the heart brain is shut down, the person loses the ability to experience other people as people. Instead, they feel just like objects, such as rocks. The experience of being able to relate to people as similar to oneself is gone. This state might be responsible for the existence of sociopathic personalities. One can imagine that if the heart were shut off at an early enough age, the person would not develop the socializations that would make them interact appropriately with other people.

Example:
> I found this state very comfortable to be in, but intellectually it was disturbing, because other people had no importance to me, nor did I care about or have any empathy towards them. I experienced others as if they were just robots, not human beings. It made me wonder if this was how a reptile, without the mammalian brain, experienced life. I could see how such a lizard would have no trouble eating its offspring, because the capacity to experience others' feelings, pain, or suffering as similar to one's own no longer existed. Empathy and connection were completely absent.

Triune Brain Peak States

In this section we look at the triune brain peak states. The states listed below have very different experiential characteristics. These different characteristics arise from the very different ways individual brains self-awarenesses can merge together. We illustrate this underlying dynamic with Perry diagrams, showing the range of brain merging that corresponds to the presence to some degree of the state characteristics.

These critically important peak states are generally not recognized as states at all, but can sometimes be found described in books on spiritual emergencies under the classification of unitive consciousness. These fusion states are intrinsically positive and in themselves do not create a spiritual emergency. However, individuals who have lost states sometimes contact the spiritual emergence network expressing confusion, grief and despair as they search for some way to regain what they've lost.

All the states below that include mind-heart fusion confer the 'invulnerability' that I spoke about in Chapter 1. This is because the person stays in the present, and past traumas don't have any emotional effect on them. It's quite possible that Underlying Happiness (heart-body fused) state also confers 'invulnerability' in a different way, but as of this writing we haven't verified this.

Although technically all triune brain states that are less than the total, perfect fusion of all brain awarenesses should be called 'sub-states', for brevity we decided to drop the 'sub-' part of the label.

It turns out that the brains tend to merge themselves in certain patterns. Many of the possible brain awareness merging arrangements occur less frequently. When moving between states, the brains tend to follow certain merging choices. The reason for this is based on the sequence of events in the coalescence described in Chapter 6. Thus, in our Perry diagrams we generally omit states where the two sub-brains, the solar plexus and the Buddha, are not fused into their respective primary body and heart brains. This is because in average consciousness or better, they are generally merged together and for all intents and purposes only the composite mind, heart, and body consciousnesses need to be specified.

The 'Inner Peace' State

This state results when the mind and the heart fuse together, with the body consciousness remaining separate. It is characterized by an unmistakable, distinct underlying feeling of peace even when experiencing other feelings, hence the name of the state. Even more importantly from a therapist's point of view, the state brings the person emotionally into the present. This means that when the person thinks about a trauma in the past, it has no emotional content *at all* for them. People exhibit reactivity in proportion to the present circumstances, rather than being 'triggered' from past trauma. Note that it is fusion of the mind and heart that gives this characteristic that the past has no emotional content—any triune brain state that includes this mind and heart fusion also exhibits this characteristic. Partial merging only reduces the level of past emotional trauma content.

We estimate 8% of the general population has this state or a better combination state called the "Beauty Way". Another 14% have experienced it enough to recognize it.

The Inner Peace state is a very important state for psychology, because of its effect of turning off all past emotional traumas. Since these mostly forgotten traumas drive most of the problems that people experience in daily life, having this state is a huge beneficial change. One way of looking at it, from everyday experience, is that we lose our 'triggers', that would normally set us off. Our reactions to events are now proportional to what's really happening in the present. Because this state has such an impact, and is relatively easy to acquire, we devote an entire chapter (Chapter 9) to this state and how to acquire it easily.

Like the Beauty Way state described in the next section, we suspect that people in the Inner Peace state do not dream and also have their mind become silent, without any internal 'mind chatter'. However, as of this writing we haven't verified this assumption.

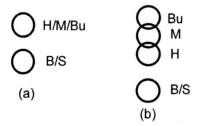

Figure 5.5: Inner Peace state Perry diagrams. Note the range of brain fusion from (a) to (b). We show the body and solar plexus fused as this is the way it is typically in our clients.

The 'Underlying Happiness' State

This state results when the body and heart consciousnesses merge. In men, it is experienced as a feeling of happiness underlying everything they experience, no matter what it is. This is true for women also, but they have a much stronger feeling of love with it. Thus, the spectrum of feelings, like sadness or anger, still occur, but with a feeling of happiness still present simultaneously to one degree or another. This brain state (or better) is especially useful for manifesting in the world.

We estimate 9% of the general population has this state, and another 12% have had it enough to recognize it.

Example:

> After doing some healing on feelings of abandonment and loneliness one evening, I became filled with extreme happiness. It was so intense that I cried actual tears of happiness most of the night, an expression that up to then I thought to just be figurative. This state lasted for months. During it, I felt an underlying happiness at the same time as I felt any other emotion, positive or negative. I could now tell that happiness was not an emotion in the way that I'd always thought it to be, but rather the sensation was a byproduct of an internal change in the connection between my triune brains.

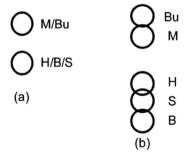

Figure 5.6: The Underlying Happiness state. Note that the state ranges from case (a) to case (b). As of this writing, we don't know if a fully separated mind and Buddha would have any effect on the state.

The 'Big Sky' State

We believe this state is caused by the mind and body merging without the heart, although we're not totally sure yet that this is the true underlying cause. The world feels huge, the sky and the land gigantic. This sensation results from being able to feel a kind of 'pressure' sensation from near and far objects, adding another dimension to sensory awareness.

We don't know the frequency of occurrence.

The 'Communicating Brains' State

In this state, each of the brains awarenesses are touching each other. The brains can communicate back and forth on whatever issue is present. This does not mean they are in agreement, just that they can share their viewpoints and desires. Communication is not done verbally. The brains still interact like a dysfunctional family. There is a feeling of being balanced, a sensation of evenness, with no internal irritation.

We estimate about 12% of the general population has this state, and another 23% have experienced it enough to recognize it.

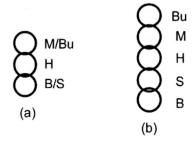

(a)

(b)

Figure 5.7: The Communicating Brains state. Although I've shown a range of merging from (a) to (b), we've never seen anything other than small variations on case (a) in practice.

The 'Deep Peace' State

This state is characterized by a deeper peaceful feeling than in the Beauty Way. It feels like the physical heart is lower in the body, and one feels more lightweight. You don't quite feel effortless in everything you do, but it isn't nearly as effortful as average consciousness. The brains are aware of each other, can communicate directly, and you are aware of each simultaneously. Brains still tend to have some interactions like a dysfunctional family, but greatly reduced. This is an intermediate state that we don't specifically target for our techniques—they aim for a lesser or better triune brain states.

In this state, all the brain awarenesses range from fully to partially merged, represented by the circles in the Perry diagram superimposed on top of each other. However, the brains themselves haven't gone the full distance into full fusion. This state is a more merged version of the Communicating Brains state. The point at which one changes to the other is somewhat arbitrarily chosen to be at 50% merged or better. The solar plexus and Buddha are fused with their respective body and mind brains.

We have no estimate of its occurrence in the general population at this time.

(a)   (b)

Figure 5.8: Deep Peace state Perry Diagram. The state ranges from (a), typical for this state, to (b) which has a reduced level of the state characteristics.

The "Hollow' State

This state results from a merging and fusion of the mind, heart, and body. Experientially, the body feels like it's made of air, without muscle, bone, or flesh. Movement and most activities feel effortless. The classical Zen phrase of being like a 'hollow bamboo' fits this, although Westerners who abruptly move into it describe it like being an empty tin can. Emotions seem more like thoughts, no longer a visceral experience. All parts of the body feel 'continuous', as described by people in the state. At a certain level of consciousness, you can see the brain awarenesses merged into a large oblong or spherical white area from the belly to the lower chest.

Estimated frequency is 7% of the population, with another 12% having experienced it enough to recognize it.

$$\bigcirc \text{ B/S/H/M/Bu}$$

Figure 5.9: The Hollow state Perry diagram. Unlike many of the states, the full characteristics of this state don't appear until all the brain awarenesses fuse.

The 'Wholeness' State

Anyone who abruptly enters this state describes it with the same word, 'wholeness'. Listening to music becomes an almost ecstatic experience. The state gives one a feeling of being totally alive, and glad to be alive. It makes life much more vivid. It's caused by merging during the death experiences of the placental consciousness with the baby at birth, and the sperm tail consciousness during conception. As good as the Hollow state is, that state feels incomplete and unsatisfying in comparison to the Wholeness state. The state also appears central to some approaches to radical physical healing.

At this time, we're classifying Wholeness as a triune brain state because it involves the self-awareness of the placenta and its merging with the baby's triune brain system during birth, even though the placenta actually dies at birth. It looks like you can get the feeling of wholeness without having the other brains merged, but the experience of wholeness is strong as possible with the other brains fused. We don't know what a separated or unfused solar plexus and Buddha do to the state characteristics, so for now I've arbitrarily restricted the Perry diagram's range for the state in Figure 5.10.

This state is indicated on the Perry diagram with a /P to indicate a fully healed placental brain death trauma—in other words, complete fusion of the dying awareness to the fetus at birth. The circle for the placenta is omitted in the other state drawings because we assume the Perry diagrams are for people after birth—the placenta has a self-awareness light in the Inner Brightness state before birth only. To indicate the strength of the state, we type in a percentage for the completeness of the merging of the placental brain to the fetus during its death. However, for simplicity we typically draw in circles for the placental brain to make it easy to graphically show the client's degree of placental merging. To avoid confusion, we draw the circles to the left of the normal ones. (If in the future we determine that the sperm tail brain contributes to the state, we'll include it with a 'T' symbol.)

Estimated frequency of occurrence has not yet been determined.

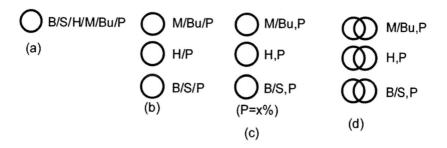

Figure 5.10: Wholeness state Perry diagram. Note that normally we don't include a circle for the placenta in Perry diagrams as its awareness is gone after birth. The state ranges from (a) to (c). Drawings (c) and (d) are equivalent.

Synergistic States Involving a Triune Brain State

Generally, other non-triune brain peak states of consciousness can be thought of as discrete packages whose specific qualities add to those of whatever triune brain state the person has. One might think of it like owning a bag of marbles, with each marble being a state. We generally describe these states as just an accumulated list of component states, for example the "Hollow, Brain Light states." If it has a well-known name, we substitute it for the list. In this case, we call the new, single name a 'combination' state. However, some states combine synergistically—they have characteristics that differ from the individual component states. If the combination state has a new, synergistic dominant characteristic, we use

that feature for the state name. We call this a 'synergistic' state to differentiate it from a combination state. An important example of this synergism
can be found in the 'Beauty Way' state.

The 'Beauty Way' (Aliveness) Synergistic State

The 'Beauty Way' state is a combination of the Inner Peace state with a
limited connection to the Creator (Creator states are covered in Volume
2). This causes an internal, unconscious decision to choose continuously
positive perceptions.

This combination of states has synergism between its component
states that creates experiential characteristics that do not exist in any of
its components. There are two major new synergistic characteristics: a
perception of beauty in everything in the physical world, even garbage;
and a feeling of 'aliveness' in oneself and in the surrounding world.

We chose to call the state 'The Beauty Way' because of its long traditional place in the Native American culture and language. Clearly, the
characteristic sense of beauty that occurs is emphasized in this label. However, if we were to name this synergistic state from scratch, we would probably choose to call it the 'Aliveness' state because this characteristic is so
pronounced. In fact, Harville Hendrix does call this state 'aliveness' in his
book, *Keeping the Love you Find*. Eckhart Tolle in his book *The Power of
Now* does a wonderful job of describing this and other characteristics of
the state, although he doesn't call it by either of these names.

Besides the huge impact of making all past emotional trauma disappear
from its Inner Peace state component, there are several other effects that
this state produces that deserve special mention. First of all, a person in
this state does not dream, or at least does not dream in the way we think of
the term. They experience brief times in sleep when the events of the day
are relived, apparently so that the memories can be sorted and filed appropriately. Dreams as are experienced by most people no longer occur. Why
is this? Because dreams are actually an artifact of the dysfunctional normal
consciousness. The 'thought' processes of the heart brain and the mind
brain during sleep feed into each other, and they create a dream 'story' to
fit, based on the many past traumas they've experienced. When the mind
and heart fuse, there is no longer this type of miscommunication, since
they're already one organism. Occasionally, there will be a dream-like experience, but it will have a numinous quality because it's not a dream in
the normal sense, but a communication from the planetary consciousness
Gaia. (Gaia consciousness is covered in Volume 2.)

Another defining characteristic of this state (as well as with more complete brain fusion states) is the silence of the mind that occurs in it.
Subvocalization can still be present, but the annoying mind chatter that is
particularly noticeable during meditation is completely gone. The reason
for this is covered in depth in Volume 3, as it has a major influence in several kinds of mental illness.

The state also gives a person the characteristic 'invulnerability' found in some children in 'at risk' situations because the mind-heart fusion. As we've said in the previous section, this fusion keeps a person in the present moment without past emotional trauma affecting them.

We estimate that both the Inner Peace state and the Beauty Way state together occur in about 8% of the general population, with an additional 14% able to recognize it from previous peak experiences.

Quick Reference List: The Beauty Way Synergistic State
- Calm, peacefulness, and physical sense of lightness.
- Past seems not traumatic—memories are without emotions.
- Feel totally alive, and everything around you feels alive too.
- Everything has a sort of beauty, even garbage.
- Spiritual truths are obvious.
- No dreaming.
- No underlying sense of fear.
- Live entirely in the present.
- No tension—like on summer vacation as a kid.
- Bird sounds are more vivid.
- Don't take on other people's emotional distress.
- Don't obey 'experts' automatically by giving up your own knowing.
- Can do many shamanic sorts of things with training.
- Silent mind, i.e., no inner chatter or voices or background murmur.

Key Points

- In a peak state, one experiences particular feelings and sensations that cannot be experienced without the state. The state *causes* the feelings. Happiness, peace, wholeness and aliveness are caused by triune brain peak states. Their degree depends on how much of the state a person has.
- The body consciousness acts in ways that it learned from associating sensations together, not through judgment. Its actions are often impossible to understand from a rational perspective because the linked sensations are generally not rationally connected.
- The body brain is the primary brain, and its influence generally dominates issues involving peak states and peak experiences.
- The associations that the body consciousness makes during trauma involving *in utero* developmental events explain why those events are important to blocking peak states later on in life. The wonderful sensations of moving towards peak states or experiences generally restimulate these old developmental event trauma responses, causing a block to any further movement into the state.

- The category of peak states we consider most important for well-being involves triune brain fusion states, that is, the internal unification of the mind, heart, and body.
- A variety of states exists depending on the degree and particular brain awarenesses that fuse together. In addition, combination states exist that build on these brain fusion states.
- To give a graphical method to illustrate the type and degree of the triune brain states, we use Perry diagrams, which allow easy visual identification, and have the added bonus that they can be seen directly by people who have the appropriate peak state.
- The Sub-average state is primarily caused by a separation of the solar plexus brain from the body brain. If true, this implies techniques to reunite these brains could have tremendous usefulness for all kinds of client populations.

Suggested Reading and Websites

On the triune brain
- Elaine De Beauport, *The Three Faces of the Mind: Developing your Mental, Emotional, and Behavioral Intelligence*, Quest Books, 1996.
- Tom Brown, Jr., *The Vision*, Berkley, 1988.
- Tom Brown, Jr., *Grandfather*, Berkley, 1993.
- Ronald Gross, *Peak Learning: A Master Course in Learning How to Learn*, Tarcher, 1991.
- G. I. Gurdjieff, *Views from the Real World: Early Talks of G. I. Gurdjieff*, Viking, 1973. Collection of his talks up to 1924.
- Charles Hapden-Turner, *Maps of the Mind*, MacMillan, 1982.
- Dr. Arthur Janov, *The Anatomy of Mental Illness: The Scientific Basis of Primal Therapy*, Berkley, 1977.
- Dr. Arthur Janov, *The New Primal Scream: Primal Therapy 20 Years On*, Trafalgar Square, 2000.
- Dr. Paul MacLean, *The Triune Brain in Evolution: Role in Paleocerebral Functions*, Plenum Press: 1990.
- P. D. Ouspensky, *In Search of the Miraculous: Fragments of an Unknown Teaching*, Harvest, 1949. A well organized outline of Gurdjieff's concepts.
- Joseph Chilton Pierce, *Evolution's End: Claiming the Potential of Our Intelligence*, HarperCollins, 1992.
- Joseph Chilton Pierce, *The Biology of Transcendence: A Blueprint of the Human Spirit*, Inner Traditions, 2002.

On specific triune brain states
- Harville Hendrix, *Keeping the Love You Find*, Atria, 1993. He talks about the triune brain structure and the state he refers to as 'aliveness' (what we call the Beauty Way).
- Eckhart Tolle, *The Power of Now: A Guide to Spiritual Enlightenment*, New World Library, 1999. His book describes the Beauty Way state very well, although he doesn't give it that name.

On the body brain's thinking processes
- Eugene Gendlin, *Focusing* (revised edition), Bantam, 1981.

On how traumas connect together
- Dr. Frank Gerbode, *Beyond Psychology: An Introduction to Metapsychology (third edition)*, Institute for Research in Metapsychology, 1995.
- Dr. Stanislav Grof, *The Adventure of Self-Discovery*, State University of New York Press, 1988.
- Tad James and Wayne Woodsmall, *Time Line Therapy and the Basis of Personality*, Meta Publications, 1988. Much is based on NLP.
- Grant McFetridge and Mary Pellicer MD, *The Basic Whole-Hearted Healing Manual*, Institute for the Study of Peak States Press, 2003.

Chapter 6

Developmental Events for Triune Brain Fusion States

Introduction

In this chapter, we apply the peak states developmental events model to triune brain states of consciousness. We start by introducing the stunning empirical observation, from trauma work, that the triune brains develop from *self-aware* organelle structures. These structures and their traumatic interactions explain much of the dynamics of triune brain separation states. These extremely important, typically traumatic developmental events are unknown to the field of prenatal psychology. We then move later in time to more familiar developmental events, such as conception, implantation, gestation, and birth for other critical triune brain developmental events.

Chapter 8 applies this information in a detailed, step-by-step procedure for acquiring relatively permanent triune brain states. Appendix B gives a time-line summary of these developmental events.

Interestingly, 16th century illustrations of the stages of alchemy turn out to be describing these key developmental events. We give some examples in this chapter.

States in this chapter:
- Inner Peace
- Beauty Way
- Hollow
- Wholeness
- Inner Gold

Grant's Story
Finding the Developmental Events

I had first realized that there was a triune nature to the brain in the early '80s when I encountered in utero trauma where the triune brains first split apart. Up to that time, I had not realized that states I was looking for were based on the multibrain's degree of fusion. Concurrently, I was also learning just how critically important remembered or forgotten trauma was to people's present-time problems. I basically started to develop the Whole-Hearted Healing process to heal myself, once I realized how much I had to heal! From these experiences, it was a small step for me to hypothesize that trauma was the block to triune brain states, especially traumas that had their origins in pre-birth events.

A few years later, I had acquired an Inner Brightness state where my body was filled with light. The state allowed me to access my pre-birth memories at will. However, knowing where to look was a problem. To my surprise, I abruptly lost the state a year later. To continue the exploration, I had to try to find people who were in states of consciousness good enough for me to use them like laboratory instruments. This was a very difficult problem—I could not demonstrate or prove anything I was saying about peak states, as I'd lost my own; anyone with the required level of ability already felt so good that they had no interest in doing anything painful, which the exploratory work required; and my ideas were in conflict with virtually everyone's beliefs about spirituality or shamanism. I couldn't find anyone to help, so over the course of time I finished developing the Whole-Hearted Healing process, and started to teach it. My real passion, peak states, was lagging behind.

Another couple of years passed. I was extremely fortunate to meet Kate Sorensen of Trauma Relief Services, who was setting up the first conferences to explore the new power therapies. She became a friend, sharing my passion for understanding peak states (her story is in Chapter 13). Because she had the Inner Brightness state, and her own insights into the problem, we collaborated in the research, sharing the excitement of discovery. She became "guinea pig number one" as Wes would put it. After she became comfortable with being aware of the triune nature of her brain, she quickly realized that the brains were constantly in conflict with each other. We spent a great deal of time looking at the reasons why her brains were unwilling to merge together. We would get temporary success in unifying one or more, but it was always short lived. Even with her excellent inner awareness and motivation, we couldn't see any way to improve on this process. And we couldn't see why, no matter what we did, something would always come up and cause her brains to split apart again. This approach was like doing basic family therapy on the conscious triune brains, but it didn't appear that this approach would result in a permanent peak state, or be very useful to the vast majority of people.

With this experience and my intuition that trauma was a critical part of the puzzle, I formulated the hypothesis that developmental events were key to permanent peak states—but I didn't have any proof. On top of that, at the time I couldn't figure out why people would lose these states at birth, which made my hypothesis even more suspect. During this period, Kate and I made a number of other breakthroughs in related areas, but eventually, to my disappointment, her life led her in a different direction.

I then met Wes Gietz, who was offering workshops in outdoor survival and native spirituality based on the work of Tom Brown, Jr. and his own native teachers in Ontario. Together, we were able to really look at the contrast between the paradigm I was developing and the traditional shamanic one—trying to understand why they were in such conflict. This was one of the most fun periods of my life, as he was a willing tool in the work, as well as sharp as a tack and able to understand the concepts and contribute. Even better from my perspective, Wes lived in the Beauty Way and Inner Brightness states most of the time, and so could examine pre-birth events at will.

To back up a bit, I had originally entered the Beauty Way state when I was 11 months old, during a near-death experience due to a blow to my head. During that experience, my heart consciousness realized it could 'reach up' and pull the mind consciousness into itself. And it did. Suddenly, I was in the Beauty Way. From then until I was 29, I had this state relatively continuously, except when I felt the disapproval of my mother. When her disapproval would stop, I'd pop back into my state.

We used Wes's abilities to try and find the origin of the Beauty Way state. We were also able to find the origin of his entry into the Beauty Way. Like my own, it happened in early childhood. He recalled looking at a bright white light on the Christmas tree. This triggered something inside himself, and his heart consciousness reached up and pulled the mind consciousness into itself. This put him into the Beauty Way state. His state wasn't as stable as mine had been, but he found that if he spent regular time in nature, it would return and last for a while. His experience and mine shared some common characteristics, and it wasn't long before we realized that what we were doing to enter the state had its analog in an early developmental event—that of conception. This was an incredible moment, when we saw the implications of what we'd found. We started looking for more of the developmental events to see what would occur. We made more breakthroughs, but soon afterwards he needed to back off from the pain he was experiencing from the work, to my regret. We had made a wonderful team, and had tremendous fun too.

I turned my hopes onto Dr. Deola Perry, whom I'd met previously at a Meridian Therapy conference. She was willing to continue the exploration, and became my next major investigative tool—"guinea pig number 3", as it were. I moved to her good friend Dr. Marie Green's porch, and the three of us really started to work. Dr. Perry made several major breakthroughs, using the model we were developing. One of those breakthroughs was in finding the existence of the precellular traumas, and the specific one that was key to the Hollow state. This seven month period with Deola and Marie was probably the most creative and amazing time of my life, as we made breakthrough after breakthrough."

The Cellular (Organelle) Triune Brain Structure

Ask yourself, why would the triune brains even have the ability to split apart? What possible evolutionary advantage could there be in having less than a peak state of consciousness? Clearly, there isn't one. So what else could it be? We thought for a time that it must be some sort of evolutionary problem, a holdover from our development from reptiles. Although there is some truth to this, the solution to this question wasn't something that we could have deduced from current information on human biology. The key turned out to involve phenomena that, as far as I know, is unknown in the field of prenatal psychology. This area is that of 'multicellular', 'cellular', and 'precellular' developmental events applied to the multibrain system.

Some of the assumptions we have in our culture turn out to be misleading. First, when we speak about the triune brains, we all automatically assume that we're talking about groups of cells located in the brain of the fetus, that later develop into the familiar body, heart, and mind brains. This model would tend to have us assume that at some early stage of development, there was not a triune brain structure. (For the sake of simplicity, I'm using the phrase triune to include the other two brains, the solar plexus brain and the Buddha brain. The 'quintuple' brain label, albeit more accurate, doesn't fit common usage.) After all, at some point we were just a single fertilized cell, with no brain matter at all. With this model, as we were taught in grade school, we might assume that there was originally just some sort of a DNA programmed sequence of events in the fertilized egg that recapitulated evolution. The unaware, primitive brain would slowly grow in complexity, from fish to lizard to mammal to primate as gestation continued. With this model, we would then look at early gestation for events that caused the developing multibrain system to fragment apart. As likely as this sounds, this idea is incorrect.

Instead, as we go back in time to early gestation, we see that the multicellular structures that become the triune brain are already present from the beginning. The evolutionarily 'newer' brain structures do *not* develop from the older reptilian brain. Instead, the cells that later form the different brains are separate from each other, as illustrated in Dr. MacLean's *The Triune Brain in Evolution* and shown in Chapter 5. Instead of the fetal development repeating evolution, it is symbiosis of very different structures which develop simultaneously.

In fact, the origin of these brain structures is *not* in early cell differentiation. Instead, we find by doing regression or using a peak state that allows us to recall this period at will, that the structures that develop into the triune brains are present in the single-celled organism as integral, functioning parts of the cell! These subcellular structures, called organelles in biology, are also self-aware and very similar in consciousness and purpose to what they become later in the multicelled fetus and adult. When regressed to trauma during this period, a client is aware that he still has a body, heart, and mind consciousness even in the single-celled zygote. (Note that these physical traumas typically cause a temporary splitting of the subcellular triune brains, which is why one can even become aware of the multiple awarenesses during this period). The mind still 'thinks', the heart still 'feels', and the body still has the 'felt sense' (using Gendlin's description of the gestalt sensation of the body consciousness's thought process).

Continuing even earlier, the self-aware triune 'brain' subcellular structure is also repeated in the sperm and the egg. Each of these single cells also has the six-brain structure inside itself (the sixth being the sperm tail or egg placenta brains respectively). These 'brains' are active in the single-cell experience just as they are active, in a more complex way, in the adult human. I want to emphasize that during regression, the client experiences these cellular-level brains as being as active and aware as they are in the client's present, just not as experienced and knowledgeable as they later become. They can get just as angry or puzzled or afraid as their more complex counterparts can in the adult.

Definition - Multicellular (in utero) developmental events

This phrase is just another way to describe any developmental event that includes the actions of the multiple-celled zygote and fetus. Thus, events or stages that occur after the first cell division fall into this category, although experientially the consciousness of the organism feels pretty much the same before and after—the transition from organelle brain awareness to multiple cell brain awareness occurs almost unnoticeably, although it starts to happen during the initial cell divisions. This period ends shortly after birth, although key experiences still occur shortly after the baby is delivered.

Definition - Cellular (organelle) brains

The six self-aware multicelled triune brains (Buddha, mind, heart, solar plexus, body, and placenta) that we are familiar with develop from six self-aware organelle structures in the single egg and zygote cell. The sperm has a tail organelle brain rather than a placental organelle brain. During regression, the organelle brains and the multicelled brains are experienced identically—only their environments change.

We use the labels of 'organelle', 'subcellular' and 'cellular' brains interchangeably in this text. We often use the label 'cellular' when talking about organelle brains because of its association with the concept of 'cellular memories' from the field of prenatal trauma. We tend to avoid using the more accurate label 'subcellular' because it can be easily confused with the 'precellular' brain label defined below.

Definition - Cellular (organelle) developmental events

These events are ones that involve the experiences of the single-celled sperm, egg, and single-celled zygote. This period lasts between the creation of the conventionally defined single cell and the first cell division. We focus in particular on the triune 'brain' structure of the organelles inside the single cell.

The Precellular Triune Brain Structure and 'Coalescence'

These and earlier events are quite possible to experience from adulthood, given the right state of consciousness. The required state of consciousness we call the 'Inner Brightness' state, and is the subject of a chapter in Volume 2. You can also experience these developmental events using regression techniques, or as out-of-body trauma images from ordinary consciousness. (These images are the basis of the Whole-Hearted Healing technique.) If you follow the egg and sperm cell development back in time, you continue to feel normal sized, with normal body parts such as arms, head, and so on, even though you don't yet have those body parts in your zygote or single-celled self. The images that clients see are what we're used to from the microscopic photography we can occasionally watch on TV from educational programs.

As we continue to regress even earlier in time, we come to scenes of ourself that no longer look like microphotography images. You are now experiencing events that probably only an electron microscope could see clearly, even though you still feel like you're normal sized or larger. The images you now see become quite bizarre. Even though the scenes are completely foreign to anything we can see as adults, clients describe the images in ways that relate them to objects they are familiar with. Thus, they might say they see a "fountain", or a "huge plain", or a "building", and so on. When doing regression using Whole-Hearted Healing or other regression therapies, many people simply disregard the images that they see as nonsense or irrelevant to healing. However, these memories/images are usually the most important to our work in both healing and in acquiring peak states. This is because trauma builds on earlier trauma, as if it were an avalanche. Eliminate the beginning of the avalanche, and later, related traumas disappear or become much easier to heal.

To our amazement, what later becomes the individual cellular brains are created separately, go through developmental events separately, and then are brought together and assembled and combined inside the body consciousness's 'body'. We call these free floating, independent organisms the 'precellular brains'. This event of the assembly of the precellular brains has no name in the literature that we know of, so we've chosen to call it the sperm or egg precellular brain 'coalescence'. Thus, the reason that the brain awarenesses in an adult have the ability to split apart is because they started out as fundamentally separate systems, and have to go through stages where they are brought together and fused. As this fusion developmental event is potentially difficult, and occurs in both the precellular egg and the precellular sperm, trauma usually results, blocking triune brain fusion states after the birth.

Let me emphasize that again. The triune brain awarenesses have a tendency to fly apart because the brains were created apart, and had to go through developmental events to become unified. These unification steps almost always occur with trauma. Thus, after birth these extremely early and fundamental unification event traumas get activated, and the brain awarenesses split apart, back to their original separate condition. Thus, we find complete brain fusion, the Hollow state, is relatively rare in the general population. We estimate only about 7% of the general population has it.

The sequence of steps that the precellular brains take in physically merging during the coalescence explains why certain triune brain peak states preferentially occur while others are less common. Restating the developmental events model for this situation, the multicellular brain *awarenesses* typically merge in the same pattern of steps that the precellular brains *physically* merged during coalescence. For example, the solar plexus and Buddha brains are formed independently in the same way that the other precellular brains are, before coalescence. Thus, giving them the label of 'sub-brains' to the body and mind respectively is misleading. They are fully independent brains in their own right. However, they *act* like sub-brains to the body and mind brains, preferentially merging with their partners independently of whatever else is happening in the triune brain system. This occurs because their self-awarenesses mimic the very first step of physical coalescence, when these paired precellular brains immediately joined together before any other precellular brain bonding occurred.

It is at this sequence of events we call coalescence that the core blocks to triune brain fusion occur, as well as problems involving the fusion of the chakras and their attachment to the meridians (covered in Chapter 7). This developmental stage of combining the different self-aware precellular 'brains' is generally not done correctly, and this separation is re-evoked during the birth (or even earlier) and locked into place. In the case of the egg, all this occurs while your mother is still in her mother's womb. A similar assembly of the brains occurs in the precellular developmental stage of the sperm, although it's only about eight weeks before conception.

Example:
> The coalescence event is occasionally mentioned in the literature. For example, Alan Watts in 1962 wrote about it in a session: "I trace myself through the labyrinth of my brain, through the innumerable turns by which I have ringed myself off and, by perpetual circling, obliterated the original trail whereby I entered this forest. (…) Down and back through ever-narrowing tubes to the point where the passage itself is the traveler—a thin string of molecules going through the trial and error of getting itself into the right order to be a unit of organic life." (As quoted by Grof in *The Adventure of Self-Discovery*, p. 100.)

Figure 6.1 shows the sequence of events that are critical to brain fusion in a schematic form. Note that fusion of all of the 12 precellular brains requires five separate events to occur without trauma for both the egg and the sperm, for a total of 10 events during their coalescence. Adding this to several required developmental events later on makes it quite surprising that even 7% of the general public has the five brains fused for the Hollow state! As I've said, these physical bondings among the precellular brains are later mimicked by the multicellular brain awarenesses as preferential triune brain peak states. Different ones tend to occur depending on whether the events occurred with or without trauma.

If you continue even earlier in time, your split brain awarenesses can be followed backwards in time to individual matrixes that feel eternal, where they are first created. This is covered in Volume 2.

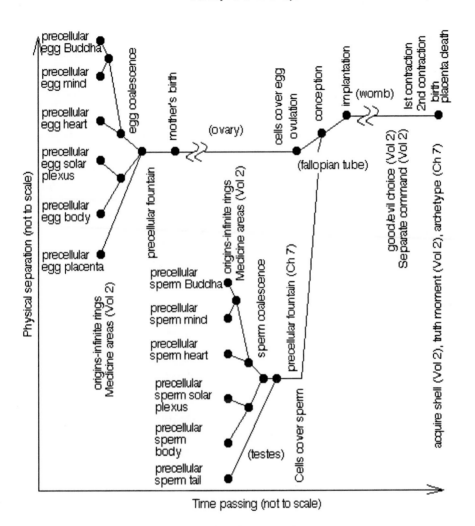

Figure 6.1: **Key triune brain developmental events**

Definition - Precellular brains

These are physically separate self-aware structures. They later combine to form a single-celled organism. They are the structures that the organelle brains develop from.

Experientially, clients in regression can experience them identically to the more familiar multicelled brains, although acting separately in an unfamiliar environment. However, the brains usually have a very different kind of consciousness, the Realm of the Shaman state (covered in Volume 2).

Definition - Precellular developmental events

These developmental events occur before the conventionally described egg or sperm cell is formed. Images from this period don't look
biological, as the scale is far smaller than we're used to seeing with mi-
crophotographs.

   Although the dividing line between these developmental events or
stages and the cellular ones is the end of coalescence, as clinicians we
tend to refer to later events that do not 'look' biological to our clients
as also being 'precellular'. (This common usage may turn out to be
more than just convenience - it is possible that there is some kind of
major change from the coalesced organism to the more familiar cell
that is more than just a change in size. If so, we will probably change
the precise definition to make the label 'precellular' extend to this later
point.)

Definition - Precellular brain coalescence

This is the developmental stage in the egg or the sperm where the biological components that will later develop into the triune brains are assembled into one package. This is quite a bit earlier than the single cell
that we're familiar with. We generally refer to this sequence of event as
just 'coalescence' for brevity.

Conception and the Male and Female Parts of the Brain

The next relevant triune brain fusion developmental event (that we know
of) after coalescence is conception. We start by addressing a key issue in
understanding how this event relates to triune brain states—the male and
female aspects of people.

   Although we typically assume that after conception we're either male
or female, the truth is more complex. Experientially during regression, the
sperm feels male, like a young version of the father, while the egg feels female, like a young version of the mother. When fully healed, conception
feels like a royal wedding. The sperm feels like a 'royal' king, and the egg
feels like a 'royal' queen. When the sperm enters the egg, its tail detaches,
and its head splits open, allowing the chromosomes (they look like little
wires moving around inside the egg) and its cellular brains to leak or squirt

out and merge with the egg's. Unfortunately, for most people there is trauma at this moment, and so to the sperm this feels like real, traumatic, awful death! The five cellular organelle brain structures from the egg and the five cellular organelle brain structures from the sperm combine to form the five new structures that develop into the fetal brain. Although the egg and sperm cellular brains unite, they don't quite become five unified structures. In later development, there is still a 'left' and a 'right' side to each of the brains, left over from this developmental event.

Several meridian-based therapies (and therapies like EMDR) note the fact that there is a left and right integration problem in many people during some traumas. Conception is the event that creates this, if it occurs with trauma as it usually does. This is compounded by the first cell division which splits us right down the center axis from right to left. It's due to the fact that the right side (left half brain) of a person remains identified with the 'male' sperm, and the left side (right half brain) identified with the 'female' egg. In fact, you can see this with clients who note that their pain or tension is on one side of their body with an abrupt edge at the center line of their bodies. If the problem is on the right, it's an egg trauma, and if on the left, a sperm trauma (assuming it isn't due to being hurt on only one side of the body later on in life, of course!)

Example:
A male client had pain across his chest that just stopped along the midline of his body. Unless the client had a very odd injury, this means that the symptom came from just an egg (or just a sperm) trauma before conception. In his case, it was a sperm trauma involving being hit in the 'chest' by the whipping tail of another sperm while moving in the father's reproductive organs.

Example:
When dealing with people undergoing a sensation of feeling frantic during Kundalini awakening, there is a fast, albeit temporary, fix. Holding the head motionless, you have them make several infinity signs with their outstretched hand while they watch their hand move from one side of the head to the other. Crossing the visual field from one eye to the other in this way causes the left and right hemispheres of the brain to reunite, making the frantic feeling vanish.

Interestingly, men typically tend to identify with sperm memories and actions, while women tend to identify with egg memories and actions, even though we're composed of both sperm and egg. For example, men are drawn to team sports (mimicking the team actions of the sperm in going to the egg) and warfare (blocking other men's sperm from the egg). Women tend to interact with each other in a way similar to how they communicated to other eggs in the ovary, and so on.

Have you ever wondered about the patterns men and women play out that are so well described by John Gray in the book *Men are From Mars, Women are from Venus*? When the man feels a lot of intimacy, he pulls away. This is because the conception trauma with the man identifying himself as the sperm is being activated, and he 'knows' that deeper intimacy will result in his death! Healing this trauma has a profound effect on this behavior.

There is yet another way in which conception affects our internal experience of being male or female. After conception, the heart brain tends to experience itself as female regardless of whether one is a male or female. Similarly, the mind brain tends to experience itself as male, again irrespective of the person's real sex. This creates problems that show up in therapy and in interpersonal dynamics. It's also central in understanding how conception relates to mind-heart fusion, covered in the next section. The reason why the brains have these sort of 'pretend' self-identities is beyond the scope of this book, but is covered in Volume 2.

Conception is Critical for the Inner Peace and the Beauty Way States

We can now turn our attention to the triune brain peak states that are involved with conception. For simplicity, I ignore until a later section the sperm tail brain death and the placental brain during conception. I also ignore changes not relevant to the triune brain peak states, such as changes to the chakras (see Chapter 7), and the interaction with the Creator (See Volume 2).

How does the experience of the ten precellular brains merging during conception relate to peak states? After all, in the previous chapter we said peak states were caused by a 'vertical' fusion of mind, heart, and body, not a 'lateral' fusion of sperm and egg mind to mind, heart to heart, and body to body. Like many things, the peak state mechanism is indirect. Healing conception fully causes more than half of our clients to acquire mind-heart fusion. Healing just a certain part of conception gives those people the Inner Peace state (mind-heart fusion), and healing all the conception gives them the Beauty Way state (mind-heart fusion with a limited connection to the Creator).

To understand this, let's look again at my description of my entry into the Beauty Way when I was 11 months old. I was hit on the side of my head so hard that my skull was crushed in and I had a near-death experience. At about that moment, my heart realized it could 'reach up' and fuse with my mind in my head. And after a moment of indecision, it did so. I would stay fused in my daily life unless I felt disapproval from my mom (and later on from other women I was involved with), upon which I would split apart. I would fuse again when the disapproval stopped. Wes also went into the Beauty Way for the first time as a young boy while he was looking up at a bright Christmas tree light. His heart reached up to his head at that moment and fused. Like me, he would leave the state for various lengths of time.

So, how did Wes and I get into the Beauty Way? We were both replaying the conception trauma moment. The heart brain was taking the part of the egg/mother, and the mind brain was taking the part of the sperm/father. (Volume 2 covers why the brains assume 'pretend' self-identities.) Although it's not well known, during conception the egg chooses the sperm it wants to be fertilized by. It recognizes the correct sperm because to the egg's 'vision', the correct sperm is brightly lit, and all the others are dark. This memory was activated in Wes with the Christmas tree light acting like the lit-up sperm. When the sperm arrives at the egg, the egg opens a passage in its chest, and 'reaches' out with what feels like arms to pull the sperm into its 'heart' region. After birth, the heart brain acts like it is the egg, and the mind brain acts like it is the sperm, with the heart brain 'pulling' the mind brain's awareness into itself. That's one reason you can't use your mind to go into the Beauty Way—it's an action the heart takes, not the mind.

As I've said, to the sperm conception feels like it really dies. That's why my own near-death experience allowed my mind-heart merge to happen—the sperm conception death sensation and my near-death experience had about the same level of trauma, and allowed me to revisit that earlier trauma and make a new choice. However, I don't recommend this method—I was very, very lucky to have changed the outcome.

The most straightforward way to acquire mind-heart fusion is to heal the conception trauma. Chapter 9 describes the Inner Peace Process, which gives a very simple and fast method to do just that. A bit over half of our psychotherapy clients gain the state when they use it, often permanently. However, what about the other half? This is an important area that we're still researching, but here is what we know so far. There are a variety of possible reasons the other half don't move into a triune brain peak state when they heal conception:

- The most common cause is coalescence trauma, especially during the sperm and egg precellular heart and mind brain coalescence.
- To my surprise, another cause can be tension in the solar plexus area. I've had success returning people back to the Beauty Way state after they've lost it by simply getting their solar plexus/diaphragm to relax. I believe coalescence trauma is involved with this effect. The solar plexus brain facilitates the connections between all the other precellular brains during coalescence. It is reasonable to suppose that trauma to this brain can *un*-facilitate mind-heart connection.
- Other blocks to mind-heart fusion also block other triune brain states: umbilical poisoning and birth canal trauma. They are covered in sections below. Note, however, that trauma in general has no effect on the triune brain fusion states. *Only traumas that are associated with underlying key developmental events have the potential to activate the splitting process between the triune brains.*

- Finally, there are other blocks to peak states that are covered in Volume 3, which only indirectly depend on the developmental events trauma.

Finally, why does healing the full conception trauma give the Beauty Way, not just the Inner Peace state? Briefly, during conception a 'ball of light' comes into the suddenly more complex organism. It's a piece of the Creator that you experience as being 'you'. Healing any trauma as this occurs gives a partial connection to the Creator. (This is covered in depth in Volume 2.) This in combination with the Inner Peace state of mind-heart fusion causes one to acquire the Beauty Way.

Example:
> Recently, there has been great interest in Eckhart Tolle's *The Power of Now*. He went through intense trauma before moving into being completely in the present. From our experience with clients healing conception, the trauma he describes is almost certainly conception trauma, although he doesn't label it as such. Assuming this is true, and it probably is, this illustrates how people explain their experiences from what they know as adults. Very few people recognize long-forgotten cellular and precellular trauma when the symptoms just erupt into their lives without preparation or training. After his trauma passed he moved into the Beauty Way state—which usually occurs when conception trauma is healed.

Implantation is Critical for the Underlying Happiness State

Recently we discovered that we could put our volunteers into the Underlying Happiness state by healing the implantation event. As with the conception, the reason is not directly obvious. We're still investigating this, but as of this writing we think it again has to do with the identifications that the triune brains have with the mother and father. It appears that to the body brain, the heart brain and the mother are experienced as being synonymous. Thus, heart-body fusion and implantation of the zygote to the mother's womb wall are linked by a similar sensation to the body consciousness. Of course, trauma in implantation is then also linked to any attempt by the body brain to fuse with the heart.

Example:
> Scott McGee describes implantation: "Implantation feels like home, at the moment it feels like nothing can knock you from the center. The heart is happy, and the body just wants to feel that. It's the same 'happy' as results from the body-heart fusion."

In Utero Umbilical Poisoning Can Cause Triune Brain Fragmentation

In this type of trauma, the mother eats, breathes, or is injected with something that the fetus finds toxic, that goes through the womb/placental barrier and into the fetus. In an attempt to pull away from the poison entering the belly button, the mind in particular, and possibly the heart, pull away from the triune brain fusion awareness centered around the belly button. Essentially, the entire organism is trying to escape the pain in the umbilical area, and this gets translated into the brains pulling away from fusion in that area of the body. Recall that the body brain 'associates' events together, even though such an association makes no sense from a logical perspective. The body can make an association between safety and withdrawal from the location of the pain near the fused triune brain center of awareness. At least in my own case, the separation between the mind and the heart-body brain awarenesses stayed after the toxin stopped coming.

This brings up an apparent contradiction—we've said that it's only at birth that older trauma material gets activated. And in general this statement is true. Yet in the previous paragraph we note that the poisoning trauma can stay activated in the fetus. There are three main reasons why this occurs. First, pre-birth physical injury leaves a kind of damage to the physical body that is seen as a black, deficient emptiness, or 'hole' where the injury occurred. This hole does not go away after the trauma ends, and causes the body consciousness difficulties afterwards as it tries to work around it, or avoid it. Secondly, generational traumas exist which can't be ignored by the pre-birth body consciousness and interfere with development. Third, and probably most important to peak states are trauma-induced triune brain self-identities and identity projections. These factors all continuously affect the pre-birth sperm, egg, and fetus. Although it might seem that these factors don't have much of an impact, remember that as clinicians we see a very biased sample of pre-birth trauma—all of our clients encountered trauma that they could handle in some way and still survive. The others simply perished.

The brain self-identities and projections deserve special mention. After the trauma that creates one of these ends, these identities and projections remain. Because of this, if the trauma was a key fusion event, it will still interfere with brain fusion even in the womb. Similar feeling traumas 'stack' or connect together and create similar self-identities which accumulate in a brain. Clients who are healing a fusion trauma will sometimes experience the identity and/or projection that the brain unconsciously holds as the trauma dissolves. Thus, healing connected fusion trauma also causes these variations of self-identity to arise multiple times. That's why when we originally worked on merging the brains by coaxing them into letting go of their separate self-identities and projections about the other brains, the change would only be temporary, usually ending by the next morning. Although this material of self-identities is of major importance to a number of peak states, we just don't have the space to cover it in this volume. It is covered in depth in Volume 2.

Birth Trauma Can Cause Triune Brain Fragmentation

Birth is the last significant event in our lives that has a direct bearing on triune brain fusion states. As I've briefly mentioned, two unique events during the birth activate developmental event traumas, causing a loss of triune peak states. Volume 2 goes into this in detail. But there is another type of trauma during birth that can contribute to a person's fragmentation of the triune brain system. In the birth canal, we often find that the individual brains pull out of the fusion state. Apparently, it's a survival struggle, with each brain trying to deal with the intolerable conditions of birth on its own. For those of you who don't already know this, birth trauma not only involves severe physical injury but is coupled with oxygen starvation when the oxygen supply is cut to the fetus due to uterine contractions, and chord compression. Instead of each brain staying focused on the body consciousness for overall direction during this trauma, the brains turn their 'attention' outward, away from the body brain. This 'turning away' tends to remain there permanently. Like other, later traumas, this situation is probably set up by earlier triune brain developmental events.

Example:
    I discovered the existence of the Buddha brain while working on this particular trauma. I was in the birth canal, feeling my mother's emotions, when I suddenly perceived what seemed like a huge, massive, immovable statue of Buddha over my head. As I watched in amazement, this massive statue picked itself up and moved from facing outward to facing inward. Afterwards, I felt like I was constantly feeling the same feelings I used to get while sitting meditating in a Buddhist temple. This eventually faded away after a few months, as at the time I had absolutely no idea what I had done, or what had occurred. I hadn't completely healed the birthing trauma, as at the time I didn't know that this was an expected outcome, and the remaining trauma reasserted itself.

Example:
    Paula Courteau writes about her healing work on this issue: "I went straight from conception trauma, where the sperm had seen its own tail rising to blissful death and realized it could merge with it and rise with it… to an episode of my birth. I'm stuck with my head out and my body still wedged in the birth canal. My body and heart decide that my mind can do all the living, and they'll stay in the spirit world, still merged with the sperm's tail. All the brightness gets shoved into my head, as if I was a paint tube being

squeezed. I decide at this point not to ever allow anyone to touch my body or heart in a deep way, so that nobody will ever find out that I'm not there." This injury didn't release fully and neither did the split that took place in conception. She had to go all the way back to the egg and sperm coalescence to find the real source of this profound injury.

We have found that in most people, after earlier developmental events are healed that involve the fusion of the brain structures, this birth event doesn't appear to cause a significant problem. Apparently, this event can only cause problems in triune brain fusion because earlier developmental fusion events are still incomplete. However, even if the earlier fusion events are not healed, healing this event can still cause a degree of merging in the brains. Occasionally, this physical trauma is so severe it has to be addressed separately.

Example:
A client healing the egg's coalescence found that when her mind awareness tried to take its place incorrectly, it felt a lot like having her head jamming sideways while coming down the birth canal. The same client had a birthing injury that felt like someone was trying to push her head back into the birth canal at the crowning stage; this injury hadn't released and she'd been unable to finish healing the birth traumas. She found it again in a later session of the same coalescence healing. It involved the Buddha brain unfolding incorrectly; it felt like a balloon inside the top of her skull pushing the mind awareness down, and causing pain down the cervical and lumbar spine.

The Placental Death Event and the Wholeness State

Occasionally, clients doing trauma healing would temporarily go into a state where they would spontaneously say "I feel whole!". Interestingly, the first time I entered the state I just knew that the word 'whole' fit the experience I was having, without question or doubt, even though I had never consciously experienced it before. For years we searched for the developmental event that was responsible for this state without any luck. One day Preston Howard of the Institute found the answer on a website in an article by Nemi Nath (www.breathconnection.com.au) at http://www.i-breathe.com/thb42/placenta_trauma.htm. Her personal experience of becoming 'whole' is in Chapter 13. My thanks to Ms. Nath for her great work.

To sum up Ms. Nath's discovery, the key developmental event for the Wholeness state is the release and death of the placenta. To our surprise, It turns out that the placenta is a self-aware 'brain'. Our cultural assumptions got in the way of recognizing the importance of the experience of the placenta itself when healing trauma, let alone its impact on triune brain fusion states. Without our realizing it, the birth developmental stage was never completed in our work. Thus, because the placenta is one of the brains that has to fuse with the rest for a unified brain system, we classify Wholeness as a triune brain fusion state. Note too that the Wholeness state does not require fusion of the other brains to manifest itself—it only depends on how the placental brain is fused with the other brains, which in our limited experience occurs equally to all of the other brains.

After birth, the Wholeness state is blocked when the placental brain's awareness does not fuse correctly with the rest of the organism as the placenta dies. One might well ask why should this matter? After all, the placenta is dead, so a fusion of its consciousness with the other brain awarenesses shouldn't make any difference in the present. Yet it does, and we suspect this occurs because of the nature of the brains' consciousnesses in a phenomenon called the 'Realm of the Shaman'. This topic is beyond the scope of this book, but is covered in depth in Volume 2.

The trauma around placental death involves both the separation shock of the cord being cut from the baby's perspective, and the reaction of the placenta's awareness itself as it detaches from the mother and dies. The symptoms in the adult include sensations in the stomach area of the belly, and separation trauma that is usually and apparently mistakenly ascribed to separation from the mother, when it is actually separation shock from the placenta. This separation often feels like a burning sensation on the entire back from both the placental and fetal perspectives. As adults, people use others in their lives as substitute placentas. The severity of the separation and death trauma is greatly increased by the way current medical practices treat the baby during birth. They almost always cut the cord too soon, causing tremendous pain and shock in the baby. This also is experienced as a life-threatening event to the baby, not only because of the abrupt loss of oxygen, but also because blood in the placenta doesn't have a chance to drain into the baby.

WARNING:

We've tracked suicidal feelings in several of our clients to this period of the birth. These can be so intense even well-integrated people who have never felt suicidal before can be overwhelmed by them. In particular, we've seen these feelings in the moment that the umbilical cord was cut, and during the birthing when the cord was wrapped around the baby's neck. See Chapter 8 for more details.

Example:
    While healing the placental death trauma, Paula first did the healing from the fetal perspective only. She then got the sensation of wholeness only at times when she was relaxing. After healing the

placental side, she felt whole all the time. The other brains were merged but not fused during this work.

Note that the Wholeness state also requires the death trauma of the sperm tail organelle 'brain' to be healed for stability. In terms of trauma, this is an earlier trauma that sets up the later placental death to be more traumatic than it is normally. Interestingly, injuries during the sperm tail death are reproduced in the placental body later.

Alchemy, Developmental Events and the Inner Gold State

Quite to my surprise the principles of medieval alchemy apply to our work. Carl Jung's *The Psychology of the Transference* has illustrations from one of the early alchemy texts, the *Rosarium Philosophorum* of 1550. The wood-cut illustrations from it make sense once you see that each frame illustrates critical *in utero* or earlier developmental events for acquiring peak states of consciousness. Recall that the alchemists who were undergoing these pre-birth experiences had no idea of the nature of cellular objects—this was far, far before the invention of the microscope and our modern understanding of biology. Their drawings reflect their experiences, and give a road map for the fetal, cellular, and precellular developmental events.

If we let go of the idea that the alchemists were talking about transmuting metallic lead to metallic gold, and were instead talking about inner, spiritual development, the illustrations make perfect sense. From this perspective, during the process of alchemical development (i.e. going through the developmental events without trauma) you become completely golden inside (your 'lead' turns to 'gold'), and at the end you find the philosopher's stone, a golden ball at the belly which is what the brains look like in complete fusion. I've chosen a few of the alchemical stages to illustrate their connection to developmental events.

Figure 6.2 shows a woodcut image of an alchemical stage of a fountain. How would this relate to developmental events? It turns out that there is a precellular developmental event (described in detail in Chapter 8) for both the egg and the sperm involving what 'looks' like a fountain. Of course, there isn't a fountain in everyday terms, but rather a structure that 'looks' like a fountain as seen from a precellular perspective. When the developing precellular organism encounters the fountain, it goes into the flow of liquid, as if it were a shower, and absorbs the 'water'. This causes a major change in one's body in the present—when the inside of the body is viewed from the Inner Brightness state, it now has a rich, metallic golden color. We call this the Inner Gold state. This change has been permanent in all of our volunteers. Most of our volunteers doing deep work encounter these events spontaneously in the course of their trauma healing. We suspect that this golden state has something to do with physical healing, or equivalently a better connection to our species consciousness, although we are still investigating. Whatever the real purpose, we feel this state is an important one for our personal work, and apparently the alchemists agree with our conclusion.

Example:

> Some time after I first encountered this event and absorbed the 'water', I was working on a severe physical trauma to my diaphragm. In it was a 'hole', an area of what feels like bottomless deficient emptiness. Normally when healing holes, the black emptiness transitions to a smoky grayness, which finally fills with normal flesh. Instead, this time and for every time afterwards, the hole filled with a golden, almost liquid substance before finally becoming normal flesh. This golden material felt, in a very deep way, that it was what I really was made of, as if it were my true substance. I noticed later that my Inner Brightness state also had changed to having a golden shade to it, instead of the clear white light it had been.

Figure 6.2: Alchemical transformation stage from Plate 1 of the *Rosarium Philosophorum* (Rosary of the Philosophers), 1550.

The woodcut in Figure 6.3 is one of a series that illustrates the developmental moment of conception. Recall that a healed conception feels exactly like a royal wedding. Experientially, the symbols fit the experience—the sperm is the King, and the Queen is the egg, and they merge into one body at that developmental event in the liquid medium of the fallopian tube. An additional level of symbolism is probably used, with the woman as the heart brain, the man as the mind brain, and the throne as the body brain. The crows likely represent the placental and the sperm tail brains.The descending figure from the clouds probably represents a piece of the Creator that enters the organism during this event (see Volume 2 for an explanation). Figure 6.4 is a revised drawing a little further in the sequence done 72 years later—note the inclusion of the 'Grim Reaper', Death, in the revised image. During conception, the sperm experiences itself as dying, a very traumatic experience which the artist obviously felt was important to include.

Figure 6.3: Alchemical transformation stage from the Plate 16 of the *Rosarium Philosophorum* (Rosary of the Philosophers), 1550.

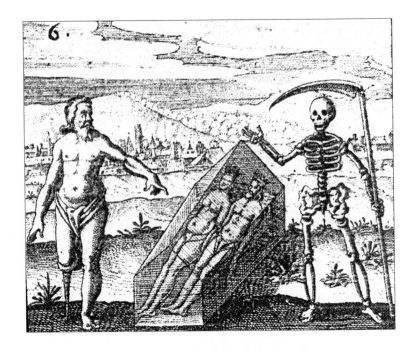

Figure 6.4: Alchemical transformation stage from Illustration 6 of the Mylius *Rosarium Philosophorum*, 1622. Note the addition of the figure of 'Death' on the right in this version.

I recognize several of the developmental events that are illustrated in the original woodcuts, but there are several illustrations whose developmental event we haven't identified yet. Crosschecking our results with theirs might be very valuable for identifying missing developmental events in our own work.

Practical Difficulties in Finding Developmental Events

As we mentioned in a previous chapter, when a state is the result of more than one developmental event, a very peculiar phenomenon can occur. If the earlier events are not done correctly (i.e. without trauma), later events will not be experienced with the full developmental changes that should occur. Thus in general during regressive healing, if you know where the earlier events are, you should start with them first.

For example, how is conception affected by trauma in coalescence? If you heal conception before completely healing precellular coalescence, you will still eventually get to the experience of a beautiful 'royal wedding'. However, the state of fusion of the egg and sperm brains remains at the level that they came in with—if they were separated, they generally stay separated during the conception. On the other hand, if you come into conception having healed the precellular coalescence traumas, so that the egg and sperm cells have the fused brains already as balls in their 'bellies', the balls in turn fuse into a larger single ball. The chakras also exhibit this effect.

We suspect that there are several more developmental events that we haven't yet found. They are hard to find, because our investigators have no trauma response around them, so they don't stand out in any way. We continue to investigate, but it's a slow process.

Triune Peak States and Permanence

One of the more interesting discussions among technique developers is the question of whether people *can* have peak states permanently, and if so, *should* they be permanent? I'll start by addressing just triune brain peak states. However, the observations I'll make below appear to apply to all of the peak states that I'm aware of.

Can people have permanent peak states? As I've said in previous chapters, lots of people can and do have them permanently. So why is there debate on this issue? I suspect that most spiritual teachers and researchers rarely if ever see examples of permanent peak states. People with good states feel unusually well for the most part, so don't generally have any interest in seeking anyone's help. Instead, spiritual teachers and technique developers generally only see the people who are suffering in some way. The people who do use currently available techniques like meditation and so on don't keep the states without continuous maintenance, since this approach only temporarily shuts off trauma responses that block peak states. Thus, based on observation, teachers naturally conclude that permanent peak states are not the normal course of affairs. It becomes natural, based on their experience, to argue that average consciousness is the base from which peak states rise from and return to, instead of realizing that average consciousness is a state of ill-health.

Another clinical observation can confuse the issue. I've seen many clients get one of the lesser fusion states, but then lose it when trauma material that blocks a better triune state emerges into their lives. These people typically have a lot of pre-birth traumatic material to heal. Thus, for someone who is trying to achieve a better fusion state, we often see an improvement alternating with partial or complete loss of their state. Others who have been born with a state may lose it temporarily, but have it return when the stressor that triggers other unhealed developmental events stops, and ends the trauma response.

On the other hand, just as many of my clients don't lose a previous state but instead make a brief, smooth transition into the new state by healing the new material that arises. As their state improves, it becomes easier and easier for them to move through any blocking material, which improves their state even further, and so on. Their biggest limitation is in knowing what to heal next! They typically have little pre-birth trauma to heal, the state they started with makes healing particularly easy, or they don't have other complicating factors like interfering generational trauma to deal with.

There is another observation that is germane to this discussion. We know of a number of cases where people who have unusual states and abilities lose them when people find out. Of course, it doesn't happen to everyone, but I suspect a significant part of the general population is affected by this. For example, Jack Schwarz lost his well-documented abilities later in life. For that matter, it happened to me! Wes and I hypothesize this problem is at least partially responsible for one of the primary taboos in shamanism—to not revealing unusual abilities. Volume 3 covers several of the blocking mechanisms that we've identified. These mechanisms are not directly related to trauma, and have nothing to do with any particular state or any issue around the use of the states.

Next, *should* peak states be permanent? Many feel that even if it were possible, permanent states would be a block or hindrance to further spiritual growth, and so states should only be only temporary. As we've seen in previous chapters, full fusion of the triune brains is our natural state, our birthright, and not something that we have to evolve to acquire. Their loss makes our lives unnecessarily miserable, and makes it much harder to grow spiritually, or in any other way for that matter. And as I've said, I've had a number of volunteers whose states just keep getting better and better—their current states help them acquire new ones. Thus, there is no spiritual or psychological advantage to moving out of our birthright states, Hollow and Wholeness.

Having said that, there are some states in particular that do act as a potential block to improved peak states:

- First, I've seen examples of people with the Beauty Way state (just the mind-heart fusion with a limited connection to the Creator) who find it nearly impossible to access trauma deliberately in order to improve their state, because they cannot feel any trauma to speak of. In their case, the state does act as a block to further growth. It can still be done, but it's much more difficult than for someone in a lesser or better triune brain state.
- Secondly, we've discovered that a good connection to the Creator can cause people to have the feeling that "everything is OK and as it should be" no matter what. This attitude not only blocks their own growth but any motivation to help others in a focused way. (We go into this in depth in Volume 2.) Although it isn't a triune brain peak state, a connection to the Creator often occurs as a byproduct in our work on triune states so I felt it was important to mention it. I can speak from the difficult personal experience of losing many volunteers who moved into this awareness and then left our work, before we understood what caused this and how to fix it. Zivorad Slavinski has also encountered this problem. I'd like to acknowledge Scott McGee of the Institute for finding the solution to it.

- Third, and a more psychological problem, is the fact that people in many triune brain peak states get used to feeling great. In fact, they get so used to it, they resist anything that might cause them even momentary discomfort, even if it would improve their state. Others in our workshops have the legitimate concern that if they continue to heal, they might lose their new state and so tend to stop any healing work at the place they're at. Most of these people who come to our workshops just want to feel better, and having achieved that, are perfectly content to stop. At some later time, circumstances or new motivation for something better may arise in them, and then it would be appropriate to continue. I know many of my best experimental subjects had such miserable lives that they won't quit, because they see a progression of better and better states. Others who have always had a great state tend to fall by the wayside quickly in this work, as discomfort is so alien and distasteful to them.

As far as other peak states are concerned, I believe the same arguments apply. However, since our way of approaching spiritual and shamanic states is so new, I won't commit myself to this position in every case. Perhaps there are some purely spiritual or shamanic peak states that people should move in and out of—I just haven't encountered them yet. Future dialog on this issue with other technique developers should prove very fruitful.

Summarizing These Key Developmental Events

An analogy can help put this material in perspective. Imagine that we're looking through a tunnel from one side of a mountain (our creation) to the other (our birth). If we're very lucky, there are no cave-ins, and we can see clearly from one end to the other, and we have our advanced 'Hollow' peak state. How about people without that state? At places where the tunnel was made larger (as we became a more complex organism), the roof suffered a bit of a collapse (a trauma). Thus, when we dig out the cave-in (heal a particular developmental event) that we might have thought would give us some particular state, such as Inner Peace, instead we get a much better state, for example full brain fusion and the Hollow state, because this was the only cave-in (trauma) on the whole journey. In other words, healing any given key developmental trauma generally gives you the expected target state, but it might not because other key developmental events either need to also be in place, or more are in place than you expected. As it's more likely that other developmental events are traumatic, it's more usual to get the target state or lesser. We see about 20% or so of our clients overshoot, in other words get better states than they were expecting.

To repeat, the different triune brain states we see after birth are usually partial states due to the individual not going through all the critical developmental events without trauma. The intermediate states, like the 'Inner Peace' or 'Underlying Happiness' states, although much better than normal, have characteristics that are still distortions of the correctly, fully fused triune brain system. Many of these characteristics disappear as more complete states are achieved because they were due to the partial or incomplete nature of the intermediate states. Thus, for example in the Hollow state, emotions themselves are no longer experienced as emotions, but almost as some sort of thought. Although this might sound disturbing from average consciousness, this is experienced as much more balanced, effortless, and pleasant. In essence, you give up aspects of your experience that shouldn't have been there in the first place, were you totally healthy from birth.

Healing conception usually results in the Beauty Way state or better. The Beauty Way state is a composite state that includes the Inner Peace triune brain state with other aspects, described in the next chapter.

Healing the precellular coalescence events usually results in very profound peak states and abilities. Healing both these, conception, implantation, and the placental and sperm tail death usually results in the Hollow and Wholeness states. In Chapter 8 we'll go through a step-by-step process for healing these key traumas using regression. 'Visual' descriptions will be given to aid in localizing the specific developmental events.

We've emphasized in this chapter the idea of using healing techniques on developmental event traumas to acquire triune brain peak states. However, people can bypass or heal these traumas in a variety of ways. Often, these traumas can spontaneously erupt in people's lives, generating emotional and physical pain ranging from mild to devastating. This almost always happens without any recognition by the person that the symptoms are caused by long-forgotten traumatic experiences. Some people end up unconsciously healing these traumas, and gain a peak state.

Example:
   Melissa Proulx is 19. She first moved into the Beauty Way when she was 17 when she started to practice not judging people (what we call the 'conscious choice approach for peak states'). "For example, I used to judge the people owning industrial farms. Now, I don't judge them. I just understand that they are just not aware yet. They are not bad people. They just don't know." She soon noticed that her past traumas no longer had any emotional feeling. She and the world around her felt very alive. Then, during a 7 day 'Arise and Shine' fast at age 19, she experienced extreme weakness, nausea, and soreness in her arms and legs. Her legs wouldn't support her. She nearly quit the fast before the process was complete. On the sixth day, she suddenly felt very happy. Her physical symptoms either went away, or she no longer cared. The next day, she noticed that she felt hollow inside, without a body inside her skin (the Hollow state). "I feel really good. I feel like I have no problems. Anything that is a problem isn't a problem for me any-

more. It's great! I stay happy no matter what." Paula had a chance to talk with Melissa the next day, and found that her symptoms matched Paula's own trauma around a coalescence event. Apparently, Melissa had accidentally triggered this old trauma during her fast, and been lucky enough to heal it in her own way during the fast.

Unfortunately, we suspect we don't have all the developmental events for total fusion of the brains, although we think we have the most important ones. This limits the success rate we have with people, as those who get the target states are the ones who don't need the events we're still missing. We'll be updating this book and our website www. PeakStates.com as new discoveries are made.

Key Points

- From an experiential viewpoint, developmental events important to peak states occur in three phases of biological development. The earliest we call 'precellular'. This occurs inside the parent that creates the cell, but before a cell is actually made. The next is cellular, and includes the egg, sperm, and zygote. The next is the multicellular organism, often referred to as the *in utero* phase, and it ends shortly after the birth.
- The organelle and *in utero* 'brains' are conscious and self-aware.
- The organelle 'brains' are constructed separately, and assembled in an event we call 'coalescence'. This is one of the key events for triune brain fusion.
- Healing certain critical developmental events results, for most people, in peak states.
- The tail of the sperm, and the placenta of the baby have their own 'brain' awarenesses. Healing their death traumas is key to the Wholeness state.
- Working in this area is potentially life threatening. Several of these events, such as birth, involve experiences that can induce overwhelming suicidal feelings in the adult.

Suggested Reading and Websites

On placental death trauma
- Nemi Nath, "Placental Trauma" in *The Healing Breath: A Journal of Breathwork Practice, Psychology and Spirituality*, Volume 4, No. 2, 2002. The article can be seen at http://www.i-breathe.com/thb42/placenta_trauma.htm
- Shivam Rachana, *Lotus Birth*, Victoria Australia, Greenwood Press, 2000.

On the effect of the conception trauma
- John Gray, *Men are from Mars, Women are from Venus: A Practical Guide for Improving Communication and Getting What You Want in Relationships*, HarperCollins, 1993.
- Eckhart Tolle, *The Power of Now: A Guide to Spiritual Enlightenment*, New World Library, 1999. His book describes the Beauty Way state very well, although he doesn't give it that name.

On medieval alchemy
- Carl Jung, *The Psychology of the Transference*, Princeton University Press, 1969.

On fetal, pre-, and perinatal events and trauma
- Association for Pre- and Perinatal Psychology and Health, www.birthpsychology.com. Excellent material on the topic of *in utero* regression.
- Early Trauma Treatment and Trainings by Terry Larimore, www.terrylarimore.com. Her website also contains excellent material.
- Emerson Training seminars, William Emerson, www.emersonbirthrx.com. He is one of the leaders in pre- and perinatal psychology in my opinion.
- William Emerson, "The Vulnerable Prenate", paper presented to the APPPAH Congress, San Francisco, 1995, published in *Pre- & Perinatal Psychology Journal*, Vol. 10(3), Spring 1996, 125-142. An online copy is at www.birthpsychology.com/healing/point2.html.
- Peter Fedor-Freybergh and M. L. Vanessa Vogel (eds), *Prenatal and Perinatal Psychology and Medicine: Encounter with the Unborn; A Comprehensive Survey of Research and Practice*, UK: Parthenon, 1988.
- Michael Gabriel and Marie Gabriel, *Voices from the Womb: Adults Relive their Pre-birth Experiences - a Hypnotherapist's Compelling Account*, Aslan Publishing, 1992.

- Stanislav Grof, *The Adventure of Self-Discovery*, State University of New York Press, 1988. Excellent coverage on the stages of birth and other spiritual and shamanic experiences.
- Terry Larimore and Graham Farrant, "Universal Body Movements in Cellular Consciousness and What They Mean," originally published in *Primal Renaissance*, Vol. 1, No. 1, 1995. An online copy is at www.terrylarimore.com/CellularPaper.html
- Sheila Linn, William Emerson, Dennis Linn, and Matthew Linn, *Remembering our Home: Healing Hurts and Receiving Gifts from Conception to Birth*, Paulist Press, 1999.
- Elizabeth Noble, *Primal Connections: How our Experiences from Conception to Birth Influence our Emotions, Behavior, and Health*, Simon and Schuster, 1993.
- Bill Swartley, "Major Categories of Early Psychosomatic Traumas: From Conception to the End of the First Hour" from *The Primal Psychotherapy Page*. An online copy is at www.primal-page.com/bills-1.htm. Excellent with great references.

Images of sperm, egg, and *in utero* developmental events
- *Journey Into Life: The Triumph of Creation* (a 30 minute video),1990, by Derek Bromhall, distributed by Questar Video, Inc. This is an exceptional video on the journey of the sperm, egg, zygote, and fetus. The material is filmed with the same viewpoint and image size that people recalling trauma around these events see.
- Lennart Nilsson, *A Child is Born*, Delacorte Press, NY, 1990. Still photos of the journey of the sperm, egg, zygote, and fetus. The images are of scenes that people recalling trauma around these moments see. Recommended.

Chapter 7

Applying the Model: Chakras, Meridians, Past Lives, Auras, Archetypes, Native Imagery and Aging

Introduction

In this chapter we apply the developmental events model to some important peak experiences and abilities. In particular, we focus on phenomena that are seen when using powerful therapies or spiritual practices, but which are outside of our conventional Western belief system—chakras, meridians, past lives, aging, aura layers, and archetypes. Our work has given us surprising information on these phenomena that, as far as we know, is unique to the field.

States in this chapter:
- Past Life Access
- Flow Awareness

Grant's Story
Collateral Discoveries

When I first started the project to induce peak states and heal trauma, I fully subscribed to the dominant Western belief system. I admit I rolled my eyes when acquaintances who were into 'new age' concepts would talk about things like past lives, chakras, and all the rest. I just assumed that these things were vague, dreamlike impressions that were a product of people's vivid imaginations. Although this may be true of some, my students and I have a very different experience—we can see this material with the same clarity that you have when looking at this book. At the time, I didn't understand that one's state determines whether one can 'see' these out-of-the-ordinary phenomena, and that the degree of the state determines the clarity. I can still recall my stunned surprise when I suddenly, completely, and in full 'surround-sound Technicolor' re-experienced a traumatic moment in a past life. It happened during a tantra workshop, when I suddenly relived the gut-wrenching sadness at the recent death of my wife in that life. My tantra partner was that 'same' woman, and I realized I'd been looking for her for my entire lifetime. Later, I found I could access that lifetime at will.

But, being a skeptic, I figured that even though there was something to this 'past-life' stuff, it didn't mean that any of the rest of it was true. Sometime later, I was in bed when I saw what looked like a silver old-time ship captain's wheel slowly spinning in my chest. I had no idea what this was, until I read up on the literature on chakras, and found out it was the classic description of the heart chakra. As time passed, more and more spiritual, shamanic, and transpersonal experiences occurred, often leaving me puzzled on exactly what they were about.

So far, my story is no different than that of many people who embark on a spiritual quest, who start by using meditation or shamanic techniques and grow into new levels of perception. What happened later is much more interesting and unique. My colleagues and I started to apply the newly created developmental events model to all of these non-ordinary experiences and abilities. That's when things really became exciting! We started to ask ourselves when we'd encounter something new, "OK, does the developmental events model apply to this?"—and sure enough, it would. I think it was with these experiences that I really, really started to trust my own model. Of course, I expect that it will take many people years of more work to fully explore this new material.

Yet our work hasn't made me a 'true believer' by any means. I still have a skeptical, practical engineer's viewpoint that needs measurable, useful applications to test for validity. The need to delude oneself to avoid pain is a constant problem in this kind of work, one which I've encountered over and over in myself and my colleagues. In fact, going towards pain is probably the safest direction to travel to avoid this problem, although clearly not the most comfortable. Delusional material can be so convincing, and get such consensual agreement that the only real test is objective physical reality—does it cause a change in the real world?

The Chakras and Meridians

Introduction

Many of my clients have come to me with symptoms that lead to pre-birth trauma involving a chakra. As we healed the trauma, they would usually be able to 'see' their own chakra. While still regressed to the *in utero* experience, they would often learn the unconscious internal cue that controlled it by observing their mother when she unconsciously used them herself. This material is covered in more depth in our *Basic Whole-Hearted Healing Manual*. Although of great practical significance in healing, this healing work didn't answer any of the theoretical questions about the chakras. Nor did it lead to any global treatments for chakra-related issues.

However, our work with fusion brain states and coalescence revealed the connection between chakras, meridians, and physical symptoms that we almost certainly would never have discovered any other way. This is of great theoretical importance, particularly the material on the meridians. Meridian therapies like acupuncture and EFT make use of them without a theoretical understanding of exactly what they do and why. Not only is this due to a lack of understanding of the material in this chapter, but it's also likely that it has historical roots—the Chinese focus on the meridians, but not the chakras, while the Hindus focus on the chakras but not the meridians. Thus, neither group sees the full picture of the relationship between the two.

We've found that a fully developed chakra system is one where they're fused into a disk located in the solar plexus area. This fusion creates an experience we call the 'Flow Awareness' state. We've also found that the individual chakras are supposed to anchor into the meridians, and problems in this anchorage creates excessive tiredness or hyperactivity. Correctly anchored chakras results in a fully restful sleep which only lasts three or four hours.

Chapter 8 gives specific details to enable one to heal the relevant developmental events.

The Chakras - Shortcomings of the Traditional Model

Our work has shown that the chakras as described in Hindu yogic texts and by groups such as the Berkeley Psychic Institute and in Barbara Brennan's *Hands of Light* exist and are key to a set of abilities that are our birthright. In this conventional understanding, different chakras act differently and have different functions. For example, experientially the most commonly felt chakras at the heart and solar plexus are able to emit energy that feels like water flowing out of one's body from those areas. Traditional illustrations show the seven major chakras are distributed in a line along the vertical axis of the body. These chakras are 'energy centers' that have distinct shapes which can be seen in the Inner Brightness state. These groups work with healing and learning how to use the abilities of each of the chakras for full health—each chakra has to be 'spinning' correctly, in the right direction, at the right speed, be unblocked, and so on.

However, the material on chakras that is commonly available has major shortcomings that are not obvious to even experienced practitioners. The most obvious problem with the traditional model of chakras is due to ignorance about the triune brain system. Proponents of the classical chakra model don't realize that the chakras are 'devices' run by their corresponding brain, so instead they develop a model that somehow the chakras are self-aware—essentially, putting too much into one basket.

Another shortcoming involves not realizing that there is a layer with changeable permeability at the skin that blocks chakra energy. Its impact on our lives extends far beyond the chakras, however. This material is covered in depth in Volume 2.

The biggest flaw in traditional models isn't obvious. It turns out that a fully developed chakra system does not look as shown in the literature. Rather, the chakras should all fuse together into a single disk-like shape in the solar plexus area. The conventional model can be compared to the model a biologist might make of an adult tadpole if he had never seen a frog. Rather than showing it had legs to jump with, he would naturally extrapolate that it was simply a larger, more robust version of the tadpole, still with a tail. The situation is quite parallel. It turns out that, just as our model says, there are a few, critical developmental events that very few people do without trauma. These traumas limit the chakra system and result in the commonly seen illustrations on the subject. We'll describe what a fully developed chakra system looks like in the next section.

The Chakras - Developmental Events

The key developmental events that we know of so far for the chakra system are the egg and sperm coalescence, and conception. However, the qualities that you get with brain fusion states are not the same as the qualities that a fully healed and developed chakra system from the same stages gives you. The chakra and brain systems can be healed independently, giving different kinds of results. However, since so few people have gone through the necessary developmental stages without trauma, a fully functioning chakra system and its impact on physical well-being is not described in the Yogic literature that we know of.

The key event is during precellular brain coalescence. Before coalescence, each of the precellular brains brings with it one or more chakras that are inside the respective precellular brains. They 'look' like glowing balls of light inside, or superimposed on, the physical precellular brain. (Closer examination of these chakras might give features, but we haven't yet investigated this.) The brain awarenesses, the 'balls of light' that we've mentioned in previous chapters, have a different appearance from the chakras.

In the case of the egg coalescence, during the entry into the body brain container the seven chakras align themselves in a vertical pattern along the axis of the precellular body, in alignment with their respective brains. The chakras look just like the classical illustrations. As the events continue, the chakras converge into a single smooth-edged chakra in the solar plexus area, about two thirds below the solar plexus and about one third above.

Interestingly, there is a difference between the precellular and cellular egg and sperm chakras. The egg has just the seven major chakras that we are familiar with from the literature, but the precellular sperm has something quite different—the heart brain has a series of chakra balls that extend upwards and downwards (in alignment with the precellular brains inside the body container) for as far as one can perceive. This was a totally unexpected result. Although we are not yet certain why this is the case, we suspect that it has something to do with a sperm's connection to all of the other sperm that help it fertilize the egg. As coalescence progresses, they converge into what looks like a ball of fog in the same area of the solar plexus as the precellular egg.

The next major developmental event is conception. During it, the chakra disks from the sperm and egg combine into a single chakra disk located in the solar plexus area of the zygote. This chakra disk has a regular pattern of indentations on the rim. (Of course, the zygote doesn't have a solar plexus area *per se*, but during regressions the clients experience the zygote as if it were their body in the present, with the zygote's internal parts aligned with their bodily parts in the present.)

Note that there are eight permutations in these events, if you assume that the events are done with or without total trauma: the egg coalescence is fine, but the sperm is traumatized, while conception is fine; the egg coalesces fine, but the sperm is traumatized, and the conception is traumatized; and so on. In reality, partial trauma causes a great many intermediate states, causing imperfections in the final chakra fusion. Since the chances that all of the chakra fusion events happening without trauma is so unlikely, we get the typical seven chakra pattern in most adults.

During gestation, most people have separate chakra balls. The fetus learns how to use or control the individual chakras by watching the mother use hers. Since most mothers are not aware that they are using the chakras, the fetus learns by associating with the body sensation that the mother experiences while she uses them. The problem with this is that it is fairly indirect control, and if the mother didn't use the chakras while the fetus was gestating, then the fetus wouldn't learn how to use them. This has an interesting implication in our clients—if they heal and get a chakra disk, will they unconsciously know how to use it properly? After all, their mother didn't, so they have no associations to learn. At this time, we don't know the answer to this question.

Example:
> My own mother would turn on her crown chakra during sex, and her heart chakra while bending over patients in the hospital she worked at. By feeling those sensations in my own adult body, I would turn on the associated chakra.

How do we apply this material to improving people's lives? It is possible to actively heal these event traumas. At this time we only use methods that require regression. Chapter 8 goes into the steps in great detail. Iteration of the healing process is usually required. One goes through the relevant traumas several times since the later ones build on the earlier ones. Note that you often can't access the earlier ones until the later ones are done as far as they can be, which is where the need to iterate comes from.

The 'Flow Awareness' State

(Although we're still investigating this, I've chosen to include in this text our current results. Note that this may change in the future as more data comes in.) When the chakras combine into a single disk, it gives one what we've chosen to call the 'Flow Awareness' state. In this state, one feels a 'flow' of water-like energy coming through the body from back to front. How this flow is perceived depends on what one's triune brain state is. If one does not have fusion of the brains, the flow direction feels like it originates from outside of oneself. Thus, conscious effort is required to align oneself with the external flow, which is perceived as being a better state of affairs than to not come into alignment.

However, in the Hollow state, the flow no longer feels like it's directed by outside forces. Instead, the person is always aligned with the flow from back to front no matter what one does.

Example:
> Scott McGee describes it like this: "Flow is like an ocean current. When you get it, it takes you somewhere. You have to be aware if it's a slow or quick flow to go with it, to synchronize with it. You can move to different parts of the flow that are quicker or slower. How does one recognize it from our own visceral experience? It's like thick syrup out of a bottle, it just flows, not pours. It feels like that in the body, pulling you along, in the back and out the front. If one gets in synchronization with the flow, there is no longer a feeling in back or front as one's whole body is flowing with it. You can notice the flow around you but it doesn't affect you. There is a kind of feedback—you can go with it or resist it, but you can sense it. Also, it makes things look more three dimensional."

How is the chakra flow state experienced with different kinds of brain fusion? In the case of average consciousness but in the Flow Awareness state, you feel the 'flow' as being either quick or slow, and this affects what you can accomplish. With the Hollow state, but without the Flow Awareness state, there is a sensation of effortlessness, but you still have to intend your actions. With both the Hollow and Flow Awareness states, everything feels effortless, and you don't have to think about it for it to be effortless. It just is.

At this time, we believe that the chakra flow state is not what athletes feel—that it isn't the 'zone', as it's called. We suspect that they are actually describing the Hollow state, which is characterized by effortlessness. And how does it compare to Mihaly Csikszentmihaly's work on 'flow'? We don't know at this time, but it is clearly a fascinating area to pursue.

The Meridians and Their Relationship to Chakras

Returning to the chakras in the egg and sperm coalescence, something occurs that we never expected and which is even more dramatic than the changes in the chakras. The chakra balls anchor themselves into a matrix of lines that appear and expand, linking the brains and their chakras as the brains are incorporated into the body container. To our amazement, this network of lines is the meridians! 'Visually', one of our investigators described the chakra balls anchored into something that resembled a webbing, or an electronic printed circuit board. The meridians continued to grow as the coalescence progressed, finally terminating into a completed webbing with the chakra balls embedded into it.

Effects of Healing Meridian/Chakra Developmental Events Trauma

As we've mentioned, one of the main problems in this work is continuing the healing long enough to get the full changes during the developmental stage. Coalescence is no exception. Potential problems can occur during this healing. The primary problem is in getting the chakra balls to be seated into the meridian webbing without trauma. There are many possible combinations of problems that can occur since there are a lot of chakras that might or might not be anchored correctly, but one really obvious symptom can be either profound exhaustion or extreme manic energy.

Example:
> The first time we experimented with anchoring the chakras, our 'guinea pig' had the two extreme reactions in the present, representing unhealed problems in the anchorage. In the first case, she found herself completely exhausted, and could hardly stay awake enough to continue the healing. As she continued the healing, she did something else incorrectly, and instead became over-energized, so much so that she had to run around the circular driveway to let off some of the energy while we continued the process!

Warning—Potential Physical Reaction
Working on the precellular coalescence trauma to heal the chakra systems can end up in one of two extreme experiences—completely draining one of energy, or giving too much energy if not

done to completion. Either case is a major physical problem for the experimenter. So beware when you do the process, and give yourself enough time to make mistakes and recover from them.

Since we tend to heal the chakra traumas along with the meridian traumas, it's a bit hard to separate them out. However, we believe at this time that healing the anchorage of the chakras in the meridians alone has another unexpected effect in our experimenters. They have found themselves only sleeping three or four hours a night, and feeling fully rested afterwards. This is a dramatic, unmistakable and clear change in people. This showed to us that the people who work with chakras in traditional processes are missing the full potential of what is possible. We found this fascinating, as differences in sleep amounts in the general population may reflect the distribution of these stages being done without trauma. We'd heard about people who only slept a few hours per night, but we'd assumed that all of them had some sort of major psychological problem causing sleeplessness. Instead, it looks like average people who need about 8 hours of sleep a night are actually the ones who are demonstrating a problem. (We differentiate here between insomniacs who are always tired, and people who hardly sleep but are "fresh as daisies".)

Changes in visual perception can also occur from healing these meridian/chakra developmental events. That visual perception can be so radically different is something that isn't realized in the dominant culture, but is stunningly obvious when you go quickly through these changes and experience what is really possible. The changes range from vision that can see behind objects to other, more common enhancements like the ability to see with peripheral vision as clearly as with direct vision, or enhanced three-dimensional vision. Both Zen Buddhist walking meditation and Tom Brown, Jr.'s shamanic 'wide-angle' vision try and get people to use their peripheral vision to improve their state of consciousness. From our results, trying to use peripheral vision would act to stimulate the traumas associated with the loss of these abilities, which are the same events whose trauma would block triune brain peak states. Essentially, healing the one gives the other because they both occur in nearly the same time during the critical developmental events.

For example, we've seen enhanced three-dimensional vision (i.e. the ability to see and know where exactly in three dimensional space oneself is) in one individual from birth. He also had the Beauty Way state of consciousness. This makes us want to investigate if a fully healed conception might give this to people, or does it require other stages also? The advantage to this change in vision is that it is relatively minor. More dramatic changes in vision can be experienced as frightening by some people.

Example:
One of our team, Frank Downey, was a fighter pilot who was in the Beauty Way his entire life, which means he had gone through

the conception event with little or no trauma. It turns out that he also always had an experience of vision that is much more three-dimensional than that of an ordinary person. This peak ability is probably why he excelled as a pilot in the first place.

Example:

When one of our volunteers had finished healing the precellular egg developmental stage, she found she'd acquired a 'peak ability' in the present—she was now able to see through things or actually behind things. It was very hard to put into words, but space became visually quite different—everything became very three-dimensional, no longer like images seen by the eyes. Our experimenter found this to be quite disturbing, as it conflicted with her religious belief of what was acceptable among 'ordinary' people.

Exceptional Strength and Ability

How does healing the chakra stages apply to extremes of physical strength and endurance? From our work so far, we haven't seen sudden changes in this area with healed stages. Regardless of the chakras, you can easily imagine how important peak states (especially ones like Hollow with its aspect of effortlessness) are for sports performance. One of our investigators who can 'see' the degree of brain fusion reported that the unexpected winner of the Olympic gold for skating had a solid fusion of the triune brains, while the favorite who lost had her mind brain pull out of the fusion. We don't know what the state of her chakras were, but we might expect that when the mind pulled out of fusion, it pulled out its associated chakras too.

Yet, what about 'superhuman' physical ability states, the classic mother lifting a car off her baby? Do levels of physical abilities far outside the norm really exist? The answer is yes. We have known people who exhibit these types of phenomena. One of our workshop participants shared an experience he had had a few years previously—one day while he was pitching to his dad at a baseball camp, he clicked into a peak ability for 20 minutes or so and repeatedly threw the ball at well over the normal world's record. The catcher, his father, asked him to slow down as it was painful. He tried just lightly tossing the ball, and it was still moving in the 80-mph range. Along these lines, Tom Brown Jr. regularly teaches his advanced students how to run at full speed for days without tiring.

Several of our volunteers report improved physical strength and endurance as a byproduct of healing developmental events, but still within the 'normal' range. At this point in our work, we haven't seen exceptional physical abilities manifest. Are they involved with the chakras? We don't know. Given that our model is correct, there will be a key, or multiple key developmental events that would give this level of physical ability. The application of our model to sports performance has huge potential, and someday we hope to explore this more fully.

Past Lives

Background

For this discussion, we're going to assume that you've encountered the phenomenon of past lives or have already recognized its existence for other reasons and have gotten past the paradigm conflict in our society. A number of good books have been written on the subject, especially from a therapeutic standpoint, but I will review some of the more unusual features of past lives that are generally not known even among people who deal with them.

Several religious traditions say that people in advanced spiritual states of consciousness recover memories of all their past lives. As you will see shortly, this is a reasonable statement based on our work. If you assume the model of this book is correct, an awareness of past lives is included in our natural state, thus certain kinds of developmental traumas must block the awareness of past lives. The development of the awareness of past lives probably goes hand in hand with the development of peak states using traditional processes. It might also be that certain peak states unblock the traumas that make past lives inaccessible, perhaps in the same way that the Inner Peace state eliminates emotional trauma from the past. However, if this is the case, we haven't noticed it yet in our experimental subjects.

The Nature of Time

The next difficult-to-accept part about past lives is regarding the nature of time. We'll be going into much greater detail in Volume 2, but for now I'll just give an outline of what we've discovered. To our surprise, we found that the present is not as our culture assumes it to be. There is no exclusive present, moving from past to future, as we have been taught. To give a visual representation, imagine time as a river running from the past to the future. The present is totally arbitrary, and depends on where you choose to put your attention by stepping into the water. You can choose any particular moment in the past or future, and when you put your attention there, it is 'in the present' just as it is right now. Every moment, past or future, is experienced by the observer as being 'in the present'. What this means for past lives is that when one re-experiences a past life, or for that matter a trauma in this lifetime using one of many regression processes, you are sharing the present moment of someone who is actually living it. They are not just static memories. And the events at that moment can be changed. The future can go back to affect the past just as much as the past can affect the future. This means that in certain peak states you can interact with people in the past in exactly the same way that you can interact, say by phone, with a neighbor down the street in the present. In fact, one can actually give oneself advice and guidance from one lifetime to the next, the ultimate example of raising oneself by one's own bootstraps!

The other major implication of this model of time is that you can also interact with lives that have not yet happened—in the future as we think of it. Although of course, for someone in the future, it's their present and we're in the past. The best example of this experience that I know of is written by Hank Wesselman in the book *Spiritwalker*.

Another natural question arises at this point. Is there some sort of oversoul or being outside of time that is experiencing each of these lives simultaneously? To answer that question, we need to look at a relevant developmental event.

Past Lives and Developmental Events

Using the model of this book, we can hypothesize that people don't recall past lives because of some sort of developmental event trauma. Secondly, we would expect a distribution in awareness of past lives in the general population due to the varying amount of trauma in critical developmental stages, in the same way as there is a distribution of peak states in the general population. Thus, we would expect to see some who could recall all their lives, some who could on occasion, and the majority who could not access them at all. And sure enough, this appears to be the case.

Wes Gietz decided to see if this hypothesis was true. From his exceptional peak state, he was able to regress to the moment where he could feel the block to his awareness of past lives occurring. Before that moment, he had full awareness of all his past lives, although it turns out that he had to experience them from the perspective of an egg in the ovary. He found that this awareness was lost when the egg was being ejected from the ovary. As this was happening, there was some sort of protective coating forming over the egg. It started from his 'head' and as it came downward, he could feel the awareness of past lives being reduced, until as the coating was complete there was no more access to other lives. He healed this event, and to our surprise, he found that in the present he had full awareness of both his past and his future lives. Wes described this about the same as having memories of his own life, no more intrusive than that—although he spent some time noticing that people he knew in the present were people he'd known in the past.

Example:
  Paula Courteau went further into this event, looking for the reason why it was relevant to past lives. She found that at a certain level of consciousness, she could 'see' a relatively flat webbing extending infinitely through space. She encountered this by healing egg coalescence, at the moment when the heart awareness comes

into the body container. She feels that it is related to the Creator level of awareness in some way, although exactly how she isn't yet sure. After she induced the Wholeness state into one of her past lives, she noticed the webbing became bright in patches. These areas were her past lives. Her own lifetime was just another one of these areas.

After more healing, the web grew a brighter golden color and she could view her past lives as either brighter patches of webbing or as dim silhouettes, as if they were people seen at dusk. Interestingly, the lit up patches closest to herself were not necessarily recent lives—rather, they had similar issues to her in the present. With further experimentation, she found there was a chronological order, however—the ones on her left were past, on her right were the future. Behind her were lives that died before birth. Directly in front were only shadows, constantly shifting. She felt that they were 'possible Paulas'—the lives she would have lead if she had taken a different path. There was a lot of fear associated with merging with those lives. I find this account fascinating, as both myself and Zivorad Slavinski in our healing work have clients access these types of 'alternative' lives. After more healing, Paula's entire mesh became golden and the past and future lives partially merged with her. Since then, she repeatedly had the impression that all her lives are getting the benefit of her healing.

With more coalescence and other healing, she now sees the webbed plane as a continuous sheet of orange-gold light. She mentions this because other investigators who are less traumatized might not see the intermediate webbed stage.

Paula writes: "It was David Burnet who put words to the way I access special abilities and different 'ways of seeing': to work from the Creator state, he said he regresses to the moment where he first became aware of Creator. I realized this morning that regression is what I do also, but not entirely consciously. When I want to see past lives I surround myself with a certain atmosphere. I realise now that it's the atmosphere of the *in utero* events I healed when I first discovered my past lives. If I want to feel the planetary consciousness, I surround myself with a different atmosphere - that of the moment just before I took my first breath. I've forgotten what most of the developmental moments were, but I don't need to remember the time; all I have to remember is the feeling of that particular moment. It's a shortcut, but strictly speaking it's definitely regression to the moment the phenomenon was first seen."

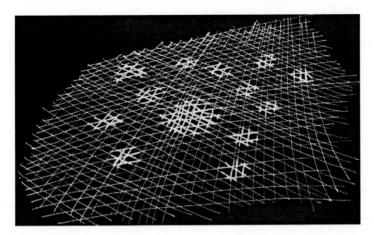

Figure 7-1: Paula sketched her observations. The pattern on this draw-ing resembles the pattern in the webbing that contains past lives. The largest patch is the present life, with past and future lives around it.

How does this relate to the developmental event of ovulation? In the ovary, the egg is tied to its 'sister' eggs via a webbing that feels and looks very similar to what Paula saw as a webbing that contains past lives. The eggs all communicate to each other, like girls and women do in groups, sharing information between each other. Recall that it is association, not logic or reason that the body uses to learn with. In the case of ovulation, as the coating comes over the egg, it cuts the communication channels to the other eggs. This loss of communication to the other eggs is carried over to the similar feeling loss of communication with past lives simulta-neously.

Is there an equivalent developmental stage in the sperm that blocks past lives? The sperm is also coated with a protective layer of cells, but at least as of this writing it doesn't appear to have the same effect on past lives as the coating on the egg does. As you might guess, developmental stages that are not experienced with trauma are hard to find, as to the ob-server they are non-events. Only people in good enough states that they can access and heal the traumatic material, and who yet have event trauma that interferes with what we're looking for, can notice the relevant events. It's been a slow and hit-or-miss process so far.

Are there other developmental traumas relevant to past lives? We sus-pect there are, as not everyone who heals the ovulation trauma recovers their past-life memories. But again, more work needs to be done.

The 'Past Life Awareness' State

As we've mentioned, when relevant traumas are fully healed, the individual experiences the merging of all of their past and future lives into their present. Obviously, there are degrees of this merging, from no ability to access past lives, to complete awareness. In this book, we've chosen to call this state the 'Past Life Awareness state'. As one can access future lives also, the label is a bit incomplete, but as the concept of past lives has already taken root in popular culture, we chose to label the state with the common name.

Healing Past Lives En Masse

After a few years, we'd come to realize that there were so many past lives that it was both futile and pointless to try to heal their relevant trauma. Given so many lives, virtually everything that could be traumatic had been experienced at least once at some time. Empirically, we'd found that issues that clients had that were traceable to past life trauma were actually triggered by more fundamental trauma in this lifetime. The client would go to the past life first, because the past-life experience is less traumatic to the person as it's happening to somebody else and doesn't feel personal. We could force the client to go to the originating cause of the problem in this lifetime, and the past-life material would become irrelevant to them.

Dr. Perry made another amazing discovery. She found that she could induce the Wholeness state in one of her past lives, and then that person in that lifetime would induce it into another of her past-life lifetimes, and so on in an expanding chain reaction. As she watched, her entire past and future history of her other lives was rewritten. This was an amazing result and helped us feel better about ignoring all those lifetimes of misery we've all had.

Implication for the Future of Our Civilization

One of the most fascinating implications from this work is again about the nature of time. We find that after going into the right peak state, Inner Brightness, people can then experience their own futures to varying degrees. This is because from that peak state perspective, the future has already happened. With frightening uniformity these people see the end of our civilization and the virtual extinction of our species in their own lifetimes. Hank Wesselman, Tom Brown, Jr., and Christopher Bache all do a good albeit disturbing job of describing this catastrophe. Even Dr. Raymond Moody's psychomanteum work, which is designed for a completely different purpose, that of communicating with the dead, is causing people to see these events.

Is this real? Well, it doesn't take an unusual state to see that our society is destroying the biosphere that sustains our own species at a frightening rate, so we can expect such a result to be rather realistic. However, the same results offer hope—the past and the future can change. In fact, one can ascribe a probability to future events based on this model of constant change. Unfortunately, the probability of global catastrophe appears to be nearly a certainty at this time. Yet, perhaps the outcome will change if enough people heal.

A Developmental Event for Native American Art and Music

While exploring developmental events of the sperm in the testes, I came across one of the most numinously beautiful and awesome experiences I've ever had. I found myself flying rapidly through a series of gigantic intertwined tunnels, which felt like they were hundreds of yards wide. There was the sound of native American chanting music that I knew was in praise of the Creator. The walls of the tunnels were covered with angular patterns, the same ones found in Plains and Southwest Native American artwork. Of course, these tunnels, artwork, and music were all from the perspective of the sperm, so the dimensions are quite tiny, but from my sperm perspective, it was stunning!

This event has no particular use that I'm aware of, but I mention it here because of its striking beauty.

The Developmental Event for Old Age and Death

Growing Old

To our great surprise, one of our contributors found a developmental event where we choose to grow old, and choose the time at which we will die of old age. This occurs during the birthing trauma, right after the first birth contraction. (The label of the first contraction assumes a simple delivery.) She found the experience quite frightening, and ended up choosing not to try and change the outcome.

Example:
"During a session I encountered a decision I'd made to age and grow old. I was focusing on a lack of wholeness, opening my heart, really letting go to my heart energy, then I started to feel myself dying, as in aging dying. Then I realized aging was a constriction, and I saw it didn't have to be that way. In order to go there, I had to let the internal wave go and expand outward. I'd have to give/surrender myself to the universe, to this giving/receiving. Membrane-less in that giving and receiving, not invested in anything. A death,

who knows were I'd end up. I decided to wait on the decision to let go of aging, to put it off till later! (There was a lot of fear around making that decision to not age.)"

Later, Scott McGee was able to verify her findings. He went through the trauma of the event, and changed the outcome. As this is all experimental work, we didn't know what to expect. He reported suddenly needing to eat tremendous amounts of protein over a period of weeks, and sleeping quite a bit. His body spontaneously regained the musculature and shape of a younger man's. We don't know how far this can go, or if other developmental events are involved, but we watch the progression of the changes with extreme interest.

Is it possible to actually stop or reverse the aging process by healing this developmental stage trauma? We just don't know.

As an aside, the babies born via Caesarean section also go through the same developmental stages as the normally born baby, but the events are compressed into just a few moments as the baby is being removed from the mother. It's actually harder to deal with than regular birth, as it's experienced as a terrible shock with all the stages crammed into just a brief interval. Thus, empirically we've found that Caesarean babies are no more fortunate than normal births, and may in fact be more impaired around stages involving birth than children born normally.

Archetypes and the Music of the Spheres

As our model predicts, there is a developmental event for every possible peak experience, and an awareness of archetypes is another example of this principle. The event is accessed just after the birth. As you move forward in time after leaving the birth canal, there is a short moment in time that has a strong archetypal feeling to it. It's quite a unique experience—your awareness goes to a 'place' where you become aware of differently-sized spheres that appear to be almost planetary sized, that move forward and back in a sort of dance. Each sphere is an 'archetype', and emits a musical note, or tone. Together, all the spheres make a harmonious cacophony that shouldn't sound pleasing, but does. On the other side of the 'space' one finds oneself in is Gaia consciousness, made up of what looks like an apartment building with the wall removed—each room being a species consciousness. Humans as a species are in one of those spaces.

I've tested this event on other volunteers. It's fairly easy to have them slowly re-experience the birthing sequence to find the moment when they need to access this experience. Like so many events, healing the trauma around it doesn't mean that you automatically know how to use it in any way. This experience is used in certain kinds of shamanic activities beyond the scope of this book.

I can only assume that the Greeks were aware of this peak experience based on their languaging that fits it so well. As far as I can tell, these archetypes are not related to ones that are referred to in psychology books—these are much more fundamental. I suspect they are related to transit astrology, however.

The Layers of the Aura and Their Biological Counterparts

Introduction

One of the key purposes of the work in this book is to define a model that ties all psychic and spiritual experiences into an underlying mechanism. One such experience is the layers of aura described by a number of people, most notably Barbara Brennan in her *Hands of Light*. This phenomenon is useful in understanding and healing certain kinds of emotional and physical problems. See Volume 3 for specifics on this topic.

Our model suggests that these sorts of phenomena exist due to biological events, and that's exactly what we've found in the cases we've looked at. Even though the layers of the aura are non-physical, these layers have a sensation to the body that mimics an underlying pre-birth biological experience. As far as we know, these layers are not formed by developmental biology, but the body experiences them as being identical to the biological layers and handles them in the same way. The biological layers come into existence during early developmental stages *in utero*, during the single or few cell period. The non-physical layers have a characteristic egg shape to them, even thought the adult does not look egg shaped, because their origins are during biological developmental stages when the body *was* egg shaped, as during conception or implantation. Interestingly, the originating developmental stages generally have to be healed for the non-physical layers to function or be used properly.

The 'Egg Shell' Barrier

There is a non-physical membrane that surrounds the human body. It can be 'seen' as an off-white, hard layer that looks like and is shaped like an egg shell. Although its dimensions can be changed or even extended to surround another person at will, it normally assumes this egg shape about a foot or so from the body, completely enclosing it.

Damage to this layer usually looks like a burned, blackened area.

This layer functions more as a barrier. Its origin is during conception, when the newly fertilized egg solidifies its outer membrane to keep any other sperm from entering. This is why the non-physical barrier has the characteristic shape of a human egg cell. There is a possibility that this barrier has its prototype in coalescence.

This barrier is particularly important for healing and diagnosing certain kinds of emotional and physical problems. This is covered in more detail in Volume 3, and in Volume 2 with reference to 'cords'.

The 'Slippery Surface' Barrier

This layer of the non-physical aura is experienced as a boundary layer that has a slippery or greasy surface. One person describes it as feeling like egg white. It also has an egg shape to it, and it lies inside of the previously mentioned egg shell barrier. Unlike the egg shell barrier, its surface can also have a rotational effect, as if a wind or dust devil were surrounding the body at the barrier. If this wind effect is not happening, it can look patchy and porous.

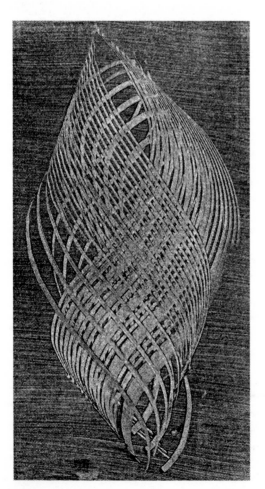

Figure 7.2: An approximate visual impression of the coating applied to the egg or sperm as they leave the ovary and testes respectively. It looks the same after conception. The impression of it persists to the present.

This layer is important in certain kinds of physical problems, and is useful and relevant to phenomena that occur in the spaciousness state of consciousness. This is covered in depth in Volume 3.

Its developmental stage origin is in three different events. The egg receives a coating as it leaves the ovary. The slippery surface is formed underneath that new layer of cells. The sperm also receives a coating as it leaves the testes. Likewise, it also creates a slippery layer when the cells cover it. The two layers are merged during conception. Finally, the slippery coating is activated during the time just before implantation when the zygote sheds the layer of nutrient cells that surrounds it. The zygote makes its outer boundary slippery to disengage the surrounding cells.

Key Points

- Chakras and meridians exist. The same developmental stages that are key to triune brain fusion states are also key to the correct development and utilization of the chakras and the meridian system in our bodies. Trauma around their development needs to be addressed, else many of our natural abilities are impaired. Consequences of healed developmental stages are changes in vision and a radical decrease in the need for sleep.
- Having a peak state or potential ability doesn't always mean that you know how to use it effectively. Training is often required. If your mother didn't unconsciously use it while you were *in utero*, your fetal self doesn't learn how to use it. Using the chakras is a good case in point.
- Blocks to awareness of one's past (and future) lives is also due to trauma in at least one developmental stage. This stage occurs right after ovulation when the egg is coated with a protective covering.

Suggested Reading and Websites

On the near-death experience
- Dr. Raymond Moody MD, *The Light Beyond*, Bantam, 1989.

On past lives
- Grant McFetridge and Mary Pellicer, *The Basic Whole-Hearted Healing Manual (third edition)*, Institute for the Study of Peak States Press, 2003.
- Winafred Lucas, *Regression Therapy: A Handbook for Professionals, Volume 1: Past-life therapy*, Deep Forest Press, 1993.

- Dr. Stanislav Grof, *The Cosmic Game: Explorations of the Frontiers of Human Consciousness*, State University of New York Press, 1998.

Communication with the dead
- Dr. Raymond Moody and Paul Perry, *Reunions: Visionary Encounters with Departed Loved Ones*, Ivy Books, 1994.

Chakras and the layers of the aura
- Barbara Brennan, *Hands of Light: A Guide to Healing Through the Human Energy Field*, Bantam, 1993.
- Karla McLaren, *Your Aura and Your Chakras: The Owner's Manual*, Red Wheel/Weiser, 1998.

Descriptions of out of the ordinary abilities and experiences
- www.ehe.org, the Exceptional Human Experience Network

On the possible future
- Christopher Bache, *Dark Night, Early Dawn*, State University of New York Press, 2000.
- Tom Brown, Jr., *The Vision*, Berkley, 1988. Non-fiction.
- Hank Wesselman, *Spiritwalker: Messages from the Future*, Bantam, 1995. An account of a future life, excellently written. Non-fiction.

A 'Trauma' Approach: Regressing to Developmental Events for Triune Brain and Associated Peak States

Introduction

This chapter is included in this book specifically for professionals and people who are taking training from the Institute. This chapter is for educational purposes only, and is *not* intended for use by the general public. The process in this chapter is designed to be used only with *trained and qualified supervision* because there is a possibility of long term emotional and physical pain as well as life-threatening suicidal feelings. If you are a layman reading this book, we refer you to Chapters 3, 9, 10, 11, and 12 for processes for acquiring peak states that have already been tested on large groups of people and are relatively quick, simple, safe, and effective.

The process covered in this chapter is our core regression process for acquiring triune brain peak states and related states of consciousness. Specifically, the peak states it is designed for are the Hollow state, the Wholeness state, the Inner Gold state, and the Flow Awareness state, all of which are explained elsewhere in this volume. As of this writing, the steps in this process are still under development, and we fully anticipate that they will be changed and improved by the next edition. We include it in this book because the process below is central to our work in discovering the origin of new states and thus improving our Gaia instruction processes (see Chapter 9 for an example of a Gaia instruction process).

We also hope that other technique developers will take this information, improve on it, and incorporate our findings into their own work.

States in this chapter:
- Wholeness
- Hollow
- Inner Gold
- Underlying Happiness
- Beauty Way
- Flow Awareness

About This Regression Process

Essentially, the process in this chapter is just a list of detailed descriptions of key developmental stages that we've found are critical for triune brain and related peak states, along with the solutions to some other specific problems that need to be dealt with. In essence, this process is just an expanded version of material described in Chapter 6 and 7. Healing these stages has the effect of giving the states listed above to many, but not all, of the people doing the healing. To do the process steps, we have assumed that you are already in a state of consciousness that allows you to regress at will, or that you can get help in doing so. The prerequisite state for being able to regress at will is an Inner Brightness state and is covered in Volume 2. For people who can't regress at will, we've had some success using the images and music we will be describing. We also assume that you know a healing technique that can heal any relevant trauma. Any process that works quickly, effectively, and completely to heal trauma such as a meridian therapy or Whole-Hearted Healing would be fine.

What You Can Expect to Achieve

Most people who finish this process will perceive big internal changes. They include:

- A deep and wonderful feeling of being 'whole' as you enter the Wholeness state.
- You enter the Hollow state or one of the lesser triune brain states such as the Beauty Way or Underlying Happiness. If you go into the full Hollow state, you feel like your body turns to air with a skin covering, and everything becomes effortless. If you already have the Inner Brightness state, you are likely to be able to perceive that your five brains coalesce into a ball around your belly button. In terms of the Perry diagram, all the circles superimpose as the brain awarenesses fuse together.
- You become a golden color inside your body. However, we believe this change is only visible with the Inner Brightness state, or while healing physical injuries using the WHH method.
- The chakras will coalesce into a ball just above and superimposed on the brain fusion ball, giving the Flow Awareness state. To see this chakra ball also requires the Inner Brightness state, although it can be felt as a feeling of flow going through the body from the back to the front.
- Assuming you heal the meridian-chakra connections during the coalescence stages, you can expect to only need about three or four hours sleep to feel well rested.

The Effectiveness of the Process

We can say for certain that most people will not find this process as it's written effective in giving them the desired peak states. This is because people in average consciousness need a fairly rare peak state, the Inner Brightness state, to easily regress to the correct moments in time. We believe that other approaches for doing regression might bypass this problem, but as of this writing we rarely do the process with people in average consciousness and so we haven't optimized it for them.

Even among people with the Inner Brightness state, we know that not everyone is successful in getting the states listed. At this time we don't have good statistics on how effective this process is for acquiring states even among this unusual group. We generally do this process one on one and so tailor it to people's individual needs, dealing with any unusual problem on the spot. This gives us better results than just a rote following of printed steps would.

As we suspect that some of the required developmental stages are not yet identified, we don't expect that this process will give the Hollow state to everyone. However, it is quite likely that it will at least give one of the other lesser triune brain peak states, which you may recall build up to the Hollow state.

Even taking all of this into account, not everyone with the Inner Brightness state is able to acquire the target states. We don't know why this is, but we have several hypotheses: missing developmental stages in our process; incomplete healing of any given stage, perhaps due to inadequate mastery of the power therapies; inadequate healing of related pre- or post traumas that relate to the developmental stages for the particular person; generational traumas interfering with the healing (covered in detail in Volume 3); unresolved earlier traumas described in Volume 2; the trauma that can occur at the start of birth, described in Volume 2; other unusual phenomena covered in Volumes 3; and reasons unknown.

Choosing to Acquire a Subset of the Listed States

It is possible to just heal some of the developmental stages to acquire specific states. However, since the stages build on each other, skipping steps, especially the coalescence stages may block the effect that healing later stages can give.

- The Wholeness state: Placental death trauma is key for this state. Do Steps 2, 7a, 9, 10, and 11. This seems to work fairly well on its own.
- The Underlying Happiness state: Healing implantation is key for this state. Do Steps 2, 8, 10, and 11. However, as this is a recent discovery, we don't have data yet on how effective these steps are by themselves.

- The Beauty Way state: Healing conception often gives the Beauty Way (or Inner Peace) state. Do Steps 2, 7, 10, and 11.
- Flow Awareness state: It is possible to just heal the chakra and meridian parts of the coalescence and conception to reduce the need for sleep or get the Flow Awareness state. Do Steps 2, 3e, 5e, 7b, 10, and 11.
- The Inner Gold state: Do Steps 2, 4, and 6, 10, and 11.

POTENTIAL RISKS

Do not use this process unless you are fully and completely willing to accept anything that happens to you as a result of proceeding. Do not use this process if you've had the previous experience of suicidal feelings.

We've used this process (excluding steps 8 and 9) on about 50 people with no ill effects. However, these were not randomly chosen subjects, so we make no predictions on what will happen if large groups of people use this process. It is still VERY experimental. We have NOT tested Step 9, the death of the placenta on more than a handful of people as of this writing, and we suspect this step may induce suicidal feelings in some people. The stage occurs during a period of time that sometimes holds extreme suicidal feelings. When this material gets triggered by going to the stage, the suicidal feelings can overwhelm a person. We suggest that you do not do Step 9 unless you are with competent assistance, and do not already have a problem with suicidal feelings to start with.

We recommend at the minimum doing the process with a trained and licensed therapist who is familiar with healing *in utero* trauma and, if you add Steps 7 and 9 into the process, is also familiar with suicidal clients. We are not liable for your use of this process if you chose to use it. Do NOT use this process unless you are prepared for the potential consequences. This process is not safe, and can be very dangerous to even well-adjusted individuals. It is given in this book only as a research tool for professionals who are familiar with and prepared for what can happen. A much safer, faster, and simpler process for just the Inner Peace state is in Chapter 9, and an expanded version of that process for the Hollow state is in Volume 2. If you are not a professional accustomed to this kind of work we recommend you use those other processes instead.

Another problem with this regression process is that it puts you very close to a major set of traumas that involve intense and often terrifying feelings of annihilation. For most people, these traumas occur earlier in time, so we note in the steps where to avoid going earlier. For more on

these traumas and the states they confer, see Volume 2 on the Sacred and
the Realm of the Shaman states.

The potential risks or problems in using this regression process are:
- Suicidal feelings arising that may cause you to kill yourself.
- You might find as you work with your chakras that you either become physically manic or completely exhausted. Continue to heal
  the relevant traumas until this disappears.
- You might experience extreme physical pain, and become nauseous
  and vomit while healing some of these stages (especially during
  birth). Prepare for this!
- If you don't fully heal the traumas, you might find that you have
  'new' physical and emotional symptoms and problems in your life
  until you finish the healing. Persistence may be required.
- You may encounter the terror of being annihilated before or during
  the coalescence stages. Persevering will cause extreme changes in
  consciousness as you move into states that you were not expecting.
  Do not continue healing these annihilation events before reading
  about the Realm of the Shaman state in Volume 2. You need to be
  able to make an informed choice on whether you want these very
  dramatic states now or not.

The Choice of Therapeutic Healing Techniques

In this book, we make the assumption that you've already been exposed to
the leading edge in healing techniques, especially the power therapies, as
used for both post-birth and pre-birth trauma. We also assume you are already aware of modern prenatal information, such as: the conscious
awareness of the fetus, sperm, and egg; the tremendous impact prenatal
injury has in people's lives; etc. If this is news to you, we recommend you
review some of the journals or books at the end of this chapter.

We derived the process in this chapter using the basic Whole-Hearted
Healing (WHH) technique, and so it is optimized for use with WHH. This
therapy is available from the website www.PeakStates.com, or from *The
Basic Whole-Hearted Healing Manual* by Grant McFetridge and Mary
Pellicer. But any technique that can totally heal a trauma should work.
Examples of such therapies are Traumatic Incident Reduction (TIR), Eye
Movement Desensitization and Reprocessing (EMDR), Tapas Acupressure Technique (TAT), Emotional Freedom Technique (EFT), any of the
other meridian therapy techniques, etc. Regardless of the technique used,
the end point of the trauma healing should be a feeling of calm, peace and
lightness, with a sense of bright inner light in every part of your body and a
sensation that you're very large. If you can't get to this type of endpoint
with the therapy that you are using, switch to one of the others.

We recommend Terry Larimore's and William Emerson's work, especially the use of body motions for particular developmental stages. As precellular stages are still virtually unknown even in the field of pre- and perinatal psychology, we hope to see new techniques and data evolve soon. See Chapters 4 and 6 for more on this subject.

Although this fact is not well known, due to the kind of consciousness you have in the womb (or earlier) the only events that are experienced as traumatic always involve physical injury. The injury can sometimes be easy to miss, so don't forget to stay with the trauma until the injury is found and completely healed. You will know that the injury is fully healed when you feel very large and bright everywhere in your body in that past moment. Since the process involves only pre-birth developmental stages, all traumas in them will have a physical injury component.

Changing the Past

Some healing therapies have the ability to actually change the client's past. This statement is completely outside of our cultural beliefs, but this phenomenon is encountered in almost all of the powerful therapies. We mention it here because you will see this when doing this process. What do I mean? Our cultural belief about trauma is that it's just a memory, and when the healing is done, the memory is still exactly the same, but the emotional charge is gone. Although this is an adequate model for most processes, this idea would cause the client doing this regression process to quit too soon before the fusion state changes come into effect. In particular, as you go through the healing, iterating to completion, you'll find that totally new experiences that were not there when you started will arise. You have to continue the healing process until these changes no longer occur.

For example, most people who heal the conception trauma take the events that happened and simply take the emotional pain off it. However, if it is fully healed, the actions of the sperm and egg can change, and the experience becomes almost a dance between a royal couple, an egg that feels now like a queen, and a sperm that feels like a king.

Having experiences that are outside the dominant paradigm are not always comfortable. You can choose to ignore our interpretation of events (i.e. changing the past), but you still need to incorporate the observed phenomena. This means that the final events sometimes bear little or no resemblance to what was first experienced.

The Developmental Events Regression Process for Triune Brain and Associated Peak States
Revision 1.0, August 2003

- Outcome: The Hollow, Wholeness, and Inner Gold peak states, or lesser triune brain fusion states.
- Required state: Inner Brightness, although it can sometimes be done from ordinary consciousness.
- Dangers: Evokes major trauma in many people that may take weeks or even months to heal. In some cases, it may evoke suicidal feelings. Should not be attempted without qualified support and guidance.
- Success rate: Probably 50% of the people using this approach are successful.
- Comments: The process is probably still missing key developmental events.

There are five main developmental events that have to be done correctly for fusion of the brains and fusion of the chakras. Two occur before the egg and sperm become single-celled organisms, during stages called coalescence. The third happens at conception, the fourth at implantation, and the fifth at birth. Iterating on each of these developmental stages will almost certainly be required to heal them completely. In addition, there is a birth developmental moment that can sometimes interfere with the process. This is the moment where birth is initiated by the fetus. We're putting this off until the chapter on Gaia consciousness in Volume 2 because more background is needed to understand what the problem is and how to deal with it.

We've included a step that causes one to become a golden color inside the body. We're not totally sure why it's important, but both the alchemists and people doing extensive inner work get to the point where this state occurs, so we've included it below. The step is primarily from a single developmental moment in the egg and sperm's precellular existence.

We suggest using music at each of the developmental stages, but you'll have to decide if this is an aid or a hindrance. Using our music selections might be more of a problem than a help, because the auditory music only bears a relatively slight resemblance to the actual 'spiritual' non-audible music. This spiritual music also usually changes as the stage progresses, making our music selection sometimes inappropriate for the entire course of the stage. You might want to experiment with and without music.

Although the process is shown in steps with the implication that they can be done fully one at a time, many people find they have to iterate through the steps due to the interactions the stage traumas have with each other. Some people do all the steps in a day—others take many months to go through them all. It is preferable to heal the earliest material first if at all possible, as it makes doing the later stages easier, and so we've laid the steps out in that sequence. However, not everyone can do this. Many people find they need to work with later trauma first before going earlier.

Step 1: Record Your Experience

Use a tape recorder, or take notes while doing the process, or have someone with you who will record what you have to say. It's important that you take notes for several reasons. First, you need to have them so you can recall what happened when you write up all the details of the work afterwards. In particular, healed issues often fade away by the next morning. If you put it off, the details become impossible to recall.

These notes have several uses. Material that wasn't healed the first time can be located as you go over your notes. For some people, strong emotions or physical sensations will arise from reviewing unfinished issues. You will also want this material for your work with other people in the future. Unusual events may happen that you want to study with colleagues later, and so a written record is essential. And as this work is still under development, we'd appreciate hearing about any new discoveries that you might make!

Step 2: Clear Out Blocking Issues

Heal any 'big issue' that you have first. This allows your attention to be fully on the developmental traumas. If you need several sessions to complete the process, you might have to heal the 'big issue of the day' at the beginning of each session. In most cases, you will probably find that whatever the issue is today, it is related to one of the developmental stages covered in this process—although not necessarily the one you were working on at the end of the last session. This principle that you need to work on the material that's at the top of your attention list before being able to move to new areas successfully is something that is also recognized in TIR processing.

Using Gaia command peak state processes (described in the next chapter) on large numbers of people uncovered an odd phenomenon. Some of our clients won't go into a peak state even though they've eliminated the developmental traumas UNTIL they also heal their 'big issue'—even if they heal it after the peak state process! Then they just pop into the peak state automatically and stay there. This problem occurs in about 10 to 20% of the studied people. Oddly, in most of these people there generally is just one particular issue. We suspect that this same phenomenon occurs with the process in this chapter, although we don't know for certain.

Example:
> Paula Courteau describes her experience doing this process: "My
> healing was not straightforward at all... For one thing, I'd already
> done the placenta's death. BUT I had a whole pile of very severe
> traumas that took place before the egg and sperm fusion, while the
> individual awarenesses were still in their timeless 'rings'. Ovary
> and sperm formation traumas and serious implantation and birth
> problems were also in the way. These traumas were not in neat,
> consequential 'stacks', but in untidy, interdependent piles, with
> physical injuries at each stage. The entire process took months. If
> this is your case, just keep picking at it... Find someone you can
> consult with on a regular basis. The transitional peak states you'll
> get on the way will give you good incentives for continuing."

Step 3: Heal the Precellular Egg Coalescence

To set yourself up for the right trauma, I recommend playing the music
listed below. We've tried to fit real music to the 'spiritual' music that occurs during the stage, but of course the match is not perfect. For simplicity, we picked common tunes that most people know. Each one applies to
a particular moment in the trauma, and so there are several tunes for the
same developmental experience. Choices are *Somewhere Over the Rainbow, Clair De Lune, I Wonder Who's Kissing Her Now, Rustle of Spring Piano*, or Roger Williams' *Autumn Leaves Coming Down*. I like *Somewhere
Over the Rainbow* the most for this part of the process, although it isn't really the best choice for every moment in time to be healed. It's just simpler
from a practical perspective.

Follow the egg backwards in time to when it is in your mother's womb
in her mother's womb. (In case you didn't know, the eggs are formed when
the mother is still growing *in utero*.) To make regression into the egg easier, it's sometimes helpful to use the feeling that you as the egg are a young
version of your mother. Other people find it helpful to stay aware of their
mother's body surrounding them so they don't accidentally move into
their sperm memories as they regress. Move past ripening and ejection out
of the ovary, then a long regression while in the ovary, past the contraction event that your mom goes through while being born. When you regress far enough, there is a sudden sensation of your mind, heart, and body
brains splitting up and apart.

For the steps that follow, to heal any particular brain consciousness
you need to put your center of awareness (CoA) into the physical location
of the brain you wish to follow backwards in time. Your CoA is where you
would point your finger if you had to tell someone else where 'you' were located in your body. (See Volume 2 for more on this phenomenon.) With
practice, you can maintain your awareness inside more than one brain at
once even though they become physically separated. Beginners usually
have to focus on one brain at a time, and shift back and forth to the others,

moving forward and backwards in time over and over to complete the healing. It's a bit like doing a slow motion replay of a sporting event, first with the camera on one player, then repeating the play with the camera on a different player.

Step 3a: Heal the Mind, Heart, and Body Fusion

You've come to a precellular memory that looks like a large flat space with a sort of long flat table. The precellular 'body' brain looks like a clear flexible distended polyester bag with wrinkles. Near the body bag are the precellular mind and heart brains which look something like turnips, with a root sticking out at the bottom. The mind and heart 'turnips' touch and start becoming circular, sliding together and through each other. They haven't completed moving together as they start moving into the body bag. The mind and heart piece moves into the body bag at what feels like the appendix region, and pain can occur there as they enter. Now, you have a body bag with two rounded turnip structures vertically stacked. The heart turnip continues to change shape into a more rounded structure, as does the mind turnip, and the heart enfolds and encloses the mind. The outer body becomes rounded also. It's a bit like they transform into three concentric spheres. The solar plexus brain becomes elongated like a long skinny egg or a rounded obelisk, and maintains an attachment to the body brain as it goes into and through the other brains, tying them together. At this point, they become one organism and their separation ends.

For people who can't get an outside image of these events, from the inside the brains feel like balloons made of soft leather.

Step 3b: Heal the Precellular Egg Body Brain and Solar Plexus Brain Fusion

Put your CoA into the the lower abdomen and solar plexus region. From the body, heart and mind fusion moment continue going backwards in time as the body and solar plexus (SP) brain. As you continue backwards, the body and solar plexus brains suddenly split apart. (**CAUTION!** Avoid going any earlier in time until you've read the material in Volume 2. Avoid the separation of the brains from the 'infinite ring' where they are first created.) These precellular brains have just separated from their adjacent source matrixes, which look like large rings. The rings are very close together, and the precellular brains come together almost instantly like magnets attracting each other.

Run through their fusion into one physical precellular organism until this stage is healed. The body brain will look like a jiggly sack. The solar plexus brain looks similar, made of the same kind of material but a darker color and smaller. They both look translucent. When they come together and unite, the precellular walls between them dissolve and they then form a continuous wall that surrounds them both. The body and the SP precellular brains remain separate in their own areas. Where they touch, the body sends hundreds of finger-like connections towards the SP, and the SP sends similar fingers that have more of a charcoal color towards the body brain. The thin area between the two brains is filled with these connections.

Step 3c: Heal the Egg Precellular Mind and Buddha Brains Fusion

Move back towards the present to where the mind, heart, and body coalesce. Put your CoA into your head. Go backwards in time as the mind moves out of the body bag, then further to the time where the Buddha brain suddenly separates from the mind. (**CAUTION!** Avoid going any earlier in time until you've read the material in Volume 2. Avoid the separation of the brains from the 'infinite ring' where they are first created.) The precellular brains have just separated from their source matrixes, which look like rings. The precellular brains detach from the rings and then float together. The mind looks like a big donut, and the Buddha looks like a smaller donut. The mind donut has slots in its center. The Buddha donut has protrusions on its outer surface. The Buddha moves into the mind, connecting the protrusions and slots together. It's like a little donut inside the opening of a large donut. Repeatedly run through these events until they are fully healed.

Step 3d: Heal the Egg Precellular Placental Brain Fusion

Move backwards in time from the mind, heart, and body coalescence. Go back in time into the placental brain awareness before it merged with the other precellular brains. This regression is a bit tricky as there is no easy place to put your CoA in the present as in the previous steps. Since this brain dies at birth, usually with considerable trauma, the 'sense' of this brain can be a bit unfamiliar. It's helpful to already have had some experience in merging with this brain while it is attached to the fetus. However, it's not necessary—you can deliberately move your awareness into the precellular placental brain once you can perceive it using the description that follows.

The time zone we want to heal is just after the precellular placental brain has just left its 'infinite ring'. (**CAUTION!** Avoid going any earlier in time until you've read the material in Volume 2. Avoid the separation of the brains from the 'infinite ring' where they are first created. Unlike the other brains, this one comes off the ring with a sort of slow, rolling, deliberate 'spin' to it.) The infinite ring that the placental brains come from has a very 'etheric' quality to it, and can be hard to notice. The placental precellular brain is also hard to perceive—it also has a very etheric quality to it. In fact, it has the same sort of quality that the children's cartoon 'Casper the Friendly Ghost' portrays. You can see things behind it, and you can notice it more because of the disruption on 'light' bending around it, not because you're easily 'seeing' it like the other brains.

The precellular placental brain looks like a transparent bag, like the body bag but bigger. The other brains come into the body bag and then the placental bag comes into the body bag and surrounds or 'goes over' the other five brains while they are merging, with the sense of being a sort of protection. When the other brains finish merging, the placental bag then merges with all of them simultaneously. It has no chakras of its own.

Example:
> Paula continues; "At first, the placental bag failed to open. Instead, it wrapped itself like a closed plastic bag, snaking between each brain and isolating them from each other. After I healed the placental brain's trauma, I also had to go heal the physical injuries sustained by each brain. I hurt at the top of the head, diagonally across the head from the bridge of the nose to the nape of the neck; across the neck; along the diaphragm to the back; and across the belly at umbilical level."

Step 3e: (Optional) Heal the Meridians and Chakras

This is an optional step to get the Flow Awareness state and radically decrease the need for sleep. If used, it needs to be done in conjunction with Step 5e and Step 7a for full effect. (**CAUTION!** This step has the potential problem of hyperactivity or complete exhaustion if the healing is not done correctly. Do not do this step without qualified supervision. See Chapter 7 for more information.) Each of the 'turnip' brains has several glowing balls (chakras) associated with it, and they move with their respective precellular brains. As the chakras come in to the body bag a webbing forms (the meridians from Chinese medicine) that anchors these glowing balls in place. This anchorage is quite physical. The webbing is like thick silver-white silken or woven cord. It looks like a webbing as soon as it appears. Healing the anchorage of the chakras into the webbing correctly is what reduces the need for sleep.

As we've said previously, the brain awarenesses fuse together into a ball as the precellular brains physically merge together in the body bag. As the brain awarenesses fuse together, the chakras also start to move together. The chakra balls then fuse together into one ball inside the precellular egg. It looks like a white silvery colored ball with a distinct edge. To the person doing the regression, about 2/3 of the ball feels like it is located below the SP, and about 1/3 is located above the SP in their body in the present. Note that for most people, on the first pass through

this event the chakras do not form a ball. This occurs only after traumatic
material is healed. However, some people can will the chakras into a ball
in spite of traumatic material. The problem with this is that the chakras
will come apart as soon as the effort is released. Be sure to heal this stage,
not force it to be what you want.

Example:

> Paula continues: "At times I found it very hard to tell which
> precellular coalescence I was in, since I kept jumping from stage to
> stage. Internally, both felt like the individual parts were soft
> leather balloons with tails on them. A couple of times I saw myself
> as transparent, vaguely cubic blocks. I always felt like myself, not
> my mother or father. My main landmark was checking who was on
> the outside of me: if I was in sperm fusion, I would feel my father,
> young, and as I healed further I'd often feel him intensely loving
> my mother. In egg fusion I'd feel my mother, often as a baby or a
> fetus, and my grandmother around her. There were severe genera-
> tional traumas on both sides, and I needed to heal those before I
> could proceed. My grandmother had a bad leg injury, and after I'd
> healed her I felt her legs like two strong pillars, a solid and safe
> base to grow up on.

> The main injury in the egg fusion was a split at mid-body. My
> mind and heart had joined outside of the body container, and my
> solar plexus was painfully holding on to the heart awareness from
> within the container, as through a bag. Also, my heart was on
> backwards, possibly in both fusions, which may have caused oddi-
> ties at later stages: as a sperm, I happily swam on my back; I also
> tried to implant on my back.

> I saw a young version of me, standing defiantly, holding a gun
> and surrounded by war paraphernalia. I merged with 'her' and dis-
> covered she was to be the oldest sister in my family…and had died
> at this egg fusion stage, due to a terrible emotional trauma to my
> grandmother… and she was me! A very recent past life, and a
> good example of the non-linear quality of time: my present self,
> the youngest sister, still had to run through the terrible constric-
> tion of my grandmother's emotional shock.

> Each brain pretended to be something else: my solar plexus
> pretended to be my heart, since my heart was outside the con-
> tainer, and felt harried by the extra work and unable to do its own.
> My Buddha brain tried to be useful and built a crude version of the
> mesh of meridians, something the solar plexus was supposed to
> do. My body brain looked like a swamp monster. In the sperm fu-
> sion my Buddha brain pretended to be a baby.

> In the earlier stages of healing, it felt like a lot of injuries were
> analogs of birthing traumas: my head feeling stuck and crushed as
> it tried to force its way down a narrow passage, that sort of thing…

In later repetitions of the sequence this was replaced by wonderful impressions of my heart awareness being massaged and squeezed lovingly and infused with physical sensuality as it passed through the body container, and my mind receiving the same treatment plus a strong dose of emotional love as it made its way through both."

Step 4: Complete the Alchemical Gold Precellular Egg 'Fountain' Stage

From the precellular fusion moment in the egg, go forward in time, and you will come to a place that looks like a fountain. The precellular egg goes into what looks a bit like a basin that collects the fountain 'water', and turns a bright golden color as it 'absorbs' the 'water'. (Another of our experimental subjects found herself also becoming the fountain. Some experimentation may be required.)

We know this stage is important, as afterwards healed areas fill with a golden substance that we recognize as ourselves. Apparently, the alchemists agreed, as there is a woodcut print showing this developmental stage from the 1500s. However, we're just not really sure why it's important yet. One of our experimental subjects felt the golden color was a permanent reconnection to the Creator energy (see Volume 2), rather than a momentary experience as occurs in previous developmental stages.

Step 5: Heal the Precellular Sperm Coalescence

The music for this developmental stage is "76 Trombones". I don't have any alternatives, although there are probably many.

Go back in time, past conception, to when the sperm is still in the father's testicles. The event that we're searching for occurs about eight weeks before conception. As an aid to telling the egg stages from the sperm stages, you might try regressing past conception with the sensation that you've become a young version of your father. Others report they don't feel like their father, but can get there by feeling their father around them. Go back in the sperm's life to its precellular existence. The sperm, like the egg, is assembled from precellular body, solar plexus, heart, mind, and Buddha precellular brains that are all grown separately. As you reach the right time, the mind, heart and body suddenly feel like they split apart.

I'll repeat the relevant instructions from Step 3 on using your center of awareness (CoA). To heal any particular brain consciousness you need to put your CoA into the physical location of the brain you wish to follow backwards in time. Your CoA is where you would point your finger if you had to tell someone else where 'you' were located in your body. (See Volume 2 for more on this phenomenon.) With practice, you can maintain your awareness inside more than one brain at once even though they become physically separated. Beginners usually have to focus on one brain at a time, and shift back and forth to the others, moving forward and backwards in time over and over to complete the healing.

Step 5a: Heal the Precellular Body, Heart, and Mind Brain Fusion

The precellular sperm brains look differently than the precellular egg brains. All the precellular sperm brains look like rounded boxes and are different sizes. The mind brain is a box with the Buddha brain inside looking like a smaller box. The body brain also looks like a box with the solar plexus (SP) brain looking like another much smaller box attached to the outside. The body box is the biggest, the mind the next largest, and the heart the smallest box. During this part of the coalescence, the mind and heart first touch and start connecting, before they touch the body. Then the heart end of the brain boxes comes together with the body brain box, a bit like a totem pole, with the body, heart, and mind stacking on top of each other, with the SP a small box attached to the body at the side. This series of events happens at almost the same time.

The boxes then move inside each other, with the mind in the middle, the heart surrounding it, and the body surrounding everything. The SP floats free in the outermost body brain box. The SP then becomes an elongated rectangular shape, and hooks all the boxes together by stretching into the other boxes while remaining attached to the body container.

Wes Gietz described the start of the sperm coalescence as follows: "Just before coalescence, the precellular brains are each in their own compartments but very adjacent to each other, and recognize their relationship to each other. They're like clear plastic boxes that are side by side and luminous." I have also heard this scene described several times by clients healing trauma at this moment as side-by-side blobs quivering in fear.

The other major difference from the egg stage is that there are what looks like an infinite number of chakra balls going up and down into the distance.

Repeatedly run through these events until they are fully healed.

Step 5b: Heal the Precellular Sperm Body and Solar Plexus Brain Fusion

The steps and scene for this stage are similar to the corresponding egg stage. Put your CoA into the the lower abdomen and solar plexus region. From the heart, mind and body fusion, continue going backwards in time as the body and solar plexus (SP) brain. As you continue backwards, the body and solar plexus brains suddenly split apart. (**CAUTION!** Avoid going any earlier in time until you've read the material in Volume 2. Avoid the separation of the brains from the 'infinite ring' where they are first created.) The precellular brains have just separated from their adjacent source matrixes which look like large rings. The rings are very close together. The brains come off as rings, and change to baggy looking structures. They almost instantly snap together like magnets attracting each other. Run through their fusion into one physical precellular organism until this stage is healed. As the body and SP quickly snap together, the walls between them dissolve. The baggy shape squares up, and like the equivalent egg stage, the two brains send interpenetrating 'fingers' into each other at their mutual boundary. Repeatedly run through these events until they are fully healed.

Step 5c: Heal the Precellular Sperm Mind and Buddha Brain Fusion

Move back towards the present to where the precellular sperm mind, heart, and body coalesce. Put your CoA into your head. Go backwards in time as the mind moves out of the body box, then earlier to where the mind box separates from the others, to the even earlier time where the Buddha brain suddenly separates from the mind. (**CAUTION!** Avoid going any earlier in time until you've read the material in Volume 2. Avoid the separation of the brains from the 'infinite ring' where they are first created.) The precellular brains have just separated from their source matrixes which look like rings. The precellular brains, looking like donuts, detach from the rings and then float together. The mind looks like a donut, and the Buddha brains looks like a smaller donut. They hook together and become boxy looking, with the Buddha inside the mind box. Repeatedly run through these events until they are fully healed.

Step 5d: Heal the Precellular Sperm Tail Brain Fusion

Go to the fusion of the precellular sperm brains again. This time, put your CoA into the sperm tail brain. It doesn't quite feel like a brain as the others do, but still feels like an intelligence. This probably requires you to have the Inner Brightness state to have enough awareness to do so, but we'll give a description for people in average consciousness as an aid. (**CAUTION!** Avoid going any earlier in time until you've read the material in Volume 2. Avoid the separation of the brains from the 'infinite ring' where they are first created.) Like the other brains, the precellular sperm tail brain is formed and detaches from its own infinite ring of other sperm tail precellular brains.

The precellular sperm tail brain floats outside in the fluid surrounding the other brains after they coalesce. As this progresses, the tail brain attaches to the outer surface of the newly coalesced sperm. It looks like a long squiggly snake that's quite small in comparison to the rest. To the person doing the regression, it feels like the tail brain hooks 'behind' the body on

the spinal column. Repeatedly run through these events until they are
fully healed.

Step 5e: (Optional) Heal the Meridians and Chakras

This is an optional step to get the Flow Awareness state and radically decrease the need for sleep. If used, it must be done in conjunction with Step
3d and Step 7a for full effect. (**CAUTION!** This step has the potential
problem of hyperactivity or complete exhaustion if the healing is not done
correctly. Do not do this step without qualified supervision. See Chapter 7
for more information.) Each of the boxy-looking precellular sperm brains
brains has several glowing balls (chakras) associated with it. Unlike the
precellular egg brains, the precellular sperm heart brain has a series of
chakra balls going up and down apparently to infinity. As of this writing,
we believe these balls have something to do with the other sperm, as the
sperm act like a group intelligence later on in development.

This part of the coalescence happens just as the fusion of the brains
into a ball is ending. The meridians (from Chinese medicine) first appear
as very fine, white-silver looking threads just as the chakra balls first start
coming together. As coalescence proceeds the threads form a webbing.
Unlike the egg coalescence, the chakras do not anchor in physically, but
do energetically and quite solidly. Healing this anchorage is what changes
the need for sleep.

The chakra balls then fuse together into one ball inside the precellular
sperm. It looks like a white ball of fog without a distinct edge. To the person doing the regression, about 2/3 of the ball feels like it is located below
the SP, and about 1/3 is located above the SP referenced to their body in
the present. Repeatedly run through these events until they are fully
healed.

Example:
> Paula continues: "In sperm fusion, once origin traumas were out
> of the way, I soon felt the chakras lined up and continuing above
> and below me. I got the impression that some of the extras were re-
> lated to the consciousnesses of the other sperm."

Step 6: Complete the Alchemical Gold Precellular
Sperm 'Fountain' Stage

Like the precellular egg, the precellular sperm has a nearly identical 'alchemical fountain' developmental stage. From the precellular fusion moment in the sperm, go forward in time, and you will come to a place that
looks like a fountain. The precellular sperm goes into what looks a bit like
a basin that collects the fountain 'water', and turns a bright golden color
as it 'absorbs' the 'water'. (Another of our volunteers found himself ab-

sorbing the 'water' as if flowed out of the basin, in what seemed like a narrow trickle. Some experimentation may be required.)

Step 7: Heal the Conception Stage

As of this writing, we've found that many people get the Beauty Way state by healing a single developmental stage trauma—conception. If this is your purpose, just doing Steps 7, 10 and 11 will often suffice. However, the Hollow state requires the healing of a variety of developmental stages and conception is just one of them.

The music to assist in healing this event starts with "When you Wish Upon a Star".

You can get to this trauma by imagining your parents are getting married (with an extreme sexual charge), and your sperm self feels like a young version of your dad, and your egg self feels like a young version of your mom. You can heal them either individually or simultaneously. The egg can see the sperm as a bright light approaching. The egg knows to choose the sperm that's brightly lit up like a white Christmas tree ornament.

A lot of people believe that the first sperm to dig through the egg's covering wins, but this is not correct—the egg chooses the one that has 'light'. The egg opens a passage in the center of its chest. The egg pulls the sperm's head in, the tail detaches from the sperm in what feels like your upper back, and then the sperm head opens along a line splitting the left from the right side, and folds back.

As the sperm head splits open, your sperm self feels like it's dying, and it can be very intense the first few times! Most people have great difficulty in facing this event without assistance. The first movement of Beethoven's Fifth Symphony is a good choice for the sperm death event. To locate the moment, imagine your dad dying just as your parents marry. Around this time, the egg seals its shell around itself. The leftover sperm-covering then moves out to the egg wall and adheres there. Then what feels like wires move around inside 'you' as the chromosomes move, and the chakras coalesce. At this point conception is finished.

Repeat it over and over, as you will almost certainly miss subtleties at first. This developmental stage needs to be healed until the egg and the sperm each feel like a king and queen having a royal marriage, without any trauma. The first few times, you probably won't get the royal wedding part, but as you heal the physical damage and change the past it evolves into what it was supposed to have been.

Step 7a: Heal the Sperm Tail Detachment and Death Trauma

Healing this event is often required so that the placental death trauma
can be fully healed in Step 10. Music to help evoke the sperm tail death
experience is Robert Gass's *Gate Gate*, and *Beyond the Beyond*. For the
sperm side of the experience, use those songs and Gass's *A Sufi Song of
Love*.

Stay at the initial part of the conception as the tail detaches from the
sperm. To stay with the sperm, recall it feels like a young version of the father. Keep your awareness in the sperm tail and in the sperm at the same
time if possible. If not, move your CoA alternately between them until
they are both completely healed. The tail detaches from the area around
the bottom of the shoulder blades, and often detachment injuries occur.
The tail is self-aware and as it dies, its trauma has to be healed. At its
death, an experience of its essential self reabsorbed by the remaining
sperm body that is inside the egg has to occur. It appears to give people an
ease with using different visual orientations, such as when looking at engineering drawings that are reversed or mirror imaged.

There may also be trauma from the egg's point of view as the tail detaches and dies.

Step 7b: (Optional) Join the Sperm and Egg Chakras Together

We recommend healing any conception chakra trauma. For most people,
doing this with Step 3d and Step 5e reduces the amount of sleep they need
and gives them the Flow Awareness state. The chakras from the sperm
and the egg come together and form a disk with indentations just above
your navel. To locate this event in time, we go to when the sperm opens its
head and the material starts mixing into the egg, and both brain awareness
balls come together. (There are only brain balls if you've done coalescence, otherwise there are five separate brains coming together.) Both of
the brain balls slightly misalign within themselves, like circles in a bullseye
becoming off center, but they don't unfuse or come apart. This misalign-
ment allows the egg and sperm brains to slide together. Then the sperm
and egg brains merge together, heart to heart, mind to mind, etc. Next, as
the brains are almost finished merging, the chakra balls come together
and flatten out to become more disc like. The indentations form simultaneously as they come together. As the disc starts forming, the meridians
sort of wobble or shimmer together, as if they were tying to figure out how
to come together properly. This happens almost simultaneously with the
formation of the chakra disc.

As the disk forms the scalloped edges, the disk cements into the meridians so that the energy inside the meridians moves in synch with the rotation of the disc, a bit like water being pumped by a water wheel. Some of

our experimental subjects have reported suddenly being able to see behind objects in the present immediately after this disk is formed when they
fully heal this material.

If you haven't already healed the chakra material in step 3d and 5e, you
will see separate chakras merge together from the egg and sperm (assuming you have the Inner Brightness state and can see them). Although the
seven chakras come together they are not perfectly fused. The other chakras from the sperm remain, looking like a series of balls that continue up
and down to infinity. The seven chakras are a little bit brighter than the
ones from the sperm that go to up and down to infinity. Staying in these
moments until everything is fully headed causes the chakras to come together into a disc temporarily, but any unhealed chakra trauma in the coalescence events causes this disc to fall apart later once attention is
removed from it. The remaining coalescence chakra trauma keeps this
process from completing fully and correctly.

Example:
> Paula continues: "At first the egg felt like it had been raped. The
> sperm entered it through the throat chakra, feeling like a solid ob-
> ject that choked me.
>
> I was quite surprised, then, to experience the sperm, not as an ag-
> gressive bully, but as a happy, loving being, full of pale-blue light,
> headed to his big date with the cellular equivalent of flowers and
> chocolate... and swimming on its back.
>
> The egg is analytical and has a clear, long-range view of causes and
> consequences. While still in the ovary it can see its whole future
> like a tubular movie screen, where any event you focus on jumps
> into the foreground. The sperm, by contrast, is very emotional,
> loving and romantic. Rather than general egg/sperm characteris-
> tics, I wonder if this isn't simply a reflection of my parents' quali-
> ties. Certainly you can find both these sides in me.
>
> Conception itself is a case of mistaken identity. I see a beautiful,
> dim structural sphere, like a geodesic dome. I think I've popped
> out of body, and try merging with it. It is uncommonly difficult.
> After three tries I find myself embracing it in a way that can't be
> reversed: I am in fact the sperm, and a completely bizarre trick of
> time has caused me to mate with this cold lifeless sphere. I'm com-
> mitted, and dammit I haven't even had any fun.
>
> I feel an emptiness in my jaw. Then it seems like my jaw's been
> shot to pieces.
>
> I'm the sperm again... but just the sperm's tail. Its head is happily
> merging, and meanwhile with excruciating slowness the tail is get-
> ting ripped out. Later on I will find out that this is due to a prema-
> ture hardening of the egg's outside cover.

I relive the time when someone tried to kill me by throwing me
into a large window. I want this pain now, to liberate me from the
slowness of this death. I am full of destructive, and self-destructive, rage.

Finally I fill with brilliant blue light. Then the light dims, to a
beautiful transparent slate-blue shot through with white flecks. I
ascend, darkened, ecstatic, to what specifically seems to be the
feminine aspect of the Creator. (Go figure.)

The next trauma is very difficult to attribute at first, because I still
feel female, and what turns out to be the egg feels male. (For almost all of this healing I've felt sort of genderless.) As the sperm
opens up inside the egg, it originally feels like it is being attacked.
It is overwhelmed by self-destructive feelings (in the present I very
much want to bang my head on the wall until it is a bloody pulp)
and thinks that if it throws those feelings out it will harm the egg.
If it doesn't, it will certainly die. In the end it does both. Its awareness ends up sprayed all over the walls of the egg. It's like a murder
scene. Actually, it's very easy to imagine that some really grue-
some murders and suicides are a reenactment of this trauma.

In a later repetition of this, I realize the stuff on the walls is in fact
just my outer covering. My 'self' is a bunch of wiry bits inside this.
In yet another version I simply swell to a huge size and feel my own
bone structure as bits of wire.

A yet later repetition sees all this as a loving dance... but it is my
parents doing this, and I'm excluded.

Yet later, the sperm is swimming the right way up, again feeling
loaded with gifts. The egg feels like a beautiful bride with flowers
in her hair. They recognize each other easily. Both of them are me.
There is a happy and very 'ornate' feel to the whole scene.

Later, I was cleaning up the conception trauma. I got to a place
where the sperm's brains blew apart due to a collision with the fallopian tube wall. I was already in the Underlying Happiness state
after healing the implantation. After healing the body brain, I had
my first experience of a 'state dependent response'. Now, when I
ask myself "What is the reason for living?," it's obvious that the
answer is "To love.""

Step 8: Heal Implantation

This developmental stage is critical for the Underlying Happiness state
with its body-heart fusion, and can be healed by itself to acquire just that
state. Of course, this particular brain fusion builds on the preceding
precellular egg and sperm coalescence stages, so preexisting trauma may
block Underlying Happiness if you only heal implantation. Healing this

stage is also required for the Hollow state as all the developmental stages involving brain fusion need to be trauma free for it.

Implantation starts as the zygote approaches the womb wall. It 'sees' a spot of brightness on the womb wall, and that's where the zygote will implant. From close up, that section of the womb wall looks like roots or fingers of light, a bit like the exposed root base of a toppled tree. As you move towards implantation, the coating of protective cells from the mother on the zygote loosens. You approach implantation from the front of your body—of course, a zygote looks like a round bundle of cells, but from the experiential viewpoint of an adult doing the regression, it feels like it's the front of your present body. As you implant, facing the implant area, the coating splits in front of your body and slides off. It's like taking a long coat off that opens from the front. The coating comes off like a snake shedding its skin just as you touch the womb. Note that many people have trauma at this point due to not being able to anchor into the womb wall the first time they touch it.

Your face touches the womb wall first. You anchor on with the sensation you get when you lay face down on a soft, comfortable mattress. It then feels like a coil of tubing uncoils from the lower belly, and the end of the tube inserts into the womb wall. Then there is a release of fluid through the tube, which feels just like talking a pee. The end of the hose feels like it is merging with the universe, not just the mother, as it anchors into the womb wall. From the placental brain perspective, it feels like you are connecting to the mother from your back, although from the zygote perspective it's like laying on your stomach. These sensations happen simultaneously.

A combination of material from the zygote and the mother form to grow the placenta. The placenta's growth occurs rapidly. The hose expands to form the placenta yet the front of the body is involved also. It feels like placental 'energy' and biology expand outward from the hose, expand down the hose. At the same time, the placental 'energy' is also expanding from the front of the body to the outside layer of the body through the protective layers of the zygote. All the front of the body is involved in what feels like exchanging energy between the zygote and the mother. This energy flow is at least partly a flow of nutrients.

The amniotic sac is forming all around the outside of the body at the same time. The sac is also part of the placenta's awareness.

It's critical to heal the adhesion of the placenta to the womb wall. Incorrect growth at this point makes miscarriages and placental separation problems more likely to occur later in development. As this event progresses, you heal it by smoothing the layers as the placenta expanded outwardly, making sure that everything is connected without any imperfections. It's a lot like taking out the bubbles on a piece of scotch tape that was pressed on something. It feels like the zygote and the womb and the placenta become one, even though biologically they are separate pieces.

Fear around too little or loss of financial income often come from trauma at this stage.

Example:

Paula continues: "Implantation was no picnic. I tried implanting on my side and got kicked off of the uterine wall twice. First the endometrium seemed too thin, like a cheap foam mattress with a hard plank underneath. The second time I was the one holding off in fear. Imagine lying on a thick carpet but somehow holding off with every cell of your body so you just touch the fibers' ends instead of sinking in. Pretty awful.

I had a twin who died in implantation. Elizabeth Noble, in her book Primal Connections, noted that undiagnosed twins are a fairly common occurrence. In my case there were awful dilemmas. I feared that my successful implantation would spell my twin's death. At the same time there was an intense jealousy and fear: if he implanted first, then I would die.

In a later healing I saw the root-like fibers described in the text, but they were unlit and looked jagged and threatening. I found a spot between them and implanted... on my back. In further sessions I healed traumas involving the placental brain. The placental awareness finally turned around and faced my zygote self: I was facing me. Now I implanted on my back, from the placental perspective, and on my front, from the body's point of view. An nutrient layer peeled off cleanly for the first time. There was a deep, deep feeling of union. Something uncoiled from my abdomen; the connection felt sexual and reached way out into the universe. My chest filled with light. The world filled with light.

I felt my hands and legs sink into the mattress as the placental connections formed themselves. My soul expanded. I saw my mother as a sister-soul, an equal. "Are we part of God? Are we that sacred?" I screamed in surprise because, by waves, I encompassed everything."

Step 9: Heal the Placental Death Trauma

Healing this developmental stage usually gives the Wholeness state regardless of the degree of fusion in the other triune brains. Music to help evoke the placental death experience is Robert Gass's Gate Gate and Beyond the Beyond. For the fetal side of the experience, use those songs and Gass's A Sufi Song of Love.

WARNING

This is a major trauma for nearly everyone, and assistance should be used if it becomes necessary to do this step. Be sure to do this only with qualified supervision. THIS TRAUMA CAN POTENTIALLY EVOKE EXTREME SUICIDAL FEELINGS. CONTINUE HEALING WITHOUT STOPPING UNTIL THEY ARE GONE. THEN LOOK FOR ANY EARLIER TRAUMAS WITH SUICIDAL FEELINGS THAT ARISE AND HEAL THEM UNTIL THEY ARE ALSO GONE. Don't stop healing until you are completely free of the emotion, as this feeling can be so strong as to cause a person to kill himself.

This birth stage can evoke suicidal feelings even in clients in whom everything went well during the delivery. In about 20% of births the cord is around the baby's neck. Hospital routine has the doctor cut it while the body of the baby is still in the mother's body.

As this cuts off oxygen to the baby, this creates major, severe additional trauma. In my experience with many clients, regressing to a cord around the neck trauma (in midwifery, a wrapped-cord trauma) usually evokes very strong suicidal feelings. Suicides by hanging are usually related to this trauma.

Come forward in time to the birth, after you've left the mother. Heal the cutting of the cord which usually involving tremendous pain in the umbilical region. There is also the feeling of having the cut cord waving around afterwards, trying to reattach to someone. Stay with this till it feels like the cord withdraws back into the abdomen.

Next, put your attention into the placenta. It is experiencing death shock as it leaves the attachment to the womb wall. Clients report there is usually a very bitter taste as they work on this trauma. As it detaches from the womb, the placenta feels a bit like it flips itself inside out as its concave shape becomes convex. When this trauma is healed, there will be the sensation that the placenta's essence moves from it into the baby body. Note that this trauma may activate earlier related trauma such as implantation that will also need to be healed.

Chapter 13 has a detailed story by Nemi Nath about her experience on healing this trauma.

Example:
> Paula continues: "I started healing this developmental stage by accident. I was working on issues of abandonment by men, and relationships that didn't work. It led to an image of my life being made

up of salvaged scraps, a rickety vessel I called my 'ship of fools'. After healing trauma related to getting insufficient nourishment in
utero and having to 'steal' my own body cell by cell, I found myself
on a beach, newborn by the wreck of my old life. Beside me was my
placenta, with its amniotic sac, like a dying jellyfish. The grief was
extreme. It had been like a lover to me, a traveling companion,
protector, source of warmth and nourishment, partner in crime. It
felt genderless, but then I felt genderless too. From triggers in the
present having to do with relationships to other people, and over a
period of a week, I grieved aspects one after the other. I also went
through anger, and rejecting the placenta. At a key point, I had the
feeling of music coming as a gift from the placenta. It also gave me
a 'blue mesh' or 'blue shroud', which seemed rather useless at first,
like a deceased friend's favorite sweater that comforts, but makes
one grieve even more. The mesh and the music seemed to stream
out of the placenta and into my heart. As I completed the healing,
the blue mesh took permanent residence, and with it came a feeling of safety, a feeling that I would never be homeless again. In my
heart was a big white light, and the placenta later merged with it,
its essence was there. It was incredibly bright and beautiful. This
led to a series of healings about being able to handle and accept
this new material, especially from a spiritual standpoint.

Later, I still had birthing injuries to my neck, back, upper sternum
and chin that were not healing; all I felt was fear and "I can't" and
"Don't!" I found the injuries were actually in the placenta itself,
and that the placenta was self-aware. The neck injury was the cord
being cut, the back injury was the placenta tearing from the uterine wall, the heart injury was the placenta being worried because it
knew it was going to die and that the baby wouldn't be well taken
care of. The sternum was about the placenta losing its
'personhood'; the placenta was becoming a thing, a piece of meat
being thrown in the trash, whereas it used to be a part of a person.
My 'solar plexus' felt like the place where the cord exits from the
placenta. After the cord was cut, the cord felt huge and empty. At
this point I felt an extremely strong urge to cut my neck for real, to
end the excruciating and ghostly pain of the injury. I dealt with
this by absolutely forbidding myself to rise from the couch until
the injury had healed. Resisting the urge to harm myself was very
difficult, even though I had lots of experience in dealing with suicidal feelings.

After detaching from the uterine wall, the placenta suddenly went
from a convex shape matching the wall, to concave, as if it were
flipping itself inside out. Meanwhile, it was full of light and wisdom having to do with divinity. Because the cord was cut, it didn't
have a way to pass this on. When the placenta died, it felt really
peaceful. I saw my father's death during the same healing. The
music that evoked and matched my experience of the placenta dy-

ing was 'Beyond the Beyond' by Robert Gass. The music for solving all the issues the placenta had was 'Gate Gate' also by Robert Gass.

There was some sort of correspondence between the baby and placenta. After healing the placenta, I now could heal those injuries sites in the baby. The baby had the cord wrapped around its neck, and was willing and wanting to die because the only way to save itself (the baby) was to cut the cord, killing the placenta. The complete phrases turned out to be "I can't do this", and "Please god don't ask me to do this". The cord is cut, the placenta dies, and the baby feels responsible. A lot of grief and guilt, ending up with an exhausted baby that doesn't want to live.

I had also found suicidal feelings during an in utero trauma where I was experiencing severe pain that seemed unending but wasn't enough to kill me. It was from my mom drinking coffee. One of the ways I tired to kill myself was detaching my placenta from the womb, which didn't work, like trying to choke oneself. (Although it sure makes me wonder about the causes of placental abruption...) I then found myself trying to tear at my face and head to kill myself. And I tried to harm my mom in anger."

Step 10: Bring the Changes Forward to the Present

The process in this chapter is a good example of 'trolling' that I discuss in The Basic Whole-Hearted Healing Manual, where you go into the past without starting the healing from symptoms in the present. If you are using the WHH regression technique to heal this material, in many cases it will not heal completely unless the way that the trauma was affecting you in the present is brought to consciousness. Let me emphasize this point again—it is critical to become aware of how these early stage traumas have been affecting you in the present. This is a vital and required step, otherwise healing the past may have little or no effect on you in the present moment.

This may also be true if you are using other healing modalities, but this is something we haven't checked on yet. If you are using other modalities, it would probably be a good idea to do this anyway just as a precaution.

For those of you using WHH, you will need to follow the natural flow of time forward from each stage you've been working on after you've finished the healing. You'll find that as you move forward in time, towards the present, traumas that were related to these earlier stages will sequentially and spontaneously come into your awareness and then dissolve. Others, especially ones involving significant physical injuries may need to be intentionally healed. This step will probably have to be iterated a number of times until nothing else changes as you come forward in time. The traumatic events that will arise after healing a developmental stage vary from person to person. For example, after healing conception, Wes had

the first cell division spontaneously come into awareness. After he healed
it, implantation then arose in his awareness, which also required deliberate healing.

Alternately, some people find that as they heal past traumas, brief images of the more recent related traumas will spontaneously appear, often
with an 'updated' version of the phrase attached to the originating
trauma. Take a moment to consider these images and their relationship to
the developmental stage trauma, and then let them go.

Many people report that healing these very early and fundamental developmental stage traumas causes them to suddenly remember their life
occurring very differently than it actually did. This new lifetime is what
would have been the result if they'd been born without the traumas that
had such a major effect on their lives. (Incidentally, this effect of having a
new past also occurs with completely different peak state processes like
the PEAT Past/Future Rundown process.) Be aware of the new past as
well as the original past, and stay with it until there is a sense of the two
time streams converging into the present. The two will eventually merge
together like a 'V' into this present moment of time.

Step 11: Check for Any Other Blocks

If after the above steps you are not in the Hollow state, follow yourself as
you grow and develop from the earliest developmental stages we've listed
to birth, making sure that you don't lose fusion of the brains. If you do,
stop in time, like a freeze frame on a TV show, and heal these traumas as
you go. Iteration might be required, so be sure to record the trauma, including a 'visual' description, a sense of where in the time sequence it's located, the emotional and physical pains involved, and any other details
that you can notice so you can return to it later as required.

Generational traumas also appear to play a part in blocking not only
the complete healing of a given stage but acquiring peak states in general.
Volume 3 covers in detail methods to heal this type of problem.

We would appreciate your contributing to more understanding of potential blocks in the process, so sending us an e-mail of your experience
would be greatly appreciated. Our email address can be found at our
website, www.PeakStates.com.

Example:
> Paula summarizes her new states of consciousness: "After healing
> the placenta's death, I could see glowing, overlapping disks where
> the triune brains are. At first they were pale-gold, with a definite
> boundary of short light rays. The feeling was of happiness and
> wholeness; there was a slightly 'jangly' overtone, as if I'd drunk
> too much coffee. On the second day the lights softened to cloudy
> white balls, without definite edges, and I became very calm. The
> blue mesh I had received from the placenta turned golden, wider

and brighter. At first I was timid about going out: I felt lit up like a Christmas tree and couldn't believe this wouldn't be visible from the outside!

The placenta's loving had been altruistic to a fault: it gave and gave until nothing was left of it. The baby's loving, in contrast, had been about grabbing and holding and wanting to consume. Formerly I had embodied these two extremes, but after the healing I started loving in a much more genuine and balanced way.

Next I tackled the conception, coalescences and implantation, all mixed together. Wholeness disappeared as severe traumas surfaced in my consciousness. The first weeks brought out a variety of fascinating inner-light pyrotechnics: gold and red rays around parts of my body, clouds of soft-colored light, a feeling that each of my cells was individually alive and lit up in green and white; shimmery multicolored rays extending several feet outwards from my body. Some of these patterns were similar to the 'layers' of the aura as described by Barbara Brennan in her book Hands of Light (color plates 7-7 to 7-13).

Each state was unstable, lasting a few hours to a few days, but overall my sense of peace increased. A few times I woke up during the night feeling completely hollow, as if my body was made of air.

I healed trauma to the egg as it exited the ovary and felt my skin peel away! Now my body feels boundaryless, and other people's behavior doesn't affect me personally anymore. Instead of judging, I've become curious and compassionate about my own problems and other people's. This change seems permanent. [Editors note: This state is covered in Volume 2.]

One morning, after a week's hiatus, I returned to my orchard-pruning job. Something important was missing... It took me half an hour to figure out what it was. My fear of heights was gone! I'd healed several things in the interim, but I suspect the 'falling' into the uterus, just before implantation, was the key trauma. This change also has been permanent.

I healed the stages where the egg and sperm get coated with a protective substance as they leave the ovary and the testes. This coating is translucent and seems to spin around the egg and sperm's bodies. When I brought the changes forward to the present, they greatly influenced the conception and the implantation. The feeling of 'spinning' remained and I came away from the healing feeling very happy. I have my usual range of emotions, but in the background is an underlying happiness that is constant. The 'spinning' feel came forward to the present and makes me feel... well... ornamental. Like an Art Nouveau print, maybe. If I focus on it, it adds an excitement to the happiness.

I did a strange session where I tried incorporating Zivorad Slavinski's concepts to Whole-Hearted Healing (see Chapter 11). I had become aware of one big set of polarities in my life: 'alone' vs. 'together'. So I used WHH but focused on this dilemma instead of on a single trauma. I rapidly moved through developmental stages, healing this particular aspect in each of them. Although I didn't eliminate the dilemma, I greatly diminished the gulf between these opposites and reduced the emotional charge. I ended up even happier and very, very peaceful. My predominant emotions now have to do with love and compassion. This change also seems permanent."

Key Points

- It is possible to use regression to acquire peak states by healing particular *in utero* and earlier developmental stages.
- The Inner Brightness state allows easy access to the *in utero* developmental stages, making healing fairly straightforward. People without it find the regressions much harder or impossible to do.
- A variety of effective therapies that heal trauma now exist and can be used to heal developmental stages. As a group, they're called 'power therapies' in the psychological literature.
- During the healing of a developmental stage, the experience of what happened can change to incorporate events that didn't originally occur.
- As early stages are healed, later traumas will sometimes heal spontaneously, unless significant physical injury was involved in the later traumas.

Suggested Reading and Websites

On the fetal, pre-, and perinatal events and trauma
- Association for Pre- and Perinatal Psychology and Health, www.birthpsychology.com. Excellent material on the topic of in utero regression.
- Early Trauma Treatment and Trainings by Terry Larimore, www.terrylarimore.com. Her website also contains excellent material.
- Emerson Training seminars, William Emerson, www.emersonbirthrx.com. He is one of the leaders in pre- and perinatal psychology in my opinion.

- William Emerson, "The Vulnerable Prenate", paper presented to the APPPAH Congress, San Francisco, 1995, published in *Pre- & Perinatal Psychology Journal*, Vol. 10(3), Spring 1996, 125-142. An online copy is at www.birthpsychology.com/healing/point2.html.
- Michael Gabriel and Marie Gabriel, *Voices from the Womb: Adults Relive their Pre-birth Experiences - a Hypnotherapist's Compelling Account*, Aslan Publishing, 1992.
- Stanislav Grof, *The Adventure of Self Discovery*, State University of New York Press, 1988. Excellent coverage on the stages of birth and other spiritual and shamanic experiences.
- Terry Larimore and Graham Farrant, "Universal Body Movements in Cellular Consciousness and What They Mean," originally published in *Primal Renaissance*, Vol. 1, No. 1, 1995. An online copy is at www.terrylarimore.com/CellularPaper.html
- Sheila Linn, William Emerson, Dennis Linn, and Matthew Linn, *Remembering our Home: Healing Hurts and Receiving Gifts from Conception to Birth*, Paulist Press, 1999.
- Elizabeth Noble, *Primal Connections: How our Experiences from Conception to Birth Influence our Emotions, Behavior, and Health*, Simon and Schuster, 1993.
- Bill Swartley, "Major Categories of Early Psychosomatic Traumas: From Conception to the End of the First Hour" from *The Primal Psychotherapy Page*. An on line copy is at www.primal-page.com/bills-1.htm. Excellent with great references.

Images of sperm, egg, and in utero developmental stages
- *Journey Into Life: The Triumph of Creation* (a 30 minute video), 1990, by Derek Bromhall, distributed by Questar Video, Inc. This exceptional video on the journey of the sperm, egg, zygote, and fetus. The material is filmed with the same viewpoint and image size that people recalling trauma around these events see.
- Lennart Nilsson, *A Child is Born*, Delacorte Press, NY, 1990. Still photos of the journey of the sperm, egg, zygote, and fetus. The images are of scenes that people recalling trauma around these moments see. Recommended.

Regression techniques and therapies
- Leslie Bandler, *Solutions*, Real People, 1985. About the VKD (Visual Kinesthetic Dissociation) power therapy.
- Gerald French and Chrys Harris, *Traumatic Incident Reduction (TIR)*, CRC Press, 1999. See also the website www.tir.org.
- Winafred Blake Lucas, *Regression Therapy; A Handbook for Professionals, Vol 1: Past-life Therapy*, Deep Forest Press, 1993.

- Winafred Blake Lucas, *Regression Therapy; A Handbook for Professionals, Vol 2: Special Instances of Altered State Work*, Deep Forest Press, 1993.
- Grant McFetridge and Mary Pellicer MD, *The Basic Whole-Hearted Healing Manual*, 3rd edition, 2003.
- Francis Shapiro and Margot Forrest, EMDR: *The Breakthrough Therapy*, HarperCollins, 1997. See also the website www.emdr.org

Chapter 9

A 'Trauma' Approach: Using Gaia Instructions in the Inner Peace Process

Introduction

In Chapter 8, we described a regression process for acquiring peak states. Clearly there are major drawbacks to that approach: 1) most people lack the ability to easily access the proper *in utero* moments; 2) it can take an immense amount of time to heal the traumas; 3) there is a risk of suicidal feelings erupting; and 4) it is impossible to run the process on large groups of people because of the need for trained facilitators and clients working one-on-one. In this chapter, we introduce a method that heals specific developmental events *without* any of the drawbacks of regression. It uses a virtually unknown phenomenon called 'Gaia instructions' to accomplish this goal.

To introduce this approach to the general public, we offer in this chapter a detailed, step-by-step procedure to put oneself or one's clients into the Inner Peace State. We include the entire process in the form we give to clients to make it a 'stand-alone' handout that doesn't need any other explanation. You are free to copy and distribute it to friends, clients, or students. The only conditions are that you do not sell it, that you acknowledge our copyright, and that you reproduce it in its entirety. This last condition is to make sure that people who receive the document are informed of the process's potential difficulties.

We chose to limit the process in this chapter to just one extremely useful yet non-disruptive state, the Inner Peace state. The process is fast, simple, relatively safe and side effect free. It puts around 55% of the psychotherapy client population into the Inner Peace state of consciousness, and is permanent for most of that group. The process takes between 30 minutes and two hours and can be run on large groups of people simultaneously with laymen facilitators. We've minimized the complexity of the process in this chapter to make it simpler to apply—the tradeoff being the number of people the process works on.

The Inner Peace state puts people completely in the present, causing all past traumas lose any emotional content. Clearly, this process has great utility for both psychotherapy clients and ordinary work and home situations. For the clients, it eliminates most post-traumatic stress disorder symptoms simultaneously, regardless of the number of traumas involved. For the general working population, it eliminates most of the emotional over-reaction known as 'getting your buttons pushed'.

The process does not use regression, but rather the commonly available Emotional Freedom Technique (EFT). The process can be done by simply reading this chapter and following the written instructions, or we have made a video available that can be used as if it were an exercise tape. It can be purchased if desired via our website at www.PeakStates.com.

We explain in Volume 2 how the method is derived, which requires the use of an unusual state of consciousness. Fortunately, once someone does the development anyone can apply the results, in the same way we can throw a light switch without having to learn electrical engineering. The method we used for the 'Inner Peace Process' (IPP) can be extended to a variety of other states of consciousness and disease processes as described in Volume 2.

States in this chapter:
- Inner Peace

Grant's Story
Creating the Inner Peace Process

The first application of the process was to my Aunt Elaine. I'd derived the idea totally from theory, so I was stunned when it actually worked—not only that, but because she already had the Underlying Happiness state with its body-heart fusion, this added Inner Peace state with its mind-heart fusion popped her into the Hollow state!

One of the big problems in this work is getting enough people to experiment on. I had several ideas on how to improve the process, but when it worked on someone I'd lose my experimental subject as they would now be in the state all the time. Then I'd have to wait till someone else showed up to try changes on. And I didn't see any way to get large enough numbers of subjects to have statistically valid results. We knew it worked, but the theory said it wouldn't work on everyone—but was our ratio of success to failure the result of this theoretical limitation, due to poor technique, or from an inadequate process?

As with so many things, help came out of the blue. Harold McCoy from the Ozark Research Institute had heard about what we were doing, and asked me to come and teach for a week at his biannual school. I'd never heard of him before, but he's a very likable guy and after I got over my surprise at the call, said "Yes!". During that week, I ran exactly 100 people through four different versions of that process, which was much more complex than it is today. I also had the volunteers sign a non-disclosure and liability form, as at that time I was concerned that the process might induce severe suicidal reactions in some people, and I certainly didn't want them taking it home to try on their friends and relatives! To my great surprise, this cautionary agreement turned out to be a real hot potato and the subject of a lot of mealtime criticism. To this day I have no idea why people felt that way, as I felt I'd explained my position quite clearly. All I can guess is that very few of them understand the research and development process, and also that they have the mistaken belief that powerful inner work processes are intrinsically harmless. I knew better—I'd already lost two of my friends to suicide in the course of this work, so I was being very, very cautious.

Because I hadn't yet quite figured out how to write a foolproof questionnaire for the state, the resulting data was a bit sloppy. All I knew was that about a third to half the people had entered the state. This was well below my target of 80 to 90%. I also decided I'd made the process too complex, so I drastically simplified it. Over the course of the next few months, Dr. Mary Pellicer MD tried this new version on her clients. Eventually, she figured out what we'd been doing wrong, and those changes are incorporated in the current process. It was great fun to listen to her describe her results, as the clients often had experiences that could only be considered outside our cultural assumptions of reality.

Again, serendipity took a hand. Dr. Pellicer and I were presenting our work at a conference for physicians on spirituality and medicine at a Toronto medical school. One of the attendees, Dr. David MacQuarrie MD, was fascinated. He purchased our IPP training video, took it home, and tried it on his group psychotherapy clients without any one-on-one sessions. His success rate is included in this chapter. We should be able to improve it in the future, but it's adequate for now—especially as a demonstration of the principles.

I'm going to end this section by pointing out that the IPP approach can be modified to acquire any state. Dr. Deola Perry was not only instrumental in formulating these changes, but had the ability to monitor the client's brain states so we could get immediate, accurate feedback to improve the process. It was one of the most creative, exciting periods of my life as we tried out the new processes on our workshop participants. Her version of the process is included in Volume 2.

The IPP is Important For Both Laymen and Therapy Clients

The Inner Peace process puts many people into the Inner Peace state. This state eliminates any emotional feelings that occur when a person re-calls past traumatic events. It puts a person completely in the present, with enhanced ability to plan for the future. Clearly, using the Inner Peace Process to acquire this state has huge value for psychotherapy clients. Ob-viously, people suffering from overt post-traumatic stress symptoms, espe-cially people who have numerous traumas in their past, would benefit greatly by having all their emotional pain and symptoms just vanish. What many lay people, and even professionals in psychology don't realize is that most of the problems we see in our practices are due to this post-traumatic stress problem in one degree or another. These past traumas surface in ways that conceal their origins. However, this problem also occurs in the *non*-therapeutic population—most of our emotional responses to situa-tions in the present are driven by feelings that occurred during past, for-gotten traumas. We call it "having one's buttons pushed," and it is the direct cause of most of the suffering that we generally consider to be our normal lot in life. This book isn't the place to prove this statement, but it's been demonstrated empirically—a variety of power therapies use this in-sight to permanently and completely heal a broad range of what in the past were considered normal human responses to life situations.

The problem with these new power therapies, fast and effective as they are for everyday situations or the kind of problems clinical psychological patients have, is that there is so much to heal! The IPP eliminates these 'land mine' feelings wholesale in a brief amount of time, and gives the added bonus of a sensation of peace during our day and even during diffi-cult moments. Of course, if one loses the state, the problems come back, but fortunately for most people the IPP is relatively permanent.

Testing the Effectiveness of the Inner Peace Process

So, just how effective is the current version of the Inner Peace process? The answer is a bit complex. First, how effective is it on psychotherapy cli-ent populations? Using the rote version without any other intervention, we see about 55% of the group enter the state fully. There is also a number of people who only partially enter the state. The percentage who fully en-ter the state can be improved by working individually with the clients who don't respond fully to the process. How about the lay population? We're not exactly sure, but it's a higher percentage offset by the fact that some people have the state to start with.

What other effects does it have on a person's problems? Interestingly, it has no effect on issues that are due to body brain responses. For exam-ple, the cravings of addictions don't change. However, we are often sur-prised by what it does affect—a woman who was suicidal found that this completely vanished after the process, even though she later left the full state.

I thought it would be interesting to give the statistics on our first large scale test of an earlier, more complex and less effective version of the process because it gives some results for the general public as opposed to psychological client populations. This also illustrates the nature of the research and development cycle, which is ongoing for this process. The IPP was tested on a hundred people at the Ozark Research Institute in 2001. These people were close to an average cross section of the population. We ran five groups of about 20 people each for roughly one hour and 15 minutes each. This state has a feature that is unmistakable and simple to test for in groups—the state must eliminate all emotional content to every past traumatic memory. We had them list two major traumas with a rating of the Subjective Units of Distress (SUDS) from 0 with no distress to 10 with maximum possible distress. (In later tests, we expanded this to five traumas to avoid any mistakes.)

Since we were working with large groups of people, we made the process totally generic without any individual instruction or support. We predicted that about a third of the volunteers would achieve the target state. And in fact, of the 100 volunteers, we got 31% confirmed into the state (their traumas went to 0), another 6% almost got into the state (one of their traumas wasn't quite to a 0), another 21% had better than 50% reduction in their trauma scale, another 23% didn't fill out the questionnaire properly so we don't have any idea if they made it or not, and we eliminated 5% because they were already in a peak state of one type or another before the process started. Thus, for an hour and 15 minutes effort, somewhere between 31% and 54% of the volunteers went into the state.

This first large-scale test was encouraging, but demonstrated that we needed to simplify the process and do a better job of measuring the test subjects. We did so, but still were not getting the success rates I considered acceptable. A bit later Dr. Mary Pellicer, while using the current process on test subjects, realized that we had not been doing the process long enough on many of the test subjects. As they had had traumas blocking the state their whole lives, they considered the symptoms of that trauma 'normal' and didn't realize that they had to continue the process to eliminate them also. With this change, we started to get better results, in the 60% range on client populations. Note that these people are in general *not* a well adjusted, normal group of people. However as clinicians we are particularly interested in the success rate with this group, as these are the people who need the state the most. As I've said, we get a higher success rate if we do individual sessions with people, in particular by going longer and by healing their current 'major' presenting problem using a power therapy before or after the process is run.

For the new version 1.0 of the IPP, we were unexpectedly fortunate to run into David MacQuarrie MD. David runs a wellness center near Toronto, Canada, and was willing to run the rote process on groups of psychotherapy clients. From our perspective this was a wonderful test as he had no training on our theories or processes and would run the process totally rote. This was a wonderful test of the clarity and simplicity of the process, with the added bonus that as he was not associated with our Institute, he had no biases. He also had access to a large client base to test the process with. For this book, I asked David to write up a short summary of his results below. In summary, he reported 55% success rate with on a test group of about 80 people.

Results of a Test on the Inner Peace Process by Dave MacQuarrie, MD, a Therapist Doing Full-Time Private Practice Group Psychotherapy.

Enthusiastic after attending a brief workshop by Grant and Mary on the work of the Institute for the Study of Peak States, and after reviewing their videotape on the Inner Peace Process, I decided it would be useful to test the process with my ongoing groups. Following the instructions of the videotape (and with time constraints because of the nature of my groups), I gave a brief introduction of the basic premises and then facilitated the process for about 40 minutes to each of the five groups.

Thirty-three people attended and 28 gave feedback 1-2 weeks later (5 didn't respond). Of the 28, 21 people reported a major shift in peacefulness for at least two days, 9 considering the shift to be major. 3 people reported side-effects (2 with increased irritability, 1 too peaceful).

At a later date, a second test was initiated (with a more detailed introduction and a 90 minute process), open to anyone who wanted to come. Thirty-eight people attended, 19 of whom gave feedback at 2 weeks (some repeaters from the original groups). Fourteen people reported positive effects, 13 of major impact; 4 people reported side-effects (ranging from apathy to severe agitation).

Although difficult to evaluate because of the shifting terrain of therapy, 11 people have reported a sustained (3-4 months) life-changing shift which they attribute to the Inner Peace Process. One person describes it as "I'm no longer peaceful but I am calm and in control; I wasn't before." Another says "For the first time in my life, I have a focus and am not in such a hurry...."

Individuals reporting side-effects all responded to individual processing of their issues.

Overall I know of no other process that could have given these results and I shall continue to use the process as part of my armamentarium.

Long-Term Stability of the Inner Peace Process

As we've said, we expect about 55% of the client population to move into the Inner Peace (or better) state with one application of the process when done in group. However, what is the long-term stability of the process? We suspect that the percentage of the total client population that will move into the state *and keep it without maintenance* is closer to 40%. This is just a guess based on very minimal data, however. We find it difficult to follow our test subjects over time. Unfortunately, Dr. MacQuarrie also has the same problem following his client population, and can't offer any more information on long-term stability than he has above. We do know for a fact that our first test subjects have maintained the state since we first invented the process four years ago without any maintenance whatsoever. There is a tendency to find the IP state so commonplace after a few weeks that they no longer realize they are in the state, which can skew the self-reporting.

However, we've also seen some of our clients leave the state. Interestingly, of this group that we've tested, almost all regain the state once their current 'major crisis' is healed using a power therapy. The Inner Peace state becomes their fall-back state—they don't return to average consciousness after the current issue is dealt with.

Both Dr. MacQuarrie's and our own clients were instructed to contact us if any unexpected problems showed up after the IPP—and so far, none have. There *are* what I consider relatively minor problems that can occur in some people during the process. These consist of previously suppressed traumas becoming activated and showing up as physical or emotional symptoms during the process. Although they should fade with time if untreated, we recommend that clinicians heal them on an individual basis with the client, usually with fast-acting EFT.

A Personal Story of What Happened After the Process

As I've said, when we were first creating the Inner Peace process, we had the wonderful opportunity to try it on a hundred volunteers at the Ozark Research Institute (ORI). Although this first version only had about a 30% success rate, Patricia was one of those and she sent us an email describing her experience. Note that for most people, this new state is almost unnoticeable since it's mostly a lack of past emotional material. But I thought this account might be useful as an example of a more extreme reaction from a person who never had an Inner Peace experience, and couldn't recognize it from our description.

"Dear Grant:

Greetings! I was in your ORI class on day 4, one of the frustrated ones "spitting nickels" in the morning and a "bliss bunny" in the afternoon after the experimental session you gave us. I had to sleep in the corner of the classroom for nearly 1 1/4 hours and could not go out and face the light of day. That evening I had one of the deepest, calmest periods of sleep in memory, that I had not experienced in years and particularly profound considering I have chemical sensitivity and regularly get up 2 or 3 times a night and sleep and breathe on the shimmery surface of life.

The next morning I awoke utterly calm, quiet, centered and peaceful, such a contrast to the anxiety and fear that usually sculpts my conscious waking moments. I felt happy in a silly light kind of way, as if I had been high on something. Really a contrast again because I did not know what a peak state was and could really not understand all morning what you were talking about. In fact I had been so agitated that it was showing, and the evangelical young man had asked me at break if I had ever experienced joy, to which I replied I wasn't sure I had and I didn't know what these peak experiences were.

The following evening I also slept quite peacefully and awoke feeling quite refreshed and managed the air flight home without much problem.

The 3rd day after the treatment in your class to address the core traumas of conception, I went to Sylvia for a shamanic journey. When she asked for me to set an intention for the journey I told her a little about ORI and the kind of experiences I had been having there and I asked to address the core trauma which I identified as fear and abandonment which underlies my chemical sensitivity. Sylvia and I lay on the floor with the drumming and rattles and deep breathing....

The next day I had an oil massage and a steam using sandalwood and rose oil for cooling. On the way back home I noticed that I could see all the details of the leaves on the trees, and the color of the flowers seemed brighter and my perspective widening while driving back and forth to Concord.

These are my experiences the 3/4 days following your session at ORI. It seems to have catapulted me into a deeper healing of my chemical sensitivity and a clearer wider presence in the process of life. I want to thank you very much for this, as I believe that your session was pivotal for me. It is very powerful work that you are developing and I can certainly testify to that. I hope that you continue on with it full speed ahead. It will be of great benefit to many people.

Thank you very very much.
Best wishes,
Patricia Vanderberg"

Introducing the Inner Peace Process Handout

We follow this introduction with a stand-alone handout form of the process. Please bear with the repetition in the handout of material elsewhere. It is provided for people who haven't had the opportunity to read this book.

Is there anything that a facilitator should know about? First of all, a video of the process actually being used on volunteers is available from our website www.PeakStates.com. Secondly, I recommend that people planning to run the process on others learn how to use EFT on people—you might need it to help someone who has unusual symptoms arise. Third, it is always possible that new techniques like this one can cause unforeseen problems in a few individuals. I recommend having people who want to run the process under your supervision fill out a release of liability form; and, if you are a layperson, make sure that you know someone you can send them to who is trained in these sorts of trauma issues. Other than these normal precautions, the process is pretty self-explanatory and, based on our tests so far, safe. Fourth, be sure to explain that it doesn't work for everyone—don't set up false expectations, because someday we plan on having a more effective version to use, and we want them to try it again!

As I've said, feel free to copy it and hand it out with the proviso that I stated in the introduction. Good luck!

The Inner Peace Process

Revision 1.1, March 2004
Copyright © 2004 by Grant McFetridge

Welcome to our work at the Institute for the Study of Peak States!

We'll briefly cover in this manual the theory and application of the process. We've designed this process to be as simple as possible. However, to do this we had to accept that it wouldn't work for everyone. At the present time, the procedure you have in your hands is somewhere between 1/2 and 2/3 effective. By this, we mean that in any 100 people, you can expect that from 50 to 66 people will actually acquire the full state of 'Inner Peace'. Folks who don't may need more time with the process, or individual attention, or in some cases we can't help them at this time with this simple procedure.

A video on the Inner Peace Process is available. It covers what is in this handout. The first 30 minutes covers the theory of the process, and the last hour and thirty minutes actually shows an audience in a group setting using the process. It's designed to be used at home like an exercise video—you just follow along, making it more convenient for many people. It can be purchased via our website at www.PeakStates.com.

Potential Risks

After three years of testing with large groups of people, we haven't found any unusual problems with the process. Having said that, there is always a risk in using a new procedure, and if you are unwilling to accept any and all of the consequences to using this process, then you must stop and not use this process. By using this process, you are accepting this risk, and we are not legally liable for your choice to do so or any consequences that may arise.

We have identified three difficult experiences that you should be aware of:

1. By the nature of the process, it brings up uncomfortable feelings and body sensations during the process. This is to be expected, and they should go away with the use of the Emotional Freedom Technique (EFT) procedure as you proceed. If you have trouble making the feelings go away, we suggest you either study the EFT process at www.emofree.com, or find a therapist who knows the EFT process. In any case, these feelings that have come up during the process and couldn't be eliminated with EFT will eventually subside without treatment, although you won't get the benefit of the process or enter the Inner Peace state.

2. Rarely, by using this process you may acquire even better and more dramatic states of consciousness. These states are ones of increased health and wellbeing, but they may give you experiences and abilities that you've never had before. Typically, in a few days you will become comfortable with these new states of being.

3. Some percentage of the public who successfully enter the Inner Peace state may lose the state later. Returning to 'average' consciousness can be experienced as somewhat difficult and unpleasant until they get used to it again. These people may feel depressed or upset returning to the kind of consciousness they always had before. Rerunning the procedure or using the other suggestions in this manual will usually restore the state. As we create improvements, we'll make them available via our website at www.PeakStates.com.

For More Information:

For more in-depth information, please go to our website www.PeakStates.com. When we publish or create new procedures we'll keep you updated via our website.

Thanks for participating in our work!

All our best to you,

Grant McFetridge and the staff at the Institute for the Study of Peak States
November 2002
Hornby Island, British Columbia, Canada
www.PeakStates.com

Peak States of Consciousness

Understanding Peak States of Consciousness

Have you ever noticed that some people just seem to be happier, healthier, more successful, able to weather life's ups and downs more easily? In the current psychological paradigm, it's believed these people had better childhoods, had fewer traumas, better genetic backgrounds, nicer friends, and so on. In this model, it boils down to two factors—better genes or a better environment. And recently a third element has been added, better prenatal care. Although these elements are important, the main reason why some people live an amazing life independent of outside circumstances is outside of psychology's current paradigm.

In the 1960s, Dr. Abraham Maslow identified moments where people feel remarkably better. He called these moments 'peak experiences'. It turns out that one can have these peak experiences continuously. We re-

fer to these long-lasting wonderful experiences as 'peak states' of consciousness. People who live in these wonderful states most or all of the
time are exceptional people. It's not their personality that makes the difference, it's the state they're in! We've identified 15 major states so far,
with a variety of substates and combination states. Any one of them is remarkably better than average consciousness. Without them, people deep
down inside don't really feel like life is worth living, and they spend their
lives in culturally approved ways that don't get them what they really
want, since our culture doesn't even recognize the existence of these
states. Each of the states has different fundamental characteristics that
are the same for everyone.

Peak States and Psychological Healing

In the last few years, a number of very powerful and fast healing modalities
have been invented, called as a group "power therapies". These processes
are transforming the way that psychological healing is done worldwide.
Using these or other therapies can remove specific, identifiable problems
that you (or your client) have. The basic Whole-Hearted Healing
(WHH) process is one of those very powerful therapies, and can be
learned for free from our website, www.PeakStates.com. However, WHH
was actually developed for a very different purpose. We were working on
the problem of how to achieve permanent peak states of consciousness.
Instead of trying to heal people so they could function normally, what we
really want to do as healers and therapists is to bring people into states of
consciousness where they not only are free of most of the issues people suffer from, but are living a life that is exceptional. To use an analogy, it's like
most people are in hell with a bunch of pitchforks in them. They've been
there so long it feels normal. Power therapies can take the pitchforks out,
which is good, but leave them still in hell. What we wanted to do is find
easy ways to move them out of hell and into heaven on earth.

   If you decide you want to learn more about our Institute's work, and
perhaps contribute to improving and discovering new processes, we recommend you learn a variety of these 'power therapies', especially the basic
WHH process, so that you can gain an understanding of the psyche and a
fundamental research tool that we use to work on the peak states project.
Most of our work in the area of peak states of consciousness builds on this
material. More advanced material not yet available on the website is in
our book *Peak States of Consciousness*, Volumes 1 to 3.

Types of Peak States

There are two distinct groups of peak states. The group that's the most relevant for this pamphlet involves fusion between the multiple brains in the
triune brain system. To explain, the brain is divided into three distinct biological parts—in everyday terms, the mind, heart, and body. What isn't

commonly known is that for most people, the brains are separated and individually self-aware. To illustrate this from an everyday experience, you might recall being attracted to someone (the body brain's reaction), whom you didn't like (the heart brain's reaction), and feeling very confused about the situation (the mind brain's reaction).

For a certain class of peak states, these awarenesses can 'fuse' or 'merge' together, which means the brains involved lose their individuality and become a single awareness. Which brains merge and to what degree determines a number of different states. A 'Perry Diagram' can be used to explain the different types of brain states. It's drawn as a vertical row of circles whose overlap and distance from each other indicate the degree of fusion of awarenesses among the brains. Below is a very brief description of several of these brain fusion states. The first state on the list is the one the Inner Peace Process is designed to give you, but in rare occasions one or more of the others can occur from doing this procedure. Thus, we've included a description of ones that might occur when you use our process:

1. Inner Peace (Mind-heart fusion)—You have an underlying feeling of calm no matter what you're feeling, hence its name of 'Inner Peace'. This state causes past traumas to no longer feel emotionally traumatic. Your emotional reactions are dictated by present circumstances and not by past trauma. Interestingly, when you do healing and get a temporary sensation of calm, peace, and lightness (CPL) afterwards, it's actually a momentary experience of this or an even better state.
2. The Beauty Way (Aliveness)—This combination state includes the Inner Peace state, and additionally gives a feeling of 'aliveness' and a lack of negative judgment about people as well as an automatic knowledge of spiritual truths. Everything has a sort of beauty to it, hence the state's name. The 'noise' of 'mind chatter' in the head goes away.
3. Underlying Happiness/loving (Body-heart fusion)—This state gives a permanent feeling of happiness that doesn't go away no matter what else you feel. In men, it's mostly happiness, in women it mostly feels very loving.
4. Brains Communicate—You can communicate between your mind, heart and body just as if there were three children talking to each other inside of you.
5. Hollow (Mind-heart-body fusion)—The interior of your body suddenly feels like it's made of air but still surrounded by skin. Activities get very effortless. In some cases, the skin boundary feels like it also disappears (which is yet another state not related to the fusion of the brains).
6. Inner Brightness—You experience the interior of your body and head as filled with bright, white or golden light.

Peak states that don't have anything to do with brain fusion are covered in Volume 2 of the textbook *Peak States of Consciousness*. If you're curious, you can also check the www.PeakStates.com website for brief descriptions of these other states.

The Inner Peace State
Induction Process

Benefits of the 'Inner Peace' State

In the Inner Peace state, the client comes emotionally into the present moment. This means that all your past trauma suddenly stops feeling traumatic, no matter how hard you try to evoke feelings from the past. You now have an underlying sense of peace and calmness, and your emotions are in proportion to whatever is happening to you—you've lost your emotional 'buttons'. Since the vast majority of people's daily problems are created by past emotional traumatic material surfacing into the present, you can imagine how much better they would feel if they were in this state. Although this is true of everyone, it's particularly true of people suffering from a number of emotionally-based issues. Rather than try to fix individual emotional issues one at a time, this process just turns *all* of them off all at once. You can imagine that applicability to a therapy practice. We suspect that certain trauma-based physical problems would also go away while the client is in the state. This is an area we're just now exploring. Please let us know of any of your results, and we'll post this information on the www.PeakStates.com website.

Clients don't find the change disturbing or unusual when they enter the Inner Peace state, as it's characterized more by an absence of problems, rather than an addition of new experiences and abilities as can happen with other states. We've also had enough experience with it now to consider it relatively free of side-effects.

Why the Process Works

What causes the Inner Peace peak state to occur? In the Inner Peace state, the mind and the heart are fused together into one consciousness. It turns out that the Inner Peace state will generally be present in people continuously from birth if they experienced conception without trauma. Unfortunately, regressing someone to this developmental event trauma in order to give them the state is relatively difficult and time-consuming, making it too difficult for the average therapist to do in an office setting in a reasonable time. Instead, we've come up with a shortcut that still gives a great many people the Inner Peace state. The tradeoff here is speed and ease of use versus the number of people who will achieve the state. Since energy therapies are used to release the conception trauma with this process, another disadvantage to this fast and simple process is the small chance that the process may come undone sometime in the future.

The shortcut works by taking a critical moment in this developmental event, and describing the biological activity at that moment as a phrase in English. (Translations into other languages work, but the wording is critical and just using a translation dictionary may or may not be successful.) In this case, the phrase is "Join forces in Glory." I know that the phrase sounds strange and rather religious—but it is the best fit to the underlying biological process. We also include a visualization and music in the process to make it work more quickly and thoroughly. The music is similar to something that can be 'heard' at a spiritual level during conception. Likewise, the visualization is similar to a process that actually occurs during conception. Some people actually hear the 'real' music and see the 'real' experience the visualization is trying to portray during the process. Understanding what causes peak states, and how we derived the particular developmental event, phrase, music, and visualization is beyond the scope of this manual, but is part of the advanced Whole-Hearted Healing training available through the Institute for the Study of Peak States. We have the client repeat the phrase, or listen to it, while they visualize and listen to music. This puts the client back to the trauma at the correct moment, generally without their conscious awareness, and emotional and physical symptoms that occurred during their conception start coming into their bodies. As this happens, we have them use meridian therapies like EFT (Emotional Freedom Technique) to eliminate the trauma symptoms.

The Inner Peace Process Steps:

Liability:
If you are reading this manual and use this process on yourself, by doing so you have implicitly agreed to these liability and responsibility conditions below. If you are working with clients, we suggest you start the process by getting a written liability agreement. You must make totally clear to your client that this is a new, experimental process, and has no historical basis upon which to determine long-term effects or consequences. The client must be willing to take complete responsibility for whatever effects might happen, even though we have no idea what they might be, or how to fix them. Again, they need to understand that you and by extension the Institute are not responsible for consequences from the use of this process. Although we've been testing the process and have encountered no unusual problems, this doesn't mean that you or your client won't have something unexpected happen.

Step 1: Choose Past Emotional 'Indicator' Traumas
Pick three or four major past emotional traumas, ones the client can easily feel. WRITE THEM DOWN, else it is likely that you'll forget what they were. Rate the pain you feel in the present when you think about them on a scale of 0 (no pain) to 10 (the maximum possible pain). These are your indicators of how completely you are entering the state. When you're fully into the state, these 'indicator' traumas will have a rating of 0. Generally what happens is that people gradually move into the state, and this is reflected by the trauma ratings going down as you work. Note that we don't want you to use EFT or TAT on the traumatic memories themselves—we just want to have you pick traumas to use as measurement tools to see if you've entered the state. The pain will go away on these and all the other traumas that you didn't pick roughly simultaneously.

Step 2: Play the Required Music
The music is Beethoven's Fifth Symphony, first movement, (although we're working on a better choice of music). This particular piece of music is important, don't substitute. Unless you're incredibly lucky, choosing other music will not help and will probably interfere with the process. The music is played continuously during the process, and greatly helps evoke feelings and speed things up. Occasionally, a client may say that the music is disturbing to them, but this generally means the traumatic material from the conception experience is coming to consciousness and is to be expected in some people. Occasionally, due to negative cultural experiences such as with forcible assimilation of minority groups into the Western culture, clients might reject the music. Explaining how the music was chosen, and that other choices from different cultures could be used if someone knew how, can help here.

Step 3: Do a Visualization
As the process is run, you should try to visualize a chain with large links about a foot in diameter, running vertically though the body. Have the client imagine the chain is linking and unlinking in their body. The chain looks a bit like the large rings that a magician links and unlinks during a magic trick. It turns out that this visualization is what is actually occurring at a certain level of consciousness, and a good percentage of clients will be able to perceive this as it happens. When the process is done, the chain will be linked up and the client who could see the rings will find that they can no longer imagine it unlinking. This part of the procedure isn't critical; if you forget to do the visualization the process should still work reasonably well.

Step 4: Say the Required Phrase
While you are doing the procedure, you will repeat over and over the simple phrase "Join forces in glory." Don't change the wording—it's critical

that you repeat it just as it's written. We realize that after a while, it gets really boring, but the phrase and music are critical parts of the process.

Step 5: Use EFT

You will be using the Emotional Freedom Technique (EFT) process on yourself to heal the feelings and sensations that will arise as you do the process (although any meridian therapy would probably work adequately). You will simply repeat the phrase over and over while you tap on meridian points while listening to the music, and if you can, do the visualization. The tapping process is shown on the video, or can be learned by getting the EFT manual from www.emofree.com. In a group setting, have everyone tap and repeat the phrase in unison. For this process, we generally omit the psychological reversal step of EFT. However, we have found that the psychological reversal step using the phrase "even though it feels like I will die if I heal this, I deeply and completely love and accept myself" is necessary for some people. We recommend using it at least at the start of a new round of music. If you don't experience any change in sensations or feelings while the process is running, you may need to include all of the EFT steps. If you don't know them, review the manual or seek out an EFT practitioner. We've found that having someone tap on you as you do the process can increase your chance of having the EFT process work—remembering where to tap can distract you from feeling the sensations and emotions that should arise. For those of you who are working alone, practice EFT on yourself beforehand with other issues until the process itself doesn't distract you from what you're trying to heal.

Step 6: Run the Process

The procedure will almost certainly cause you to feel discomfort, both emotionally and physically. Rather than this being a problem, it's a sign that the process is working! You need to deliberately focus on and feel the discomforts, pains, and emotions, rather than try to avoid them. The EFT is used to eliminate the feelings, new ones arise, are eliminated, and so on until no more arise. The process won't work if you successfully ignore any symptoms that arise. Note that a number of people try to explain the arising sensations as due to what's going on in the classroom. For example, you might feel the choice of music is bad, or too loud, or that you need to leave to take care of some business, and so on. This can fool you and block the process from working, because you are not focusing on your feelings while you're doing the process.

Step 7: Check Your Progress

At the end of every few rounds of the music, check to see if your rating of your indicator traumas has gone to zero. (Remember, DON'T think about your indicator traumas while doing the process, or you might find that you've healed those few traumas accidentally. If you're not in the Inner Peace state all your other life's traumas will still be painful.)

Step 8: Continue Until There Are No Additional Changes
Generally, the process takes a minimum of 30 minutes, and can take up to 4 hours. You will need to continue the process even after your indicator traumas all go to zero. For most people, change will continue to happen. You continue the EFT for at least a couple of rounds of tapping past any additional changes in your body sensations, and preferably go an entire round of music with no additional changes. Not going long enough *is the single biggest mistake* people make. Since you've had the traumatic feeling from conception for your entire life, you consider the trauma sensations in your body to be normal. Thus you generally don't realize that you do have symptoms that you need to continue tapping on until they go away. Several hours of tapping spread over a couple of sessions works fine, and in fact can be required to get the full change that can happen. Continuing in this way also makes you less likely to fall out of the state.

If the Process Doesn't Work

What happens when you (or your client) thought it over, got excited by the possibilities, was willing to try this process, and it didn't work? Generally, you (or they) may feel like they are intrinsically defective, or doomed never to get what so many other people have. THIS IS NOT THE CASE! These and other peak states are actually everyone's birthright, and the reason why a particular individual does or does not have the state has nothing to do with their intrinsic ability or worthiness to have it. You (they) have just been unlucky in accumulating life experiences that block the state, and it will require more detective work to find out what else needs to be healed. Or you will have to wait until we come up with better procedures. However, there are other reasons why some people don't have peak states, and the Institute is currently investigating this problem.

For improvements and updates on this technique, please check in on the www.PeakStates.com website occasionally. We also suggest that you sign up for our very infrequent newsletter to be notified of new material. Additionally, if you are interested, there is an email group for people using the basic Whole-Hearted Healing (WHH) process which is particularly useful for healing pre-birth traumas like conception, and you can sign up by going to the website section on the WHH process. Here are some specific things to try:

- Try putting a combination of the essential oils spearmint and juniper berry on your 'karate chop' point while you're doing the process. That point is at the edge of your palm, and one of the EFT tapping points. Be sure to not get it in your eyes, it stings!
- You might need someone else to tap on you, or you may need to use the full EFT process. You might want to visit an EFT practitioner to get assistance.

- Try another power therapy in addition to the EFT, like the Tapas Acupressure Technique (TAT), Be Set Free Fast (BSFF), Eye Movement Desensitization and Reprocessing (EMDR), and so on.
- You might have been ignoring the sensations in your body while tapping. EFT won't work if you don't consciously place your attention on your body and emotions that arise.
- You may have forgotten to tap while doing the process. Just saying the phrase, listening to the music, and doing the visualization only accesses conception trauma—the EFT tapping is what eliminates it.
- If your birth language isn't English, you may have to translate the phrase into your birth language. This may not work, as the translation might not be accurate enough.
- You might have a 'dominant' trauma. In this case, there is some major issue going on in your life that is holding you out of the state. Further work with any powerful healing modality to eliminate the issue is required. Fortunately, the Inner Peace process that you've done wasn't wasted, as now that state will occur when the dominant trauma is eliminated. In other words, you will return to the Inner Peace state when those major traumas are healed, instead of the 'average' consciousness that you were used to.
- Some people still won't respond to this process. They might need to work with a professional who can help them access and heal the conception trauma directly. This sometimes works, and gives the better Beauty Way state as an added bonus—although usually it's something else in their life that is blocking the state. As we improve the process, we'll issue updates on the www.PeakStates.com website.
- A variety of organizations have processes that can induce peak states, albeit usually temporarily. If the Inner Peace Process was unsuccessful, or if you would like to add other peak states, you might try these other processes. Our website, www.PeakStates.com, has links to the ones that we know work at least for some people. Probably the easiest and simplest one is taught by Jacquelyn Aldana in her book *The 15 Minute Miracle*. In the future, we will be releasing more peak state processes, and you can find out about these by checking in with our website or signing up for our infrequent newsletter.

Recovering the Inner Peace State If You Lose It

For the people who moved into the Inner Peace state during the process, most will find that this state is relatively stable. Others may leave it for brief periods when some current stressful situation occurs, but they go back into the state as soon as the situation ends or they relax a bit. However, some people leave the state and it doesn't return. Their calmness leaves them, their traumatic past returns, and they go back to what they had before. This latter case can be a problem as they've had a chance to experience life in a better way and don't feel very good about living as they used to. For this group, we have some advice that will help most to get their state back:

- Do EFT or WHH or a hybrid combination on whatever issue drove you out of the state. You will generally pop back into the state once this issue is resolved.
- Repeat the Inner Peace process. If the process again works, you've probably left the state because the healing effects of the EFT became undone, or you didn't run the process long enough. This may be because your breathing was done in a way that reverses the effect of EFT. You can read about the correct way to breathe by reading Gay Hendricks *At The Speed of Life*. Another way to reverse the effects of EFT is by encountering a substance your body reacts to, called an 'energy toxin'. Review Gary Craig's manual or see an EFT practitioner for help in these areas.
- Focus on any negative judgments against self or others that occurred when you lost the state. Focusing on letting them go, or using a power therapy to help you do it, generally will pop you back into the Inner Peace state quite quickly. *This is the most successful method of returning to the Inner Peace state.*

Suggested Reading

- Grant McFetridge, *Peak States of Consciousness*, (Volumes 1 and 2), Institute for the Study of Peak States Press, 2004.
- Gary Craig, *Emotional Freedom Techniques: The Doorway to the New Healing Highrise: The Manual (third edition)*, 1999. See www.emofree.com for a copy.

Acknowledgments

The breakthroughs needed for this process came from the dedicated hard work of the following people: Grant McFetridge, Wes Gietz, Dr. Deola Perry, Dr. Marie Green, and Dr. Mary Pellicer. Thanks also to the numerous volunteers who worked with us to test out these ideas over the years.

Chapter 10

A 'Choice' Approach: Aligning with Peak States Via The 15-Minute Miracle Process

by Jacquelyn Aldana

Foreword by Grant McFetridge

I've had the delight to have first met Jacquelyn several years ago, and feel extremely fortunate to have her contribution in this book. Her work is the best example of what we call the 'conscious choice' approach for acquiring peak states that I know of. In it, you deliberately choose to feel the qualities of the state you desire, and continue to make that choice. From our perspective, we suspect her process combines several states—at a minimum, the 'Underlying Happiness' state and a solid connection to Gaia, which she includes in the term 'Life'.

In this chapter she briefly talks about her process for how to choose to have a peak state of consciousness, and to keep it by using simple maintenance steps. The name of the process, The 15-Minute Miracle, accurately describes how little time is required per day. Her process is generally so successful that her workshop offers a money-back guarantee. And she doesn't stop with just feeling wonderful— she shows how to use the state to manifest dreams and desires in the physical world. In fact, the ability to manifest is woven into her method for having peak states. Jacquelyn clearly shows that the right state of consciousness (or equivalently, the right feeling sensations) is required to manifest your desires.

Jacquelyn is a pioneer whose work shows a simple, easily used method to live 24 hours a day, 7 days a week in states of consciousness that make this world a heaven on earth. Her process has come to incorporate the latest therapies, like EFT, to help people gain and maintain the state she lives in even more easily. This is an incredibly exciting time to be involved with this work, as new discoveries and synthesis between approaches are just starting to take place.

Of course, in this chapter we don't have the space to fully explore her process—for that, I refer you to her well-written and easily followed books such as *The 15-Minute Miracle Revealed*, *Miracle Manifestation Manual II*, and the short *Shortcuts to Miracles*. I also highly recommend her wonderful

'Playshops' as she so delightfully calls them, which can be enrolled in through www.15MinuteMiracle.com.

About the Author:
How The 15-Minute Miracle Came to Be

Jacquelyn Aldana is one of the happiest people you'll ever meet, and it isn't because her life was always picture-perfect. Her biological parents abandoned her at an early age; she had a pretty poor self-image most of her life; and she had lots of ups and downs like most everyone else. Oddly enough, however, her greatest blessing came when she had to face the three biggest challenges of her entire life all at once.

- Her husband Ron was dying of a virulent cancer.
- Their 20-year marriage was falling apart at the seams.
- Their family business was on the brink of financial disaster.

As she completely surrendered and released all attachment to possible outcomes, she felt an inexplicable sense of peace and well-being come over her. That same day she was inspired to write something on a piece of paper, and then it happened! Something shifted! All of a sudden, she began to experience a series of incredible events – one right after the other! It was as though she had tapped into an inexhaustible reservoir of amazing miracles.

- Ron completely regained his wellness (he is now radiantly healthy).
- Their marriage on the rocks became a marriage made in Heaven.
- The family business suddenly took a 180° turn and began to flourish.

Not only did Jacquelyn discover ways to access amazing miracles in her own life, but she also found ways to make it easy for the rest of us to attract and create major miracles in our lives as well. She is convinced that the process she affectionately refers to as The 15-Minute Miracle was given to her as a Divine gift to be shared on a global basis. She was inspired to call it The 15-Minute Miracle because it takes only about 15 minutes a day to do; it seems to work wonders for most anyone who merely experiments with it; and the results are often so dramatic and life-changing that most people refer to them as MIRACLES!

How Every Day Can Be a Great Day

Have you ever had one of those EXTRAORDINARY days that made you wish it would never end? You know, one of those days when everything just magically fell into place no matter what you did or how you did it? Wouldn't it be wonderful if only there were a way to experience days like these more often? Just imagine how glorious that would be. What usually happens, however, is that we go through our lives thinking we have no control over such things—that some days are just better than others. Right? WRONG!

You'll be glad to know that you have the power to call these miraculous days into being as often as you choose. The book *The 15-Minute Miracle Revealed* promises to show you how to create remarkable days, one right after the other. In fact, you will be able to do "these and even GREATER things" by merely applying a few simple principles. All you have to do is understand how certain universal laws operate so you can enjoy the benefits of working in harmony with them. Yes, we know, this all sounds too good to be true, so please don't take our word for it. Just follow the instructions in this book and see what happens. Don't be too surprised, however, when people begin to ask why you are happier, more energetic, and more productive than usual. Next, they will want to know how they can accomplish these things!

The next few pages will give you a better idea of what The 15-Minute Miracle is all about. We invite you to discover how you can deliberately attract and consciously create a desirable quality of Life on a consistent basis. Learn how every day can be a wonderful day and how you can easily experience your highest purpose for being. Prepare for an adventure that will very likely inspire you to view Life through the eyes of awe and wonder. Get ready to fall in love—in love with Life and everything in it (including yourself). Life absolutely adores you and is eager to respond to your every desire. All you have to do is figure out what truly makes you happy—the rest is relatively easy. Life wants you to thoroughly enjoy your experience here on earth, because you are the Divine Creation in whom your Creator is well pleased!

A Brief Overview of The 15-Minute Miracle

If you can answer "yes" to the seven questions below, you are a prime candidate to benefit from The 15-Minute Miracle. Doing this simple process in writing usually takes less than 1% or your day (about 15 minutes) and it seems to work wonders for most anyone who playfully experiments with it. See how many questions inspire you to say "yes"!

1. Is there anything you are grateful for today?
2. Can you identify how you love to feel and why?
3. Would you like to strengthen your intuitive abilities?
4. Are you willing to allow your higher power to assist your?
5. Are you willing to release and let go of negative emotions?
6. Are you willing to take time out to be kind to yourself and others?
7. Can you daydream and play in your imagination (even if only for a few moments) until it feels like you are already living the life of your dreams?

The quickest and easiest way to master this simple process is to utilize the easy-to-read books and gifts in the Deluxe Miracle Starter Kit. See www.15minutemiracle.com for details.

How to Know When You Are in the Flow

The following statements represent what people often say when they feel in the flow of Life. Please check off the statements below that describe how you feel most of the time.

- My work feels like play!
- I have boundless energy!
- I feel "on top of the world"!
- I am unaware of time passing!
- I feel authentic and true to myself!
- I feel impelled to pursue my dreams!
- Life is fun, exhilarating, and rewarding!
- I think about positive possibilities 24/7!
- I feel much happier than I have ever felt before!
- Things seem to fall into place for me more easily!
- I am eager to make a positive difference in the world!
- I live in a state of constant gratitude and appreciation!
- I have a sense of just "knowing" that I am on the right track!
- I now perceive so-called challenges as opportunities in disguise!
- I feel strong, confident, clear, and unstoppable about my mission!
- I feel as though I have Divine Assistance in all that I choose to do!
- I am able to make decisions more quickly with greater confidence!
- I am so excited and extremely passionate about what I have to offer!
- I have never felt more confident or committed to anything in my entire life!
- I always seem to be in the right place at the right time. It's just the story of my life!
- I am able to feel happy and stay in the flow of Life, regardless of circumstances!

Total Number of Check Marks: _____
     The more statements you were able to check off, the more you are "in the flow of Life" at this time.

With Regard to the Word, "Life"...

When I use the word "Life" in this chapter, I am referring to that which I consider to be The Infinite, Divine Oneness, and The Creator of All That Is. To me, Life is synonymous with God, Holy Spirit, Gaia, the Alpha, and the Omega. In my opinion, there is nothing bigger, greater, or more powerful than LIFE!

Joining the Flow of Life

Three years prior to discovering The 15-Minute Miracle, my life was like watching reruns of a bad movie on a TV with poor reception. Just about the time when I thought things couldn't possibly get any worse, THEY DID! When I stumbled onto a simple way to manifest miracles into my life through the power of thought and prayer, I was sure I had found Aladdin's Lamp. As I spent just 15 minutes each day simply writing a love letter to Life, everything began to fall into place for me easily, effortlessly, and magically! It wasn't until much later that I realized that all of the amazing manifestations that surprisingly showed up were merely byproducts of seeking "sustained joy." As I made it my ongoing intention to find ways to become "The Happiest Person I Knew," everything else took care of itself with little or no effort on my part.

Although this intriguing process often results in manifesting desirable circumstances and wonderful material things, the real value of The 15-Minute Miracle is that it creates a divine connection between you and your Higher Power, you and your magnificence, and you and Life (in other words, you and You)! When this happens, things begin to align perfectly and fall into place easily. This is probably why so many people associate what they begin to experience with miracles. The best part is that miracles can happen to YOU (when, that is, you are ready and willing to experience them).

Allow us to save you a lot of time and energy that you might otherwise spend pushing, pulling, struggling, swimming upstream, running uphill, and trying to control the outcome of circumstances. Simply surrender your worries, doubts, and fears to your Higher Power and trust that Life will reveal Its grandest plan to you in just the perfect time. The difference between trusting and controlling is this: trusting is equivalent to hiring a team of experts to get the job done, whereas controlling is equal to trying to do all of the work yourself. Until I let go of my need to control everything in my life, everything in my life continued to control me! I finally had to resign as "CEO of the Universe" in order to transform my stress into peace of mind. We hope the success stories on the following pages will inspire, uplift, and encourage YOU to do the same.

Why "What We THINK and SAY" Really Matters

Although there are many languages throughout the world, the one that can enhance our lives the most is the "Universal Language of Life." To master it, we must choose purely positive words as we speak. It is equally important for us to think purely positive thoughts even when engaging in "self-talk" in the privacy of our own minds. This purely positive language is based upon a universal law called the Law of Magnetic Attraction that is at work every second of every day, whether we are aware of it or not. When we understand how to work in harmony with this immutable law,

Life is much easier. When we are ignorant of it, however, Life can be rather challenging. This law says, "What we think about is what we bring about and what we fill our minds with our lives are full of." In other words, whatever we think about, talk about, observe, or even imagine, is the very thing we (knowingly or unknowingly) attract to ourselves! Furthermore, Life interprets everything we think or say quite literally, so we must be very aware of our language in order to attract what we truly desire. To thoroughly learn this language and to be able to speak and write it fluently, you may want to consider attending the Level I Miracle Mastery Playshop. If you prefer to study at home on your own, you'll find the Deluxe Miracle Starter Kit (see the website) to be a great resource.

What Do Happy People Do?

- They always see the magnificence in each and every person they meet.
- They see the beauty and benefits in Life, regardless of circumstances.
- They appreciate all that they already have before asking for anything else.
- They find something to love and admire about everything and everyone in every moment.
- They allow themselves to feel all of their feelings so they can choose which ones to keep and which ones to release.
- They view Life through the eyes of awe and wonder like a small child who absolutely knows beyond a shadow of a doubt that all things are truly possible.
- They embrace all aspects of life, both positive and negative, because contrast is an extremely valuable tool. By simply knowing what they don't want, they can better identify what they prefer instead. What could be easier than this?
- They totally release and let go of whatever no longer serves them in a positive way: things like resistance, resentment, condemnation of themselves and others, fear, and attachment to outcomes. (When you let go of them, they let go of you!)
- They hold the space for themselves and others to regain their balance in just the perfect time in ways that bless and benefit everyone. This is one of the most loving and supportive things we can do for ourselves or anyone else.
- They love others even when others are less than loving toward them. When other people do something that could be considered offensive, they just say to themselves, "That's just them not knowing a better way at this time. If they could do better, they certainly would do better." This is what we call unconditional love at its very best.

If you make it your ongoing intention to practice these principles, you may very well become "The Happiest Person You Know," as well as an "Irresistible Magnet for Miracles!"

Life's Best-Kept Secrets

- You always, always, always get to be right!
- What you fill your mind with, your life is full of.
- You always get more of whatever you sincerely appreciate.
- Whatever you focus upon usually gets much bigger in your life.
- You increase the odds of achieving your goals by simply writing them down.
- Always look where you are going, because you'll always go where you are looking.
- The quickest way to get back into the flow of Life is to find something (anything) to appreciate.
- You automatically invite more of whatever you think about, talk about, observe, or imagine.
- You can feel good right now by remembering something pleasant from the past.
- You can feel good right now by envisioning something you look forward to in the future.
- To experience joy and sweet inspiration, release and let go of all condemnation.
- If you want to successfully travel the distance, you have to let go of both fear and resistance.
- Attachment to outcomes evokes fear and doubt, which only results in your doing without.
- If you want to experience peace and contentment, you have to let go of both hate and resentment.

A Closer Look at Step #1 of The 15-Minute Miracle - The Appreciation Step

"Miracles are happening everywhere all the time, but only those with an 'Attitude of Gratitude' seem to notice them."

Author Unknown

The Appreciation Step is the first step in The 15-Minute Miracle process for a very specific reason. It is number one because it opens the door for all the other steps to work to our greatest advantage. Instead of just making a typical "gratitude list," this step asks us to explain why we are grateful. As we ponder our blessings in this way, we can't help but deepen our sense of appreciation, which makes us realize how very fortunate we are already. Some people feel they are able to access a more profound sense of appreciation by using the word gratitude. If this is true for you, simply rephrase this step as follows: "I am so grateful...because..." Gratitude is the magic bridge to a more sustainable sense of joy, and joy is the key to becoming "The Happiest Person You Know."

We find that most people who are drawn to The 15-Minute Miracle are in a state of longing and yearning for things to be different in their lives. As it turns out, most of them either want something they don't have or have something they don't want (or both). Unfortunately, in their state of needing and pleading, they unknowingly attract more of the very things they don't want—more lack, limitation, and not having! For a more fulfilling life, we recommend that you make it your ongoing intention to transform all longing, yearning, and needing into appreciation, gratitude, and succeeding.

Appreciation Saved Our Marriage
The stress of struggling to make ends meet and trying to keep Ron alive for three years began to completely overwhelm both of us. Everything in our lives began to fall apart, including our 20-year marriage! A health practitioner friend of mine suggested that I go to a quiet place and write down everything that I appreciated about Ron. It took me quite some time to release my resistance and resentment long enough to write anything very complimentary. Once I got started, however, I wrote several pages of glowing comments about the man I had married 20 years before. Although I never showed it to him, nor did he ever read it, the very next morning Ron responded to me with enormous warmth and tenderness. As a result, all hostilities and misgivings completely dissolved. Only 12 hours after I did this little writing exercise, our failing relationship was completely healed and our love for each other was greater than ever before. This was truly a miracle when you consider the fact that we barely spoke for nearly eight months. In my opinion, appreciation is to well-being what oxygen is to breathing!

Gratitude Saved Ron's Life
When Ron was suffering from cancer, he found it very difficult to appreciate much of ANYTHING. Finally, one day after the doctors said that he might not even make it through the night, he made the decision to do something different. Because he wanted to make the most of whatever time he had left, he consciously turned his attention from death, dying, and devastation to life, living, and loving every moment he had left. The most amazing thing happened! He not only made it through the night, but he also began to feel a bit better the following day. As he celebrated another glorious day, he experienced a little more strength and encouragement. After a few more days, he was finally released from the hospital. Ron faithfully wrote his 15-Minute Miracle every day for three months

then returned for his regular checkup. The doctors were utterly dumb-founded! After a plethora of tests, they could not find even a trace of can-cer anywhere in his body. They pronounced him totally cancer free! Although the doctors called it a "spontaneous remission," Ron and I KNOW that it was nothing short of a miracle!

We Always Get MORE of Whatever We Appreciate
Things for which we express LOVE, GRATITUDE, and SINCERE APPRECIATION naturally expand. Life humorously emulates my be-loved grandmother when she used to serve the evening meal. If I compli-mented her on a particular dish that she had lovingly prepared, she would instantly provide me with second helpings. Life does exactly the same thing—it always makes sure we get MORE of whatever we LOVE and APPRECIATE!

Benefits of Appreciation
- It only has positive side-effects.
- It provides a delightful shortcut to miracles.
- It floods your body with immune-boosting endorphins.
- It puts you back into the flow of Life at the speed of thought.
- It is the lantern that shines the brightest light in your darkest hour.
- It provides a totally legal way for you to enjoy a "natural high."
- It causes you to feel a wonderful sense of "coming home".
- It provides an immediate sense of well-being.
- It is the primary cause of "sustained joy".

15-Minute Miracle Success Stories

The following success stories are from our readers and Miracle Playshops graduates who have applied the simple principles of The 15-Minute Mira-cle. This is just a small sampling of stories to give you ideas of what YOU have to look forward to.

Health
Ron Aldana, who was told by his doctors that he had a very poor chance of survival, completely regained his wellness and is now totally cancer-free.

Stephanie Coffin, who suffered the pain, spasms, and fatigue of multi-ple sclerosis for over a year and a half, overcame every symptom of MS in only three weeks.

Debba Boles, who had symptoms of clinical depression and intense sui-cidal feelings for over five years, is now grateful to be alive. She is truly "living proof of living truth".

Laney Boyle, who experienced an average of 28 severe migraine headaches a month for over 32 years, says her migraine episodes have diminished dramatically.

Gemma Bauer, who suffered for over 10 years with chronic pain from rheumatoid arthritis, reports that she is much happier and healthier than ever before. As a bonus, she also achieved her ideal body weight, shape, and size.

Vocation

Dr. Kim Jameson, who desired to have her own practice and a cute and cozy cottage in the country, was able to realize both of her dreams at the same time.

Carol Gibbons, who became very discouraged after repeated episodes of unemployment, landed an exciting job that far exceeded her wildest expectations.

Debbie Voltura, who loved the idea of singing for a living, was hired by Louise L. Hay to provide musical inspiration for audiences all over the country.

Well-Being

Cheri Carroll, who spent over $100,000 and 30 years searching for personal fulfillment, is now ecstatically happy and successful in every major area of her life.

Judy and Kenny Dotson, who longed for more harmony in their marriage, fell in love all over again as a result of doing their 15-Minute Miracle each morning.

Gayle Marie Bradshaw, who was unable to speak in front of groups, is now able to address audiences of any size comfortably, confidently, and dynamically.

Lisa Racine, who found many areas of Life extremely challenging, now enjoys abundant prosperity, loving family relationships, and radiant health.

Brent Carroll, who had completely given up on Life, himself, and God, is so grateful to be alive, because he now sees that everything in Life is a precious gift.

Prosperity

Alice Cabral, who asked for exactly $625, won $626 in the lottery less than 24 hours after she attended her first Playshop (the extra dollar paid for her lottery ticket).

Glenda Dean, who desired to set extraordinary sales records in her insurance business, quickly exceeded her wildest expectations. Not only that, but she also attracted over $17,000 worth of unexpected income.

Sheila and Arnold Estep, who desired greater financial freedom, became multi-millionaires only days after attending their first Miracle Playshop.

What Do These People All Have in Common?
- Every one of the individuals did their 15-Minute Miracle in writing.
- They all said they felt better the minute they engaged in the process.
- They saw themselves *already* enjoying their desired quality of life.
- They all had a desire to experience more JOY in their lives.
- They were all willing to experience the goodness of Life.

How to Become an "Irresistible Magnet for Miracles"

Magnetizing miracles into your life is much easier than you might think. I feel qualified to say this, because I became an "Irresistible Magnet for Miracles" at a time in my life when my whole world was upside down. It was BECAUSE of the challenges that I discovered an incredibly simple way to raise my energy and get into "the flow of Life." It was BECAUSE my husband was dying of cancer, BECAUSE our 20-year marriage was "on the rocks," and BECAUSE we were nearly bankrupt that I finally surrendered and asked for help! It all started one day when I shouted right out loud to Life, "Either show me a way to experience more joy in my life or just come and take me right now!"

In other words, I wanted Life to either show me a way or haul me away, and I had absolutely no attachment to the outcome! Just moments later, I was inspired to write something down on a piece of paper that ultimately resulted in my husband completely regaining his wellness, our relationship becoming a "marriage made in heaven," and our business getting back on its feet almost overnight! What I wrote down that day turned out to be the forerunner of the magical process we now call The 15-Minute Miracle. Listed below are the five most important things for you to know in order to become irresistible when it comes to attracting miracles into your life:

1. Clarify your dreams and desires by writing them down.
2. Appreciate what you already have before asking for more.
3. Think about, talk about, and envision only what you do want.
4. Notice how you feel in every moment (feelings of comfort or discomfort).
5. Make it your ongoing intention to be "The Happiest Person You Know."

Shortcuts to Manifestation

The quickest and easiest way to transform your wishes into realities is to consciously appreciate what you ALREADY have before asking for more. Herein lies the key to success and personal fulfillment. Focus upon what IS working in your life and what IS right with the world, no matter how small or seemingly insignificant it may be. Before long, more things will fall into place with little or no effort on your part. Because you cannot possibly experience negative emotion when you are expressing gratitude, it is a wonderful tool to use when you want to feel good in a hurry!

A Sample Step in Manifesting:
The "Tell-A-Vision" Step

> "All things for which you pray and ask, believe you have already re-
> ceived them, and they shall be granted you."
> Mark 11:24

Since I can be, do, and have absolutely ANYTHING, I see myself ALREADY enjoying the following:

- I have plenty of time to indulge in the things I love to do!
- I am able to make a prosperous living doing something I enjoy!
- My body is in better shape than it has ever been in my entire life!

Have fun as you take an all-expense-paid "Creation Vacation" in your imagination. Allow your mind to playfully explore the positive possibilities of the future. The quickest way to attract miracles into your life is to see your dreams already realized and your wishes already granted. Bask in the feeling of appreciation and contentment as you create your perfect life in the playground of your imagination. This innovative step enables you to manifest things beyond your wildest expectations, because it invites you to build your dreams at "the speed of thought". Anything you can visualize in your imagination has the potential to become real in your life, so be sure to take ample time to honor your dreams and desires. Remember… "You have to have a dream to have a dream come true."

Experiment with the fascinating principles of positive expectancy. Just believe in your heart that your wishes have already been granted (even though physical evidence may not yet be apparent). This is truly the most powerful ingredient in your recipe of deliberate creation, because it actually causes your subconscious mind to carry out your conscious desires. Just think—if you can successfully change the programming of your computer (your subconscious mind), you can successfully change the printout of your life. What you can accomplish in just minutes with this step often takes several weeks, months or years of repeating affirmations to accomplish the same thing!

Just decide what you want and call it forth by reveling in how wonderful it would FE-E-E-EL to experience it. Focus only upon that which makes you smile, laugh, and feel fully connected with Life—those incredibly wonderful feelings that cause the floodgates of well-being to fly wide open for you!

Your job is to know what you are ready to be, do and have. Life's job is to attend to all of the details (the who, when, why, where, and how). Therefore, just focus upon that which you desire, then leave the rest to the discretion of the same magnificent Power that created all that is. Since you are very likely to get whatever you ask for, be sure to invite it to come to you in ways that are in harmony with your well-being. For instance, request that things come to you in just the perfect time and in ways that totally delight you. Otherwise, you may get what you want, but NOT in the appropriate time or in a way that is convenient. As Walt Disney often said to those who longed to turn their creative ideas into physical realities, "If you can dream it, you can do it!"

Ron always tells me, "Life is just one big canvas—put as much paint on it you like." The American billionaire Donald Trump says, "Since you have to think anyway, you might as well think big!" Since you can be, do, and have absolutely anything your mind can conceive, what do you choose for yourself right now? What does your biggest dream look like? What do you choose to bring from your past that you want to carry forward? Look at things as they CAN be—not limited to what they ARE right now. Visualization allows you to experience everything you desire in the privacy of your own mind. Since all amazing manifestations begin in the imagination, we recommend that you allow yourself to go there to play as often as you possibly can. According to Albert Einstein, the ultimate genius of the 20th century, "Imagination is more important than knowledge!"

Let's imagine for a moment that you are the director, producer, and star of your own television show. Tell me all about yourself and what is going on in your life. By answering the questions below, you can paint a colorful word picture to describe the life of your dreams. Create your declarations to reflect what you desire to experience as though it were already so. By writing or speaking in the first person/present tense, you greatly amplify the effectiveness of this step.

Examples of Your Declarations
- I am by far "The happiest person I know".
- I enjoy multiple streams of residual income!

Based upon what you desire, answer these questions in the first person / present tense using complete sentences:
- What is your overall state of being?
- What degree of prosperity do you enjoy?
- What are you currently doing vocationally?
- What is the current status of your love life?
- What are you most proud of and excited about?

- What are you doing that is most rewarding for you?
- What is your latest and greatest accomplishment?
- How is your physical, mental, and emotional health?
- What complimentary things are people saying about you?
- What are you doing to contribute to the well-being of others?

CONGRATULATIONS! You are now an
"Irresistible Magnet for Miracles"!

I absolutely LOVE the Tell-A-Vision Step, because it allows me to create a sense of Heaven on earth. By looking at reality through the lens of my imagination, troubles vanish, obstacles fall away, the lost become found, the sick become well, dark becomes light, and rough places become smooth. The imagination is the power we all possess in which we are able to see the harmony, unity, and beauty in things. It's what links us to The Divine and brings into existence an indescribable sense of awe and wonder. Best of all, it enables us to see through "what APPEARS to be" to the positive possibilities of "what CAN be".

"Imagination is the most POWERFUL word in the dictionary.
It's the magic lamp that lights up the mind.
It spotlights great ideas. It banishes darkness.
It is the very heart of creative thinking."
Wilferd A. Peterson

15 Simple Ways to Miracle-ize Your Life

1. Focus primarily upon that which you DO want to experience.
2. Notice how wonderful you feel when you express gratitude.
3. Envision Life as you prefer it to be for at least 15 minutes a day.
4. Appreciate everything you ALREADY have before asking for anything else.
5. Learn to work in harmony with the natural laws that govern the quality of your life.
6. Decide what you want to experience; then step aside and allow Life to take care of the details.
7. Understand the Law of Magnetic Attraction that says, "What you think about is what you bring about."
8. Release resentments – holding on to them is like drinking poison and expecting someone else to die.
9. Allow Life to consistently and abundantly fill your cup so that you can help others to fill theirs.

10. Remember to be proactive; being FOR something greatly strengthens you and attracts solutions.
11. Accept others just as they are by completely releasing your desire to judge and control them.
12. Commit your goals to paper and you will likely achieve them more quickly and easily.
13. Recognize how you love to feel and ask to experience more of this feeling.
14. Emulate the positive qualities you admire in highly successful people.
15. Create a specific intention prior to taking action on things.

Common Blocks to Manifesting Your Desires

Why "Positive Thinking" Just Isn't Enough

Although success certainly begins with positive THINKING, we must eventually take positive ACTION in order to bring about positive RESULTS. The final step to personal fulfillment, however, is achieving a state of positive BEING. So many of our clients tell us that they used to think of themselves as very positive minded until they began to pay attention to the way in which they expressed themselves. They were quite shocked to realize that they most often talked in terms of: 1) what they DIDN'T like, 2) what they DIDN'T want, and 3) what they most FEARED. After learning the "Universal Language of Life" (a purely positive language), they soon realized that they had to think and speak more about what they DID want, instead of focusing so much upon what they DIDN'T want. Once they began to redirect their attention exclusively upon what they PREFERRED to experience, Life suddenly became a game that was much more fun to play. Not only does positive focus yield much higher dividends, but it also provides a way to accomplish more by doing less! What could be more ideal than this?

Why Affirmations Don't Always Work

Affirmations, although very empowering, often fail to fool the subconscious mind into believing something is true when all evidence points to the contrary. Most people require a bridge to believability before affirmations provide much benefit. Although the words, "I am" and "it is" are extremely powerful, they often invite IC (your Inner Critic) to have a regular field day at your expense. For instance, if you were overweight and out of shape and you repeated to yourself over and over and over again, "I am my perfect body weight and size," IC would probably mutter, "Oh yeah? Have you looked at yourself in the mirror lately? Get real!" If, however, you rephrased this statement and said, "I love it when I am my perfect body

weight and size," IT (your Inner Teacher) would likely say, "It is my pleasure to always give you MORE of whatever you love, Magnificent One.
Please allow me to show you how to create a fit and trim body in ways that
are fun and easy." As silly as this may sound, it has proven to offer enormous benefit to those who practice it. Without changing anything other
than prefacing her affirmations with "I love it when..." one of our
Playshop graduates released over 35 pounds in less than 10 weeks!

Why Journaling Sometimes Backfires

Several of our readers have said, "I have been faithfully journaling for
years and, if anything, my life has become even MORE challenging!"
There is actually a very logical reason for this. If you are writing about how
BAD everything is, you are unfortunately attracting the very people,
places, and things you dread most. The only time I feel comfortable refer-
encing something of a negative nature is when I am writing about it for the
sole purpose of **releasing** and letting go of it. The act of writing is a wonderful power tool when you use it to describe what you desire. When,
however, you use it to vent your hostilities, it becomes a self-sabotaging
weapon that is destined to undermine your joy. In other words, anything
you are FOR empowers you; anything you are AGAINST weakens you.
This is why it is essential that you make wise choices when it comes to
putting things in writing. Ancient people of the Nile were convinced that
writing made things real. If this is the case, what do you want to make
REAL in your life today?

Why Traditional Therapy Isn't Always Effective

Although traditional therapy can be quite valuable, it often invites us to
focus upon things that are NOT working, things that distress us, and
things that cause us to re-experience fear and pain. Since "Whatever we
FOCUS upon with FEELING gets BIGGER," focusing too much upon the
negative aspects of Life causes us to attract the very things we DON'T
WANT! If, for instance, we allow an unhappy childhood to dominate our
thoughts in our adulthood, we literally rob ourselves of the joy that Life is
so eager for us to have. When we dwell upon "what's going wrong in our
lives," we inadvertently invite many more things to go wrong! That's why
it is so important for us to understand the magnitude of the power we possess. When we begin to focus upon our blessings, we attract MORE blessings. When we redirect our attention to "what is right with the world," we
begin to experience a much higher quality of life. If you are ready to live
the life you love and love the life you live, we invite you to appreciate all
the goodness of Life that you already have and then bask in the positive
possibilities that are awaiting your discovery. Take only 1% of your attention to focus upon what you don't want and 99% to focus upon what you
prefer instead. Herein lies the key to experiencing a more sustainable

sense of joy. As it turns out, love, joy, and laughter are truly the best therapy, because they make you feel great and offer only positive side-effects!

Why Getting What We Want Doesn't Always Make Us Happy

I used to think, "If only I could have everything I want, THEN I would be happy." It wasn't until 1995 (when Life brought me everything I asked for at the speed of thought) that I realized that this was definitely not the case! It was like going to my favorite restaurant and ordering everything on the menu and trying to eat it all at one sitting. Although everything was delicious, it was also extremely overwhelming. It was like trying to satisfy my thirst by drinking from a fire hydrant! Even though I received everything I wanted, I often didn't want it once I got it. That's when I was inspired to make the following request of Life: "Please bring me only that which serves me best at this time, in the most appropriate ways that express the highest good for All Life Everywhere. Instead of always getting what I want, please arrange for me to want what I get." By allowing Life to unveil Its grandest plan this way, I am much happier and far more content.

Why the Rich Get Richer and the Poor Get Poorer

Have you ever wondered why some people are very successful in life in terms of loving relationships, good health, and prosperity, while others seem to have overwhelming challenges in one or more of these areas? Coming just a little closer to home, have you ever wondered why YOU sometimes feel absolutely invincible, while at other times you feel like a helpless victim of circumstance?

To unravel this unsolved mystery, we must first know how we unknowingly attract unwanted stuff into our lives in order to better understand how to consciously attract what we prefer instead. This single awareness will provide us with an invaluable gift more precious than all the gold in Fort Knox. When I first became aware of how I acquired MY so-called "lot in life," I was both shocked and amazed! As you read the next paragraph, you may be taken aback at first, but when you read a little further you'll discover how YOU have the power to create a happier, more fulfilling life in ways that are easier and more rewarding than you have ever dreamed possible!

The shocking news is: WE are the creators of our OWN experience. WE are the ones who attract and create both what we don't want as well as what we do want! Everything we experience is based upon what we CHOOSE to think about, talk about, observe, and imagine. What we believe also has an enormous influence over what prevails in our lives. Anything we say "yes" to, we automatically invite into our experience (ah yes). Likewise, whatever we say "no" to, we ALSO invite into our lives (oh-oh).

In other words, whatever we choose to give our attention to (whether it's something wanted or unwanted) is what we are knowingly or unknowingly asking to become real in our lives. When you finally realize that "energy flows where your attention goes," you will be highly motivated to keep your attention exclusively upon that which you desire!

It's true! Our thoughts have the power to create our realities—both good and bad, wanted and unwanted! We are certainly not implying that anyone intentionally attracts and creates undesirable experiences. For that matter, most of us are seldom aware of how we attract positive circumstances into our lives. If we neglect to consciously choose what we prefer in life, we are doomed to live life by default. Whatever we give our attention to is the very thing we can expect to call forth into being. Therefore, it is in our best interest to make it a habit to visualize the positive possibilities of Life instead of dwelling upon things that worry us. If the state of "what is" doesn't appeal to you, then consciously shift your attention and clearly envision "the life of your dreams." Above all, it is essential for you to imagine that your requests have already been granted. This is the golden key that opens the door to miraculous manifestations. Since we can attract a quality of life that matches the quality of our thoughts, we can consciously create favorable conditions in our lives. We can use the power of our thoughts, words, feelings and imagination to intentionally improve the quality of our lives. This means we are NOT victims and that NOTHING can really hold power over us without our consent.

It is so exciting to realize that most conditions in our lives are usually nothing more than expressions of our thoughts, feelings, and beliefs. Once again, whatever we think about and talk about is what we are asking to bring about!

So why is it that "the rich get richer?" Perhaps it's because they have a tendency to focus upon prosperity, and in doing so, they attract more abundance. And why do "the poor get poorer"? Maybe it's due to their overwhelming fear of scarcity, which causes them to stay focused upon poverty. Unfortunately, their limiting beliefs cause them to unknowingly attract the very things they fear most, which results in even more lack and limitation in their lives. It helps to remember when we are feeling overwhelmed that it's just temporary and fear is just an acronym for "Forgetting Everything's All Right"!

When we are positively focused, we naturally attract an abundance of good into our lives. When we are negatively focused, however, we are more likely to see abundant evidence of lack and limitation. Both scenarios are perfect examples of the Law of Magnetic Attraction in action. Remember...this immutable universal law is always at work. How you experience it is all based upon how you choose to focus your attention. Take time today to focus upon things you desire, such as: abundance, balance, health, happiness, harmony, peace, playfulness, prosperity, love, beauty, and sustained joy. Now notice what you begin to magically attract and create!

Suggested Reading and Websites

Jacquelyn Aldana's work
- For Playshops and ordering information for Ms. Aldana's books, see www.15MinuteMiracle.com
- Jacquelyn Aldana, *The 15-Minute Miracle Revealed*, Inner Wisdom Publications, Los Gatos CA, 2003.
- Jacquelyn Aldana, *Miracle Manifestation Manual II*, Inner Wisdom Publications, Los Gatos CA, 2003.
- Jacquelyn Aldana, *Make Room For Miracles*, Inner Wisdom Publications, Los Gatos CA. (Forthcoming)
- Jacquelyn Aldana, *Shortcuts to Miracles*, Inner Wisdom Publications, Los Gatos, CA, 2003.

Other authors using a similar approach
- Lynn Grabhorn, *Excuse Me, Your Life is Waiting: The Astonishing Power of Feelings*, Hampton Roads, 2000.
- Lynn Grabhorn, *The Excuse Me Your Life is Waiting Playbook*, Hampton Roads, 2001.

Chapter 11

A 'Resolving Dualism' Approach: Neutralization of Opposites Using the PEAT Process

by Zivorad Slavinski

Foreword by Grant McFetridge

Although there have been a lot of people looking at how to acquire what we now call 'peak states', there are only a small handful of people who have actually developed effective working processes. Zivorad is one of those people and has one of the most important of the current processes.

I feel very blessed to have this chapter about Zivorad's work, because it illustrates a very different and important approach to the whole field of peak states. His PEAT process not only gives very radical results swiftly, but works on most people that have used it. In this short chapter, we don't go into the steps of his process. The specifics can be found in his book, *PEAT and Neutralization of Primordial Polarities—Theory and Practice*, by Zivorad Slavinski. It can be purchased at www.spiritual-technology.com.

I first became aware of Zivorad's work before his current process came out, through a workshop participant of mine, Evertt Edstrom. Evertt had been trying to heal a severe physical problem as well as change his consciousness for the better. Evertt's comment was that of everything he'd tried, Zivorad's and my work were the only ones that had had a dramatic effect on his state of consciousness. This caught my attention, and I began to hear similar stories from other people I knew. I have to admit I had a momentary feeling of inadequacy when I started hearing about his results!

I suspect that Zivorad has found a way to work with phenomena that actually underlie the mechanism of the creation of the separate spirit from the Creator itself, as is reexperienced during the first contraction of birth (or its equivalent in C section babies—see Volume 2). Investigating this and putting it into an understandable framework, along with other discoveries in this field, will keep us busy for years to come. I wouldn't be surprised if in the future, when various methods become more integrated, PEAT or one of its successors will be a first or primary step in acquiring peak states of consciousness.

Zivorad also has the distinction of being one of the few breakthrough pioneers that doesn't live in California, USA, but rather in Yugoslavia. I want to make a special point of honoring the breakthroughs he made without the close synergy of nearby colleagues, all during the turmoil that his country has been in.

One of the most wonderful things about this work is the joy of sharing exciting discoveries with peers, and then seeing what can grow out of it. The computer industry went through this in Silicon Valley in the '70s, power and energy psychologies went through that stage while Kate Sorensen was nurturing them via her conferences in the '90s, and the field of peak states of consciousness is now in a similar state of flux, change, growth, and excitement. Zivorad's contribution will spur that growth on. Welcome to these amazing times!

Zivorad's Story
A Lifetime of Searching

I'm now 65. In my lifetime (since I was 17), I have practiced many different things: from classical yoga and Zen to Scientology, EST, thelemic magic, Access, shamanism—you name it. I am also a clinical psychologist.

From about 1980, I practiced and led the so-called Enlightenment Intensive, developed by Charles Berner (aka Yogeswar Muni). Its goal is direct experience of Truth or Enlightenment, by mainly focusing on four fundamental questions: Who am I? What am I? What is life? and What is another? Fifteen years ago I wrote and published a book with the title Encounters with Truth: Enlightenment Intensive. For ten years, until about 1990, I practiced just that Enlightenment Intensive system. I led many Intensives and trained many masters as well. Today, there are more masters in Yugoslavia than in the rest of the world. I participated in and led many 3-day Intensives, some 14-day, one 30-day and even one six weeks long.

After 1990 I started developing my own systems but even today I hold the Enlightenment Intensive in high esteem. Ten years ago I developed it further and five years ago I created the 'Alternative Technique of Intensive', which shortened it tremendously and made it more efficient at the same time. It's difficult to say what all my material covers, because I developed almost ten different systems, each one coming out of the previous one.

People still keep those systems I developed in high esteem. However, even with all those different systems I was not able to solve my most fundamental life problem. Then I created PEAT, which probably falls into the category of the Energy Therapies. And I finally solved my crucial problem, which had been with me in many of my previous lifetimes, as well as in so many of the people whom I process with PEAT.

Introduction to the PEAT Processes

PEAT is an abbreviation for 'Psycho Energetic Auro Technology'. It is both a therapeutic technique and an efficient method of spiritual development.

I created PEAT four years ago from different systems of Energy Psychology, Yoga and Vedanta. Shortly after its creation I made the essential creative breakthrough which allows one to transcend dualistic consciousness and to effectively and permanently solve hard core problems; most of all, one's fundamental life problem. The newest PEAT process is called PEAT-3 (or DP-3 for short).

DP-3 has since evolved into specific processes that put people into a variety of peak states. One in particular causes people to no longer have emotional charge on their past or future—in essence, they report that the past and the future just vanish. These processes we call 'rundowns', and are described towards the second half of this chapter.

Definition - PEAT

A process using an energetic deep-diving approach that eliminates the underlying cause of a variety of core and repeating problems in one's life. PEAT stands for Psycho Energetic Auro Technology. The original PEAT process is considered a 'light' PEAT.

Definition - DP-3

The third PEAT process developed after the first version. The DP-3 stands for Deep PEAT third level. It results in eliminating the core attraction/aversions a person has, and eliminates many core symptoms that express this inner conflict.

Definition - Rundowns

Processes using PEAT-3, consisting of specific steps with definite and intended end phenomena. Certain kinds of peak states result.

Definition - P/F RD

Short for Past/Future Rundown. This one eliminates the emotional experiences of the past, and the future as well, while the memory of the
past remains intact. Similar to, but possibly not the same as, the Inner
Peace state described in Chapter 9.

The Background Problem - Dualism and Unity

One of the shortcomings of the majority of therapeutic and personal
growth methods is that one should always be at cause, never at effect. In
other words, these methods want to attain just positive polarities. In fact,
the habitual way of trying to solve human problems is by attempting to
eradicate one of the opposites. As Ken Wilber points out in *No Boundary*,
"...we suppose that life would be perfectly enjoyable if we could only eradicate all the negative and unwanted poles of the pairs of opposites. If we
could vanquish pain, evil, death, suffering, sickness, so that goodness, life,
joy and health abound—that indeed would be the good life, and in fact,
that is precisely many people's idea of Heaven." But in vain! Modern
physics, hand in hand with oriental mystic philosophy, points out that reality can only be considered a union of opposites. Reality is not found in
the crest nor the trough of the wave, but in their unity.

True, some researchers tried to find a better solution to the fundamental problems of human existence. They tried to reconcile fundamental polarities and they had some success in their endeavor. (I don't take into
account traditional systems of Oriental philosophy, which destroy the
whole of mind stuff, but which also demand the investment of one's entire
lifetime). But only in DP-3 (as far as I know) have we so far gotten it into
an operative method. To one who knows Perennial Philosophy, the only
permanent solution in this dual universe is not to try to get just the positive side (it's impossible, because the negative one follows it as a shadow),
but to transcend polar opposites and experience them as two sides of one
and the same reality.

Mystical Traditions and the 'Primordial Polarities'

There is no definite theory about the genesis of 'Primordial Polarities'.
From an experiential perspective, when a Spiritual Being for the first time
enters from the Unmanifested universe (Void, Brahma, Sunyata, Tao) to
this universe of matter, energy, time and space, the Spiritual Being posts
two energetic pillars at its entrance, his/her first Yin and Yang. They de-

fine the Being's playground and from that moment on the Being plays his/her fundamental game of life between them.

Oriental philosophers of ancient times knew that we had to understand yin and yang in order to work with the manifestations of creation. When we go back to the Tao or the Source of All, yin and yang become One and distinctions cease to exist. In the Void balance and imbalance cease to exist. When dealing with all the manifested things, we have to understand imbalance (extremes) in order to find balance. Ultimate balance presupposes neutralization of all polarities, where all that is left is the shifting between emptiness (Void, Tao, Quantum Vacuum) and fullness (manifestations) in the universe of energy, matter, space and time.

A Being's 'Primes' are the highest goals a Being wants to attain, again and again. They are a Being's most powerful attractors. But the main characteristic of a Being's fundamental game of life is that it is unconscious and compulsive. In endless situations of life, Primordial Polarities make his/her life seesaw back and forth unconsciously and compulsively between Primordial Polarities. The Polarities are not fixed values, rather they are like alternating electric current. For a period of time, one Polarity seems to be the positive goal (Being strives with all his/her power to attain it) and another the negative (and Being does his/her best to avoid it). But after some time their values change, and the effort is reversed. Different Beings have different Primordial Polarities, but some Beings share the same ones.

Definition - Primordial Polarities ('Primes')

The most fundamental paired attraction/avoidance themes in one's life. They are called 'primes' for short.

Neutralization of the Primordial Polarities

One can't solve one's most fundamental problem in life until one attains neutralization of Primordial Polarities. This is the most important goal for both a person's spiritual development and their everyday life. By practicing different spiritual disciplines one can destimulate the problem of the Polarities for a short time, or in other words truncate it, but sooner or later it gets restimulated again. When one gets a Neutralization of their Primes with PEAT Deep Processing, one sees his/her previous life as a series of compulsive and unconscious oscillations from one Primordial Polarity to another. Of course, neutralization of Primes doesn't solve all your problems, just the most fundamental one. I'll emphasize that again: It solves the most fundamental problem in your life.

There are many others problems based on dualities, but they can be easily and quickly solved with the same Deep PEAT process.

Until recently only a small number of selected people knew about this. The reason for this is simple. Neutralization of one's Primordial Polarities was a secret for many centuries, from Taoism and Tarot to middle age alchemy and 19th-century occultism. The whole Kabala is about neutralization of opposites—one must neutralize them and bring one's own consciousness to the central point, encompassing both of them on the so-called Middle Pillar. In its quintessence, alchemy is about the neutralization of polarities, which is the biggest secret of that spiritual science. Advaita Vedanta, the most profound system of practical philosophy there is, speaks only about non-duality. ("Advaita" means non-dual.) This secrecy is why just a few selected individuals knew about the possibility of solving the most fundamental problem in their lives. That's no longer the case.

The Origins of the PEAT Process

About 30 years ago, in some paper I read the following words: "If you want to create an efficient system for handling human problems, you must not forget that this is a dual universe." I felt as if I got a strong punch into my face. There was some jewel inside those words, but I was not able to take it out from the mass of thoughts I had in my mind. Yet, I never forgot those words.

Some time later I had a funny experience. Passing by a garden on the outskirts of Belgrade, I noticed two men trying to bring down a large upstanding wooden pillar. Its lower part was buried deeply in the ground. They swung it left and right, forward and backward and in about five minutes brought it down. A question came to my mind: "How long a time would they need if they tried to do it by pushing that pillar in only one direction? Much, much more. Hours or perhaps days." In that moment I had valuable cognition and the whole idea of new, more efficient methods of therapy and spiritual development came to my mind. I called them by one name, "Alternate technique", and indeed they proved to be very fruitful. They later developed into the PEAT process.

How PEAT Works

In this section, we'll describe a bit about the process so you can get a feel for what happens. It would be impractical to cover the detailed procedure for the PEAT process in this short chapter. However, we have books on the process that can be purchased by going to our website at www.spiritual-technology.com. We also have an email discussion group for people using the process, which can be joined by also going to our website.

There are two levels of PEAT: Shallow and Deep. Shallow resembles EFT very much, as it was my starting point, but that process is now an uninteresting part of my work. I use it very rarely, just with phobias and similar problems. Even in shallow PEAT, the main point is the "I" point, in the middle of chest (as in Grant's Whole-Hearted Healing work) and there is no tapping, just putting the fingers on the points.

Deep PEAT is quite different. I give credit to EFT as a starting point, of course, but I don't apply EFT in Deep PEAT (or in DP3, Past/Future Rundown, etc.), which is now my main "forte". I use only three points (around an eye), and if a client's processing goes smoothly, all the mind stuff comes to the surface on the first point (under an eyebrow). That's the reason I call this point the "Insight point". The Deep PEAT processes are developing all the time.

So far, I've developed two levels of deep PEAT: DP-2 and DP-3. I use DP-2 in my practice when I have intellectual-type clients, the ones who experience difficulties in separating thoughts from emotions and body sensations. DP-3 (which is an abbreviation of Deep PEAT Third Level) is much more efficient than DP-2.

In PEAT Deep Processing you start with a problem and you uncover, not new aspects of the same problem, but deeper and quite different contents on the chain of problems. This finally leads to the deepest cause of the problem you started with (or if you prefer, the highest cause of it). In other words, you don't try to eliminate pain, sickness, disturbance or other problems directly, but instead you uncover the negative core beliefs, or, if you like, roots and metastructures behind the problems. When you work with a problem using PEAT, all kinds of material comes up to consciousness. In many other therapeutic systems people usually ignore this material. But in PEAT they are the crux of the matter! The PEAT session lasts from 15 minutes to one and one-half hours, the average being 30-50 minutes. When you get to the deepest cause, the problem vanishes for good.

Now, the following is very important. In one to three sessions of PEAT Deep Processing with a client, you uncover, make conscious, and neutralize his/her Primordial Polarities ("Primes" for short). Neutralization of one's Primes solves one's most fundamental problem forever! You can't avoid it even if you want to. It is an extremely important experience which liberates a human being from the deadly grab of the fundamental forces of duality, which the huge majority of people on planet Earth seem to know nothing about. Just before that moment there is a short confusion. A person doesn't understand usual questions, and becomes a bit dizzy and disoriented. It's natural, of course, because the limits of the playground on which the game of life was played have vanished. It is like the walls of the house you lived in as a slave for your entire life have suddenly evaporated.

At the moment when one discovers one's own Primes there is a neutralization of opposites. One sees one Primordial Polarity inside another and vice versa. They become ONE. That experience is always different from what one expects it to be.

DP-3 has a number of very good characteristics. Its main strength is the ability to directly neutralize specific pairs of polarities in a very short time. Here are some examples of Primes: Creating and Destroying; Potential and Actual; I and not-I; Tiny and Endless; Power and Powerlessness; Unity and Duality; Consciousness and Unconsciousness; Knowledge and Ignorance; Justice and Injustice; Spiritual universe and Material universe; I and Another; Giving and Receiving; Advancing and Retreating; Liking and Disliking; Happiness and Unhappiness; Tolerance and Intolerance; I want to smoke and I don't want to smoke; Desire to be faithful to one's partner and desire for exciting adventures with another; Scarcity and Abundance; and so on. Using both polarities from the beginning of the process, you destroy the mind stuff (*chitta* in yoga terminology) between them very quickly. DP-3 is very fast. A session to finish neutralizing the pair rarely takes any longer than 10 to 30 minutes

What is the value of such experience, which is no doubt a peak experience? Exaltation doesn't last long, it's true. But you see your whole life become clear. You see through the fundamental game of life you unconsciously and compulsively used to play in many different variations. You are set free from your main compulsions. You could still play the same games, but now you can choose other games as well. You have freedom to... and freedom from...

In addition, after uncovering and neutralizing your Primes you become more conscious of new and old problems, but all your problems are solved much more quickly. Their structure often follows your fundamental game of life in endless variations.

Since I created PEAT more then 900 people have neutralized their Primes and gotten freedom from the most fundamental, unconscious and compulsive problems of their whole life (and many lifetimes before). Changes in their lives were profound and substantial.

Reports of Some Members of My Research Group Using DP-3

Bojana reports:

> Yesterday in the Omega group Zivorad explained the new DP-3 method and it was a smashing success. Just for one pair of people it took a little more than ten minutes to do the process. Everybody else did it in just ten minutes. But one woman did it in only four and a half minutes. It is a wonder. What is more interesting, after the process, no one can do another process immediately, because one gets key-out. It shows that a large amount of mental masses has been removed or destroyed. I'm glad I can tell you that the new DP-3 method is a really golden key for spiritual, emotional and psychological liberation of a human being. It's so simple, efficient and quick. It opens the door to completely new dimensions of therapy and emotional freedom. It's amazing when you watch what happens after a neutralization of some polarity. If it was some compulsive behavior, and you try intentionally to experience

that compulsion again some time after the neutralization, you can't! It simply slips out in a second.

Lune reports:

My wife and I have been members of Zivorad's Omega group for several years. We had a wonderful experience today and would like to share it with other list members.

First I would like to say that from my point of view DP-3 is the most effective method in dichotomy neutralization we ever practiced. In my case the whole process took about seven minutes to complete neutralization. Both dichotomies dissolved in endless space of white light. My body was flooded with energetic sensations and an unforgettable feeling of absolute peace and liberty.

After the process I realized that all great things are very simple and effective and DP-3 is definitely one of them. With this powerful tool any dichotomy problem can be solved in minutes.

Recently I led three workshops in the USA, which were PEAT Processors' training courses. On the first one, in Charleston, WV, I had opportunity to "blind" process a lady. What does "blind" mean? Simply, she preferred not to tell what the trauma from her childhood was about. It was a very heavy one, with a lot of very bad emotional charge. In my estimation it was some bad abuse or incest. But such estimation is not important at all. What is important is the following fact: In PEAT you can process a client 'blind', without knowing what the problem is. You just start from "Your problem." Although it was a blind process, it was a most successful one. In only 20 minutes she made conscious and neutralized her Primordial Polarities. Let's take a look at the process:

"My problem." There was a lot of charge. Lady started to cry and screamed terribly, but was able to follow instructions.

"I'm shaking and freezing." Continues crying and actually she is shaking strongly.

"I'm scared." She is trembling all over and cries.

"I feel pressure in my stomach."

"My heart is beating very hard."

"I feel sinking down." Still she looks a little bit uneasy.

"I'm becoming very, very small."

"Strange thing happens. I now feel very big!" Her expression completely changes. She looks now positively surprised and she is smiling.

"From a great height I'm looking at myself as very, very small."

"My big 'I' and my small 'I' are coming closer to each other."

"They are merging."

"They are one!"

Her Primordial Polarities were Big and Small. There was applause in the group of participants. When I asked her: "What's the matter with your problem we started from?", she laughed and said it seemed to her empty, stupid and unimportant, not a problem anymore. I had to explain to the group that all processes don't go so quickly.

I'll give another example of a man doing a session. I asked him not to give up on whatever came up, as the day before he'd left before the end of the process. And we had a wonderful session lasting only 19 minutes. Below is a transcript of it. Pay attention to his experience of the first polarization after the beginning problem.

His problem was: "I lead therapeutic groups and when everything is not as I would like, I get attacks of uncontrolled anger"

"I can't control my anger"

"I am angry at myself for not being able to control my anger." Processor's comment: Polarization begins.

"Two angers are moving back and forth."

"There is the anger toward others and the anger toward myself moving like two blocks."

"One block moves forward and the other moves behind and I feel torn between them."

"There are two parts pulling in the opposite directions and a shade between them."

"Now these parts are turning around me and I'm shaking."

"These parts represent me and others and I don't know what to do."

"I feel ambivalence, don't want to choose."

"I feel being in the column of light, separate from the world. These parts are circling around."

"Now everything disappeared. There is only me in the huge ball of light."

His Primordial Polarities (Primes for short) were "Me and Others."

Long-Term Effects of DP3

Three years after neutralizing Primes, one person comments: "Piora asked us to post our experiences we have had after Primes neutralization. During this period of time, more than three years, I neutralized a lot of different polarities, but recently I became aware of one strange situation. When I want something, I have nothing against the opposite polarity of that thing. I do my best to get something, but at the same time I am not fighting with its opposite side, it is not opposition it is a complementary thing. Therefore, I have more energy for anything I want."

Permanent Change and States of Consciousness

One idea runs like a thread through all systems of psychological and spiritual development: How to get permanent results? Is it possible to keep our wins stable, without losing them after some time?

A great majority of system originators state just that. Their systems of development, they tell us, give permanent results: Good feelings, positive attitudes toward life, ability to cope with problems, a higher level of understanding of life and huge expansion of consciousness, etc. The fact is they don't. As the old Chinese Book of Change or I Ching taught humans thousands of years ago—only change is permanent.

I was stimulated to post this on our lists because recently one PEAT Processor asked me that old question: How to anchor the state, to make the satisfaction and happiness of his clients permanent?

The fact is that permanency and development are mutually exclusive ideas. With many systems you can get relatively permanent states. But if you wish to continue developing, spreading into new dimensions, spaces and dynamisms, you encounter new problems and your previous satisfaction and happiness disappear.

Other Outcomes of the PEAT Process: The Great Space

Neutralization of Primordial Polarities is not the end of our adventures with PEAT. After neutralization, for a short period of time in front of you opens the so-called Great Space (Quantum Vacuum, Tao, Source of All, Void, Oneness, Sunyata...) or corridor to the parallel universes. In it one becomes huge, omnipresent or limitless, in Union with everything. It is Non-dual consciousness. But after the first moment of that Non-dualness, the very threshold of Great Space seems to be the crossroad to the parallel realities or parallel worlds, where relations are quite different and hard to compare with what exists in our world.

At first, only a few of my associates succeeded entering the Great Space. But now, after many months of PEAT research, I am able to say that there is a simple, easy and quick way of entering the Great Space for every diligent practitioner. There are three means for that: 1) Care with 'unpolluted' language we use in processing; 2) Using metaphors as doors or corridors for entering the Great Space; and 3) the PEAT Technique.

'Unpolluted' language: From much of NLP research we know that we process everything that is said to us by trying to duplicate it. When a processor uses 'polluted language', as they mostly do, he/she forces his/her map of the world on the client. For example, in a well-known Scientology process (Traumatic Incident Reduction or TIR) we use the command, "Go to the beginning of that incident...What do you see?" Well, some clients don't see (at least at some periods of their lives), but they hear of feel. In such a case a client's true experience has been ignored. When one gets such a command, one has to go through a 'translation process' to reorient to the processor's presuppositions, his school of thought, or his system. Thus therapy goes to the direction of the processor's map of the world. As Abraham Maslow said: "If you only have a hammer, everywhere you will see only nails."

Metaphors: Metaphors are frozen structures in an individual's subjective universe; they are frozen rivers of information and once we melt that ice, a lot of precious and hidden information comes to the field of our consciousness. In contrast to this, 'unpolluted' language must leave the greatest possible freedom for movements of the client's mind, and at the same time elucidate his/her metaphors. When during a process a client says "I'm empty...", "I'm stuck..." or "There is nothing...", we now know that there is rich and valuable information in that emptiness, stuckness and nothingness. Such metaphors are frozen corridors to the new universes behind them. They make a Wall of Ice which we are now able to melt and pass through to the new dimensions of freedom.

This system has a tremendous potential for further development.

Discovering the PEAT 'Rundowns'

I made the breakthrough working with my wife Alda (Jadranka). I applied DP-3 for just a couple of minutes on her past time, and then both Alda and I had a real shock. To explain, I will give you a short description of the session. When I asked her to describe her experience of present time, she said: "Nothing, I just feel myself as empty space, like some line, separating past on the left-hand side and future on the right-hand side." When she tried to recall her past, she got an emotionally dry memory of some street she had walked on one day. That was all. Her experience of present time stayed the same in all repeats of the process. Her experience of the past changed in that the memory of the street became shorter and shorter and in her fourth attempt it became just a minute point and then vanished. *For her it was a moment of strong shock, because at that moment the whole past vanished.* She was stunned, and for a couple of minutes she could not speak. The strangest thing of all was that the future vanished as well, although we did not touch it in the process! After Alda recovered herself, she started to speak fervently and could not stop for almost an hour, discharging huge masses of energy.

What follows is a small part of her communications: "I have a strong impression of not being able to repeat anything, even this that I'm saying to you now. Now I understand how past time 'holds' the future in itself. I destroyed the past, and the future vanished at the same time. I feel as if I untied some knot which connected past and future. Now I have no place in which to put anything... When I try to remember, it is more recreating the past then remembering. Before, when I remembered something, I had an impression of entering the room of memory and taking some memory with me. Now, I can't; it is like entering into an empty room. I feel that I have to reconstruct the past—like being on an empty stage, forcing myself to take some elements and reconstruct the scenery."

Varieties of PEAT Rundown Processes

After this breakthrough, I started creating a series of Rundowns (that is, processes consisting of specific steps and with definite and intended end phenomena) which have as the final goal the greater liberation from the physical universe. As everybody knows, the four main components of the physical universe are matter, energy, space and time. The process which I call Past/Future Rundown pretty much handles time. The Space Rundown seems promising, although just a few people have experienced it. Next come Energy and Matter Rundowns which seem to me to be more difficult to develop. Since I recently started leading DP-3 workshops, more people are equipped with simple and efficient methods for developing next-level processes, so it's reasonable to expect that we are at the verge of a new expansion of consciousness.

My idea behind the Past/Future Rundown (P/F Rd for short) was as follows: In his/her life a human being has experienced innumerable traumas and unpleasant incidents. Trying to resolve them one after another is a Sisyphean task. The highest goal a researcher can have is to eradicate all negative charge from one's whole past with just one shot, in one session. Perhaps it's hard to believe, but it seems I got just that. Thus, in a nutshell P/F Rd is a holographic process. The smallest is in the biggest and by eradicating the charge in the smallest part of the person's past we eradicate it in the whole of his/her past as well. A very old dream finally came true!

Experimenting with this method, I have noticed one thing which is important for the development and perfection of the methodology: after the past vanishes with this rundown, some people will discover just one incident in their past which attracts their attention. It is usually a very charged one. It's like a nail having its head out of the otherwise smooth and empty surface of the past. When the P/F Rundown is applied once more to the specific incident, it gets flattened very, very quickly and the person gets an additional sense of psychological and spiritual freedom.

Although we're enthusiastic about the results of our experimental work here, we must be cautious as well! These Rundowns are not for everybody, especially not for emotionally unstable people!!!

Naturally, I will have to do a lot of experiments with this system and procedure. For example, I need to check if the freedom from the past phenomena will be permanent, or could it become weaker and weaker after some time? But, to my knowledge, there is nothing so simple, so easy to learn and with such far-reaching consequences as DP-3. I can't help remembering my endless hours of other kinds of processing with some of the much advertised systems. Now, it seems, they belong to history.

Individual Experiences with the Past and Future Rundown

Alhor writes:

> In everyday life, like before the process, I work, read my books, practice my sport, live with my family, but all is somehow clear, especially the past. I checked myself by recalling memories of the worst events in my life, and I was able to recall them fully with many details but there was not a bad emotion in them. That is a strange thing: now they are not unpleasant events! They are just events like pictures from the dust disseminated by the wind of absolute acceptance. No charge, no feelings.

> How nice to be free from any charge that comes from the past!!!

Bogdan, an electronic engineer describes his experience with Past/Future Rundown this way:

> Yesterday we had a meeting of the Omega experimental group. I was one of several clients that were processed by Zivorad using his new technique. The process was very short, not longer than 15 minutes. However, it will probably make deep changes in my personality and the way of my thinking generally.

> During those 15 minutes, visions and feelings were changing frequently. From "I'm sitting in the chair" to "I'm the top of the mountain" and "There isn't anything." Finally, I forgot literally everything. I wasn't able to talk for moments. On Zivorad's questions of who are my mother, father, or cats, I wasn't able to answer. Even now, several hours later, I can hardly recall what was going on in the process, so I can't tell much about details. Furthermore, I've mixed my memories with visions, sensations and feelings of other members of the group who were processed.

> So, the process was fascinating, but what came after was really unbelievable. I'm able to remember all facts from my past, but facts look just like some data from a database. No charge, no feelings. All the time I'm wondering was something really happened or is it just my imagination? I can recall good and bad experiences, but all charges about negative experiences just faded away. It's hard to believe, but now I haven't any unpleasant experience in my lifetime. Happily, memories about pleasant experiences are intact, only without any charge.

> I've tried to compare my current feelings with those that I had after Primes neutralization, but I can't remember how it was. It's a little bit tricky because I'm not able to compare anything with similar events that happened before.

> Also, there isn't any fear or doubt that may come from the future. Freedom is complete, I enjoy in endless pleasant emptiness.

Lune, another member of the Omega Group, wrote after P/F Rundown:
When thinking on past or future, I feel now like a movie director able to create things by my own free-will. Past doesn't influence me in the same way as before the process. I always had a feeling that past influenced my life in some way, now it's gone. When Zivorad asked me to remember something from my past it was an unbelievably strange question for me. I had some idea of past but no contents at all. It looks to me that all my past data are now reassembled in some different way and have no charge—just pure facts. This gives me freedom to search through my new database whenever I decide it's necessary, without being connected all the time.

Now I can change my past, getting completely different influences in my present and future life. There is no feeling of time track as I had before, it looks like the present point got bigger and past and future tracks vanished. I am pretty amazed that the whole process took only 25 minutes. By the way, I was a slow one compared to some other Omega Group members. People used to say for somebody in deep trouble: 'He is a person without future.' After my experience today, I think having no future is excellent.

After experiencing end phenomena of P/F Rd, Jerry Pegden, famous teacher of the Light Language system, said:
Ten days ago my wife Olga and I visited Zivorad and Alda in Belgrade for PEAT processor's training, DP-3 training and Past/Future Rundown and some surprises. It was a wonderful experience on many fronts and we look forward to returning to Yugoslavia in the coming months. I wanted to wait a few days before posting my observations.

In a nutshell, I found his methods astonishingly simple, elegant, powerful and practical. They are easy to use with others and with yourself. Zivorad is a master teacher. He doesn't quit until he is satisfied that the student got it. Zivorad and Alda opened their hearts and home to us. It is obvious that they use their tools. If you forgot or never knew what nurturing and support means in a relationship, just spend five minutes in their presence.

After Zivorad neutralized my Primes (a set of core polarities) I felt a new lightness and I couldn't readily distinguish between me and outside of me. I instantly understood how I have moved between these two poles all my life but mostly out of body. Now instead of bouncing between them I have choice and I feel I am a part of the universe rather than separate from it.

Deep PEAT

Zivorad has processed thousands with his tools over the years so watching him do real "demos" was a treat. All the pieces from the

PEAT manual and more came together after the demos and a bit of practice. He taught many nuances and cleared up many questions I had from the manual. He also covered things not in the manual and expanded on some of the overlooked gems in the manual. The most obvious one was the simple method for working with a group of people at the same time.

DP-3

After learning DP-3 I thought, "This is so simple and obvious (in hindsight) why did no one ever think of it before?" There are many uses for DP-3. One of my favorites is to clear false dichotomies such as scarcity/abundance, dark/bright, and drowning/breathing. I have a list of hundreds of these which I am selectively going through with myself and others.

P/F Rundown

If you remove the charges from the past and don't focus on the future what is left? Only now. And that is what I heard and read happens with the P/F rundown. And so I was prepared for just that—so I thought. I was not prepared to see events and images meld together and literally vanish and be left with a feeling of only the void and a big smile. It has been 10 days and I can say the past rarely comes up for me now. It almost feels like there is an energy barrier keeping it out. I talked to a gentleman in Belgrade who had his P/F Rundown five months ago and it is still holding.

All my push-buttons are not gone but there are fewer and a clarity about those that remain. They don't seem to be part of the physical me but the energy me just waiting for release.

Bottom line—we will be returning soon to learn more (and we miss Alda's unbelievable sauces!). The universe continuously feeds Zivorad ideas for testing. He is continuously expanding his tool kit with simpler and more powerful technologies. Find a way to take his classes and be transformed.

Make no mistake though. While there are major benefits during the classes, to receive further big results and be able to help others you need to practice.

Questions and Answers on the Past/Future Rundown

Question: When the past vanishes, what happens to acquired data in the memory? One might suppose (I assume erroneously) that Bojana couldn't remember how to make dinner after 'losing her past'. Or how to write her name. But because there is no mention of any such disability, and indeed, your wife wrote a message to the lists, I assume that such data is NOT lost along with the past. Therefore am I to assume that all past data and knowledge have moved into present time in some manner?

Answer: You are right in your assumption that data from the past is NOT lost. Yes, all past data and knowledge have moved into the present in some way. Which way? I really don't know. Perhaps we will know that soon, or someone else will search it out. I will not, I'm not interested in it. I'm satisfied with what happens in this Past/Future Rundown. If Bojana had not been able to make dinner or write her name, it wouldn't have been a Past/Future Rundown, it would be a process of some terrible brainwashing, or for making people into idiots.

Question: Has there been any loss of acquired motor skills, like the ability to drive a car or use a typewriter after the process? You are an old-timer like me, and I am sure you recall the early Clearing Course 'clears' who had to reteach their bodies complex skills which had vanished along with their reactive minds.

Answer: No, nothing has been lost. I was involved with Scientology in London in 1977. That time I did only dianetics. Seven years later, at David Mayo AAC in Santa Barbara, I discovered that I was a dianetic 'clear'. So, I did not have any bad experiences which happened on the early Clearing Course, neither I ever heard about it until I read this post of yours. But neither Bojana nor Alda (Jadranka) lost any motor abilities, or any other kinds of abilities. There was shock in Alda's process because we did not expect what happened, especially so quickly and suddenly, but after a short time of communication with me she calmed down completely. With Bojana, I expected the same phenomenon, so it was less shocking for her. But both were quite amazed with that experience. Bojana was a dianetic clear as well and she remembers long processing, clearing engrams, implants and all such stuff. And now she removed all her past in less than 20 minutes! If I try to explain what happens with the past, it is this: You are *free to choose* from it whatever you want. In choosing something, you have a very strong impression that you recreate it. There is no compulsive stuff coming up. I guess someone could be able to recreate even some bad experience, but it's not probable. What is important is this: One has the freedom FOR the past and the freedom *from* the past. A new, higher level of freedom. The same as the Sixth Patriarch of Zen experienced—there is no place for dust!

Preliminary Results Using the Space Rundown Process

After some time I started experimenting with space. I have done it with only three persons so far (this is written on February 10th, 2003). Here is one sample experience:

Recently Zivorad got the idea to apply the DP3 method on four basic elements of this physical universe: matter, energy, space and time. As you know, he started with time. Few days ago he started experimenting with space. I was his second client, after Alda. This is what happened to me:

In some 10 minutes the process was over. I started with some definite and specific space but very soon it started to be transparent and blurred and at the end it vanished completely.

Several days passed and from time to time I tried to find out what was happening with space. For this what happened to me I am not able to find a single attribute, it is not empty space or infinite space nor anything else, not even emptiness. Simply there is not anything.

Now with open eyes I experience the space around me as unreal. Physical objects that should occupy some space I experience as designs on some transparent matter and I see through them. It is as if I have created them. I simply see through them. The illusory experiencing of things creates certainty and peace in me. This is the best I can say about the whole thing in this moment."

Now it becomes evident that past and future are impersonal, general, cosmic polarities, which can't exist one without other. The same with "here and there." We create them from the void and they go back to the void when we apply DP-3 on one of them.

Long-Term Results of the Rundown Process

Five weeks after I processed members of Omega Group with P/F Rundown, I checked with them on the results. What could be said? Separation from the past seems to be permanent. Their past is available, but has lost all its attractive power. It is uninteresting, boring mainly, and one has to force oneself to think about it, to remember it, or to enter it. One person compares it to a soap bubble. Her past somehow evades her intention to enter it and if she forces herself to, that part of the past just bursts like a bubble and disappears. Another says, "I tried to enter into some incidents from my past, but they don't touch me at all and I can't find an explanation for that." Still another keeps the knowledge of the past, but when he tries to think about it or to remember it, he has an impression of watching pale photos of someone else's life.

The majority of group members (almost all) have started to live in the present ("here and now") fully. One says: "Before the Past/Future Rundown I used to spend a lot of time thinking compulsively about what I did, what I said, what I should not have done, what others did to me and I did to them, what could happen tomorrow or what could not... Now it's over, I live absolutely here and now."

One member from our discussion list posted the question: "It's well known that many sicknesses are caused by traumas, etc. Do they vanish now since the traumas are empty of charge?" I have not noticed that happen. My opinion is that health concerns are mostly about genetic entity material and this Rundown doesn't handle it in this period of my work (or, if it does, I have not noticed it). One can turn the question upside down and ask: "One's good health is a result of past positive influences; now when the past is empty, does the health deteriorate?"

I noticed some mild problems which seem to be a result of this Rundown. Sometimes a person gives a phone call and for a couple of seconds can't remember their own name. It's as if the person, being previously widely spread around, has to make some efforts to pull oneself together into the 'I' position.

A couple of members have the strong feeling that the lives of other people are their own without any effort in identification. It's like "...vanishing limits between other people and myself."

One person says: "I used to say, destiny is what cards you get on the card table and your free will is how you play them. Now I have the feeling that I choose cards as I want to."

Dreams have changed as well. Some people dream a continuation of their day's activities, some meet many dead people (perhaps the compensation for losing one's past in the awake state?), some have the feeling that a separating line between the dream and awake state has become very thin. Some started having lucid dreams in which they know they are dreaming.

Changes to the Time-Line From P/F Rundown

Some of the group members have found their time-line has substantially changed. It is not a line leading backward-forward any more. It is like a global net, with many lines crossing each other. For example, one member of our group just changed only one unpleasant and humiliating experience from her past. After that moment, a completely new parallel or alternative world (or life or history) has come into existence and started to develop on its own without the person's interference. What is strange, but perhaps logical in some way, is that it is a completely new history, with happy and unhappy incidents, some other inhabitants, etc. In that alternative history Slobodan Milosevic never existed, neither did the NATO bombing of Belgrade happen, there are no ruins of destroyed buildings in Belgrade, and so on. What is also strange is that in that world, time is passing more quickly, so that the "present moment" in that world is more in the future. That person is a couple of years older than in "this our reality" and her children as well.

Another person has a strong feeling that this 'parallel happening' effect is caused just by one thought. In the middle of some activity if she has a thought "it could happen this way," it starts to happen that way in her consciousness as a parallel happening. Reality seems like a fan with count-less possibilities. What will become dominant depends only on one's at-tention. But there is no problem in normal functioning. To the person it doesn't matter what happens "in reality," because everything happens si-multaneously in all and every chain of happenings.

In Conclusion

What to say at the end of this chapter? A lot of serious work is waiting for us, together with a lot of pleasant surprises. That's for sure. As one re-searcher once said, we are just standing on the ocean shore trying to see what is waiting for us over there.

It seems to me that although Primordial Polarities neutralization is the important step toward spiritual freedom, the next great step forward to new and higher freedom could be the neutralization of basic polarities of time, space, energy and matter. In this kind of processing there is a lot of amazement, feelings of shock, followed many minutes after the process by a state of disbelief and awe. What is also important is that this method has a tremendous capacity for increased perfection and advancement, and such work is a real pleasure. We can now serve people in a much, much better way. I hardly can believe what has happened in these last days. We all feel that Providence leaned down, hugged us and gave us a warm and loving kiss. I'm sure that in the future you will hear a lot of fascinating news from this part of our planet.

Zivorad M.Slavinski
zivorad@spiritual-technology.com
www.spiritual-technology.com
++381 11 32 40 888
Yugoslavia

Suggested Reading and Websites

- Kenneth Grant, *Beyond The Mauve Zone*, Starfire:London, 1999.
- Zivorad Slavinski's website is at www.spiritual-technology.com. It has updates on his work, an e-list, articles, people's experiences, and available workshops.
- Zivorad Slavinski, *PEAT and Neutralization of Primordial Polarities - Theory and Practice*, 2001. It can be purchased at www.spiri-tual-technology.com.
- Ken Wilber, *No Boundary*, Shambala, 2001.

Chapter 12

A 'Meditative' Approach: Learning and Identifying Peak States Using Brain Biofeedback at the Biocybernaut Institute

by Dr. James Hardt

Foreword by Grant McFetridge

I first heard of Jim via articles he wrote back in the '70s. At that time, I was in college but fascinated with the potentials of the human brain. Jim was in the thick of it, doing exciting work with the then obscure spiritual paths of Zen and Yoga. My life took another direction, and so we didn't get to meet till 1996 during one of the Transpersonal Psychology conferences in Asilomar, California. Jim was giving a talk about brain biofeedback, and afterwards we spoke. He mentioned that he'd seen a phenomenon completely outside of our cultural beliefs—the merging of people's consciousnesses and memories when brain waves were synchronized[1]. This effect of merging consciousnesses was something that I had been taught as part of shamanic training, but had never hoped to understand from a Western hard science cultural perspective. I was filled with excitement at the promise that the work I was attempting could be understood from a Western viewpoint. I'll always treasure that moment.

We met briefly only a few more times over the course of the next decade. The encounters were brief but each time something useful and fascinating would come up from our quite different approaches to achieving exceptional mental and physical health. Last year I had the opportunity to meet with a number of brain biofeedback experts, when our Institute attempted to find ways to identify peak states using brain wave signals. To my surprise, these other experts had no idea what I was referring to, nor any belief that it was possible. This really brought home how ground-breaking and exceptional Jim's work was.

---

1 Dr. Hardt calls it "shared feedback™" which is when two or more people do brain wave feedback training at the same time and in the same chamber, thus hearing their own AND each other's tones and seeing their own scores and the scores of the 'others'.

We're very honored to have him contribute to this book. More information than can be put in this chapter, and the opportunity to have training experiences, can be found on the Web at www.biocybernaut.com.

Introduction

In this chapter, we shall examine the connection between peak states of consciousness and brain waves, known as the electroencephalogram or EEG. In addition, we will consider the extremely important topic of the cultural context in which we do our work of studying peak states and the exceptional skills and abilities that peak states confer. For most of Western history, those people gifted with the skills and abilities available in peak states, and the people who have studied peak states, have been a small minority in the mainstream cultures in which they lived. Also, good techniques for inducing peak states simply were not available. Thus, few people ever heard about peak states and even fewer had the opportunity to try to gain them. It has been rare for people with peak state abilities to become more than a tiny percentage of the people in a given culture. This means that, in the past, the benefits of peak states have not been available to make significant contributions to solving problems and contributing to the growth of individuals and their cultures. This is about to change.

Now we have an important new player on the scene in our modern times—science and technology for studying brain waves. Brain wave measurement technology can now validate the differences between peak states and ordinary states, by showing the underlying differences in the brainwaves. Brain wave feedback technology can help people who do not have the brain waves of giftedness to quickly develop those brain waves, and the peak states associated with those altered brain waves. Having a science and a technology to both *validate* and to *induce* peak states uses the beliefs of the dominant culture in science and technology to bypass some of its resistance to change.

Peak states of consciousness can be mapped by measuring the brain wave patterns of adepts with appropriately complex brain wave measurement techniques. This is something not widely appreciated by many people interested in peak states. In general, simple measurements are inadequate to this task, because the brain is so highly complex that our efforts to understand it from a scientific perspective must also be complex. Some of this data is based on techniques and technologies that are unique to our work at the Biocybernaut Institute, and are not being used by other researchers. We have conducted long-term studies here in the USA and in India with exceptional people who demonstrate brain wave patterns that would cause alarm among many researchers and licensed and certified experts. Such unusual brain wave patterns would often lead to immediate diagnoses of pathology, when in fact advanced spiritual states are at the root of these exceptional brain wave patterns.

We will also describe how brain wave biofeedback (neurofeedback)
can be successfully used for active intervention. With appropriate
neurofeedback training, one can access and heal the traumas that block
access to peak states of consciousness; or specific states can be directly accessed using the biofeedback, provided there are no obstructing traumas.
The Biocybernaut technology and methodology and those available in the
rest of the field are described and contrasted.

The Key Assumptions of Brain Wave Biofeedback Technology

One of the key insights to brain biofeedback work is that there is a link between specific brain wave patterns and specific skills and abilities. This
link is central to all brain wave technologies for measuring and training for
peak states. The most fundamental principle of this link I call the
'Psychophysiological Principle' which states:

"Any experience (conscious or unconscious) that you have as a living human
being, you have ONLY because you have a specific, albeit complex, pattern of
underlying brain activity."

Everything else flows from this. As a corollary, the only way you can
change your experience or your abilities is if there is a change in your underlying brain activity. And if your brain activity ceases, then you cease to
have any of the experiences or abilities of a living human being. Brain
death is the accepted medical definition of death. Your heart can stop, or
can even be removed, as in a heart transplant operation, and so long as
there are machines to oxygenate and move your blood, you can continue
to live and to have experiences. But when your brain ceases to function,
you stop having the experiences and the abilities of a living human being.

Operating under this Psychophysiological Principle are what I call the
Axioms of Biofeedback. The first Axiom of Biofeedback is: "Any process in
your brain, mind, or body, about which you can be given accurate, immediate,
and reasonably aesthetic feedback, you can learn to control."

The Psychophysiological Principle and the First Axiom of Biofeedback
mean, of course, that

1. Brain EEG activity is correlated with all experiences, including trauma
on the negative side and with beneficial peak states on the positive side.

It also means that

2. Changing brain activity, especially the EEG activity, changes the experience of trauma and peak states.

Expanding upon this second point we can see that appropriate changes
in brain activity allow a person to heal past traumas, and once these traumas are healed, the person then has easier access to those changes in brain
activity that change the person's subjective state (phenomenology) into
what many are calling a peak state, of which there are very many, and with
very different properties, and very different phenomenologies.

Other Axioms of Biofeedback follow quickly, including those that specify that the control might take a lot of practice to develop—and might be limited in the amplitude or magnitude of effects by the needs of the body. For example, decreasing your heart rate to one beat per day is probably not consistent with keeping your body alive and healthy, in most cases. When we talk about the Psychophysiological Principle and the Axioms of Biofeedback, we must understand that they apply fully to ordinary human beings, even human beings in many peak states. They may not, however, apply to enlightened beings who have transcended the laws of physiology and the Psychophysiological Principle. For example, Ram Dass described an event where his guru, Neem Karoli Baba, once ate a big lump of arsenic that would have killed ten men, and all the women devotees around the guru started to wail and cry, "Oh Babaji, don't leave us." The guru just laughed and said, "Where could I go?" And then nothing harmful happened to him. His consciousness had transcended the Psychophysiological Principle.

Jim's Story
My Passion for Brain Wave Biofeedback Work

I'd like to take a moment to give you some personal background about my discovery of the relationship between this brain wave technology and peak states. In 1968 I had been a subject in Joe Kamiya's alpha feedback lab on three prior occasions when our story begins. The three prior sessions (part of an ongoing study) had been on three days earlier in the week, and each day had featured about 50 minutes of actual feedback time. A laboratory technician had affixed the scalp, ear, and ground electrodes, escorted me into the sound and light reduced chamber, and monitored the equipment from an adjacent room. When instructions were given or the end of the session was to be announced, the technician spoke over an intercom.

But this fourth session was to be different. Having been intrigued in the formal experimental sessions by the warbling tone said to reflect my brain's activity, I returned to the laboratory to find that no experiments were scheduled, so I asked the lab director's girlfriend that I be "hooked up for feedback" and allowed to explore, on my own, with the feedback signals. This lab technician was agreeable, affixed the electrodes, escorted me into the experimental chamber, and then left, closing the door. She then started the electronic equipment, and, unbeknownst to me, went upstairs and became involved on another project, since I was not generating data for any of the lab's ongoing studies.

Forgetting the trainee in the experimental chamber, she went out to lunch with the rest of the lab crew. While she was at lunch, she suddenly realized, 3 hours later, that she had not checked on her subject. Everyone left the restaurant in a rush, and hurried back to the laboratory. Then the technician and eight to twelve others came bursting into the feedback chamber in some alarm and interrupted the last stages of an incredible adventure.

I was sitting in a dark, soundproof room, and there was little to do besides listen to the tone. The tone would start one of its bursts, and I would try to ignore it, but I could only do so for a fraction of a second before my attention would swing around and focus on the tone. When it did, the tone would shrink like a balloon being squeezed by my conscious attention. But that fraction of a second was a wedge for my understanding. By slightly prolonging each burst, I noticed that my scores were getting larger, so I persevered. I didn't know it then, but I was practicing the Witness, distancing myself from the processes of my consciousness, and there was no mistaking success for failure. If I failed to keep my attention from focusing on the event of a tone burst, that burst would be dramatically and immediately squelched.

That kind of almost instantaneous feedback accelerated a most difficult self-awareness learning process which might have gone on for years with less success if it had lacked the feedback. As the scores got slowly larger and the tone remained loud for a longer fraction of each two-minute epoch, I began to notice a strange sensation of lightness. Where my body had pressed against the chair and the floor, the pressure began to give way to the sensation of just a gentle touching. When I "noticed" this and focused on it and began to reflect upon it, I was at once alerted by the tone, which got quieter, softer. And I had another clue: Reflective or analytical thinking got in the way of alpha enhancement.

That clue helped enormously, because I hadn't fully realized up to then that by adopting an attitude of "not-noticing," I was suspending rational and analytic thinking. I realized that I had, in fact, been aware of tone bursts even when I didn't focus my attention on them. The real work was in being aware of, but not focusing on the tone bursts with the egoic, analytic modes of consciousness. A certain part of me, that ego center which was concerned with DOING things, with success or failure, suddenly relaxed, and I watched myself floating above the chair, which was in the middle of a little room, which was filled with the loud alpha feedback sound. Floating above the chair? Floating!?? My relaxed detachment evaporated, and I awoke back into rational and analytical consciousness almost as from a dream. Of course, as I did so, the tone volume decreased sharply from its loud intensity, so I knew I had been awake and not drowsy or asleep while experiencing this "floating". If I had been asleep or drowsy there would not have been a loud tone (indicating lots of alpha) to vanish as I "awoke" to rational awareness.

"I was floating above the chair," I marveled to myself. I realized at once that my mental focusing on what had been happening had terminated the happening, so as quickly as possible I readopted the detached attitude and the tone again started to increase. Before long, I was again looking down on my body from a position near the ceiling of the room, although how I could see anything in the total darkness I cannot explain. It wasn't a normal kind of seeing.

I was almost afraid to deal with the fascinating situation because I had learned that conceptualizing the situation I was in would catch me and pull me down, and reduce the tone and my scores. So I merely floated and observed, and tried to fend off the constant temptation to evaluate, speculate, analyze, reason, congratulate. This last one was especially troublesome. After a particularly sizable series of increases in the scores, which left me feeling indescribably high, light, mellow, clear and pure, I slipped on a fleeting prideful thought. I permitted a conceptual thought to flash through my mind, "Gee, I'm doing pretty good." And crash! I was tumbling back into my normal consciousness. The conceptualization caught me and pulled me down. While I was struggling to regain the disinterested composure of the high alpha state and its loud tone, I noticed the gradual intrusion of the demand of my body for air. I wasn't breathing. I was living sufficiently detached from my physical body that there was not enough consciousness left to run my respiration processes.

I felt poised for a plunge of prolonged ecstasy. My gaze followed the tracks downward eager to see the succession of dips and hills I imagined would follow the initial plunge. But I was startled to see that the tracks, instead of veering upward again near the ground, bore relentlessly downward, entered, and were swallowed by the blackest hole I had ever seen. The blackness lapped like a liquid at the tracks and at the edges of its pool.

As I started downward toward this engulfing, enveloping blackness, I, my ego, understood through a flash of intuition that if it entered this place, ego dissolution would occur and it would no longer Be In Control. So my ego told me the Big Lie and filled my mind with the warning thought that if I entered this place, that I would never emerge, and I would cease to be. Since I was a Physics major with a Protestant fundamentalist religious background, I was totally ignorant of mystical experiences, ego dissolution, transcendence, etc., ... and I foolishly believed my ego's self-serving warning ... and I panicked. A soundless scream of fear and unwillingness filled my mind ... and of course my alpha instantly disappeared, so the feedback tone disappeared; then the whole scene disappeared, and I tumbled back into he-who-was-sitting-in-a-chair in Joe Kamiya's feedback laboratory.

The rest of the afternoon was spent in telling and retelling the story of my adventure. For two days afterwards, I walked around feeling light and buoyant and not at all sure I was touching the ground, which remained about 2 feet below the soles of my shoes. Four months later, still moved by the realness of what had happened, and having heard that similar things can happen in meditation, I started Raja Yoga lessons to prepare for another encounter with the Unmanifest, which my ignorance and unreadiness had led me to fear and to avoid.

This experience was so profound that I have dedicated my entire professional life to the quest of creating the technology to most effectively transmit this experience to others, and to studying this process scientifically so that it can be understood, so that it can be evaluated as to suitability of methods and the range of benefit outcomes, and so that it can be ultimately accepted by the professional scientific communities. This quest led me on a course, over the last 30 years, to first establish that individuals do have an innate ability to control their own brain waves (contrary to the "conventional thought"), and then secondly to develop and to optimize a technology and methodology with which to obtain the profound and wide-ranging benefits which result from voluntary control of central nervous system activity.

Background - A Brief History of Brain Biofeedback

There have been periods of great excitement about the possibilities of such brain training (like in the late '60s and early '70s). However, there was also disillusionment when bad technology and ignorance of the required training protocols (which must be rigorous) led to many failures by alpha researchers. Because of this ignorance, a majority of those early brain wave feedback studies failed to produce increases of alpha in the volunteer trainees.

The new science of Biofeedback was actually launched in April 1962 by a report by Dr. Joe Kamiya (my former teacher, then colleague and co-author) that people could in fact learn voluntary control of their own brain waves. Brain wave feedback training was heralded primarily as promoting relaxation and mental creativity. Brain wave studies of meditation established that meditators could exert profound control over their brain waves, and brain wave feedback was thought to make possible an "instant Zen" experience. Speculations became confused with claims, and by the late 1960s a firestorm of media attention ensued. This firestorm of popular attention to exaggerated or unsubstantiated claims disturbed the conservative authorities of the medical, psychiatric, and psychological communities. They and other guardians of the status quo were not pleased with what they were hearing about neurofeedback.

As a result, a number of eminent scientists began to do alpha brain wave feedback studies to rebut the popularized claims. Many of these eminent scientists were unfamiliar with the vast classical literature of scientific research on brain waves and psychophysics, especially the work done on the psychophysics of alpha waves. As a result their studies did not employ anything approaching optimal designs or ergonomic feedback technology.

Without an informed understanding of the causes of the natural waxing and waning of alpha rhythms it proved to be quite difficult to successfully train people to increase their alpha, resulting in most alpha researchers in the 1970s failing to teach their research subjects how to increase alpha activity, obviously resulting in a flood of publications stating that alpha feedback did not work. Some of these reports even suggested that people innately lacked the ability to learn control of their alpha activity. Most of these researchers did not know that their incomplete findings were caused by non-ergonomic feedback technology and inappropriate training protocols, and virtually all employed too little feedback time. Also absent in these reports were any alpha-related benefits. If benefits come with increased alpha, then absence of alpha increase means absence of any benefits.

Some in the cultural establishment may actually have been relieved that alpha feedback was being shown not to work, given the difficulties which were experienced in countering the psychedelic drug movement and movement known then as the "counterculture." The popular belief that alpha feedback was an electronic technology for consciousness expansion and transformation was now contradicted by the existing consensus of so-called experts. So the word went out: "Brain waves can NOT be voluntarily controlled." As a result the alpha brain wave feedback movement went underground by the mid-1970s, and most brain wave training fell into obscurity as just another consciousness fad spawned by the psychedelic 1960s.

However, the considerable clinical and popular enthusiasm which had been generated for doing "biofeedback" could not be put back into the bottle. That energy and enthusiasm were blocked from going into brain wave research by the negative findings of experts, so all that energy went, instead, into doing "biofeedback" with the NON-brain activity of the body. Biofeedback came to be synonymous with the peripheral modalities of muscle tension (learning to relax the muscles), of skin temperature (learning to warm the hands and feet), and electrodermal response (learning to change the electrical responses of the skin which are induced by shallow or transient emotions).

Brain wave feedback had come to be viewed as a false hope, or worse, as a false hype, by the time of my *Science* paper in 1978, so that there was almost no interest in my work from within the USA. Almost everyone had bought the official line that brain wave feedback did not work, and that people could not increase their alpha activity. The genie remained locked in the bottle until 1989 when Gene Peniston (working with Kulkowski) published a paper showing that the worst of the worst alcoholics, the untreatable dregs of the Veteran Administration system, could be cured of alcoholism in 80% of cases using brain wave feedback training for both alpha and theta EEG. This blew the cork out of the bottle and the genie escaped again. Soon there was a whole Society for Neuronal Regulation dedicated to brain wave feedback. However, most of the people there were wanting to use the new technology to treat ailments for which there was insurance reimbursement and there was not much interest in peak states or the paranormal abilities that attend some peak states.

Understanding Standard Brain Biofeedback and Its Limitations

Although there will soon be major changes as people rediscover the power and the range of brain wave feedback training, most of the work done today by biofeedback clinicians is still done with the peripheral modalities of skin temperature, muscle tension, and electrical conductivity (or resistance) of the skin. Peripheral modalities of feedback are generally only effective in working with some peripheral symptoms. The peripheral modalities are largely ineffective in working centrally, with the brain itself. This limits the results to treatment of symptoms rather than treating their underlying causes.

Because would-be brain wave biofeedback practitioners have been limited by grossly inadequate equipment until just the last few years, and because they continue to be limited by lack of knowledge of proper brain wave training protocols, biofeedback has been limited to the peripheral modalities. Specifically, most researchers do not realize the critical importance of a short (less than 350 msec) response time between the brain wave signal and the audio-tone feedback and the critical need for long sessions to practice the feedback. Biofeedback has remained, in the official view, an interesting curiosity of limited power and limited range of applications. As a result, biofeedback has not been highly regarded by the medical professions.

The Difference Between Hardt's Biocybernaut Program and Standard Brain Biofeedback

Biocybernaut Institute intensive Alpha One Training uses state-of-the-art amplifiers and filters to analyze EEG to provide real-time auditory feedback in conjunction with detailed debriefing and mood analysis. The Biocybernaut Institute offers advanced training for all brain waves and combinations as well as shared feedback and coherence training.

1. Biocybernaut Institute has developed training protocols and advanced equipment from over 30 years of scientific research.
2. We use integration of time and amplitude, not percent time over a threshold. Thus our training has depth of feedback, not just a simple on-off kind of feedback so common in other systems.
3. Our training epochs are optimized at two minutes each. Almost all other systems use training epochs that are too short or too long.
4. Our training sessions give at least one, two, or more hours of neurofeedback each day. Almost all other protocols are too short.
5. Our training series begins with an intensive seven-day Alpha One Training. Other training programs are too short.
6. Our training programs are very intensive. They consume the better part of each day on which they occur. They include daily introductions, baseline testing, enhancement feedback, mood scale tests, post-session debriefing, EEG chart reading, score analysis, and mood scale discussion. Other training programs are not nearly as intensive.
7. Our trainings are conducted by trainers with graduate educations, Biofeedback Society Certification, and specific Biocybernaut Certification. Other systems do not provide as highly qualified biofeedback trainers.
8. Biocybernaut EEG amplifiers and filters are state-of-the-art. They are the most accurate filters in existence. Other systems can't match our specifications.
9. Some systems depend on brain wave entrainment (frequency following response, FFR, binaural beats) instead of feedback. This is not as effective, nor is it as natural as the Biocybernaut process because entrainment is enforcing external frequencies. This is fascism imposed on the brain. In the Biocybernaut process you can trust in your own brain's processes to find its own frequencies for maximum benefit. Biocybernaut Institute was able to help at least one trainee reverse mental difficulties that had been introduced by an entrainment system.
10. Biocybernaut feedback is pleasing (aesthetic) sounding to the ear, using musical instruments with 5.1 Sound Systems. Other systems use simpler audio feedback technology.
11. Our feedback is multi-modal and the modes are used in very appropriate ways at very appropriate times. Other training systems use single mode feedback, or mix modalities in ways that are deleterious to brain wave enhancement (most often using eyes-open visual feedback continuously).
12. Biocybernaut training makes extensive use of mood scale analysis with discussions. Home use systems are purely machine-driven with little human interaction.
13. Biocybernaut training clearly separates suppression training from enhancement training for greater effective learning. Some systems and trainings intersperse suppression with enhancement.

14. Biocybernaut training is done with eyes closed. When people open their eyes, alpha is nearly always suppressed. Some systems depend on visual feedback (eyes open) instead of auditory feedback (eyes closed).
15. Biocybernaut Institute uses individually applied scalp electrodes with high-quality gels for maximum sensitivity. Some other systems use ineffective electrode systems such as headbands.
16. The Biocybernaut Institute includes hemi-coherent analysis for enhancement of brain wave coherence in all trainings. Many other systems miss this entirely.
17. Biocybernaut Institute does not use any subliminal or auto-hypnotic messages. Some other systems confound their trainings with these messages. BI does not believe in using trickery. Your results from Biocybernaut training are deep and fundamental.

Specific outcomes of Brain Biofeedback processes include:
- Improving and enjoying skills and abilities,
- Improving mental clarity and effectiveness,
- Restoring youthful brain wave patterns, thereby reversing some effects of age,
- Building self esteem and self-confidence,
- Increasing emotional and physical well-being,
- Enhanced spiritual awareness,
- Greater access to forgiveness and non-attachment,
- Developing your natural intuition and problem-solving capabilities,
- Staying calm and focused under pressure,
- Performing more effectively and more creatively with less stress,
- Profiting from increased productivity.

The trainings help you to first become more aware of and then to heal your often unconscious negative emotions like sadness, anger, and fear.

Using Brain Wave Biofeedback to Achieve Peak States

No one chapter, indeed no one book, could begin to cover all the possible states of consciousness. We should note that the Buddhists describe and even have numbered over 150 states along the way to enlightenment. Each one of them would, of course, have its own brain activity patterns. Some of the brain activity shifts among states are subtle and could not ever be noticed by even a skilled clinical electroencephalographer, especially if the changes occur primarily in deep subcortical structures. Here we would need the power of magnetoencephalography (MEG) to detect changes in brain activity that occur deep within the brain. MEG can look 6-7 cm in from each surface of the brain and thus can measure, and provide feedback on, brain activity that occurs deep within the brain in deep cortical and deep subcortical material. In many instances a powerful computer is needed to detect these subtle shifts in surface and deep brain activity. On the other hand some other changes in brain activity associated with shifts between some other states are quite obvious to a moderately well-trained observer of the EEG.

Since we are not born with an "owner's manual" for our brains, we pretty much have to figure these things out for ourselves. But given the similarity of all humans, which are so much a single species that all humans can interbreed, what is discovered as the pattern of a peak state for one person is likely to be quite similar to the pattern of the same peak state for another person. Now we must allow for the very real differences between right- and left-handed people and there are developmental changes in children's brain wave activity, and age-related changes in the brain activity of older adults (which can be reversed with appropriate brain wave feedback training). However, if you can give me six highly gifted people of the same handedness who can reliably produce the same example of gifted behavior, physical, mental, emotional, spiritual, or psychic, I can make appropriate measures of their brain activity and extract from about 200 parameters enough relevant information to create a hyperdimensional map of their brain activity. This map can then be used to train other people to produce the same or very similar gifted behaviors by using patent-pending algorithms to train the brain activity of the non-gifted people to closely match the brain activity of the gifted people. And we need about a half dozen masters or experts to get a sufficiently reliable data set to produce the hyperdimensional brain maps that can then be used for training others to produce this giftedness.

The brain learns a complete pattern faster than it learns a piece of a pattern, so the more fully we can represent the brain state of the masters, the faster and easier it will be for others to learn to duplicate these patterns of mastery in some skill or ability, including the ability to enter valuable peak mind states. The surface EEG is by no means all there is to brain activity, so some peak states will require more than matching patterns derived from the surface EEG. It has been shown that with large montages of, say 121 electrodes, and powerful computers doing off-line [not real-time] processing, it is possible to derive the details of electrical activity throughout the entire volume of the brain. While this is useful for diagnostic purposes, it will not do for feedback, which must be in real time. The Biocybernaut Institute *System and Method Patent #4,928,704* on brain wave feedback specifies that feedback must be accurate, immediate, and reasonably aesthetic. And immediacy is defined as less than 350 milliseconds. Slower than 350 mSec, the learning is impaired and the feedback "feels muddy" and disconnected from the phenomenological reality of the feedback trainee.

Permanency and Transience in Brain Wave States

Any experience you have requires specific underlying brain activity. Choosing and controlling what you will experience is as easy as choosing and controlling your brain activity. Most people can control their brain activity sufficiently to go to sleep and to wake up as needed. Those who have exceptional mental abilities simply have additional subtleties of brain self-regulation available to them.

Learning to understand and control the subtleties of one's own brain function opens up vast new areas of skills, abilities, and experiential fulfillment. It is simply learning to operate one's bio-computer more effectively, and the rewards are beyond your current ability to imagine, just as a two-dimensional person could not imagine life in a three-dimensional world. You first need to make the shift into a new mind perspective, a new point of view, to understand the implications of having that new point of view.

We are considered gifted if we can turn on the ideal brain waves to deal with each and every situation. The good news is that you no longer need to be born gifted. There is now a technology and a training method that allows nearly everyone to learn the skills of changing your brain waves as the situation requires.

As we will see later in this paper, creative people have the natural ability to adopt a different [high alpha] brain state when they are working on a problem. This ability to step into a different brain state gives them a new mind state, one that is ideal for being creative. Thus they are completely interconnected. Without this ability to change the brain activity, the person is non-creative. The ability for voluntary control of our brain activity is one key. The other key is experiencing the subtleties and knowing what brain changes to make for any situation.

Ethical Purification and Peak States of Consciousness

It is important to note that there are preconditions for a person to attain such brain wave states and the associated phenomenological states. There must be an ethical purification that occurs or else the person will be unable to sustain the brain waves associated with the advanced states. In the present form of the Biocybernaut Institute neurofeedback training there is formal work on forgiveness that is a key part of the Alpha One and the Theta One Brain Wave Training Programs. The computerized mood scales identify buried and unconscious negative emotions and then the trainer coaches each trainee on how to use the interaction with the neurofeedback technology to achieve an ethical cleansing. The trainee is instructed to search for his/her own personal forgiveness method to deal with and heal the wounds of traumas and the negative emotions of anger, hostility, fear, sadness, unhappiness, and depression. If a trainee is unable or unwilling to undertake this thorough ethical cleansing, or if the trainee has an attachment to anger or one of the other negative emotions, then that trainee will NOT be able to attain the high amplitude, long sustained alpha spindles that are coherent in both hemispheres. If you are not willing to do the ethical cleansing and the purification, then the door to the higher states is closed to you. Biocybernaut neurofeedback involves profound ethical cleansing which opens the mind and the heart to the possibility of peak states.

Meditation States and Brain Wave Biofeedback

In one study in Japan by the highly respected scientists Kasamatsu and Hirai, they studied Zen monks from both the Soto and Rinzai sects of Zen. Each monk was rated for level of spiritual development by his Zen master, his Roshi. Interestingly no one was rated as "Advanced" in their spiritual development if they had less than 21 years of daily practice of zazen meditation. Then each of the monks was instrumented with EEG electrodes and his brain waves were measured during his practice of zazen meditation. The first finding was that the higher the rated level of a monk's spiritual development by his Zen master, the more alpha waves he had in his zazen meditation EEG record. And then there were subtleties and nuances. As a Zen monk progressed from Beginner toward Intermediate and Advanced, his alpha increased in power and also spread forward on his head. In the most advanced group, all of whom had more than 21 years of daily practice of meditation, there were all of these changes plus the emergence of theta waves at frontal sites on the head [F3 and F4 in the International 10-20 system of EEG site location].

This exact same pattern of alpha changes and theta changes is produced on a regular basis in the brain waves of Biocybernaut Alpha One trainees. However, instead of taking 21 or more years, it only takes seven days with the Biocybernaut technology and methodology. Using data derived from 17 right-handed, non-meditator trainees ranging in age from 20 to 64 who did the Biocybernaut seven-day Alpha One Training, we see brain wave patterns virtually identical with advanced Zen. These changes are increasing alpha amplitude, alpha spreading forward on the head, alpha slowing in frequency, and the emergence of frontal theta. We know that technology speeds things up, and now we know that Biocybernaut technology speeds up the process of meditation and the attainment of brain wave patterns and the associated mind states that characterize the most advanced practitioners of Zen meditation.

Psychic Seeing and Psychic Healing

During one period during my work at UCSF I studied numerous well-known psychics in my laboratory. Some had clairvoyant ability and abilities to see into the future. Others had medical diagnostic abilities and some could do these diagnoses at a distance without being physically present with the patient. Some of them could do psychic healing for a patient who was present or even, in some cases, for someone many miles away. All of them had unusual brain wave records, with abundant waking theta and even delta activity. And when they were doing their psychic "accessing" or "seeing" or "healing," the amounts of theta and delta increased, often dramatically. If any of them had been studied with the technique now known as QEEG [Quantitative EEG], in which brain waves are recorded and compared with "normative" databases, they would have been branded as "deviant" and efforts would have been made to "fix" their deviant brains and to make them "normal." One interesting recent story involves a gifted computer programmer who came for Biocybernaut Alpha Training. He was an expert in database design and had uncanny gifts and abilities to create powerful new software. He was involved in a study where we imported a technician skilled in taking QEEG recordings, so we could look at the results of the Biocybernaut Alpha Training through the "views" of the QEEG techniques and analysis methods, by having QEEG recordings done both before and after the seven days of the Biocybernaut Alpha One Training.

This trainee was initially like Star Trek's Mr. Spock. He was very highly rational and quite invested in his powerful intellectual abilities, which were his bread and butter for himself and his family. But in the course of his Biocybernaut Alpha Training he began to have powerful experiences that would be described as mystical experiences. Arthur Deikman has described the five hallmarks of the mystical experience: (1) Intense Realness, (2) Unusual Sensations, (3) Trans-Sensate Phenomena, which come to a person from beyond the realm of the five senses, (4) the Experience of Unity or Oneness with all of reality, and (5) Ineffability, or inability to be described in words. This gifted computer database designer began to have powerful experiences that contained elements of all of these five categories of the mystical experience. And at one point he, his rational mind, became alarmed that these new phenomena might become so powerful and so commonplace that he would not be able to shut them off. So he tried shutting them off. And of course they all quickly went away, and then he was even more disturbed that he could not immediately call them back. This is one of the powerful lessons of Biocybernaut brain wave training: You only get as much as you can handle.

Even though he had only begun to invoke some of the aspects of mystical experience, his understanding of the nature of reality was profoundly changed, and he was later to come back to do more Alpha Training to gain skill in exploring these new-found dimensions of reality. But before he did that, he had a follow-up QEEG recording taken the day after he finished his seven days of Biocybernaut Alpha One Training. The QEEG records were then sent off for analysis by those skilled in QEEG interpretations. About a week later I got an alarming phone call from a Medical Doctor who was skilled in reading and interpreting QEEG recordings. He said that there was frontal delta activity in the initial QEEG record that suggested a brain tumor. And he added in a very alarmed way that this delta activity had increased so much in just one week [the week of the Alpha training] that it must be a very aggressive, dangerous, and rapidly growing brain tumor. And this MD QEEG specialist urged me to immediately contact this person and tell them they must have a CAT scan immediately to see if the brain tumor was operable and if not, then to start radiation and chemotherapy at once.

This is not the kind of news you want to bring to anyone, but I dutifully and as gently as possible transmitted the alarming information, and the gifted computer database designer immediately went out and got a series of very thorough CAT scans, which found absolutely NOTHING.

He was and is completely free of any brain tumors.

However, this delta activity which increased in his right frontal brain associated with his beginning explorations into profound mystical experiences was considered so deviant by this MD QEEG specialist that he was talking about having that part of the man's brain cut out or destroyed by radiation treatment.

Peak states are routinely misunderstood by a very wide range of traditional professionals and lay people and this is simply one very carefully documented example of this common misunderstanding.

Kundalini[2] Brain Wave Profile

This story of discovery begins with a training that was going to include a Zen Master and one of his friends (JH), who was not a Zen meditator. The Zen Master was unable to attend and JH came alone. JH was a quiet and unassuming man. He was a veritable milquetoast. In a crowd of two you would not notice him. And yet he was very highly sought after by IBM. He had worked for IBM and was presently on a three-year paid leave of absence, by which IBM was hoping that he might decide to come back and work for IBM again. We were curious how such a plain, placid and unassuming man could be so valuable to IBM.

Then we heard his story. He had been a mid-level functionary in IBM and had been working in Marseilles, France. It was summer and he got caught in one of those horrendous French traffic jams where horns blow for hours and the French get out of their cars and have fist fights with each other. During this ordeal, in the heat, noise, and distress, he had an out-of-body experience (OBE). His astral body separated from his physical body and he flew around and ended fights and helped people calm down. Thereafter he was profoundly altered.

Suddenly this mid-level functionary had awesome powers that were quickly recognized and exploited by IBM. Before JH took his leave of absence he had been performing miracles for IBM. For example, IBM wanted to have a factory in an Asian country to make certain IBM prod-

---

2 For a detailed description of kundalini, see Gopi Krishna's *Kundalini: The Evolutionary Energy in Man*, Shambhala: 1971.

ucts. Single-handedly, JH would go to that country, find the land, negotiate for the purchase of the land, find the contractors to construct the buildings, negotiate all the constructions contracts, obtain all the regulatory permits and governmental permissions, supervise the construction, and then hire and train all the people needed to run this operation, bring in all the necessary equipment, again dealing with all the regulatory agencies involved in such imports; then he would get the newly hired people to set up the production equipment, while he was finding, hiring and training the local management staff to run the operation; and then he would turn over to IBM a complete facility that was running efficiently producing the products that IBM desired. No wonder IBM was willing to give JH a three-year paid leave of absence in the hope, and that is all it was, a hope, that at the end of the three years he would come back to IBM. He had no obligation to do so.

OK, so this unremarkable looking and acting milquetoast of a man had some awesome powers. But, initially, in the first several days of training, his brain waves looked unremarkable. He had some alpha on his occipital channels (O1 and O2) but it was fairly small in amplitude, even though he could stretch out and sustain the alpha spindles for several seconds. But the other six channels (C3, C4, T3, T4, F3, F4) had very low amplitude alpha and it was intermittent. However, day three was to bring a great surprise. Suddenly, out of nowhere, those other six channels burst forth into very high amplitude rhythmic delta activity. Sometimes he had a whole body twitch just before the delta emerged or just as it went away; sometimes not. Since he was getting four-channel alpha feedback from O1, O2, C3, and C4 cortical sites, there was no reflection in his feedback tones of this remarkable delta activity, which did not pass through the alpha filters. At the end of the day his interview contained no clue as to the nature of this remarkable high amplitude synchronous delta activity over most of his head. His two occipital sites, O1 and O2, continued along with his normal modest alpha activity during these phenomenal delta episodes. That alone was one for the record books: alpha and delta together in the waking brain. Most neurologists would say this was impossible and if they saw the polygraph record they would be alarmed and say it was dangerous and surely pathological. (This actually happened later in this story where a Harvard neurologist was alarmed by such an EEG record).

When JH was shown his polygraph records, which is an important part of the debriefing that follows each session of Biocybernaut neurofeedback training, he offered no useful information and simply shrugged his shoulders and said nothing. I was not prepared to let the most amazing brain wave record I had ever seen go into oblivion unexplained so I told my assistant Maureen, "We are going to fix him tomorrow. We have 16 speakers in that training chamber and we can send any combination of brain waves to any or all of those speakers. Normally we only use four speakers during the Alpha One Training, but tomorrow we are going to turn on six more speakers. Each one of those six EEG channels that showed the delta activity are going to provide feedback from any delta activity that may occur on any of those channels tomorrow. And if he does what he did today, he's going to get BLASTED in there because that delta activity he showed today was really big and it will translate into very LOUD tones if it occurs like that tomorrow. And every time he does that delta thing he will immediately be blasted by the loud tones and he will not be able to shrug his shoulders and tell us he does not know what he was doing during those events."

And this we did. We told him what we were going to do and asked him to notice and to remember what he was doing IF those extra six speakers went off and emitted loud tones. And again on day four, JH made those huge delta waves synchronously at six sites on his head while his occipital sites O1 and O2 continued to show their modest alpha activity. And when he did this there were very loud blasts of tones from the delta speakers.

When the session was over and I began to interview JH about his session, my first question was, "OK, what were you doing when those delta speakers made loud sound?" JH raised his bird-like voice just a little and said, "Oh, that was when the kundalini was coming up." I was astonished and delighted. I had studied Yoga and practiced Yogananda's meditation for seven years and I had heard and read a lot about the powerful energy of kundalini. I exclaimed, "Well, why didn't you tell me you had kundalini?" JH shrugged his shoulders diffidently and whispered, "Well, I didn't know if you'd know what that was." He did not say a lot more, but he did tell us that the emergence of his remarkable powers that were of such great value to IBM were coincident with the emergence of his kundalini energy, all of which began after his out-of-body experience during that horrific six-hour traffic jam in Marseilles.

It was many years before I presented the data on JH's kundalini brain wave record in a scientific conference, and when I did, I chose Rob Kall's annual Winter Brain Conference. After I had told the story and shown overheads of the remarkable EEG records, Dr. Gary Schwartz of Harvard and Yale and now of Arizona State University came up to whisper in my ear. He told of a time back at Harvard when he was a Professor of Psychology there, when a student came in to see him. This student said he was practicing Kundalini Yoga and he insisted that Gary record his brain waves. Gary was insightful enough to accede to the student's request. And he was rewarded with seeing an EEG record, he whispered in my ear, that looked remarkably like the EEG record I had just shown to the Winter Brain Conference. I asked Gary what he did with that record. He said he was alarmed, knowing that the conventional wisdom was that it was not possible to have both alpha and delta activity in the waking brain. So he took the alarming "impossible" EEG record, the paper tracing, to a friend of his who was a neurologist at Harvard. The Harvard neurologist was indeed alarmed and he warned Gary, "Don't let him do that again on University property." But the neurologist asked Gary to lend him the polygraph record so he could show it to some of his colleagues in the Neurology Department. Then he promptly lost the polygraph record. This is emblematic of how science often deals with anomalous data.

After hearing Gary's entire story, I noticed people gathering near us, and I realized that the last event of the night was about to take place. This was to be a panel discussion and both Gary and I were on this panel. I asked Gary if he would be willing to tell the entire assembled conference this same story he had told me. Gary had never spoken of this in any scientific setting before and he was a little nervous and reluctant. However, I encouraged him and then I was so delighted when he agreed to tell this story publicly. This did many useful things. First it validated in a powerful way the reality and the validity of the remarkable polygraph record I had just shown in my preceding talk, and it shed a bright light on the all-too-common ways that mainstream science deals with anomalous data: destroys it, censors it, classifies it, loses it. Peak states, even ones that are of great value to corporate giants like IBM, nonetheless have the power to strike terror into the hearts of neurologists and other Keepers of the Gates, Arbiters of Reality, and Censors of the Anomalous or Unusual. All of us who are interested in and who study peak states must be aware of this. We must not pretend that we can study these phenomena in a protected Garden of Eden. We must be willing to share with each other the remarkable phenomena that fascinate all of us who share this common interest, and we must be willing to be open with each other, and with the larger audiences that we want to reach.

Brain Waves and Personality

Let us look at the relationship between EEG changes and changes in personality. In 1973 I completed an analysis of a research study that trained two groups of college-age males: Very High Anxiety and Very Low Anxiety. In this study I was working with college men who were in the top and bottom 10% of the Anxiety Scale. I used the Welsh Anxiety Scale, which is the first factor of the MMPI (Minnesota Multiphasic Personality Inventory). What I saw was that when men in the high anxiety group increased their EEG alpha, their anxiety went down. Anxiety and alpha were significantly and negatively correlated, but only in the High Anxiety group. In the Low Anxiety group, alpha increases were associated with a sense of being "high" and more conscious. The Low Anxiety men reported alpha-related feelings of flying, floating, light, lightness, and vast space, and some of them got into such bliss states as their alpha increased that they experienced spontaneous orgasms, while sitting alone, not moving, in the quiet and dark feedback chamber. This was the my first strong evidence that brain wave feedback could move people away from dysfunctionality toward hyperfunctionality and that there were stages people had to go through as they did the work. It seemed that no one got the bliss states until they had resolved their personality dysfunctions, which they could do through the Alpha Training that I was developing, testing, refining, and improving. In 1978 I published a paper in *Science* magazine documenting the changes in Anxiety Traits and States that were reliably produced by learned changes in EEG alpha activity.

Some states are complex and are characterized by many different kinds of brain activity and many locations of the brain, and others are simple enough that changes in EEG alpha activity at one or a few sites of the brain can significantly shift those states. By giving people batteries of personality tests twice before their Alpha Training and once (at least) after their training, I was compiling the data to begin to determine the correlations, maybe even the causal connections, between brain activity indexed by the EEG and dimensions of personality as indexed by respected and widely used personality tests, such as the MMPI, the Myers-Briggs Type Inventory (MBTI), the Personality Orientation Inventory (POI), the Clyde Mood Scale (CMS), the Multiple Affect Adjective Check List (MAACL), and the Profile of Mood States (POMS). As you may guess from this list, some of the tests measured personality *traits* that were thought by most psychiatrists and psychologists to be stable over the adult life-span. Other dimensions, called moods or mind states, were understood to be temporally variable and subject to sudden changes. Intriguingly, both traits and states were showing changes that were correlated with the changes in brain activity that I was producing in my research subjects (or they were producing in themselves) with my increasingly effective technology and programs of brain wave feedback training.

Healing Traumatic Material Using the Biocybernaut Training

One of the developments that made the Biocybernaut training different from other systems was a significant change in the computer programs administering and scoring the mood scales, and a related significant change in the way the results of the mood scales were presented to the trainees. Response latency timing information on a trainee's responses to each of the mood scale items was already being collected with a precision of one-hundredth of a second. To this software capability I added the calculation of descriptive statistics for each of the different responses. Suddenly it became possible for the trainee and the trainer to know subtle details of the trainee's response patterns. To this was added statistical significance testing on the responses. I soon recognized that some of these statistical patterns were pointers to an alternate part of the mind that was filled with unacknowledged (and thus buried) anger or fear or guilt or sadness or whatever else.

Equipped with these new tools I was able to function as though I were telepathic or psychic, but with the added advantage that my insights were supported by measured data derived scientifically from the trainees' own responses. Once the buried emotional blockages of a trainee had been identified by the new computerized mood scales, they often came very quickly to consciousness. And once the emotional blockage had come to consciousness, it then quickly became possible for the trainee to work through the "charge" or valence on the emotion in the next day's Alpha Training.

Bringing to mind some highly-charged emotional topic in the Alpha Training would, at first, block or suppress the alpha, and the feedback tones would shut off and the scores would drop. But then the challenge for the trainees would be to discover new ways of relating to their own experiences of that emotion and the events behind it. This is one of the key growth experiences of the Biocybernaut Process, and the trainees would grow through their fear or anger or guilt or sadness much faster than believed possible.

What does it mean to grow through an emotion like anger? We all know suppressing anger does not work. That leads to heart attacks, ulcers, unhappiness, and occasional violent outbursts of anger. On the other hand "expressing" anger does not work very well either. If someone practices expressing anger, then they usually develop the habit of expressing anger, they become too good at it, and it becomes a form of public littering. What is needed is to get to the source of the experience of anger in the mind and to learn how to adopt a new point of view about that experience.

In the Biocybernaut Process, trainees have daily assessment of their emotions by computerized mood scales together with in-depth interviews by highly-skilled trainers to help them become aware of hidden, buried, and latent emotions. Once the awareness of these emotions has been raised to the level of conscious self-awareness, then the trainee can begin to use the brain wave training process to gain control of his or her emotional processes.

When individuals receive Brain Activity Feedback, they can change in ways that give them greater objectivity, increased self-honesty, greater self-responsibility, more choices, and a degree of freedom from cultural conditioning, all of which can have surprising and beneficial consequences. With appropriate Brain Activity Training, individuals can improve their skills and their abilities, and they can learn both how to have new desirable experiences (happiness, vigor, contentment) and how to stop having undesirable old experiences (like anxiety, depression, paranoia).

Indeed, people can learn how to change the core dimensions of their personality, by changing their brain activity, just as a computer's basic characteristics can be changed by loading a new operating system. By changing their brain activity, people can change their behavioral characteristics and they can learn how to regulate almost any process in their minds and their bodies. An individual with such a range of capabilities is far outside the range of the cultural norms.

Suggested Reading and Websites

An extensive list of milestone papers is available at Dr. Hardt's Biocybernaut Institute website at www.biocybernaut.com. We suggest the following publications for interested lay people:

- Doug Boyd, *Conversations with a Cybernaut* (forthcoming).
- Barbara Brown, *New Mind, New Body: Bio Feedback: New Directions for the Mind*, HarperCollins, 1974. An early visionary in the field of neurofeedback. One of the first people to recognize the potential of biofeedback to transform humanity.
- James V. Hardt, "Pathways of the Mind: In the Master's footsteps with technology" in *Nous Letter: Studies in Noetics*, Vol. 2(1), pp. 26-29, 1975.
- James V. Hardt, "Alpha EEG Feedback: Closer Parallel with Zen Than Yoga" in *Proceedings of the Association for Applied Psychophysiology and Biofeedback*, 24th Annual Meeting, Los Angeles, CA, March 25-30, 1993a.
- James V. Hardt and R. Gale, "Creativity Increases in Scientists Through Alpha EEG Feedback Training" in *Proceedings of the Association for Applied Psychophysiology and Biofeedback*, 24th Annual Meeting, Los Angeles, CA, March 25-30, 1993b.
- James V. Hardt, "An Example of the Kundalini Experience Viewed Through Multi-Channel EEG" in *Proceedings*, FutureHealth's Key West Conference, EEG '96, Key West, FL, Feb. 8-13, 1996.
- James V. Hardt, "The Ultimate Peak Performers: Alpha Feedback Training for US Army Green Berets" in the *6th Annual Winter Conference on Brain Function/EEG, Modification & Training*, sponsored by FutureHealth, Vol. 6, Palm Springs, California, February 6-9, 1998.
- James V. Hardt, "Brain Energy Training: A Technology and Method for Spiritual Growth [the Biocybernaut Process]" in *ISSEEEM*, Boulder, CO, June, 2000.
- Peter Russell, *The Global Brain Awakens: Our Evolutionary Next Step*, HarperCollins, 1983. A visionary who has a modern perspective on Teilhard de Chardin's mystical world vision about the culmination of human development.

Chapter 13

Personal Accounts of Peak States of Consciousness

Introduction

Our work with peak states of consciousness is about real people living their lives in amazing and wonderful ways. In this section, we're going to give you a small sample—in their own words—of the life experience of several people who live or have lived in relatively permanent peak states. Due to space limitations, we only cover a small number of the possible states people have. A couple of the states are from Volume 2, but are included to give you a taste for what is to come.

This chapter tries to answer key questions that our students ask of people who are in peak states. Would I want to even have a peak state of consciousness? How important are peak states really, given that it may require a lot of time and effort? Which peak state would I want, or would I want them all? How would the peak states affect my real day-to-day life? How would my new peak state affect the people around me, especially my intimates? Would having a peak state affect my physical health? Would a peak state change the way I live my life?

Some of the people in this section have had a peak state all their lives. They show how different life can be when you grow up this way. These people illustrate what giving a peak state to your own children would accomplish. Others got their state later in life, some by attending one of our training workshops. Some of the people are in relatively minor states, others have radical new perceptions and abilities.

We hope you become inspired by what you read in this chapter. Enjoy!

A Beauty Way State Acquired During College

Rene is a man in his 60s involved in engineering. During his earlier years, he searched and found, somewhat by accident, a way to be in a permanent Beauty Way state. I worked for him for a number of years, and I have to say he was the single most inspiring manager I've ever had—it was actually fun to come to work in the kind of atmosphere he created. Here's what he had to say:

What is a peak state like? It seems like ordinary reality only less cluttered – in the same way that the realized Zen practitioner experiences ordinary reality—about a foot off the ground. Life is there with all its aches and pains, problems to solve and disappointments to experience—but it just keeps going. There is always the realization, simultaneous with the struggles and failures, that there is another chance, another day to begin; that everything that happens in life is not the end but part of an ongoing process or experience.

Think of life in this way (to use a well worn but well suited metaphor:) You are set adrift in a boat in the middle of an infinitely wide river with many rapids whose degree of difficulty is unknown to you. You may capsize, be cast ashore or drowned. But suppose you were given one piece of knowledge beforehand—every rapid is navigable if you trust in yourself. The unknown river then becomes only an exercise in attention.

I do not feel special or isolated but I do know that many—perhaps most—people do not look at life the way I do. How did I come to look at life this way? How did I get this knowledge about the river? I think it took many experiences before I realized two things: first, as a condition of living in this Universe, many forces are always acting upon us; and, second, there is only one force we can learn to direct – ourselves. I say learn because I had to discard all those ideas we are brought up with about getting help from others when we are in trouble: (when else do we ask for help?) from parents, friends, angels, God. Not that they can't give advice or that we shouldn't listen to advice. But it's up to each of us to make the choices and move on. And the next logical conclusion was simply that if I couldn't be helped by them, I certainly couldn't blame them for anything that happened to me either.

The problem with being in a peak state (if there is a problem) is that you accept ultimately that you yourself are the one responsible for you. The up side is that now that you've stopped blaming others for your life, you can get on with living it the way you want to.

Gaining a Connection to Gaia and the Creator Later in Life

Wayne Ngan is a well known potter who lives on an island in British Columbia, Canada. He's taught in Canada and China, and is a delightful elder who enjoys talking with people. He was willing to speak about his own peak state, which he acquired as a young man, and how it has effected his life. He didn't always have this state. In fact, his early years were quite painful and difficult, growing up in poverty in China. He never finished school, he struggled with English when his father immigrated to Canada, his finger is twisted from beatings he received, and he barely knew his father. As a boy, he was shamed in life and in school for his inability to 'measure up'.

His story is particularly important because the state he has and the way he got there mirror what Jacquelyn Aldana says in Chapter 10. And his advice is similar.

The following is a transcript of a conversation I had with him at his home. I hope you will enjoy this brief meeting with Wayne as much as I did.

What would you want the people reading this article to learn from you?

When I started here on this land, I sat in this bare parking lot and asked myself, how could I transform this into a living? It's not the parking lot only. It's you and what you know and what you possess within you, and hard work to bring out the harmony in you. Now, I have gardens, a pond, a home.

The garden becomes your painting. Looking at the pond, you can see the reflections in the water. You can see the bugs swimming, the light shifting. Its amazing to see all that. Being in the present, being here looking at the pond. You can look close, look for the alchemy of transformation. The sounds of the birds, the wind—it's a natural music. You could compose music, paint, recreate abstract painting. It's infinite when you feel comfort and no stress. Your being has to be free to have the natural environment help you. Everything becomes a part of you, and that's exciting.

See the little white dot on that bug? In memory, you know it has eyes and wings, but in this moment, this flash, you just see it's pure movement—it is like a star in space. You can capture its amazing lines into art. Its shadow can be transformed into sculpture, the water into a layer of glass. Everywhere is art, is sculpture. You can do so much, even writing a child's story.

What is your inner experience, so we could identify your state?

I was not well for a few days a while ago. Somehow, I asked the highest being to clean my blood system internally. My whole being felt good after a few days. When you are ready to ask, in the most honest and needed way, the highest being comes in.

I had open heart surgery a few years ago. Through that, I had an 'inner Christ' experience. It was beyond time, space—you couldn't measure it.

I weigh 125 pounds. I could be turned into a small pile of ash. Yet, what I am is something else. If you break down this pile of ash, it becomes nothingness, which you cannot see or a scale can't measure. How could you measure your soul, spirit, and love? All this is what holds everything together, breathing, being, the essentials of life. Science can only go so far.

For example, if someone calls in the middle of the night, you tumble around in a daze. Then you can pull yourself together from where ever you were and respond—that is magic to be able to see that awareness, how our own inner being operates.

Would you speak about the Inner Christ experience?

It gave to me an inner security. The physical surroundings can be a burden, too much a descriptive part of life. In the Inner Christ, you find the inner heart, who you are, that holds all things in it. Beyond substance. You're connected to all of people, nature, plants, ocean, flowers, stars, the galaxy. And that's what makes it exciting.

Would you recommend to others that they should seek out what you have? Is it so important that they should look for it no matter what?

Some people go through the education system. After they go through it, afterwards the job they worked so hard to get is no longer there, or for other reasons everything collapses. They are not in touch with who they are. When you find your own passion, your gift in life—when you find it, you can work towards expanding it. In the end, you have more, an inner security, your life feels more comfortable in the universe, because you come from the center of who you are.

Knowledge is a cold, unsatisfying side of life, and that's what modern life is like. Also, man is a vast computer, it is all there, you are connected to the universe. You don't need a piece of equipment, your connection is direct. There is more mystery, more beauty, more wholeness.

Today is about business, control like in the government, computers to run things. People forget their own body, their own soul and spirit.

Where you always like this?

I don't have much education. Though grade nine, with a D in art (chuckle). Not good for the normal system, I didn't fit, so I had to find my own direction. Surviving in a tough situation as a boy, catching fish by hand to eat. I can transcend and transform that now into harmony. It's internal, because I had to dig into a deeper level.

Kids in tough situations might commit suicide. We're not born to die, we're born to live. Choosing to live transcends sorrow into art, into life, mystery, drama.

When you have the financial opportunity, you don't need to hang onto the idea that life is hard. You can shift it to life is easy, find the Inner Christ, shift into harmony with all things.

I think harmony is connected with being connected to our inner being. When you don't connect with that inner warmth, harmony is too far out. When you are in touch with yourself, the concept of harmony becomes meaningful.

Westerners are more into Christ, the skinny body that was crucified. Buddhist revere the fatter Buddha, but the real spirit, the real soul and spirit is beyond fat or thin. You don't die, like a star, like the water we drink, the air we breath, a kind of timeless thing. Work can distract you from what is real.

You cannot kill 'Christ', because it's a way of being. The physical body can be killed, but what's real is beyond that. What's behind the Christ body is light. It holds everything together. It doesn't disappear with death.

When you close your eyes, are you bright inside?

Oh, yeah. When you close the physical eye, I see all is energy. You turn the 'TV' off, and the inner vision continues in a substance-less, weightless way. That kind of vision excites me. You close your eyes, your other senses become intensified. When that happens, your awareness shifts. Then you can transmit it into your art. You transmit it into that inner harmony. It's another way to see. Sometimes our physical eyes can be distracting.

Is there anything you would like to say to the people reading this?

I feel it's good to know your passion early, especially children. When you discover your passion, you can work towards that area. The parents don't know how to guide the children, they're working so hard. Then the schools take over, and you get stuffed like a turkey. Your being gets choked into nothing, you lose your own being and passion. It's hard to escape the box that the school puts you in, and that box gets stuck in your subconscious.

I think it takes courage to do what you like to do, because usually it doesn't pay—that's why I do so many things (chuckle).

I had so much humiliation and drama in my life. It forced me to find my own inner truth. Given enough time, I can discover my own universe—what fits me.

A Workshop Participant Goes into the Inner Peace State by Healing an Issue Using Whole-Hearted Healing

Jenny Heegel attended a Whole-Hearted Healing therapy training a few years ago. Using the WHH process, she healed an issue that caused her to enter into a relatively permanent peak state. At first, she was quite concerned because she couldn't feel any past traumas to work on during the WHH practice sessions, but was relieved to find out that this was normal for someone in the state she had just entered. It's been a couple of years since the workshop, and her state continues unchanged.

Thanks Mary,

.... I was talking to some friends after my Course in Miracles meeting about my new found "freedom" and wonderful life, love, etc. I described how I 'got it' that we are creating our own play of life from Pam's Radical Forgiveness workshop. Toward the end of our lunch, my lower back began to ache. (I have periodic intense back pain about every 3 months or so since last April). I was scheduled to go the Indigo Girls concert that evening and was desperate for that pain to go away. I called Alan to do a surrogate Reiki healing and started to cry when he began it. I got off the phone and did WHH, EFT, and worked through some traumas but my back was still hurting. I went to the concert and met with the WHH group the next day and Alan and I supported each other with WHH but the pain didn't quit.

I don't get images but I am able to feel and move through thoughts and feelings of various traumas. The one I was working on re: back pain ended up being labor and birth pain stuff. Is it weird that I am able to easily access the emotion? Pamela mentioned that I am visiting various different peak states. I am not sure where I am working out of at this point.

Also, Alan wanted me to tell you that my ADD appears to be gone, I can concentrate at work even with noise going on around me (cubicle hell). I am not irritated by noise like I used to be. I recently played the piano and was able to read the music and play and even ENJOY playing (it sounded beautiful). It was such a chore when I was taking lessons. I can stay on task at work, am calm and patient. I still chew my cuticles some but haven't bled since the workshop.

Thanks,
Jenny

(A few days later...)

Thanks Mary,

I don't know what happened about the ADD stuff. I had a lot of anxiety along with it. I currently do not experience intense fear, anger, or sadness unless I "go there" with WHH.

I went with friends to dinner and one person verbally attacked the other. In the past, I would have cringed and tried to smooth thing over. I did not feel responsible, I just watched them and realized they were both in pain—and loved them.

I can hardly remember being the person I was 3 weeks ago. This state is so liberating. I'll watch for the "chewing" emotions and let you know what happens.

Light and love,
Jenny

A Lifelong Hollow and Inner Brightness State

Susanne is a 22 year old woman who has been in the Hollow and Inner Brightness state since she was born. This is the target state of the process in Chapter 8 and the simpler one in Volume 2. It's possible that she has other states also. From our perspective, she's an exceptionally well balanced, joyful person who lives a life that can only be described from the outside as magical. Her creativity, sense of service, grace, and ability to manifest her desires has to be seen to be believed. As an adult, she notes that she rarely if ever experiences pain or injury, even so much as a paper cut.

Her account of how she experiences life is particularly important as it shows how a person's personality develops with this state as its basis. Since this state is relatively rare, this account is particularly unusual. Most of the data we have on it is from people who have acquired it later in life from our workshops or by other means.

In particular, we asked her what potential drawbacks there might be with having such an exceptional state, so that people who might be considering moving into this state themselves could judge the impact it might have in their personal lives. I was curious myself how she found living in a world filled with people in average consciousness, in such activities as finding a loving partner, and so on.

She has been kind enough to write about her everyday experience in her own words below:

Body experience

As far as my body experience in general... when I sit and simply experience the quietude of my body...there's light...and there's emptiness or vast space...depending on which way someone would interpret my experience...

Physical health

My health is healthy...my body is physically strong...my immune system is amazingly strong (even amidst continuous travels in third world countries, I have maintained good health)...and I am beautiful...

I've had very few experiences of injuries, sickness, or pain—I did get ear infections from ages 2-6 (3 to 5 times a year). I do remember a few typical skinned knees, cuts, and bumps as a child...and I had strep throat from ages 7-14 (2 or 3 times a year)...all of which hurt some in the moment, but healed quickly. I feel that I respond quite mellowly to pain...and I actually enjoyed the frozen popsicles and special treatment that I received during my sick moments...other than that..I probably have a cold once every 3 years maybe...if that...and that's about it.

Judgment

I love seeing myself as containing the same inner essence as the next soul. I don't see myself as different from others. I am often unaware if others are judging me. I believe that there are only a few people that would even confront me with the judgments that they do have of me. When someone does communicate, I love journeying into the reflections that they are experiencing. I love being available for growth that one is willing to share with me...I feel very little judgment of others.

Challenges

I love challenges...Challenges offer me a moment to reveal what was once concealed. I enjoy the growth that I experience upon undergoing challenge. I often feel more beautiful and shining after confronting myself and seizing the opportunity to deepen the realness within...Personally, I have had far and few challenges in my life. The challenges that do arrive seem so finite in respect to the infinite blessings in this life.

Material Aspects

I love the material aspects of life...I have everything, yet nothing. The material visions that arrive into my consciousness, seem to magically appear into physical reality. At this point, what I own is minimal. My material desires miraculously appear on a fun, fabulous platter right before me if I am both ready and available for a particular vision to manifest. I feel that the material aspects of life arrive in a natural progression for me...

Money

I love money...Again, I have everything, yet nothing at this point in my life. Financially speaking, funds seem to arrive in perfect timing and to fulfill their purpose in the now. I'm conscious of keeping financial balance and of keeping priorities straight when spending money. I tend not to invest in something new until I am clear that more cash income is on its way. I enjoy and feel deserving of the monetary abundance that is available for me this life...

Work

I love work. I don't know if my work arrives to me or if I arrive to my work. It seems to happen simultaneously. I simply am a soul stepping forth and right when I am available for work, work is available for me. My work seems to fulfill the links that others are missing in order to manifest their personal visions. I often make things happen...and happen in a pleasant way. I am led to an array of work experiences...all of which contain a creative, spiritual, or hospitable aspect. Even if I personally cannot be available in my body, I can usually have a contact or suggestion of assistance. My way of living is my work. The creative work that does ignite monetary gain seems minuscule compared to the greater work that is happening each moment of this life...

Drawbacks to the state I'm in

So...the downside of being this way of being...it's not a downside for me...while others may feel lack of connection with me...I feel connection with them...while others have there own journeys to experience (and some may be harmful or negative through some eyes)... I don't feel confusion for their way of being. I trust that what they are experiencing is what they need to be experiencing...and that the experience is valid for the whole...appearances and judgments can be deceiving. I feel that there is something much bigger happening...and we all have to make the full journey in order to fully arrive to our understandings.

I feel that I become like everyone else the moment that I start thinking that I'm different...

Gaining the Hollow State and Peak Abilities Using the Process in Volume 2.

Pamela Black attended our workshop several years ago. She went through the Hollow state process described in Volume 2, and had dramatic shifts in her state of consciousness and awareness abilities. Although some of the changes involving abilities that we were not targeting for faded after a while, others remained as of this writing several years later. (We've explained why this sometimes occurs when doing the trauma healing approach for peak states in Chapter 9.) She also found that she could pull the state back at will if it faded.

One of the important reasons to acquire the Hollow state is how it drastically increases one's abilities to rapidly and effortlessly heal traumatic material. Pamela gives some examples of this, healing things that a person in average consciousness would not be able to do at all, or at best with great difficulty.

The following is a copy of emails sent at the time to Dr. Mary Pellicer along with some follow-up material.

Hi, guys,

Here's some bits of real feedback about my last 24 hours and attempt to get used to this new landscape. Mary, in answer to your question, yes, I am diffused. I don't stop at my own body/skin, I spread out pretty far but differing distances (from house-sized to Mars), and it will move at will when I shift my attention but I think I pretty much stay house-sized if I'm not thinking about it. Regarding skin, sometimes I feel it more than others (like hollowness) but it seems to be a separate thing from the diffusion. Diffusion feels like 100% of the time, but hollowness and skinless feel partial, and now that I think of it, I'm going to play with whether they come and go simultaneously (connected to each other).

Driving home, 'sensed' the living energy of pavement, as differentiated from the energy of the median or berm. Experimented with predicting (based on sensing the strand of pavement) which way the road would next curve—left or right. Simple, and I had a 50/50 shot at it, but I thought it pretty amazing that I did it more than 40 times and was only wrong 3 times. In all 3 cases I was "trying really hard" to focus/sense the pavement; when I backed off and became more casual about it, or forgot until a spur of the moment check, I was 100 percent.

Also on the drive I went in/out of Hollow but was very aware of passing trucks, felt them in my field, felt when someone was inattentive and making sharp/dangerous moves. But not by sensing the other drivers, as I would have expected. It was more sensing the energy field, and the sharp movement in the field as a big object floated through it, commanded by an energy that was inharmonious (the driver's intention or carelessness or something). Very odd. It makes me understand what the planet must sense in us (humans) as we are inattentive and angry and careless.

Felt the pavement, molded my car into the pavement as "we" drove (because I drive very fast and like the sense of extra traction). Very aware of the almost-full moon and amazing clouds in this big, big, and bright sky (definitely the Big Sky state). I could reach out and feel the fuzzy treetops. When I arrived in Atlanta and drove along my favorite streets I could sense (hear?) the trees welcoming me home— they definitely know me!—and it was so lovely and unexpected I almost had tears of joy. I drove very slowly and admired their being washed in moonlight. I was also aware of small creatures in the underbrush.

Came home to an email from a 'gentleman friend' which could have been considered pretty negative. Responded at scale 3 (would have been 8 a week ago—he won't let me kiss him, can you imagine?? —but I had worked on that space over the weekend), so I still felt CPL (calm, peace, and lightness) underneath the moment. I did a 'standard TAT' then flipped back through the generations (with the 'deck of cards' and inducing Hollow trick) and got down to a 1/2 (I know it wasn't 0 but it was 4 a.m. and I was in the Crusades, okay?). Slept 4 hours, got up, felt great, went back into WHH to finish the half, went into the egg state just prior to conception, worked that "oh, god, only 24 hours, hurry, hurry" apprehension then jumped automatically back to a preconception "little speck" state with a muted sense of some fear (still some CPL (calm, peace, and lightness) under all this). Worked the speck by surrounding it (while I was also in it, like surrounding me with me) and inducing hollowness, and then starting growing until I was out in the Infinite, definitely regained full Hollow myself, as strongly as when we first finished the exercises and I went to Mars.

Decided to check for any difference in brightness, so I not only closed and covered my eyes with my hands, but stuck my face into the pillow, to be certain I was reading correctly, but careful not to touch my eyes as pressure changes the brightness, too. Found that if I gave myself the time—say 5 minutes, instead of 30 seconds—things actually got a bit brighter behind the lids. I think I had been fluctuating somewhat, around the 5-6 level, but I think it's gone up a notch, now 6-7. The scale on brightness is hard for me; I think we all have a different numeric sense, so I want to get some photographic gray scales to work with and send you, so you can tell me your idea of 7 or 10 or 3. I'll keep checking but I think waiting a bit really gives a truer read, than just doing the quick look.

I have an eye appointment on Monday and I'll let you know. I awoke this morning and panicked for a moment because I thought

I'd slept in my contacts; things were not completely clear, but much clearer with naked eyes than I remember them being. But when I put my industrial strength contacts in they're also clear, so I'm confused (and probably healing)."

(The next day, she is laughing about one of the most common effects of removing the shell—the urge to clean and throw old stuff away:)

"Mary, this is truly a warped reality.

I got home last night, and this morning, after only 4 hours sleep, I'm up cleaning my stove (of all things) and I realize I'm humming.

This is sick.

Is there more?

Twirls,
Pamela

(Two weeks later:)

"Feedback on my Hollow state: I'm not sure I'm holding Hollow well, and have gone in/out of some of the permeability (I feel some skin, though I'm still diffused) as I've had emotion come up around some things. I know the next trauma is coming up to heal and am very grateful, as I wanted a state from which I could continue to do legitimate clean-out. And very grateful as well that the emotion is much lighter than I know it would have been even a week ago, and there is a layer of CPL (calm, peace, and lightness) underneath. Perhaps this is what you mean by emotions while in a peak state being different, so perhaps I am truly retaining the peak while bringing up traumas to heal, and will pop back into full peak state when I resolve.

I also used once more the TAT/flipping back in time for the generational thing (like flipping through a picture book, or deck of cards) and also used simply a "visioning the image then filling with light" technique and quickly resolved a couple of things.

The last piece is just feedback for you and Mary to do some sort of handout on the states and what to expect, for those of us who hit them and are walking around in "holy shit!" land while stumbling over our own feet. It might help you not to have to answer 6 million individual questions.

I'm not holding my states completely or all the time, but it is hugely different, yet at the same time feels like the logical next step from where I was. Thank you, truly; language is so inadequate here.

The biggest piece I healed during the workshop was around fear/safety; I know there is more to go (lots of trauma stacks around fear, I think) but the difference in today vs. before is HUGE. It's not that I lived with fear every day or that I felt fear often, but there was an underlying guardedness about life and boundaries that I just don't feel anymore. And an underlying joy that was beginning to be present more often, is now always there.

Two weeks later, and I still feel gratitude beyond words, for the work you've shared.

Pamela

A Hollow State and an Awareness Extended Past the Skin after Individual Work

David Burnet is a volunteer living in the eastern US. He had already accessed the Inner Brightness state to some degree, and with Dr. Pellicer's help moved into the Hollow state using the regression process in Chapter 8. I think you'll find this abridged version of his email fascinating.

Age 14 or 15 —Light and brightness, for a couple of weeks.

I had been studying books by Alan Watts, and trying to learn how to develop a photographic memory. I'd intend to take mental "snapshots" of what I saw, and try to see exact duplicates of that, later. Learning to notice and recall in more and more detail, across a wider field of awareness.

Suddenly everything became very bright, and very easy. My mental abilities seemed to jump. Taking mental "pictures" and recalling them was easy. Learning and studying in school was suddenly easy, as well. There was a connectedness to everything and everyone, though I didn't particularly stress this...it was more as if the FIELD of my awareness had shifted, and hence everything in it.

I could recall, easily, anything I set my mind to recall.

I had a strong sense—this is a bit hard to put into words—that the key was in "not saying no", which allowed "yes" to happen. Like not reacting with the ego/reactive mind...just letting things BE.

Life was bright, easy, joyful...and so was I.

This lasted for a couple of weeks, then began to wear off and dissipate.

(Material omitted. Account takes up in 2003.) Through the help of Mary (Pellicer) I've come to appreciate a little bit about the "Hollow state", and experience it in various degrees. The breakthrough came, if I recall correctly, with some generational trauma healing, which apparently went in a very classical way.

My sense of body is now often (maybe even usually) larger or more extended than my physical body, my skin. It's pretty easy, easier than before, to extend even further. I can frequently take in other people and circumstances to within my "space", with varying degrees of intuitive knowing...and sometimes doing...that seems joined with them.

Warm regards and blessings,
David Burnet

Acquiring the Wholeness State Using Rebirthing

Nemi Nath is an Australian rebirther whose account below is of her discovery of what makes the Wholeness state occur. Her story is from an article focused on placental trauma, which can be found via her website at www.breathconnection.com.au. My thanks to Ms. Nath for her permission to use her work.

Wholly Whole: A Personal Case History

The first time I encountered my 'placenta trauma' was during my very first rebirthing session, which happened to be about my birth. I saw something being thrown into a white enamel bucket and was not sure what it was. At the time I wondered if it was the placenta, but because I felt so close to it, and the pain of it landing in the bucket was so immense, I interpreted it to be a dead twin that was removed without mention.

The bucket appeared many times in later sessions and each time caused the same amount of separation pain that stayed unresolved. I frequently considered whether the content could be the placenta, but discarded the thought/feeling because I believed that the placenta was a part of the mother, after all in German it is called the Mutterkuchen (mother-cake). The intensity of feeling towards this 'being' in the bucket confirmed my belief that this must be more than an afterbirth, which in 1947 was not much more than a discardable leftover from the birth.

My Placenta Trauma Symptoms

For about half a day after the talk [by Shivam Rachana, author of Lotus Birth], I wandered around pondering what the symptoms of my cord cutting/placenta trauma might be. I was sure that I would have the symptoms because I know my cord was cut immediately, and I realized that I must be attributing the symptoms to something else. During these hours a quite familiar feeling of dread developed in my belly, right in the pit of my stomach. It intensified to the point that I knew I needed to give myself a quiet space to explore this experience. Using conscious connected breathing, I was there immediately, in the womb, feeling my placenta and me as one. I reinstated my placenta as a part of me, an external organ, which had a very specific function during the passage from the universe via my father and through my mother's body into my independent existence.... I felt whole and complete, really whole, how I had never felt before... And I thought my session was complete.

However, the feeling of dread returned within minutes, this time slightly to the right of where it had appeared first. When I let my whole consciousness slide into it I became aware of two parts of me. One was the me that I usually identified with, and the other was a slightly smaller me that I also sometimes identified with, but never recognized its separateness as distinctly as now. I was able to slide from one to the other easily. The smaller one appeared not to be embodied and its feeling was that of dreaming in an awake state. The bigger one was the one I usually identify with and live through in my awake consciousness.

The Placenta has Feelings Too

I noticed that the returned feeling of dread came from the smaller part and decided to stay in there to fully experience it. I discovered that my placenta was afraid. This feeling of fear was different from experiencing fear in a part of my body. It is difficult to describe. It was as if my placenta had been a separate being with an intelligence of its own (my earlier thinking that it was a twin), and that it had feelings separate from those of the baby. It had its own separation trauma from me, hence the dread came back after I had integrated 'mine'. I also noticed that the location of these feelings of dread had been in two different places in my belly, as I described above.

The Birth of the Etheric Body

Now I remembered parts of Rachana's talk about the function of the placenta, after the cord had completely dried up and several days after the birth,.... that the etheric body of the baby is still encompassing the placenta for much longer than the time of the physical transfer between placenta and baby, and that the etheric transfer is also interrupted and incomplete when the cord is cut before it disconnects naturally, by itself, from the navel. The etheric body, invisible to the normal physical eye, is a major part of us like the Earth atmosphere is to the Earth. I could feel that I still had two separate parts to my etheric body here in current time as a result of the early cord cutting. One was inside the other, like a little balloon inside a big one, and now my task was to have them merge into one.

Merging My Etheric and Physical Bodies

This part of the session took a long time, more than an hour before I was able to get up. I assisted myself by holding a little soft cushion to feel the small part easier. The merging process was nothing I could consciously 'do'. I had sent out a prayer to ask for this to happen and it began. The sensations of this process were quite physical. Heat built up in my belly and extended up to my neck. Both parts of me had to give up their separate identity. I talked to the smaller part and encouraged it, that it would be bigger afterwards, a lot bigger and I encouraged myself in the same way. It was a loving and divine melting into Me, the real me, I was making love to myself.

There were very funny moments too. I had the sensation of my head sticking out above the two bubbles that were engaged in the merging process. Every now and then my head would slip into the bubble alchemy and the process would stop until my head was above 'water' again. This sensation of having my head above water is still with me today as I am writing the article. It helped me to continue the merging process, which continued even after I had got up from the session.

What I learned

The effects of the session continued and are still in progress (three month after the event, when I wrote this article). Daily I notice that my perception of reality is different, as I perceive my environment and myself from a Whole Self. This is impossible to describe to someone who has not gone through the process of placenta re-unification. Because we have called something whole, that is not whole, our language does not have a word for a 'better than whole'. I will call it wholly whole. 'Whole' simply feels different from before. My energy body feels clearer, more aligned and less cluttered, as if I had exchanged a few pieces of furniture for one piece that serves the purpose of all of the previous ones. I am in a permanent state of joy and my heart feels warm and I am constantly in love with myself. I believe this is the state of cosmic joy referred to in eastern philosophies as being our natural state of being. Now, one year after the experience that umbilical cord to my joy is still intact, even in intense and emotional situations. I have some grief for what I missed and sadness for all the people who are still missing being wholly whole.

As a rebirther/trainer I have a new ability to perceive the real cause of separation and abandonment trauma started by the cutting of the cord, and how the effects ripple through all we do and effect our ability to relate. To let go naturally of our placenta is to learn how to finish things, how to leave, how to complete in wholeness and move on. It is about knowing when to go and when to start something new. It is about feeling full and coming to the lover in wholeness, and independence with a full heart to give of ourselves.

Spontaneously Removing the Skin Boundary and Connecting to the Creator

Below is a transcript of a conversation with Kate Sorensen about her experience at age 22 of merging into a column of white light, going to the Creator, and losing her skin boundary. (These states are covered in Volume 2.) She vividly describes her experience of how this occurred, and what the state felt like afterwards. Although Kate returned to everyday consciousness some weeks later, we've included this transcript because it illustrates the state quite well.

We've also included this account for another reason. Kate's story illustrates one of the problems with acquiring major peak states—what happens if for some reason you lose it? People who lose a peak state, especially a major one, realize what they've lost and often describe it as "being kicked out of heaven." They struggle, sometimes in despair and hopelessness, to regain what they've lost. In Kate's case, she's tried to get back to that state for over twenty years with only sporadic success. This search has shaped much of her life, and her choice of work and activities ever since. She's the founder of Trauma Relief Services, Director of the Traumatic Incident Reduction Association, and organized the first energy psychology conferences.

> I went to Miami from Sarasota to attend an evening program of women's Sufi practices. This involved chanting the names of God and other things in Arabic (lots of vowel sounds that resonate in various chakras), at a higher pitch than I was used to. We also did some visualizations and meditations—I remember an unfamiliar one focusing on Mary, the mother of Jesus. In the previous two months I had fallen on my head on the highway and suffered through two bouts of pneumonia, and had done a cleansing fast as part of the cure. The day after the women's group I didn't feel very strong, so I stayed alone and ate very lightly. I laid down in the afternoon to rest, and dozed off, going through some dream states that I don't remember now. I then found myself in a grayish cube-like space. My father was standing quietly in front of me and to the left, and my mother stood in front and to the right.
>
> My mother was talking nonstop, on and on. Essentially, she was describing all of the beliefs she held and telling me, in various words, 'This is reality, and you just have to buy it, that's all there is

to it. I'm telling you the way it is, everyone knows this and you have to accept it, too." As I listened, and listened, I started feeling weighed down. My head was bending forward, and I felt heavier and heavier. My consciousness was getting more dull and dim as I took on what she was giving me. Then, I somehow found the strength to stand up straight. I looked my mother in the eye and said "NO". The "NO" was not particularly loud, but it felt huge, tangible, powerful, possibly coming from my throat/heart area. It traveled across from me to my mother. When it reached her, she froze. I started feeling guilty, thinking "Uh oh, I shouldn't talk to my mother like that. What if I hurt her, what if I killed her? But before the guilt got too far, I felt energy vibrations, a rush of energy coming up through my feet. It moved through my legs, up through my body, and out the top of my head

As the energy exploded upward, my awareness was lifted out with it, out the top of my head. I looked down at the scene and saw my body with my hands crossed over my chest, leaning forward. I thought for a moment, "I'd better stay there and take care of my body, it might fall over." Then I thought, "I'll let my parents take care of it, they like to do that sort of thing." With that, I felt released and swept upward in a great whoosh of white light, an extension of the same blast of energy, but all the scenery was gone. All I was aware of was the blazing column of white light moving up and down at the same time. Looking back, I could say that this felt like it had something to do with the realm of the Creator. The buzzing column was like a God-related phenomenon. I wouldn't exactly say this was God, but maybe the closest that I, as a human being, could experience God directly.

Along with the white light there was an enormous roaring, buzzing sound that seemed to be moving inward from all directions around me. As it reached the center, in the roaring there was a thunderous voice that said just three words: "ONLY GOD ETERNAL." Then the whole thing seemed to move on to something I've never had words for; maybe I went into a field of lightness and clarity, I'm not sure.

Eventually, I became aware of my body in the room in Miami and I opened my eyes. Everything was different: brighter, quiet, clear, very vivid and beautiful. I felt very, very good, with a sense of calm joy. My body felt as if it had no density, there were no obstructions inside, no barrier at my skin, everything felt unified yet with energy flows. My emotions would bubble up and move freely with no attachments. After a while people returned to the house and I noticed areas where the energy flowed, areas of turbulence, other places where it was stuck. My sense of all this was more kinesthetic than visual, but very clear. I felt like I could sense everyone's intentions directly, I could sense the energy like looking "behind the scenes" to a level where true intentions existed. Sometimes these intentions were in alignment with what people were saying and doing, other times the intentions seemed different than the appearances people were projecting. Where people were trying to do two things at once, I could say a few words to address the conflict and they would resolve it, or I could reach out with my intention and unjam it. Just by moving my body, it would shift the whole energy in the situation.

During this state, I knew, to some degree, what was going to happen in the future, I'd know what people were going to say before they said it, know when somebody was going to show up, things like that. I felt that my perceptions expanded, like I could sense things through walls, I wasn't subject to the usual limits of sight and sound. I was feeling much more present than usual. I got used to it quickly and felt a sense of grace. Barrier at skin still gone. I was happily connected to my body, but felt light, my body was a form in the whole energy field of the world, both the visible world and what might be called a world of subtle energies.

That state lasted for 2 or 3 weeks, during which time I had a lot of amazing adventures. Little miracles happened frequently. I decided to drop out of school, I had a surprisingly good time with my parents over Christmas during which time it looked to me like they were acting very differently than they usually did. I ended up back in Florida with two former boyfriends, really great guys who I still wanted to be friends with, but not lovers. They were resentful toward me and toward each other, and I felt very stuck and guilty. I remember looking at both of their unhappy faces and losing the lightness, like a balloon coming down from the sky. With all of my programming about sex and being what other people wanted me to be, I was very confused. I really felt stuck. I not only lost the light, but I felt really miserable. I had the sense that I put "it"—the shell, the fog—back on, even though I struggled and resisted it. My guess is that it had to do with a combination of earlier stuff getting triggered, and my own judgments on myself. I agreed with my mother's reality again: "Oh yeah, I'm not really good, I'm small, I'm screwing up, I can't handle power responsibly, look what a mess I made." I didn't have the skills to deal with relationship problems at that insoluble level where people were wanting different things that just didn't fit together.

It was probably not just incidental that this breakthrough came after about five months of conscientious daily spiritual practices. These involved yoga, conscious breathing, and chanting certain names of God in Arabic, which have drawn out vowel sounds that vibrate in the heart, throat, "third eye" and crown chakras.

Conclusion

This chapter is just a taste of the variety of experiences and states that we've seen over the years in our work. Although the changes in some case were very new and dramatically different to the people involved, none would be willing to give up who they now are. We hope this has been an inspiration for your own hope for a better and more fulfilling life.

For more accounts of people's peak experiences and states, and a useful bibliographical selection, I refer you to Rhea White's 'Exceptional Human Experience Network' website at www.ehe.org.

An Index of Peak States and Their Probabilities of Occurrence

Number of States

We believe that there are at least 17 major states, and a host of substates and combination states. A lot more work needs to be done in this area, as it is often very hard to figure out if a person is in a unique state or in a combination state (they don't come with subtitles, unfortunately). The list below is *preliminary*, and we're sure it contains errors. It's just the best we've got so far. In addition, we need to do a lot more work identifying the core developmental events for each of them. That should keep us busy for a couple more years.... Many of the states in this list involve Volume 2, but they are included in Volume 1 to give interested readers a feel for the range of states that we've isolated. The major variables we've identified so far are:

- Triune brain states and their degree of fusion.
- Connection to the Creator (a plane of bright self-awareness).
- Body boundary states.
- Connection to the Void.
- Connection to Gaia, the planetary consciousness/Creative Principle.
- Connection to the Realm of the Shaman and the sacred.
- Internal and external awareness states.
- Good/evil states.
- Various kinds of inner light states.
- Miscellaneous states.

Naming Conventions

As we mentioned in the Introduction, naming the states has been difficult. If the state already has a well-known name, we've tried to use it, as for example 'the Beauty Way'. We realize this may lead to problems when our definition is not quite the same as other people's, but in the future we expect the names and definitions to stabilize as more people work with peak states. An example of a potentially debatable state name would be the Christ consciousness state. For other states we've tried to use the most noticeable characteristic as its name. Some have different characteristics for men and women, and in that case we arbitrarily chose the male version, as for example with the 'Underlying Happiness' state.

When describing a state made up of two other states, we simply combine the names together with the triune brain state name first (if applicable) and call it a combination state. If a combination state already had a well-known name we used it. Note that some states, when combined, give qualities that neither alone possess. In this case we call it a synergistic state. For example, the Beauty Way is a synergistic state that already has a well-known name, and that has a quality of 'aliveness' that the separate states do not.

Estimates of Occurrence

In the short descriptive list of peak states below we've included some estimates of the probability of their occurrence in the general population, as well as a probability of how many people have at least experienced the state enough to have a conscious memory of it. They are based on Caucasian North American populations. Unfortunately, these estimates may be wildly inaccurate due to measurement problems and tiny sample sizes (see Volume 2 for our measurement techniques), but we included them as a starting place to give people a feel for the relative rarity. I wouldn't be surprised if the estimates are off by a factor of 10 to 100 especially for the rarer states! We suspect that, if anything, our estimates may be overly optimistic, i.e. there are fewer people in the general population in the state than given below. Another problem with making these estimates is in defining the cutoff point for people who are only partially in a state.

These considerations generate a list of questions. Many of these will resolve themselves with more work and the creation of better measurement tools:

- Do we include people who fall in and out of the state (i.e. the state's stability), and if so what average percentage of the time do they have to be in the state to be included?
- Where is the cutoff point for someone who is only partially in the state?
- How do we make externally verifiable and repeatable measurements that independent investigators can agree on?
- If we use self-reporting to determine percentages, how do we measure the completeness of the state in terms of core characteristics?
- Do we have an accurate list of core characteristics for each state?

As we've mentioned in Chapter 4, estimates of occurrence can also be generated theoretically based on the probabilities that any given developmental event will be encountered with enough trauma to block the peak state after birth. At the present time we haven't run any large-scale tests to measure the underlying probabilities that an average person will successfully make it through any particular developmental event unscathed. However, we hypothesize that it may be possible to measure these probabilities by using a Gaia instruction phrase with galvanic skin response (GSR) measurement equipment to evaluate the occurrence and amount of trauma. With this information, overall estimates of the occurrence of any given peak state could be calculated. This can be used as a crosscheck on actual measurements of the occurrence of the states in the general population, and might actually be used to predict the existence of unknown developmental stage traumas if the numbers don't match well in a particular case.

Another problem we have is identifying if a person actually has experienced or is in any given peak state. When we ran questionnaires in the past we found people who were not in a given state put down that they had characteristics of it. This occurred because we were forced to use common English words to describe aspects of the state, aspects that they'd never experienced before and so incorrectly translated into experiences that they did know. See Volume 2 for more on this problem and the methods we've used to measure the states.

A potentially much more accurate way to solve this problem is to use brain biofeedback equipment. Chapter 12 and Volume 2 cover the possibilities of this approach. This would give us an objective and repeatable measurement technique, and estimates that we could feel confident about. In the future, we hope to give much more repeatable and verifiable techniques to make these measurements.

Dysfunctional States Involving the Multiple Brain System (Volume 1)

'Sub-average Consciousness' state
- Characteristics: Unusually messed up, a sub-normal life.
- Cause: Body and solar plexus brain are not communicating. No other peak states are present.
- Comment: Found in psychotherapy client populations, and in many multiple developmentally challenged clients.
- Frequency: Not determined.

Brain Shutdown States:
   Note: We chose to call these states by what causes them, rather than by their dominant characteristic, as we're not sure that these characteristics might also have trauma related causes for some people. All possible combinations of brain shutdown states exist—we just list ones here that we've had personal experience with. These are dysfunctional states because they involve a loss of the associated brain abilities, although to the person they feel better than normal.

'Mind Shutdown' state
  • Characteristics: Inability to form judgments or make choices. There is a peace and calmness with the state even with the frustration of not being able to weigh choices.
  • Cause: The mind brain is turned 'off'.
  • Comment: No common name that we know of.
  • Frequency: Unknown.

'Mind-heart Shutdown' state
  • Characteristics: The body feels like it's made of air, without a boundary. However, the lower belly feels 'full' like we'd eaten a large meal. No ability to feel emotions or form judgments.
  • Cause: The mind and heart brains are turned 'off'.
  • Comment: May also be known as the 'Pearl Beyond Price' state from the Sufi tradition.
  • Frequency: Unknown.

'Samadhi' (Heart-body Shutdown) state
  • Characteristics: An overwhelming feeling of peace, timelessness, and almost no need for oxygen or breathing.
  • Cause: The heart and body brains are turned 'off'.
  • Comment: Could have been called the 'Heart-body Shutdown state'.
  • Frequency: Unknown but rare.

'Heart Shutdown' state
  • Characteristics: Inability to feel emotions. Feeling that other people are just objects.
  • Cause: The heart brain is shut 'off'.
  • Comment: Probably a major cause of sociopathic behavior.
  • Frequency: Unknown.

Peak States Involving the Multiple Brain System (Volume 1)

'Average Consciousness' state
  • Characteristics: Living in (often subtle) fear. Totally at the effect of other people's emotions. Reactivity.
  • Cause: The body and solar plexus brains are connected or at least communicating. The triune brains' awarenesses are not communicating. The Buddha brain is usually fused with the mind brain.
  • Comment: No peak states of any sort.
  • Frequency: Very common.

'Inner Peace' state
- Characteristics: A continuous feeling of peace even while feeling other, even painful emotions. Past traumas no longer have any charge associated with them.
- Cause: Mind and heart brains fused together.
- Comment: A subset of the Beauty Way state.
- Frequency: Not determined.

'The Beauty Way' (also called Walking in Beauty) synergistic state
- Characteristics:
  Calm, peacefulness, and physical sense of lightness.
  Past seems not traumatic—memories are without emotions.
  Feel totally alive, and everything around you feels alive too
  Everything has a sort of beauty, even garbage
  Spiritual truths obvious.
  No dreaming.
  No underlying sense of fear.
  Live entirely in the present.
  No tension—like on summer vacation as a kid.
  Bird sounds are more vivid.
  Don't take on other people's emotional distress.
  Don't obey 'experts' automatically by giving up your own knowing.
  Can do many shamanic sorts of things with training.
  Silent mind, i.e. no voices or background murmur.
- Cause: A combination of the Inner Peace state (with the mind and heart fused) with a limited connection to the Creator. Creates an unconscious decision to make perceptions continuously positive. The component states interact synergistically to create new characteristics.
- Comment: An important state for shamanism, and physical and mental health. A better descriptor for the state might be the word 'Aliveness' as used by Harville Hendrix, but we're choosing the better known label of the Beauty Way for now. Well described in Eckhart Tolle's *The Power of Now*.
- Frequency: Estimated that both this state and the Inner Peace state occur in 8% of the general population relatively continuously, with an additional 14% who can recognize it.

'Underlying Happiness' state
- Characteristics: A feeling of happiness underlies all other feelings. It exists simultaneously even with difficult feelings such as sadness or anger. In women, a continuous loving feeling is more dominant, although the happiness is still present.

- Cause: Heart and body brains fused together.
- Comment: Doesn't stop the past from feeling emotionally traumatic.
- Frequency: Estimated 9% relatively continuously, additional 12% recognize it.

'Big Sky' state
- Characteristics: The world feels huge. Looking at the sky, it feels gigantic. Your boundaries disappear, especially above your head.
- Cause: Body, mind and Buddha brains fused together. The sensation of the huge sky is from a body sensation of the relative distance between objects and one's body.
- Comment: I'm not sure if I've accurately analyzed this state. Treat it as possibly being due to some other phenomenon. More work needs to be done on it.
- Frequency: Not determined.

'Brains Communicate' state
- Characteristics: The three brains can communicate with each other. Brains interact like a dysfunctional family.
- Cause: All the brains' awarenesses are touching and in communication.
- Comment: A useful intermediate state, but not as valuable or dramatic as a fused one. In a Perry diagram, the circles all overlap slightly.
- Frequency: Estimated 12% relatively continuously, additional 23% recognize it.

'Deep Peace' state
- Characteristics: Deeper peaceful feeling than the Beauty Way. A feeling of being balanced, evenness, no irritation. Feels like the physical heart is lower in the body. Feel more lightweight. Not effortless, but not as bad as normal consciousness. Brains are aware of each other, can communicate directly, and you are aware of each simultaneously.
- Cause: Brains' awarenesses are superimposed, but not completely fused. No hollow sensations in the body.
- Comment: An intermediate state that we don't try to get.
- Frequency: Not determined.

'Hollow' state
- Characteristics: Body feels hollow inside the skin. All parts of the body feel 'continuous'. Emotions have a cognitive rather than affective quality.
- Cause: All brains fuse together.

- Comment: Chakras are not merged. Brains are not connected to the Realm of the Shaman.
- Frequency: Estimated 7% relatively continuously, additional 12% recognize it.

'Wholeness' state
- Characteristics: The word 'wholeness' is the most accurate for this state, and is used spontaneously by people acquiring it. A feeling of being complete, with nothing missing. Music is especially vivid.
- Cause: A fusion of the placental and sperm tail 'energy' or 'awarenesses' with the other triune brains.
- Comment: The sensation of wholeness exists independently of the state of fusion of the other brains.
- Frequency: Not determined.

States Involving the Creator (Volume 2)

'Creator Awareness' state
- Characteristics: Can 'speak' to the Creator directly and move awareness to that level of being at will.
- Comments: Related to the Creator Light state.
- Frequency: Very rare (estimated at 0.003% relatively continuously, estimated additional 0.01% recognize it).

'Creator Light' state
- Characteristics: An internal light that can in some cases extend past the skin boundary. It has more of an intense white color to it, not a broad-spectrum light like sunlight.
- Cause: A limited connection to the Creator. Probably involves the light balls that come into the body from the Creator at certain developmental events.
- Comments: In the Realm of the Shaman state, the bright white is mixed with the fluorescent black. People describe this 'light' as being intense or energy charged. Often feels like it comes from above. Can be used to regress as in the 'life review' of the Near-Death Experience. Comes in various brightnesses.
- Note: (also classified in the Inner Light category)
- Frequency: Not determined.

States Involving the Body Boundary or 'Shell' (Volume 2)

'No-skin' state
- Characteristics: No sensation of having a skin boundary. Events in general don't cause one to lose perspective, and events no longer feel personal, at least at first. Generally found with the Hollow state, so that the entire body feels like it's just made of air.
- Cause: This state is the result of removing the generational ego shell at the skin boundary and other less substantial layers.
- Comments: The most obvious layer is attached to generational traumas. We call it the 'shell' because it is usually quite impermeable. This layer can become very permeable, which can feel like it has been removed when it really has not been. The boundary feels like it 'burns' a bit when in the Hollow state.
- Frequency: Not determined.

States Involving the Void (Volume 2)

'Void Connection' state
- Characteristics: A sense that the ultimate emptiness of the Void, which is past all physical existence, is within oneself. With a feeling of finally knowing who you are.
- Comment: This is the state we do when merging with the Void during the removal of the 'shell' at skin level. The void may be called the Infinite or the Tao in other traditions, but the word 'void' fits experientially.
- Frequency: Very rare (estimated 0.005% relatively continuously, estimated additional 0.02% recognize it).

States Involving Gaia (Volume 2)

'Gaia Communication' state
- Characteristics: An ability to communicate with Gaia, via one or more triune brains (i.e. a body sensation, a feeling or vision, or hearing). At it's best, a clear transmission of information at every level.
- Cause: Full Gaia connection is a natural state. This connection is blocked by trauma around misunderstood Gaia messages.
- Comment: Called the Inner Vision state by Tom Brown Jr., apparently because he mostly communicates via images with Gaia. We changed it because it was confusing if another brain's primary style to communicate was used, and because it sounded like the ability to see one's own internal organs.
- Frequency: Not determined.

'Creative Principle' state
- Characteristics: Feeling of being the essence of creativity oneself.
- Cause: Becoming completely and wholly merged with Gaia. A deeper state than just communicating with Gaia.
- Comment: The triune brains can choose to make this connection to Gaia individually. When experienced with all the triune brains, you experience yourself as the Creative Principle itself, or equivalently 'Brahma, creator of worlds'. It feels quite different when done partially one brain at a time. For example, to the body brain this connection feels very sexual, as in the creativity of reproduction.
- Frequency: Very rare (estimated 0.035% relatively continuously, estimated additional 0.17%recognize it.)

'Unbounded Awareness' state
- Characteristics: Things in the environment feel like they are inside one's own body. People can experience themselves as anything they put their attention to, such as animals or plants.
- Comments: Descriptions often found in shamanic literature. May be a subset of the Spaciousness state, but most likely is a Gaia awareness state.
- Frequency: Very rare (estimated 0.01% relatively continuously, estimated additional 0.025%recognize it).

'Radical Physical Healing' state
- Characteristic: Gives the ability to heal virtually anything in just minutes.
- Cause: Blocked by placental death, generational traumas, and other factors.
- Comments: Ability to heal due to a strong Gaia connection, we believe.
- Frequency: Not determined, but very rare.

States Involving the Realm of the Shaman and the Sacred (Volume 2)

'Sacred Body' substate
- Characteristics: Part or all of the body radiates a feeling of sacredness.
- Cause: A partial connection to the Realm of the Shaman. Probably due to a weakening of the triune brains 'pretend' selves. In one person the state occurred with solar plexus and heart brain fusion.
- Comments: A substate of the full Realm of the Shaman state.
- Frequency: Not determined.

'Realm of the Shaman' state
- Characteristics: Awareness that each brain is the physical expression of huge, sacred beings that look like totem pole images in the Realm of the Shaman, a place filled with luminous blackness. You, as a collection of these sacred totem pole beings, experience yourself in a tiny human body. Feel extremely sacred. Can have the brains fused or separate, corresponding 'beings' for each brain in that place.
- Cause: Experiencing oneself in the Realm of the Shaman by dropping the brain self identities and shifting the CoA into the 'totem pole' beings in the fluorescent black Realm.
- Comments: A better name might have been 'sacred nothingness' or 'sacred totem self'. However, we chose to use the existing label from Tom Brown Jr.'s work. There is also the probability that the state is called the Akashic Records in the yogic tradition.
- Frequency: Very rare (estimated 0.005% relatively continuously, estimated additional 0.01% recognize it).

Sacred Body and Brain Light synergistic state
- Characteristic: The body feels sacred, and with the eyes closed, there is a sense of looking at bright fluorescent blackness.
- Cause: Same as the individual states.
- Comments: The blackness is a partial view into the Realm of the Shaman. This synergistic state makes the Brain Light state appear differently inside oneself, changing it to a black fluorescence.
- Frequency: Not determined, but rare.

Realm of the Shaman and Brain Light synergistic state
- Cause: Same as individual states.
- Characteristic: The body feels sacred, one can see oneself looking as if composed of totem pole images, and space inside is a bright fluorescent black.
- Comments: The combination of states makes the Brain Light state appear differently inside oneself, changing it to a black fluorescence.
- Frequency: Not determined, but very rare.

The states involving the Realm can all be added to other ones involving the triune brains already described. We create combination state names by just adding the individual names together. Below are some examples. These occur fairly regularly with Realm of the Shaman states due to the amount of prior work it usually takes to experience the Realm in the first place.

Sacred Body and Wholeness combination state

- Characteristics: The feeling is "I am of God". All of body feels intensely sacred. These qualities are in addition to the feeling of wholeness.
- Cause: Combination of a limited connection to the Realm of the Shaman and the triune brain Wholeness state.
- Frequency: Not determined.

Hollow, Sacred Body and Flow Awareness combination state.
- Characteristics: Same as the individual states combined. Effortless without any deliberation.
- Cause: Brains fuse into a golden ball. Chakras fuse into a single disk. A limited connection to the Realm of the Shaman.
- Frequency: Not determined.

Wholeness, Hollow and Sacred Body combination state.
- Characteristics: The body feels empty, whole and sacred simultaneously. A limited connection to the Realm of the Shaman.
- Frequency: Not determined.

Internal and External Awareness States (Volume 2)

Two states in this group are obvious peak abilities. We believe they are a result of a particular peak state, but until we can verify what state it might be, we'll leave them called peak abilities. I would expect that the state name and ability name will be the same, when we figure out what it is.

'Inner Vision' ability
- Characteristics: Seeing, feeling and moving within one's own body or the bodies of others.
- Cause: Not determined.
- Comment: Is a peak ability. Probably a substate of its own. This is a subset of Cellular Awareness ability. The name is unfortunately in conflict with Tom Brown Jr.'s choice of the communication with Gaia ability name. Perhaps 'internal focus' might be an alternative name choice.
- Frequency: Very rare (estimated 0.025% relatively continuously, estimated additional 0.03% recognize it).

'Cellular Awareness' ability
- Characteristics: An awareness of every cell in the body, but not like you're actually in there touching them.
- Cause: Not determined.
- Comments: Probably a state on its own.

- Frequency: Rare (estimated 0.01% relatively continuously, estimated additional 0.06% recognize it).

'Brain Light' state
- Characteristics: A diffuse, 'soft' clear light inside the body. Can be experienced in whatever locations the triune brains have their awarenesses centered in by moving the CoA. Feels boundaryless and appears similar to sunshine.
- Cause: Is the light the triune brains have with unobstructed self-awareness.
- Comments: This state allows people to regress at will. Also useful for a variety of other purposes like merging with other people's consciousness. When experienced with the Realm of the Shaman or Sacred Body states, creates a bright fluorescence to the Realm of the Shaman black, rather than having a light appearance. Comes in varying brightness, the full state is extremely bright.
- Frequency: Estimates are—90% are dark 90% of the time, 10% are 50% bright 50% of the time, 0.5% are fully bright 90% of the time, 0.5% are fully bright for 100% of the time.

'Unbounded Awareness' state
- Characteristics: The most noticeable characteristic is that people can experience themselves as anything they put their attention to, such as animals or plants. Things in the environment feel like they are inside one's own body.
- Comments: Descriptions often found in shamanic literature. May be a subset of the spaciousness state.
- Frequency: Very rare (estimated 0.01% relatively continuously, estimated additional 0.025% recognize it).

'Spaciousness' state
- Characteristics: The state has a range of experience from a lack of reactivity and 'spaciousness' emotionally to a deeper experience of becoming an observer whose awareness merges with a light gray medium that is spread throughout space. In this deeper level, objects, like one's body, just rest in the gray medium and are hard to perceive.
- Cause: Appears to be lost in the first contraction of birth.
- Comments: Very important state for healing (see Volume 3).
- Frequency: Not determined.

Good and Evil (Volume 2)

Good/evil choice
- Characteristics: During stressful events, an often subtle choice between choosing to feel goodness, or to feel evil—with the consequent choice in actions or thoughts.
- Cause: A choice made just before birth by each brain individually.
- Comments: This is not really a state, but rather a predetermined choice.
- Frequency: Estimates are: accessing evil to some degree—95% of the general population. Only 5% never access evil. Never accessing evil or up to a maximum of 1% of the time—only 8% of the general population.

'Christ Consciousness' state
- Characteristics: Incredible love and strength, feels like we imagine Jesus must have felt.
- Cause: We suspect it's a choice of all good in every brain. Still unverified.
- Comment: I believe this is what it feels like to have all the brains choose good, or love. It feels a lot like you are love, not just feeling love. It may be a combination state or a unique state of its own. I continue to investigate.
- Frequency: Not determined

'Medicine Area' experience
- Characteristics: A metaphysical 'place' where awareness can go and create anything.
- Cause: Access is blocked by precellular brain trauma just after the infinite rings.
- Comments: This set of traumas set up the conditions that predispose the triune brains to choose evil. The choice of this phrase is from Tom Brown Jr.'s work. The phrase "creative area' fits the experience better, but we chose the existing label.
- Frequency: Not determined.

'Inner Brightness States' - States Involving Internal Light (Volume 2)

There are several states that involve an experience of light inside (and outside) the body. We know of two presently, and suspect there are others. Getting a person with only one type of inner light to identify which one they have is difficult, as the verbal descriptions can be hard to apply to the inner experience. Thus, to help us diagnose which states a person has, we start by asking if they experience themselves as being 'bright inside', or as having 'inner light'. Then we can ask more questions to identify the particular light state they have.

Note that people in the Sacred Body or Realm of the Shaman state don't always realize they have an inner light state—their interior 'looks' fluorescent black to them. We feel the word 'brightness' captured both this quality of a 'bright dark' and the more typical inner light experience, and so often use it when identifying states in people. Note too that in our Whole-Hearted Healing therapy, we often mention the word 'light' or 'lightness' to describe one of the endpoints in healing trauma, when it feels like we've had a weight removed from our back. Thus, to avoid confusion, we tend to use the word 'brightness' when talking about the inner light experience states. Thus, we call this group of states the 'Inner Brightness' state as a overall label.

In the future, we may change this nomenclature when we find better ways to specify the states, but for now we hope this helps minimizes confusion.

These states are already listed in other categories, but are put here in one location involving light to aid in finding the states.

'Brain Light' state
- Characteristics: A diffuse, 'soft' clear light inside the body. Can be experienced in whatever locations the triune brains have their awarenesses centered by moving the CoA. Feels boundaryless and appears similar to sunshine.
- Cause: Is the light the triune brains have with unobstructed self-awareness.
- Comments: This state allows people to regress at will. Also useful for a variety of other purposes like merging with other people's consciousness. When experienced with the Realm of the Shaman or Sacred Body states, creates a bright fluorescence to the Realm of the Shaman black, rather than having a light appearance. Comes in varying brightness, the full state is extremely bright.. Also listed under the 'Internal and external awareness states' category.
- Frequency: Estimates are—90% are dark 90% of the time, 10% are 50% bright 50% of the time, and 0.5% are fully bright 90% of the time. Also 0.5% for 100%.

'Creator Light' state
- Characteristics: An internal light that can in some cases extend past the skin boundary. It has more of an intense white color to it, not a broad spectrum light like sunlight.
- Cause: A limited connection to the Creator. Probably involves the light balls that come into the body from the Creator at certain developmental events.
- Comments: In the Realm of the Shaman state, the bright white is mixed with the fluorescent black. People describe this 'light' as be-

ing intense or energy-charged. Often feels like it comes from above. Can be used to regress as in the 'life review' of the Near-Death Experience. Comes in various brightnesses. Also listed in the 'States involving the Creator' category.
- Frequency: Not determined.

Miscellaneous states

'Inner Harmony' state
- Characteristics: The flesh of the body radiates a sensation of harmony.
- Cause: Not yet determined.
- Frequency: Not determined.

'Ecstatic' state
- Characteristics: Feels like a continuous endorphin rush.
- Comment: This appears to be what the Sufi teacher Rumi was referring to.
- Frequency: Estimated 1.5% relatively continuously, 3% enough to notice it.

'Inner Gold' state
- Characteristics: The interior of the body turns a deep bright golden color to inner vision. If the brains fuse, the resulting ball has a golden color.
- Comment: We're not sure what this is for, but the alchemists clearly thought it was important. People doing extensive inner development achieve this eventually. It may have something to do with past lives or our species consciousness.
- Frequency: Not determined.

'Past Life Access' state
- Characteristics: Can access past (or future) lives, either with difficulty or at will. In the limit, all past and future lifetimes fuse with this one.
- Cause: The ability/state is blocked by ovulation trauma.
- Comments: Other lives can access this one also. See Chapter 7.
- Frequency: Not determined but happens briefly in several therapies.

'Flow Awareness' state
- Characteristics: A feeling of having energy flow from the back to the front of the body, as if coming from moving air from behind.
- Cause: Fusion of all chakras into a disk near the solar plexus.

- Comments: The characteristics are experienced slightly differently by people in the Average or Hollow state. See Chapter 7.
- Frequency: Not determined.

A Time Line of Developmental Events

This partial list of developmental events is provided as a help for putting the ones used in Volumes 1, 2, and 3 in their chronological order. For more on the developmental events, refer to the books and websites in Chapter 4. In the events below, the (Vn) coding translates into a reference to Volume n, and the (Cm) to a reference in Chapter m of this volume. A few of the major problems that can occur at each stage are included only for reference.

About 6 months before mother is born, mother is fetus inside grandmother's womb.
Precellular triune brains being formed separately in 'infinite rings'. (V2)
  • Separation trauma as they detach from the ring of other brains.
Movement through infinite ring boundary. (V2)
Access the 'Medicine Area'. (V3)
Body bag forms around precellular body consciousness. (V3)
  • Body bag acquires generational traumas. Seen as silver motes floating in fluid.
Coalescence of precellular egg brains, heart then mind enter body at appendix area. (C6)
  • Precondition for 'soul stealing' set up here. (V3)
Meridian 'webbing' grows during coalescence. (C7)
Chakras anchor into webbing during coalescence. Form single chakra ball. (C7)

A short time later, precellular egg develops further.
Precellular egg goes into a 'fountain' and becomes golden. (C8)

Mother is born, from grandmother's womb.
  • Potential egg trauma during mothers birth.

Two months before conception, inside father.
Similar events for sperm precellular brains as for egg ones as described above.

- Major differences are additional chakras and different precellular shapes.

Sperm develops. Nurse cells protect sperm.

- Often injuries involving being hit by other sperm tails.

Passage of sperm through Native American patterns in testicular tubes. (C7)

About 1 day before conception, inside mother.

Egg ripens.

Cocoon of webbing egg is carried in dissolves.

Coating of cells over egg (to nourish it) forms. (C7, V2)

Ovulation—egg ejected from ovary blister.

- Feels similar to birth and sets up some later birth trauma.

Movement down fallopian tube.

- Secretion of attraction scent for sperm.
- Potential mechanical damage during passage.
- Potential chemical damage from toxic mother.

Ejaculation by father during sex.

- Potential damage during ejaculation as sperm collide.
- Potential conflict with sperm from other fathers.

Minutes before conception.

Egg chooses sperm that appears bright.

Untraumatized event feels like a royal wedding. (C6)

- Trauma can cause chosen sperm to feel in competition with other sperm.

Egg reaches out with its 'arms' to pull sperm into chest.

- Often mechanical injury due to sperm hitting egg too hard or at an angle.

Conception.

Sperm tail detaches from what feels like the upper back.

- Trauma as sperm tail consciousness dies.
- If the egg hardens the shell too soon, it rips the sperm tail instead of detaching correctly.

Head of sperm opens and chromosomes come out.

- Experienced as a death event.

Sack around sperm goes to egg wall.

Chromosomes move across egg like a bundle of copper wires.

Chakras merge.

Cellular triune brains from egg and sperm merge. (C6, C8)

Ball of light enters new zygote. (V2)

12 hours after conception, first cell division.
Can be experienced as another death trauma.

6 days after conception, implantation.
Entry into uterus.
  • Feels like falling into a huge void or on roller coaster going off edge.
Loss of layer of nutrient cells around zygote. (V3)
Egg 'head' impacts with uterine wall. (C6)
  • Possible trauma around not being able to implant easily or at all in places.
Belly uncoils and inserts into uterine wall. Fluid ejected into wall from zygote.
Ball of light enters uterine wall then into head of zygote. (V2)
  • Potential trauma if ball of light is held by mother and doesn't move into zygote.

From conception through birth, during growth of fetus.
Numerous developmental events. Some may be related to peak states.
A variety of major traumas can occur during this period.
  • Traumas create conditions for later 'soul stealing'. (V3)
  • Traumas around trying to escape to the Realm to escape trauma. (V2)

By 6 weeks after conception.
Most pregnancies confirmed.
  • Often abortion attempts made now.
  • Morning sickness by now.
'Undiagnosed' twin usually dead by 6 weeks.
  • Twin death trauma can cause 'divine homesickness' and gets re-created in relationships.

7-9 months after conception.
Baby feels the womb space tightening. Mother starting to feel discomfort.
Later will walk around breathless with no room to inhale.

Birth (see Stanislav Grof's *The Adventure of Self-Discovery* for descriptions of the Birth Perinatal Matrix [BPM] stages of birth).
Choice between good and evil just before start of birth sequence. (V2)
Initiate birth sequence when the 'separate from the mother' Gaia instruction given. (V2)
  • Generally lose triune brain fusion states and ability to hear Gaia.
Baby moves upside down and puts head into the pelvis.
  • Can cause vertigo and nausea symptoms later in life.

Contractions start. Some movement engaging head, nestling into bony structures. (Start of BPM 2 in Grof's system.)

- Baby feels helpless, nothing it can do.
- Intense rage at the mother.
- Rape and rapist precursor trauma.
- Grinding teeth a common symptom.

First Contraction. (V2)

- Most intense trauma of the birth sequence. Unintentional separation from the Creator, the Realm, the other triune brains, and everything else. Can feel like total annihilation.
- Major trauma around first oxygen starvation as blood through mother's diaphragm is reduced.

Second contraction. (C7)

- The life/death choice is made here. Blocks Gaia connection. Choice to age and die, and of how long to live life.realm of the shaman

More contractions with cervix closed.

- 'No exit condition' of the first perinatal sequence of Grof. Usually intense rage at mother. Rape trauma activated in mother.

Cervix starts to open and motion through starts. (BPM 3 in Grof's system starts with the gradual propulsion of the fetus through the birth canal.)

- Feeling of losing connection to mother–abandonment.
- Mother typically is very upset for 5 to 30 minutes, with feelings of panic, wanting to change her mind, doesn't know what she's doing, can't do it, tears. Called the 'transition stage' in obstetrics.
- Mother is in pain, typically wants drugs. Drugs are a huge shock to baby.
- Joy is common in the baby as it starts through the cervix. Mother feels relief.

Moving through the birth canal. Fetus in descent and head rotation.

- Trauma around head rotation, and often skull damage as it crosses the mother's lower spine.
- Can cause poor 3D sense and orientation, directional confusion.

Crowning and birth. (BPM 4 in Grof's system.)

- Face to spine in most babies. Self-esteem issues as baby is seen for the first time.
- Typically, doctor twists the baby's head the wrong way!
- In the '50s, lots of grief and volcanic rage when nurse keeps baby from being born until doctor arrives.
- Often severe oxygen starvation as the cord is compressed.
- Blinding light and pain in eyes as baby is exposed to cold and fluorescent lights.

Acquires the skin boundary ('shell') as baby leaves the vagina, like a layer of tar. (V2)

Baby is out of the mother.
First breath.
- Usually traumatic due to having umbilical cord cut too soon before blood leaves placenta.

Momentary 'truth' experience passed through. (V2)
Momentary archetype access passed through. (C7)
Cord cut. (Can be before or after first breath.)
- Generally done too soon in Western hospitals. Trauma around blood not leaving placenta and into baby before cutting.
- Shell hardens with cutting of cord.

Uterus continues to contract.
Placental separation and its death trauma. (C6, C8)
- Trauma response to placental death is loss of Wholeness state.

Baby often removed from mother and taken to another room.
- Huge abandonment and loneliness trauma.
- Often trauma around being too tightly wrapped in blankets.

Glossary

Applied kinesiology: Developed for chiropractic, uses changing muscle strength to test for various problems and sensitivities to toxins. Mistakenly assumes the body isn't self-aware with its own agenda. Same principle as muscle testing or dowsing.

Average consciousness: A person who has no peak states except for some degree of solar plexus-body connection. The most common state in people.

Body: The reptilian brain, at the base of the skull. Thinks in gestalt body sensations. Experiences itself in the lower belly. Known as the hara in Japanese. It is the brain that we communicate with when doing dowsing or muscle testing.

Breathwork: Using hyperventilation for extended periods of time to facilitate healing. A variety of processes exist.

BSFF (Be Set Free Fast): Invented by Larry Nims, a spinoff of TFT involving only 3 meridian points. Also important for the technique called Instant BSFF, where the process is programmed internally to occur at a cue word.

Buddha brain: The prefrontal lobes in the brain. Experientially it feels like a huge, massive statue of Buddha located above the head. Normally fused with the mind brain.

Buddha brain structures: Looking like cables or containers internal to the body, appearing like the movie idea of an alien implant. Created by the Buddha brain during trauma. Often cause physical pain.

Chakras: Energy centers associated with different areas of the body. They 'look' like white or colored balls with geometrical features. Can be merged into one white disk near the center of the body.

Cellular brains: The self-aware organelles in the sperm, egg. or zygote cell that later develop into the multicelled brains of the fetus. Equivalent to saying 'organelle' or 'subcellular' brains.

Cellular memories: Memories of the sperm, egg, and zygote. These include sensations, feelings, and thoughts. Also applied in the literature to memories of the body consciousness alone.

CoA (Center of Awareness): Using a finger, you can find your center of awareness by pointing at where 'you' are in your body. Can be at a particular point, or diffuse, and both internal to the body and external.

Coalescence: The developmental event where the physically separate precellular brains combine into one cellular organism. It occurs for the egg about six months before the mother's birth, and for the sperm about two months before conception.

Coex (Condensed experience): Coined by Dr. Grof, describes the phenomenon in regressive healing that sensate related traumas are activated together and interrelate.

Combination state: Two or more peak states experienced simultaneously. The characteristics of the combination are the sum of the individual characteristics.

CPL (Calm, peace, lightness): The endpoint to healing a trauma, caused when the client goes into a peak state, usually temporarily.

Creator: An experiential 'place' that people encounter during near-death experiences. It looks like a plane light that is self-aware.

Developmental event: A short-duration event of biological change or experience that the developing organism, be it sperm, egg, fetus, baby, child, or adult goes through as part of the developmental process. Examples include conception, implantation, the first heartbeat, etc.

Developmental events model: Explains the presence or absence of peak states, experiences, and abilities due to pre-birth trauma.

Dowsing: Using pendulum or rod to communicate with the body consciousness. Same mechanism as in muscle testing or applied kinesiology.

DP-3 (Third deep PEAT process): Invented by Zivorad Slavinski, it is used to dissolve dualism issues and give peak states of consciousness.

EFT (Emotional Freedom Technique): A therapy that uses tapping on meridian points to eliminate emotional and physical discomfort. Classified as a power therapy, in the subcategory of an 'energy' or 'meridian' therapy.

Focusing: Invented by Dr. Gendlin, involves becoming aware of the body consciousness communicating (the 'felt sense') to release held traumatic material.

Fusion: The most connected that two or more brain awarenesses can get. When fused, they are one organism without any separate identity remaining. When all the brains fuse, their awareness can be seen to 'look' like a golden ball just below navel. Smaller and denser and feels more powerful than merged brains. Probable origin of the concept of the 'philosopher's stone' and alchemy.

Gaia: The biological consciousness of the planet earth. In certain states of consciousness, it looks externally like the flattened side of huge ball or building, with vertical and horizontal line structures on it. Our species occupies one band of the structure.

Gaia Instructions: All the steps in developmental events are directed by Gaia, and take into account current circumstances. The instructions for the steps can be translated into spoken language.

Generational trauma: Problems or beliefs passed down through the family line. Can be healed.

Heart: The limbic system, or old mammalian brain. Thinks in sequences of emotions, experiences itself in the center of the chest.

Holes: 'Look' like black holes in the body, feel like infinitely deep deficient emptiness. Encountered during some therapies. Caused by physical damage to the body.

Infinite ring: The locations where the precellular brains are first created. They are experienced as an infinite ring of similar precellular brains.

Inner Peace state: A state of consciousness where a person's emotional past no longer feels emotionally traumatic. A substate of the Beauty Way state.

Kundalini: Characterized by the sensation of a small area of heat (about an inch in diameter) which moves slowly up the spine. Can go on for months and in some cases years, stimulates traumas and other unusual 'spiritual' experiences, creating severe problems for most people.

Merging: Two or more people sharing awarenesses and memories. Feels like the person merging gets larger to include the other person. Can be dangerous, as 'soul stealing' can occur.

Merging of brains: The awarenesses of the biological brains can come together in various combinations. Fusion is a more extreme experience of merging.

Meridians: Energy channels that wind through the body. Used in therapies such as acupuncture and EFT.

Muscle testing: Communicating with the body consciousness by using muscle strength as an indicator. Same mechanism as applied kinesiology, and the terms are sometimes used interchangeably.

Mind: The neocortex, or primate brain. Thinks in thoughts, experiences itself in the head.

OBE (*Out-of-body experience*): An experience where your 'self' is outside the physical body, yet able to see.

Organelle brains: The self-aware organelles in the sperm, egg. or zygote cell that later develop into the multicelled brains of the fetus. Equivalent to saying 'cellular ' or 'subcellular' brains.

Past lives: Encountered in some therapies, the experience of having lived in the past or the future with a different body and personality.

Peak ability: An ability not possessed in average consciousness.

Peak experience: A short lived peak state or other unusually good experience.

Peak state: One of about 15 major states of consciousness that gives experiences and abilities that cannot be experienced in average consciousness. Felt as vast improvement to the average state. Can be had in combination and to various degrees. A number of substates exist also.

PEAT (*Psycho Energetic Auro Technology*): Invented by Zivorad Slavinski, a peak state process that dissolves dualistic conflicts. Results in dramatic healings.

Perry diagram: A diagram using circles to indicate the degree of connection the triune brain awarenesses have.

Placental brain: The self-aware placental consciousness.

Power therapy: Phrase coined by Dr. Figley, applied to extremely effective therapies that remove symptoms from post-traumatic stress disorder and other issues.

Precellular brains: The self-aware brains when they are independent organisms before becoming incorporated into the egg or sperm cell as organelle brains.

Precellular trauma: Trauma that occurs to the biological system that is the prototype of the egg or sperm, before the egg or sperm have formed into a cell.

Psychological reversal: The individual has a counter-commitment at the body consciousness level to healing or peak performance. In energy therapies, healing is blocked unless treated. In WHH, it causes the client not to want to heal, but does not block the healing directly.

Radical physical healing: A particular type of physical healing occurring in just minutes. Range of healing includes injuries that cannot normally heal, such as scars, cut spines, etc.

Realm of the Shaman: Home of the sacred selves; looks like fluorescent black velvet. A state that shamans enter in order to do drastic healing on others. See Tom Brown Junior's *The Vision* for more description.

Self: The part of us that experiences itself as 'I am'. It is eternal. The part of us that's in all of our past lives. Also called spirit. Also called the conscious awareness.

Self-identity: Each of the biological brains pretends it's someone or something else.

Shamanic states: States that are valued in shamanism. Typically involve the body or a connection to Gaia.

Shell: A layer right at skin level that gives us the sensation of having skin and keeps our awareness confined to our bodies. Can be experienced as burning or painful.

Sperm tail brain: The self-aware sperm tail consciousness.

Spiritual emergency: An experience usually classified as relating to spiritual or mystical traditions, experienced as traumatic or overwhelming to the level of being a crisis.

Stable state: A peak state that is retained without any maintenance.

Subcellular brains: The self-aware organelles in the sperm, egg. or zygote cell that later develop into the multicelled brains of the fetus. Equivalent to saying 'organelle' or 'cellular' brains.

SUDS (Subjective units of distress scale): Used to evaluate the degree of pain in trauma. Originally from a scale of 1 to 10, common usage is now from 0 (no pain) to 10 (as much pain as it's possible to have).

Synergistic state: Two or more states experienced simultaneously that have characteristics that are new or different from the individual states.

TAT (Tapas Acupressure Technique): Invented by Tapas Fleming originally to heal allergies, also works on trauma and other issues. Recommended for generational traumas.

TFT (Thought Field Therapy): The original tapping on meridian therapy. Also discovered the phenomenon and a fix for 'psychological reversal'.

TIR (Traumatic Incident Reduction): A power therapy that uses regression.

Trauma: A moment in time, or string of moments where the sensations, emotions, and thoughts are stored. Causes difficulties for humans as they guide behavior inappropriately. Usually painful or difficult experiences, although can be pleasurable. Trauma creates post-traumatic stress disorder.

Triune brain: The brain is built out of three separate biological brains, formed through evolution. They are the R-complex (body), the limbic system (heart), and the neocortex (mind). Each is self-aware, built for different functions, and thinks by sensations, feelings, or thoughts.

Unstable state: If not maintained, the peak state will not continue.

WHH (Whole-Hearted Healing): A regression therapy technique. Uses awareness of the out-of-body experience to heal trauma.

Index

Lightning Source UK Ltd.
Milton Keynes UK
25 August 2010
158967UK00001B/103/A